MW00666989

VBScript®

MASTER'S HANDBOOK

How to Order:

For information on quantity discounts contact the publisher: Prima Publishing, P.O. Box 1260BK, Rocklin, CA 95677-1260; (916) 632-4400. On your letterhead include information concerning the intended use of the books and the number of books you wish to purchase. For individual orders, turn to the back of this book for more information.

VBScript®

MASTER'S HANDBOOK

Christopher J. Goddard
and Mark White

PRIMA PUBLISHING

PRIMA is a registered trademark of Prima Publishing, a division of Prima Communications, Inc. Prima Publishing is a registered trademark of Prima Communications, Inc. Prima Publishing, Rocklin, California 95677.

ISBN: 0-7615-0769-8
Library of Congress Catalog Card Number: 96-70883
Printed in the United States of America
96 97 98 99 BB 10 9 8 7 6 5 4 3 2 1

Publisher Don Roche, Jr.
Associate Publisher Ray Robinson
Acquisitions Manager Alan Harris
Managing Editor Tad Ringo
Product Marketing Specialist Julie Barton

Acquisitions Editor:
Ian Sheeler
Development Editor:
Timothy Ritchey
Project Editor:
Kelli Crump
Copy Editors:
Phil Worthington
Judy Ohm
Technical Reviewer:
Dr. Donald Doherty
Indexer:
Emily Glossbrenner
Cover Designer:
Rick Wong

To those friends from our Cambridge years

Acknowledgments

The summer of 1996 has been an eventful one, and revolved around the production of this book. We hope that the end result proves to be a useful addition to your library—whether you are using it in a professional capacity or simply as an introduction to new Internet technologies.

There are many people who have been a part of this project, in one way or another, and this is our chance to give them a mention (whether they want it or not).

First in the line up is Tim Ritchey, the Harley Davidson fanatic, who we would like to thank for giving us the opportunity to do this book and for organizing much of the work for us. The staff at Prima also deserve a big thank you; especially, Ian Sheeler, Jill Byus, and Kelli Crump.

The accommodation prize must go to Sandra Gordon for providing a roof, phone lines, desks, and most importantly, food each evening. Any author needs to take a break from time to time, and we'd like to thank those who turned out to entertain two hard working guys on the essential Friday and Saturday nights. We are also greatly indebted to our friends who looked after us on our mini-breaks around the United Kingdom and Channel Islands. We will mention all of them, individually, throughout this book around examples and sample listings. To those people, happy hunting, and to our general audience, we hope you enjoy *VBScript Master's Handbook* and its accompanying CD.

Contents at a Glance

Table of Contents

Introduction

The power of Visual Basic in today's development community is unmistakable. Visual Basic is in many ways the culmination of several decade's of work in writing software for computers. This development has taken computers from the climate-controlled rooms of lab-coated, punch-card shuffling technicians, and placed them into the offices and homes of average non-technical people around the world. In turn, computer languages have evolved from the arcane scrawl of machine code, through higher level languages such as C++ and FORTRAN, to pseudo-English languages like BASIC. These advances reinforce the original principle of providing a general purpose computing machine which could be used in a variety of situations—predicated only by the people who used them. In turn, the cottage industry of Visual Basic controls made creating software controls into a viable business, and brought the long underused idea of object-oriented programs into the mainstream, if not in its purest form.

In placing the hardware and languages within financial and mental reach of the average person, the computer stretches beyond a convenient platform for marketed products, and becomes a tool for providing unique solutions on a problem by problem basis. For years, computers have been a combination of the hardware and software that vendors provide. It is not as much, "How can I mold the computer to what I need?" as it is, "What computer and software comes closest to solving my needs?" Creating unique one-off programs was a time-consuming and costly undertaking which few companies or individuals were willing to undertake. Development environments such as Visual Basic changed that, and fostered the idea that custom built apps were possible. Many small in-house MIS departments were formed around the idea of *creating* applications that would allow a *general* computing device to solve *specific* problems.

At the same time that programming computers was becoming demystified, work was underway which would radically alter the way computers would be used, and usher in the current interest in the World Wide Web.

The emergence of the Internet as an entertainment and information medium has created, in much the same way as Visual Basic controls had, a home-grown industry of individual developers creating new and exciting technologies. The World Wide Web's open platform for innovation provided new opportunities for expansion, and companies quickly moved to fill technological gaps with a wide variety of solutions. The explosion of *intranet* technology as an outgrowth of the Internet is a direct result of the wide and varied availability of these tools, which were unavailable even one year ago.

The development of VBScript and Microsoft's Internet Explorer 3.0 has combined both the development of user-friendly languages, and the advanced technologies being developed for communication around the Internet framework into a single product for creating specific solutions to individual problems in developing and distributing Web content.

Over 450,000 people downloaded Microsoft's FrontPage beta, and millions have downloaded Internet Explorer 3.0. Internet Explorer 3.0, and Microsoft's ActiveX model has created a framework for extending component development work on the Web. Visual Basic Scripting Edition is a glue which can be used to tie individual elements together to create an overall Web presence or intranet solution.

VBScript Master's Handbook explains what VBScript is, and introduces Microsoft's Internet Explorer 3.0 and ActiveX controls to the reader. It contains a complete discussion of the language structure for the novice programmer as well as more advanced integration with HTML, including coverage of forms, objects, Java Applets, and CGI scripting. The book is going to help you:

- Produce more effective Web documents.
- Perform client-side validation of forms before processing by the server.
- Include Microsoft's new ActiveX controls in Web documents.
- Create interactive, multimedia documents using event-scripting.

- Add new and exciting features to your Web sites to stay ahead of the competition.
- Get the most out of the HTML Layout Control to simplify page layout, and the ActiveX Control Pad to insert objects into your pages.
- Use the Internet Control Pack to develop complete Web applications which communicate with remote servers.

VBScript is one of many new technologies which will help the average Web developer, who may not have much programming experience, take the tools and components available across the Internet and develop exciting and innovative products.

VBScript Master's Handbook is your reference for getting a foothold on this emerging technology and integrating it into future development. VBScript is the combination of thousands of individual developers competing, cooperating, and producing technologies aimed at fundamentally changing the way we work, rest, and play. By learning languages such as VBScript, even the most uninitiated can begin to take a hand in the development of their own future.

PART I

What Is VBScript?

CHAPTER 1

VBScript—What's All the Hype About?

People's expectations are increasing as fast as the size and popularity of the Web. Static pages that crawl on the screen at a snail's pace to display a few lines of text and an occasional image are no longer impressive. Instead, users want to see full animation, high-quality sound, and aesthetic, creative pages that captivate their attention and entice them further into the cyberworld of the Internet. The dawn of VBScript and Microsoft's new ActiveX technologies bring this dream to life.

The Visual Basic Scripting Edition programming language enables you to create spectacular, smarter Web pages that are rich in active content. You can use such content to integrate multimedia (animation, video, sound, and 3-D rendering), dedicated applications, and database tools into the Web pages. You can build pages that respond to questions, validate user input, calculate expressions, control program flow, link to other applications, and execute Java applets. The world of interactive Web documents is available to create a scope of endless gripping effects.

Microsoft designed VBScript as a lightweight, high-performance scripting language to help you create active content on the Web. It's a fast, portable interpreter for use in WWW browsers and other applications that use the new ActiveX architecture.

Visual Basic Scripting Edition—The Sky's the Limit

Only a few years ago, Web pages were characterized by reams of text and a few tiny graphics—the available technology couldn't support anything more involved. Now things are different. With the latest version of Internet Explorer, Microsoft's ActiveX technology, and Visual Basic Scripting Edition, Web pages can burst into life and impress millions of users. Fancy color schemes, new layout controls, animations, graphics, sound and video add functionality to your Web pages and give you a chance to use your flair for design. The gray days are gone, the sun is up, and the Web looks enticing.

What Can You Do with VBScript?

A good way to get a feeling of VBScript's potential is to download examples from Web sites. Figure 1-1 presents one such example: Mr. Eggplant—a bit o' fun that demonstrates the use of scripting to control individual graphical elements onscreen. Users can select and attach vegetable bits to an eggplant to make it look like a person. Old style Web pages couldn't support movable graphical elements, so superposition simply wasn't possible. The new technology does, however, and scripting controls all user interactions. The positioning of the images uses the HTML Layout Control (covered in detail later in the book).

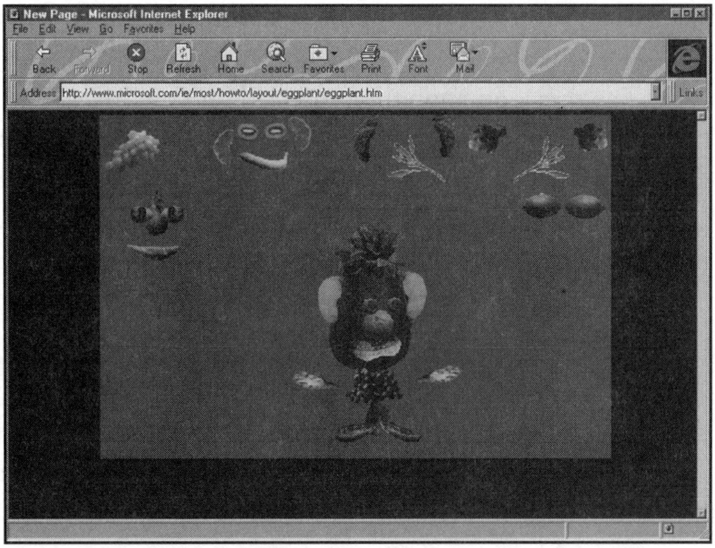

FIGURE 1-1
Scripting lets you move graphical images independently around the page.

Another example is the Internet Explorer Express, located at `http://www.microsoft.com/ie/offers/express/home.htm` (see Figure 1-2). This newspaper-style document shows many of the new controls and functions.

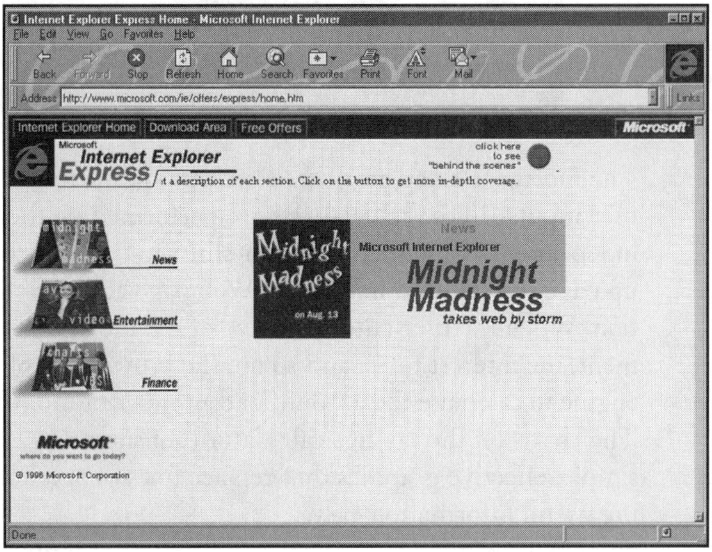

FIGURE 1-2
The Internet Explorer Express Newspaper demonstrates how to use the ActiveX controls and scripting to create professional documents.

To create a line of scrolling text at the top of the page, as well as the spinning red disc, you would use the ActiveX marquee control.

The disc is an animation inserted into the stylesheet. The other three section buttons are GIF images. When a user moves the mouse pointer over any of them, a scripting routine displays a related image to the right of the respective button.

You can bring up a special finance page that features a mortgage and savings calculator by clicking on the Finance option (see Figure 1-3).

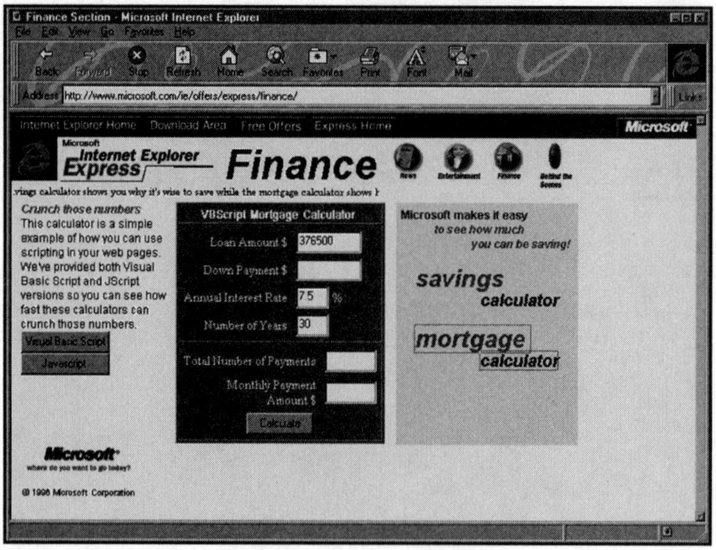

FIGURE 1-3
The mortgage calculator here uses scripting to work out the size and number of monthly payments.

The mortgage calculator uses a script to perform calculations based on user inputs. These calculations are performed on the host machine, independent of the server. Power shifts to the host computer, speeds up page refresh, and makes the Web page act more like an application. When the user enters the size of the mortgage, the down payment, the interest rates, and so on, the browser invokes the scripting engine to calculate the amount and number of monthly payments. The charts on the savings calculator (not shown in Figure 1-3) are simple, effective graphics that replace lines of text and make extracting useful information easy.

The final example demonstrates the power of VBScript and the ActiveX commands in the form of a simple game and shows how scripting is useful in applications. It's called WebZee, and is a takeoff of the popular Yahtzee™ game (see Figure 1-4). The computer rolls several imaginary, you select which dice to hold, and then you roll again. Different combinations score different numbers of points. One or two players can play WebZee.

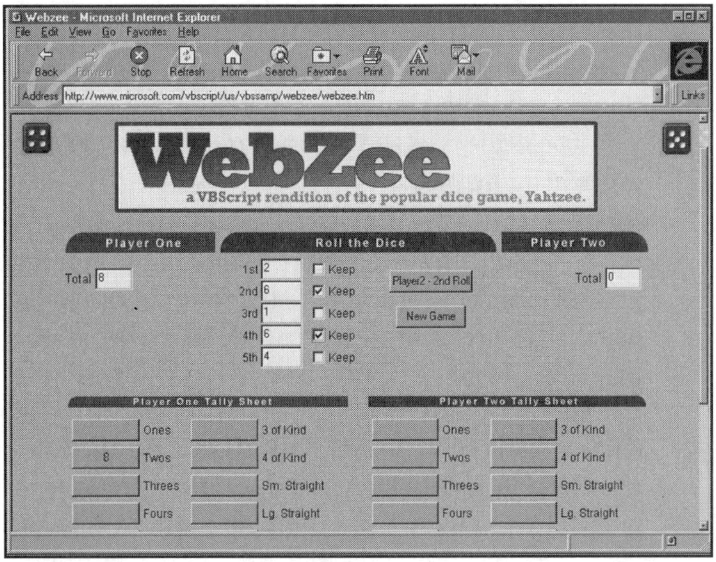

FIGURE 1-4
The popular dice game, WebZee

A script routine generates the dice values and several routines adjust the scores at the end of each round. The Web page downloads from the network like a normal document, and then the browser takes over and runs the script from inside the Web page. The script controls the whole game so you don't have server interactions slowing things down.

Why Do I Need To Know about VBScript?

The Internet has helped the computer industry become one of the fastest growing industries in the world. The technology available today enables worldwide communications at the touch of a button, accesses huge databases covering almost every topic imaginable, and improves communication in the workplace with sophisticated company intranets. Keeping up with the latest developments on the Internet will pay dividends in years to come when high performance Web technology is commonplace.

ActiveX technology and VBScript are at the forefront of the information revolution. Static pages are a thing of the past and dynamic content is in. VBScript is one of the key ways to introduce dynamic and active content into your pages. Video, high-quality sound, on-demand features, exciting graphics, and many other options are now available. This book can help you take advantage of them and demystify the overwhelming nature of the Internet.

VBScript Master's Handbook takes you through the entire Visual Basic Scripting language from short scripts and simple applications to complicated protocols that initiate file transfer and so on. It doesn't matter whether you're a corporate Web developer who wants be on top of the latest Web technology or a hobbyist who likes to dabble in forefront technologies—this book's for everyone. Experienced programmers (especially those versed in Visual Basic) may dive straight into the middle of the book while beginners may prefer to start at the beginning. The text guides you through many aspects, such as writing simple scripts, incorporating ActiveX controls into your documents, using the various browser features, and supporting programs. By the end of the book, you will understand scripting and how you can use ActiveX controls to transform your pages. Many examples, along with printed code and working samples on the CD, assist to guide you in understanding how to build scripts.

Getting Hold of Visual Basic Scripting Edition

Microsoft supports Visual Basic Scripting Edition and distributes it as part of the Microsoft Internet Explorer 3.0 for free. The CD that accompanies this book supplies Internet Explorer 3.0 and is simple to install (see Chapter 2 for more details). Over one million copies of Explorer 3.0 were downloaded from the Microsoft Web site during its first week of release. It is estimated that the market value of ActiveX technologies will be worth over $2 billion by the turn of the century. It's big business.

After you install it on your computer, you can write examples and familiarize yourself with the language. The next section looks at the Internet's humble beginnings and explores the browser's role in the WWW scheme.

How Does Scripting Fit into the WWW Picture?

If you're new to HTML and scripting, you might find terms like "Java applets" and "ActiveX controls" a little daunting. Let's first have a look at how scripting fits into the Web and see why it's a crucial step toward interactive content. Figure 1-5 shows a schematic of the interaction between the Web, the browser, and components within the browser (such as a scripting engine).

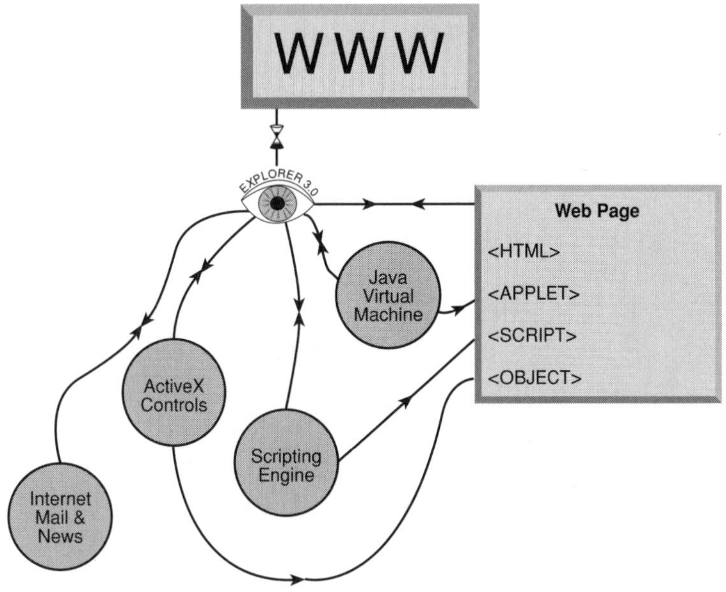

FIGURE 1-5
Fitting scripting into the picture of the WWW.

The Story behind the Internet and the WWW

The Internet, as it is known today, started out as a 1970s research project for interconnecting multiple diverse hardware technologies into a universal network. It was part of a drive by the United States government to show its commitment to high technology research. It was prompted by the launch of the Soviet Sputnik satellite in 1957. A network system that would decentralize American military information (while still keeping it top secret, of course) would give the Americans a tactical advantage in war because there would be many centers of information.

The ideal network would use a single hardware technology that would satisfy the demands of all the users on the system. Trying to implement such a hardware standard was impossible, and a method of allowing different hardware platforms to intercommunicate, independent of their physical network connections, was sought. TCP/IP was born. TCP/IP is a suite of communications protocols which include the Transmission Control Protocol and the Internet Protocol—hence TCP/IP.

The research into the development of these protocols was too risky for the private sector, so the Advanced Research Projects Agency (ARPA) undertook the task. It created ARPANET in 1969 and by 1977 had produced the TCP/IP protocols as a solution to internetworking. The global Internet began around 1980 when ARPA converted all the machines attached to its research network to use the TCP/IP protocol. The backbone of the new Internet was formed. In 1983, the Office of the Secretary of Defense mandated that all long-term network computers should use the TCP/IP protocols and divided the ARPANET into Milnet (for military purposes) and ARPANET (for research purposes). ARPANET was offered to universities at a low cost to enable transferring experimental data worldwide.

Slowly but surely, the Internet caught on. The big break came when the TCP/IP suite of protocols were implemented as part of the Berkley Software Distribution of UNIX, and they became the standard communications protocol worldwide. In 1986, some 20,000 computers at universities, government offices, and corporate companies were connected to the Internet. By 1994, this number had grown to 3 million computers in 61 countries. The universities and smaller organizations who were influential in promoting Internet technology have long since been swamped by major corporations. Internet Service Providers now are the most common means of connecting to the Internet.

No single company or organization owns the Internet, just as no one owns the world. The National Science Foundation, in conjunction with AT&T, used to maintain TCP/IP technology and occasionally make revisions to TCP/IP protocols, but these matters are now handled privately. Anyone can send in ideas to the discussion groups to work on the suggestions and produce documents called a Request for Comments (RFC). After RFCs receive a number, they become the accepted standard for a certain part of the protocols.

NOTE

A new IPng (Internet Protocol next generation) standard is being developed owing to a shortage of Internet addresses. IP addresses currently are 32 bits long and provide only 2^{32} possible addresses—4,294,967,296. Because the addresses have been split into Class A, B, C, and D networks, some classes of addresses are close to being fully allocated. IPng (or IPv4) addresses this problem by using 128 bits for an IP address, which provides about 1,500 possible addresses for every square metre of land on the planet—enough to cover the problem for the time being.

The Internet provides the powerful and universal connectivity that underlies the Web. The Web reciprocates this great connectivity by providing a powerful user model to attract people to use the Internet.

The World Wide Web

The Web is a brainchild of the 1990s and was developed at CERN (European Laboratory for Particle Physics) as a set of protocols for information transfer between research groups. It was an online system that would allow non-technical users to share data without needing to know about the interfaces and protocols (communication languages) which connected the various computer systems.

Today, the Web is a fabulous playground of information that users can visit using any of the various viewers available on the market, such as Microsoft's Internet Explorer 3.0 or Netscape's Navigator. Millions of people around the world contribute to this giant database and feed off it symbiotically. As bandwidth capabilities increase, more and more people use the Web to find facts, join newsgroups, or peruse information at their leisure. VBScript and ActiveX controls will enhance the capabilities of Web applications even further, allowing such uses as electronic banking, Internet-wide games, high-quality video and sound, and even 3-D virtual reality worlds.

Web servers and browsers communicate mainly via the Hypertext Transmission Protocol (HTTP). HTTP allows HTML documents to port between different platforms without changing appearance. These platforms are as diverse as Windows, Macintosh, or UNIX versions made by Sun, HP, Digital, or IBM. You can use other protocols to transfer files and other information, but the Web controls these features for you. If your browser needs to download a file from an FTP server, it uses the protocol for FTP (File Transfer Protocol) and automatically carries out the operation. The browser is the key to navigating the Web—just imagine what it would be like trying to wade through the millions of pages on the Web without a way to track where you've been or where you want to go. All browsers on the WWW use URLs (Uniform Resource Locators), hyperlinks, and in-frame navigation to provide an efficient means of traversing the Web.

Between 1994 and 1995, Netscape dominated the market for browsers with its Netscape Navigator product. Not only did this make surfing the Web easier, it also dictated the direction in which the Web would evolve over the next few years. Netscape wanted to push the WWW standards forward and added nonstandard items, such as plug-ins and form elements. Other standards adopted these innovations because the user community had already done so.

In 1996, Microsoft completely reformed its Internet strategy and returned to the stage with a glittering display of Internet software. Internet Explorer 3.0 was finally released in August of 1996, boasting a fast browser that supports ActiveX technology and takes Web page design to a new level. Complete compatibility with Microsoft's other software makes the browser instantly likable; and being supported by such a large company, it's bound to have an impact in the highly competitive browser market. The product is free, and without question, attractive to consumers.

Who Looks after the Web?

Maintaining the standards of the hypertext markup language isn't easy. The WWW Consortium (W3C) was set up to carry out this function on behalf of all Web users to ensure that pages look the same across different browsers. W3C's task is to evaluate modifications to the markup language and ratify which ones pass the revision process. After it accepts the draft, the IETF (Internet Engineering Task Force) accepts the standard as the official Internet standard. This body preserves the universality of HTML. The long timescales involved in drafting proposals, however, encourages many people to add their own extensions to their browsers, thereby breaking the ideal of a standardized language. In the past, this has put great pressure on the W3C, and it nearly disbanded a few years ago because software developers considered it a hindrance rather than a help.

The History of HTML

In the early days of the Web, HTML existed in two stages—level 0 and level 1. These were quickly superseded by HTML 2.0, which became the official Internet standard and is what most of today's browsers support. It includes features such as headings, paragraphs, links, lists, forms, and images.

HTML 2.0 was fine while the Web was in its early stages of development, but as browsers became more sophisticated, a successor had to be found to host the next generation of features including tables, scientific equations, and better control of page layout and design. This successor started out as HTML 3.0 and was in draft version for quite some time. It brought together many of the tags that browser manufacturers had added as their own extensions, but grew so amorphously that a consensus on which tags to accept and which to discard couldn't emerge. The proposed 3.0 standard was also changing too rapidly for browser manufacturers to implement its features without growing concerns that they would soon become obsolete. The draft for HTML 3.0 expired in September 1995 (its life lasted only 6 months) and 3.2 was drawn up as an alternative.

HTML 3.2

HTML 3.2 brings together the popular tags from draft 3.0 in a concrete way that is conducive to universal acceptance. It includes HTML 2.0, some 3.0 tags, and some Netscape extensions. The release of this standard means that smaller browser developers can implement the language with confidence instead of being at the mercy of the dominant companies such as Microsoft and Netscape.

It offers many new features, including Netscape extensions, 3.0 features, color controls, client-side image maps, and support for Java applets.

Some HTML 3.2 Features Included in the HTML 3.2 Standard

Some of the features in HTML 3.2 include better table commands, improved text alignment tags, and more control over fonts, colors, and backgrounds. The <TABLE> tag allows you to insert a table and provides better support for alignment, padding, and spacing of cells.

The font, color, and background tags mean that adding backgrounds to pages, altering the size and color of text, and assigning colors to objects are all much easier. You now can represent colors simply by typing their name—red, green, blue, silver, and teal are just a few examples.

Netscape Extensions

Netscape has been incredibly influential in taking the Web forward by adding its own powerful extensions to the Navigator browser. These include image control tags, better rule commands, list controls, impressive fonts, and stylish backgrounds. By adding their own extensions,

Netscape created a stir in the W3C. After a great deal of persuasion they agreed to comply with the standards and contribute to 3.0. Now that many of their extensions have been implemented in version 3.2, they should see HTML 3.2 become the accepted standard.

Image tags include better alignment facilities, size controls, and border features. Line rules properties now include thickness, width, and style attributes. These tools enable you to give your pages a professional appearance to set them apart. The extensions also allow greater control of lists, including the style of bullets, numbering, and indentation.

Client-Side Image Maps

Client-side image maps are images that have hotspots for creating links to other Web pages. You could use a map of the world, for example, as an image map to let a user select a country for a flight destination. Prior to client-side image maps, image maps were implemented on the server and were tedious and frustrating. The new tags let you use the <MAP> tag to map images and the <AREA> tag to define areas. They're a popular way to navigate around pages using the visual map instead of reading multiple text entries.

Java Applets

Java applets can be animations or database managers—basically anything you feel like designing. HTML 3.2 offers a high level of support for Java because Java's one of the most significant Internet-related languages. The <PARAM> tag lets you pass parameters to the applet, increasing the browser's flexibility.

The Significance of HTML 3.2

The 3.2 standard is a welcome player in the WWW arena. Browsers will add the new tags to their software, and there will be a uniform set of tags that everyone agrees on. Soon all browsers will be able to view all of the content of Web pages rather than missing out on certain sections because of compatibility problems.

HTML 3.3 draft is already underway and promises greater support for scripting and stylesheets. Future versions will add math capabilities, banners, figures, and notes. Microsoft Internet Explorer 3.0 already supports some of these, so you can get to the future today.

Internet Explorer already offers the capability to support multiple scripting languages. This book deals with one of those scripting languages in particular—VBScript, Microsoft's own scripting language, based on their popular Visual Basic programming language.

Getting to Know VBScript

VBScript is easy to learn and use because it's so similar to Visual Basic. It's designed as a strict subset of the Visual Basic for Applications (VBA) language that Microsoft's Excel and other Office applications use. VBA itself is a subset of the Visual Basic language from Microsoft's VB 4.0 Development system. The lightweight nature of the package means that it's ideal for Internet applications but still contributes new and exciting functionality to Web pages. Lightweight does not mean flimsy, but rather a simpler language structure that can be interpreted at high speed (lighter). VBScript also is intended to be a safe subset of the Visual Basic language so it doesn't include file I/O or direct access to the underlying operating system. This is a security feature most new Internet packages include.

One benefit VBScript bestows is that it enables developers to link and automate a huge number of objects in Web pages to produce amazing effects. These range from ActiveX objects that manage sounds and applications to Java applets that give high quality animations. This book shows you how to incorporate these features into your documents. Check on the Web for examples of dynamic pages—you'll definitely be impressed. Figures 1-6 and 1-7 show a couple sites that illustrate how you can use scripts to great effect. The Safari Web page is at `http://www.onsafari.com/demopg1.htm`.

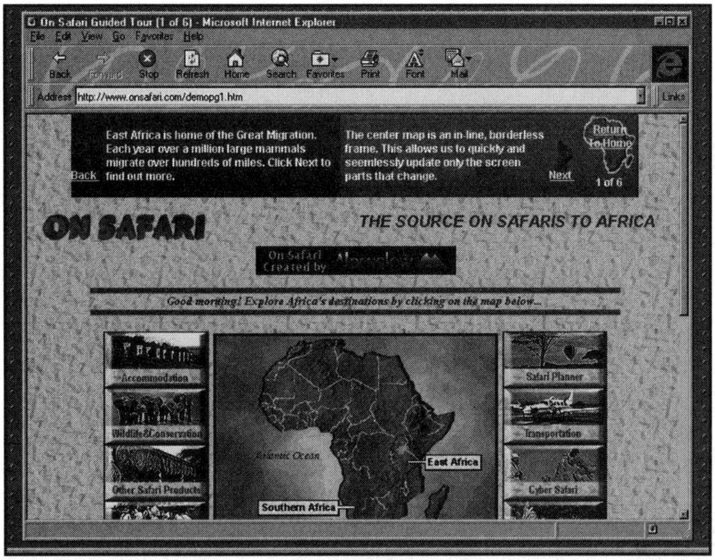

FIGURE 1-6
A safari Web page that uses frames, banners, scripting, sound, and a Java applet

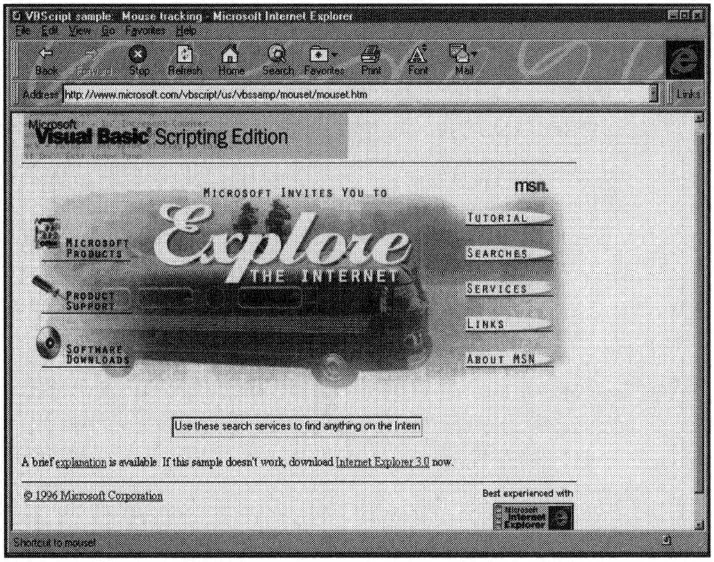

FIGURE 1-7
Clickable image maps and VBScript enable you to use images as navigation tools.

Developers can write Visual Basic code that lives in the HTML document using the <SCRIPT> tag. The code is produced in ASCII format and interpreted on download, allowing the page to become interactive. The browser needs to have Visual Basic Script support and must be able to integrate scripting with controls or applets embedded in the HTML stream. Because the script is in ASCII code, it transports across the Web like any other HTML document, and the browser processes the information on the host machine. The power thus shifts away from the server toward the host machine and greatly improves the capabilities of Web pages. Scripting can be done in several languages, using the common object and event models to dynamically produce content, aid navigation, and communicate with ActiveX controls.

Another popular scripting language is Netscape's JavaScript, a partner of VBScript. Internet Explorer supports both languages. Both Netscape's JavaScript and VBScript achieve similar features. JavaScript is possibly a little more difficult to learn whereas VBScript uses the more straightforward BASIC style language.

Which One Is Better—VBScript or JavaScript?

VBScript and JavaScript both are excellent scripting languages and powerful tools for improving the functionality of your Web pages. The answer is purely subjective, so the choice belongs to you, the Web author. Currently, Netscape Navigator doesn't directly support VBScript or ActiveX technology, but Netscape may eventually be forced to implement these changes in their browser to satisfy public demand. A plug-in available from Ncompass Technology lets you view ActiveX controls within Netscape Navigator—even though Navigator doesn't offer native ActiveX support. Meanwhile, Microsoft's Internet Explorer 3.0 is fully compatible with both scripting languages.

One of the wonderful features of VBScript is that it's just the thing for less experienced programmers because it has the same style as Visual Basic and is easy to pick up. Because JavaScript is based on the C++ language, you may find it more difficult if you're unfamiliar with C++. As many Web users are casual programmers, VBScript is an ideal way to spice up your Web pages with minimal effort. And what's more—it's free!

The Microsoft Strategy—ActiveX Technology

The ActiveX initiative enables software components to interact with one another in a networked environment even though they were created in another language. ActiveX is Microsoft's replacement for OLE controls. It's based on the COM architecture for designing software components. The ActiveX architecture is used to build container applications that can host other ActiveX modules, such as scripting engines and Visual controls. Building software components in a standard way keeps compatibility problems to a minimum.

Microsoft's Web site hosts the first visible signs of ActiveX technology, boasting multimedia effects, interactive objects, and sophisticated applications. Figure 1-8 is an example page from its Microsoft's Web site.

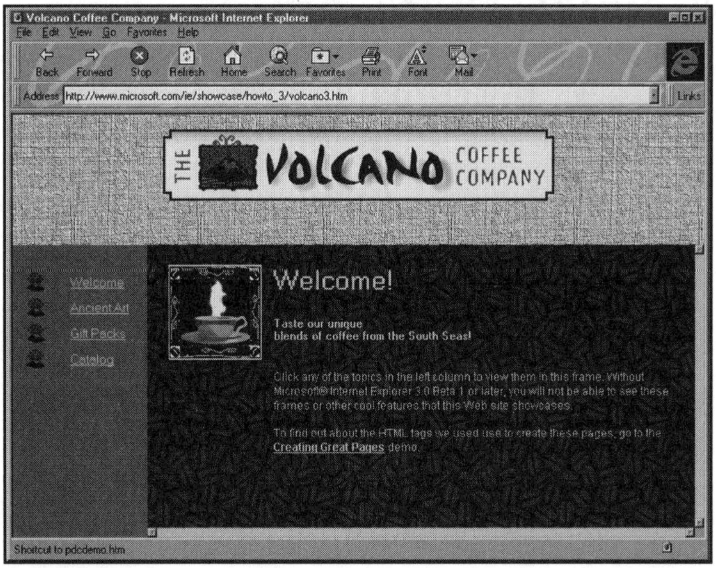

FIGURE 1-8
Microsoft's sample page demonstrates the latest ActiveX technology.

The days of a separate Internet browser, word processing package, spreadsheet, and so on are nearing an end. You can expect to see a new style of browser with the next version of Internet Explorer; a browser that permits file management and document creation without ever leaving the browser shell.

ActiveX technology is built behind the ActiveX scripting standard. This standard allows a supported ActiveX scripting engine to plug into any ActiveX-enabled product and open up a whole new world of opportunities for improvements to applications. For example, independent software developers could write components for different applications and add them to a standard application to customize it for a particular user. This technology will act as a glue, tying together a wide assortment of building blocks that enable the rapid development of sophisticated Web sites and applications.

Most Web users will experience the ActiveX standard as controls, documents, and scripts, but it also embraces client, server, and tools technologies.

Developing and Deploying Interactive Applications

Imagine that you could download an application or a specific functional component from the Web and run it within your browser. Instead of buying a copy of a word processor, you might download the latest version from the Net and pay a subscription to the vendor. Cross-platform applications could be released without the expense of creating and distributing multiple copies of the software. Using scripting languages, you can add greater client-side functionality (beyond HTML) to Web pages and complex processing can occur on the client machine. The reduction in network communication with the server will manifest itself to all users still connected by modem (and not lucky enough to have a T1 connection).

ActiveX controls and ActiveX scripting provide the infrastructure for adding behavior and scripting to Web pages in a language-neutral and tool-neutral way. They will seamlessly connect Internet-access applications and traditional desktop applications so that Web access and Internet use are an integrated extension of the user's desktop.

The Concept of the Internet Explorer 4.0 Shell

As mentioned earlier, the next version of Explorer will be a marriage of the Internet Explorer browser and the Windows file management Explorer so that all browsing, creating documents, and editing are done from within a simple Explorer shell. Applications will live inside the document browser frame as document objects. The application (document object) will borrow a page from the container (Explorer) and then the browser frame will lend itself (captions, menus, toolbars, and so forth) to the document object to use as it pleases. ActiveX technology will also allow applications to create documents that can be published directly on the Web without conversion into HTML format.

ActiveX Controls

You can insert ActiveX controls into HTML documents to provide interactive and user-controllable functions, such as animation and audio and video, without having to open separate programs. The need to download separate applications for incorporating sound and images into your Web pages will fade, because the browser can take care of them automatically. ActiveX controls will enable Web pages to update dynamically based on user interactions or events specified by their own internal state. Also, new text controls and events for handling them will greatly increase Web authors' control over the appearance of a Web page. Microsoft currently provides a fairly extensive selection of controls, and this will grow as other developers get to work writing new controls.

Examples of Some Controls

Some of the controls that Microsoft has already released include the following:

CONTROL NAME	FUNCTION
ActiveMovie Control	Enables you to embed popular video and audio formats into your HTML pages
Label Control	Enables you to insert text at various angles, follow user-defined paths, and display using different colors and fonts
PreLoader Control	Loads a specified document in the background while the reader continues to view another one
Timer Control	Lets you introduce delays and time intervals into Web pages; the event fires at regular intervals and can be used in connection with VBScript code to obtain animated effects and delays
Marquee Control	Scrolls text and images vertically, horizontally, or in both directions at once, which makes creating scrolling banners and attention-grabbing sections in documents easy
StockTicker Control	Provides real-time data acquisition capabilities for use in Web pages; downloads stock price data at regular intervals and displays it as a scrolling marquee
Menu Control	Lets you use a menu in an HTML document; enables you to add menus anywhere on a page (you can respond to user selections via execution of script functions)
Popup Window Control	Provides a preview window for displaying another HTML file without ever loading that file into the main browser window.
Chart Control	Lets you create business graphics on the Web (the charts are quite simple, but if this doesn't fulfill your needs, several excellent chart controls are already on the market)
Animated Button Control	Enables you to use moving images on your buttons to attract readers' attention or change the image when the mouse pointer moves over the button
HTML Layout Control	Enables you to control exactly where you put objects

The Impact of VBScript—What Will It Lead To?

What does VBScript mean for the future of the publishing on the World Wide Web? If that question could be answered in one or two paragraphs, you wouldn't need to read the rest of this book. We aim to present all the essential features of the language, starting at the beginning and working through to more advanced topics and larger examples. The most important thing about this book is that it is meant as a source of ideas and inspiration—we can't hope to provide complete Web sites for you to use, but we can provide you with the skills, techniques, and information you need to develop truly active content with VBScript.

For readers new to programming, or to the Visual Basic family, Chapters 3 through 7 form a complete language tutorial. Chapter 3, "Creating Your First VBScript Document," covers the essential HTML tags, the new <SCRIPT> tag, and how to write your first interactive document. Chapters 8 through 15 discuss everything from declaring variables and writing VBScript expressions to defining functions and handling events. After introducing the language, we also cover topics such as error handling, coding conventions, object models for scripting, forms processing, ActiveX controls, and using Java applets and server side scripting.

You might want to go ahead and start using VBScript straight away; if so, take a look at the table of contents and start scripting. If you want to know more about Internet Explorer 3.0 first, the next chapter should tell you all you need to know.

CHAPTER 2

Internet Explorer 3.0—The Final Release

On August 13, 1996, Microsoft's development laboratories set Internet Explorer free as a final release: IE 3.0. Although far less publicized than the release of Windows 95, more than a million copies of Internet Explorer were downloaded from Microsoft's download sites during just the first week following the release date.

Microsoft is giving it away free to encourage people to use their Internet products. The touted release of Nashville (the code name for the next version of Windows) promises an integrated browser and desktop, and familiarity with the browser setup should ease the transition from Windows 95 to Nashville. Other Internet applications from Microsoft include:

- **Visual J++ Development Suite** for creating Java applets and applications
- **FrontPage™** for creating and managing Web sites

- **Internet Studio™** for developing professional Internet applications
- **ActiveX Control Pad** for inserting ActiveX controls into Web pages
- **Office Internet Assistants™** for creating Web pages from Office files

You can download the self-extracting version of IE 3.0 from the Microsoft Web site, or you can use the CD that accompanies this book to install it directly on your computer. Whatever you decide to do, remember to register your copy with Microsoft on their Web site so that they can determine how many copies of IE 3.0 are in use and keep you informed of the latest developments. The CD saves you from having to wait around while the software downloads, and is exactly the same as the version available at the site.

NOTE

You might want to check Microsoft's site from time to time for additional patches or new components that enhance your browser:

`http://www.microsoft.com/ie/`

Installation Procedure for Internet Explorer

The CD contains a self-extracting copy of Internet Explorer. To install Explorer on your system, just run the executable on the CD. The setup program creates a temporary folder for extraction and stores iexplore.exe with other Microsoft Internet files.

To run the executable, insert the CD into your CD drive and use Windows Explorer to view the contents of your CD. Look in the directory labeled *ms_setup*, and run the file labeled *msie30m.exe*. The icon for a self-extracting file looks like this:

After the installation process finishes, you can run Internet Explorer by double-clicking on the icon. It should look something like Figure 2-1.

FIGURE 2-1
Microsoft's Internet Explorer 3.0

Try using the browser to connect to the Web and visit a few sites to get a feel for it. Peruse the various menus, and pay special attention to the Options category in the View menu (see Figure 2-2), which gives you a good idea of what features you can customize and what security procedures it uses.

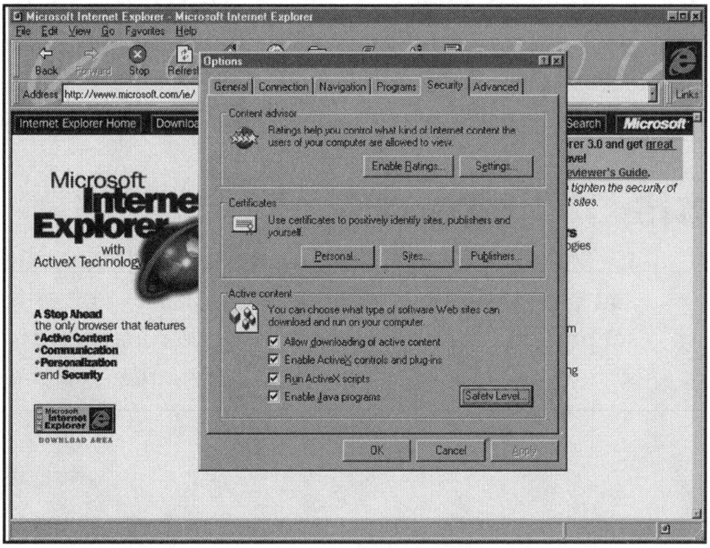

FIGURE 2-2
The Options menu allows full customization in Internet Explorer.

TIP

After you install Explorer 3.0, be sure to adjust the Internet Cache settings to reflect your needs. You can access these settings from the Options dialog box on the View menu. The cache section allows you to specify how much of your hard disk to use as an Internet cache and when to reload pages from a remote site.

You also may want to examine the Security settings (accessed from the Options dialog box) as you set up the cache. You can tailor these settings to suit your needs, but you will need to enable scripting, applets, and ActiveX controls before you can use the examples presented in this book.

To browse sites on the Web, you must have access to the Internet through a local access provider, as well as a dial-up connection. Further, you should have a Serial Line Internet Protocol (SLIP) or a Point to Point Protocol (PPP) installed on your system (you generally can acquire these from an access provider). You can run most of the examples on the CD without such a connection, because they don't require remote access.

What Does Internet Explorer 3.0 Have to Offer?

Internet Explorer 3.0 is packed with new features awaiting use by Web authors. Some are multimedia-related, some concern security, some improve e-mail communications, and others support new HTML tags (both standard and experimental). The following sections explains the features IE 3.0 has to offer in greater detail.

Loads of Features

IE 3.0 is fully compatible with the latest HTML standard (version 3.2) and supports several additional features that other browsers don't yet support. HTML 3.2 is fully backward-compatible with previous versions of the HTML language, ensuring that you can view any current Web page using IE 3.0.

NOTE *Web browsers that support only version 2.0 of HTML ignore the new commands in version 3.2, and consequently tend to lose page content. You should consider this when you compose your Web pages. HTML does have some commands that enable different styles to be used if a browser lacks support for certain features. Unfortunately, this exceeds the scope for this book. For further information, refer to a book dedicated specifically to HTML.*

In addition to HTML commands for objects, tables, colors, image tags, applets, frames, and stylesheets, Internet Explorer also offers virtual reality support, multimedia components, scripting capabilities, and the HTML Layout Control. Read on to find out more about these exciting innovations.

Using the <OBJECT> Tag to Add ActiveX Commands to Web Pages

Chapter 1 mentioned ActiveX technology and touched on its anticipated role in the future development of the Web. It did not, however, go into detail about how to infuse this new super technology into your Web pages. To do so, you use the HTML <OBJECT> tag.

The HTML <OBJECT> tag allows ActiveX objects to be inserted into the HTML source code. Whenever someone using Internet Explorer visits your Web page, it automatically checks to see whether the necessary components are installed on their system. If not, IE 3.0 automatically installs the components from a predetermined location. These controls then remain on the user's computer, but are loaded into memory only as needed, keeping valuable resources free.

You can use a special ActiveX tool that is included on the CD (called the ActiveX Control Pad) to insert the <OBJECT> tag. The ActiveX Control Pad generates all the information you need to configure the control. Suppose you want to place a timer on your page: the ActiveX Control Pad enables you to use drag and drop windows to create the timer object and set the delay in just a few easy steps.

ActiveX controls let you insert drop-down menu boxes, charts, animated buttons, and scrolling marquees into your pages, giving them a professional appearance. You can choose from more than 1,000

ActiveX controls, so learning how to use the <OBJECT> tag definitely is worth your while. Chapters 12 through 14 explore ActiveX controls more thoroughly.

NOTE *If you're new to HTML and tags, you should start out at the beginning of Chapter 3, "Creating Your First VBScript Document," which gives a brief overview of the language.*

Although ActiveX technology isn't part of the HTML language, the <OBJECT> tag is. Several other HTML commands improve the look of Web pages in general, and the next one that this chapter considers is the <TABLE> tag.

New Table Specification

NCSA Mosaic gets credit for introducing tables, but Netscape quickly picked them up, and finally they have been introduced into HTML, version 3.2. Internet Explorer fully supports the <TABLE> tag and gives the author full control over the layout of table, borders, and rules—you can even set the background colors of individual table cells.

Keeping Hold of Your Old Plug-Ins

Internet Explorer is a beauty. Not only does it offer massive amounts of new functionality, but it also lets you transport old bookmarks and plug-ins into your new browser. You can convert bookmarks into favorites in a flash, and IE 3.0 supports your plug-ins as if it was their native browser—a major plus for users who want to keep the setup of their old browser, yet want the more modern technology.

Using the Java Environment

Java has taken the Internet by storm. Although Java isn't a Microsoft brainchild, Microsoft has embraced Java and offers full support for it in IE 3.0—after all, if it didn't, who would use its browser? Microsoft even says it has produced the fastest implementation of Java on the

Web today, and independent tests carried out by Microbenchmark and Linpack (when Navigator 3.0 was in its Beta 5 release) bear out the truth of the the claim.

The support for Java in Internet Explorer 3.0 provides the following features for Web authors:

- The 32-bit Windows reference implementation of the Java Virtual Machine (VM) designed by Sun Microsystems. Microsoft's version contains several important differences from Sun's implementation. You can do some things in Microsoft's implementation that you can't do in Sun's, which leads to some compatibility issues.
- A wide range of Java applets can run reliably within the browser, providing huge scope for innovative Web content.
- Enables the integration of applets into script routines (using VBScript or JScript). The scripts can control the applets directly or link them to other ActiveX controls and applets within the same document.
- Contains built-in Java security, a primary concern that affects most corporate Web administrators and Internet users. The browser provides standard security schemes such as code signing, as well as Java-related security technologies, like Java sandbox security.
- Features fast Just In Time (JIT) support, which provides a fast and effiecient way to run Java applications. The JIT compiler provides tool vendors with rich debugging support when debugging Java source code.

NOTE

Microsoft has developed a complete development tool for Java that complements the Java support that Explorer 3.0 offers. The product is called Visual J++ *and should ship in the fall of 1996.*

VRML Support

The Virtual Reality Modeling Language is a fully supported add-on module for Internet Explorer. It lets you navigate virtual 3-D worlds on the Internet and view 3-D objects. Although Virtual Reality still hasn't caught on, it's a useful feature for developers to have at their disposal.

Microsoft now supports the VRML 2.0 standard for creating 3-D models and virtual worlds. Microsoft has licensed Liquid Reality from Dimension X and plans to include it as a part of Windows in the near future. In brief, Liquid Reality is a Java interface to VRML 2.0 and permits more interaction with virtual worlds from applets and scripts than do the current VRML implementations.

New Frame Support

The advent of frames in Web pages means that developers now can divide the window into different sections to present information more clearly. Each frame displays a different HTML document, so you can effectively view several pages without navigating between them.

Internet Explorer is the first commercial browser to support the following types of frames:

- **Borderless frames** that fit into your page almost invisibly
- **Frames without scroll bars** to allow seamless connections
- **Floating frames** that let you embed one Web page within another; you can embed a frame anywhere in a page that you might ordinarily put an image

Using multiple frames, each containing sounds, video, and different background colors, you can achieve sophisticated layouts. You can even apply bitmap patterns to your borders to give your pages that winning touch.

Cascading Style Sheets (CSS)

Cascading Style Sheets (CSS) are the HTML stylesheet standard set by the W3C, and Internet Explorer 3.0 fully supports them. They allow you to attach styles to HTML tags to revolutionize your documents.

Cascading Style Sheets separate the design elements of a page from the page content, which means you can work on the two areas independently, as in desktop publishing systems. Now you can add color, fonts, styles, and spacing to your documents much more easily than before. In addition, you can easily control margins, line spacing, and placement of design elements. You can even put color and image backgrounds on tables and table cells.

Most browsers don't yet have the facilities to display stylesheet information, but because the content and style information is separate, the content can still be displayed. In the future, the effects of this problem will decrease as more browsers add support for CSS.

Linked stylesheets allow you to apply a standard stylesheet to many different documents, giving a uniform appearance to your pages. Additionally, if you want to change the style throughout a document, just update the style in one place to apply the changes throughout.

Scripting Engines

The browser architecture that Internet Explorer 3.0 uses is built to conform to the new ActiveX Scripting standard. The browser provides a standard interface with which scripting language modules (implemented as script *engines*) can communicate. These engines can plug directly into a Web browser without modifying the browser software. Currently, Internet Explorer ships with DLLs (Dynamic Link Libraries) for Visual Basic Scripting Edition and JavaScript. Other developers are designing scripting engines for other languages (such as Perl), but it may be some time before these new scripting languages become as widespread as VBScript or JavaScript. This book covers the VBScript language and how to use it to create true active content on the Web.

NOTE *Microsoft's implementation of JavaScript has been named JScript. Although perhaps initially confusing, the fact is that JScript and JavaScript essentially are identical. The former is a specific implentation (Microsoft's) and the latter is the language itself.*

Scripting engines allow the look and feel of documents to be changed, as well as giving them "life." You can build pages that respond to user actions, validate user inputs, link to other applications, play animations, control applets, and much more. You even can build complete

Web applications that run within the browser itself and can be downloaded like any other documents. (Chapter 14, " Using the Internet Control Pack and Java Applets with VBScript," covers this topic in greater detail.)

Microsoft wants to encourage other software vendors to write and use scripting engines in their software and is making the specification and the source for VBScript freely available to software developers. This new technology is fast appearing on Web sites everywhere, and several large third-party companies already are developing products that use the VBScript engine.

HTML Layout Control

HTML Layout Control is a special ActiveX control that Microsoft has developed. It ships with the ActiveX Control Pad (available on the CD) and allows pinpoint placement of objects on a Web page. The Layout Control supports an experimental HTML standard for placing objects at exact points within a layout, so the programmer can design complex forms. These forms will look exactly the same when displayed by any Web browser capable of hosting the HTML layout control. Figure 2-3 shows an example of the control in action.

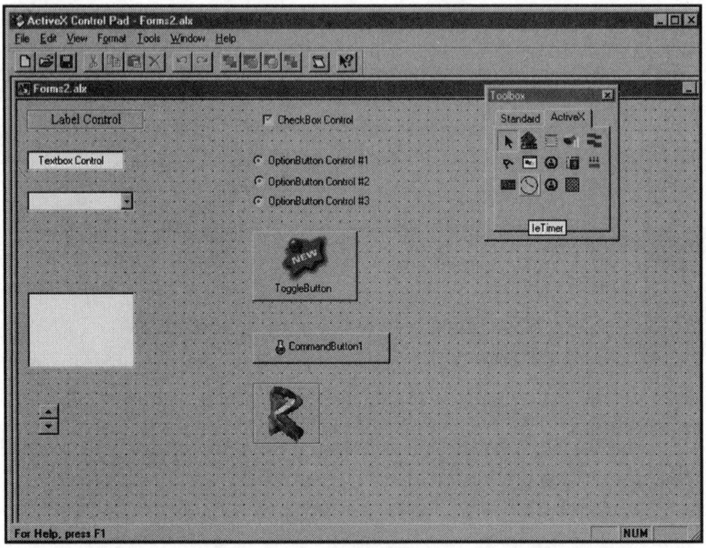

FIGURE 2-3
Using the HTML Layout Control to position objects on a Web page.

At the moment, HTML deals with relative positions, such as ALIGN=MIDDLE, <CENTER>, and so on. Sometimes you simply cannot design the page you want, owing to the limited control you have over object placement. The Layout Control removes these limitations by allowing you to specify x,y pixel coordinates for objects within a layout. Because it's only an experimental standard, Microsoft doesn't support it directly in Explorer 3.0, but rather, as an add-in ActiveX control. The real benefit of using the HTML Layout Control is that you can move items around the layout while displaying the document, which lets you use VBScript to write scripting functions that modify the document at run-time—a feature not possible with simple HTML. Chapter 13, "Using the ActiveX Control Pad and HTML Layout Control," covers this control in more detail.

Multimedia Support

Internet Explorer offers full multimedia compatibility—the technology is streets ahead of any other browser. All popular video, audio, and graphics formats are fully supported, allowing you to listen to music, watch movies, or play animations from within the browser.

It also has built-in ActiveMovie support. *ActiveMovie* is the latest digital video technology for the Internet and desktop from Microsoft. Now developers can deliver creative titles on multiple platforms with synchronized audio, video, and special effects. Full-screen MPEG quality and real-time special effects are now a reality, and when bandwidth restrictions are lifted, full movies will be available over the Internet with high-quality stereo sound.

You can now enjoy top-quality video and audio on the Net without having to use separate players or helper applications. Internet Explorer 3.0 has it all!

Internet Mail and News

Internet Mail and News are two additional fully integrated applications that ship with Internet Explorer. They provide a simple and fast way to send and receive e-mail and contribute to, or read articles from, newsgroups. You no longer must load a separate application to check your messages, because you can access Internet Mail from Explorer's menus.

The Inbox Assistant helps you manage messages and, if necessary (if you have Microsoft Exchange Address Books), you can use a conversion facility to help convert your data into a suitable format. The application uses the SMTP and POP3 protocols for sending and receiving mail, and the News component allows you to take full advantage of Usenet Newsgroups. Figure 2-4 shows the layout of Internet Mail.

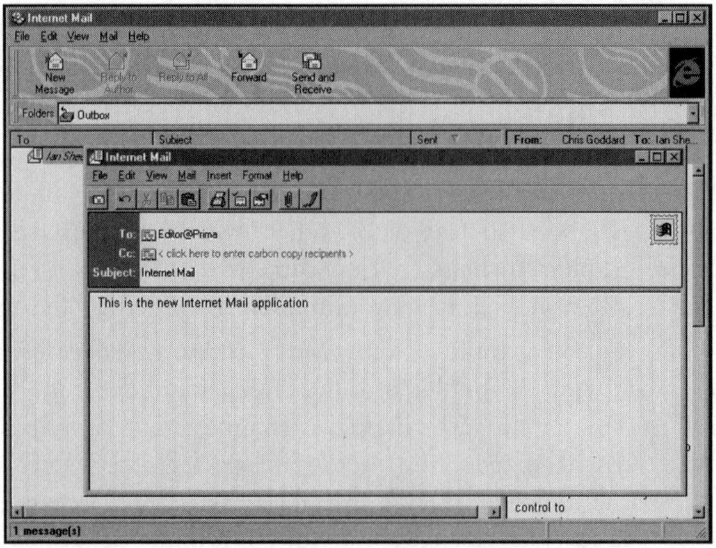

FIGURE 2-4
Internet Mail allows mail facilities from within the browser.

A handy hyperlink feature also converts any references to e-mail addresses, http:, ftp:, mailto:, telnet:, or file: in the message into a hyperlink. By clicking on the hyperlink, it automatically creates a new message that already has the address line in place if it's a mailto: reference. If it's an http: or other Web-related link, Internet mail launches the respective program and directs it to go to that URL.

Other features include:

- **Spell checking of mail**, if the Microsoft Office 95 spell checker is installed
- **Fast message preview**

- **HTML support**, enabling viewing and sending of messages in rich text format
- **International character sets** for sending and reading messages in different languages
- **Automatic signatures** for personalizing your mail
- **MIME support**
- **Conversation threads in Microsoft News** to assist with following a topic
- **Automatic decoding of binary attachments in Internet News**

Security Issues

Security on the client side of Web connections has always been a concern for both developers and users. As people become more accustomed to sending information over the Internet, most users give little thought to the possibility of espionage, fraud, or viral infection. Web security is a critical subject that goes far beyond the stereotyped image of protecting credit card numbers, and covers the following areas:

- **System security and integrity**, relating to hardware, software and operating systems on client and server machines. Attacks in this area normally make use of weaknesses in the operating system, and sometimes in the software.
- **Authentication mechanisms** are used to verify that a particular user matches up with whom they claim to be, as well as authenicating documents, applications, and source code.
- **Access control and authorization systems** prevent access to restricted areas by unauthorized individuals
- **Privacy technologies** protect against unwanted data interception over a network.

In the latest version of Internet Explorer, Microsoft has implemented security features to allow private communications, safe download code, and self-identification across the Internet.

Privacy is incorporated by using the latest SSL and PCT protocols. Secure Sockets Layer(SSL) 2.0 and 3.0 and Private Communications

Technology (PCT) 1.0 reduce the likelihood of eavesdropping on the Net by creating secure channels between two computers, enabling private, personal, or business communication to transpire privately on the Internet or intranets. This opens the way for personal banking, airline reservations, and private communications.

Privacy isn't the only security concern. Viruses are a major threat to all computer users, and Microsoft has been involved with developing the new Authenticode technology to reduce the chances of infection by allowing you to verify the source of any component you download.

Authenticode™ is the latest initiative for reducing the risk of downloading something destructive from the Internet. It enables the addition of a digital signature to software for verification prior to usage. Software publishers obtain certificates from a central authority and use them to digitally sign their software code. Internet Explorer can then verify that the software originated from the named software publisher and that tampering has not occurred. Figure 2-5 shows an example of a certificate.

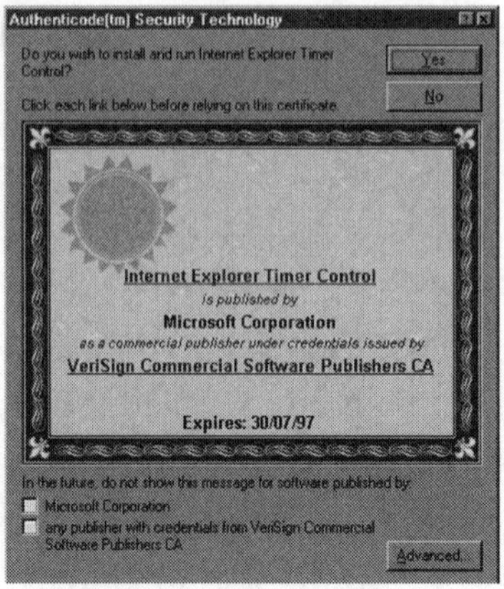

FIGURE 2-5
A security software certificate.

So, IE 3.0 supports security measures to reduce eavesdropping and downloading of corrupted files. Does it offer any further protection, say from hackers or impersonators? Yes. It includes client authentication, cryptographic services, SOCKS firewall protection, and Cookie privacy.

Client authentication lets you identify yourself to others on the Internet using a digital personal certificate. You can obtain these from companies such as Verisign, and use them to confirm that you are who you say you are. As a user of Internet Explorer, you are entitled to a free Class 1 Digital ID from Verisign (see the online setup pages that follow the Internet Explorer setup for information on obtaining this freebie).

CryptoAPI 1.0 is incorporated into Explorer, and allows you to integrate strong cryptography into your applications. Cryptographic Service Provider modules integrate with CryptoAPI and perform functions like key generation, key exchange, data encryption and decryption, hashing, and digital signatures and verification. IE 3.0 will install the Microsoft RSA Base Service Provider on Windows 95 and NT (the software that implements the RSA Encryption Algorithm used by the API).

These are some of the security features available on Internet Explorer 3.0. They are the latest cryptographic and security technologies, and hopefully will succeed in fulfilling Microsoft's aim of maintaining privacy in and around the Internet.

Behind the Scenes—The Architecture

The Internet Explorer architecture has been designed as an open, Internet standards-based platform. The browser has been designed to fit into any DocObject container applications while providing services, support for ActiveX technology, Java, and Web browsing capabilities.

When Microsoft releases the next version of Windows, code-named Nashville, it intends to provide a fully integrated Windows Explorer shell, capable of use for browsing the contents of your hard disk, office LAN, Web sites (using the Internet shell add-on), and even for sending and retrieving mail messages. All these capabilities will be possible using a single shell application, owing to the new DocObject architecture, which allows host applications to lend themselves (caption bars, menus, and window area) to another object. In the case of browsing the WWW, this object is the IEBrowser object, which plugs into the shell and takes over its drawing canvas, menus, status bars, and caption bars to provide a complete Web browser. The current container application for Explorer 3.0 is only a few kilobytes in size—all it provides is a shell for the IEBrowser object to use.

Figure 2-6 shows an overview of this architecture, including the services that the IEBrowser object provides. Besides these services, the browser provides support for the complete ActiveX standard, including ActiveX documents, controls, and scripting. All these items contribute to a fully configurable browsing environment. The new ActiveX technology leverages over five years of component software development with the old OLE standard. By extending the old standard with models for communicating over the Internet and the new user and system paradigms that have evolved, Microsoft hopes to take advantage of the huge existing base of component software and developers. By all accounts, ActiveX is tipped to be a highly successful technology.

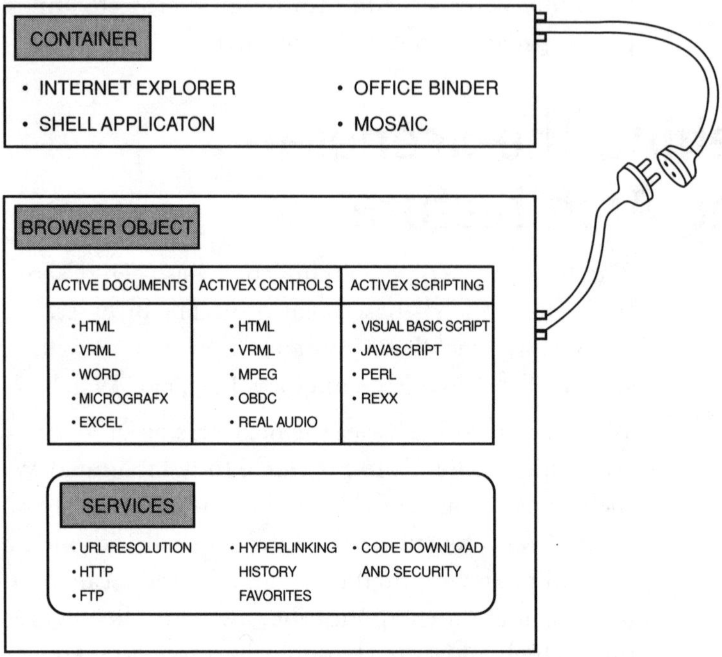

FIGURE 2-6
Microsoft's architecture for World Wide Web browsing on the client machine

Let's Get Started

It's about time to start learning at how to use VBScript. The potential benefits of using scripting to make Web documents come alive should be clear by now.

Before you can run any active HTML documents that use VBScript, you must have Internet Explorer 3.0 (or another browser that supports the language) installed. In addition to a browser, several other software tools make a Web author's life easier, including the ActiveX Control Pad, an HTML editor (such as Kenn Nesbitt's WebEdit), and various ActiveX controls. The CD that accompanies this book contains these items, and the beginning of the next chapter covers the installation process.

Because this book has been written to help everyone, ranging from HTML beginners to experienced programmers, different readers will use it in different ways. The next few pages start from the beginning with the basic structure of HTML documents and builds from that foundation to create your first active document—the ubiquitous Hello World! application.

CHAPTER 3

Creating Your First VBScript Document

If you haven't used much HTML (Hypertext Markup Language), or if you're learning VBScript for the first time, this chapter's for you. It first introduces several basic HTML elements, then covers scripting tags and setting up your first document, and concludes by furnishing an event-driven example.

The chapter discusses the following topics:

- Creating and running scripts using Internet Explorer 3.0
- Basic HTML tags
- The new <SCRIPT> tag
- Writing your first interactive document

- Placing scripts in an HTML document
- Using simple controls and responding to events

Setting Up Your Software Tools

You can create Web pages using something as simple as a basic text editor, such as Notepad in Windows 95 and NT. But if you do, you generally end up spending most of your time typing instead of designing compelling pages. You should use software tools like those on the CD, because they let you concentrate on creating pages.

The first part of this chapter deals with the installation and setup procedures you need to follow to get the tools on the CD up and running. These tools include the following:

- The example files for all the chapters in this book
- Kenn Nesbitt's WebEdit
- The ActiveX Control Pad and HTML Layout Control
- The ActiveX Gallery Controls
- The Internet Control Pack

The CD contains several other pieces of software not dealt with in this chapter. For a complete list of these programs and their uses, see Appendix D, "What's on the CD."

> NOTE
>
> **WINDOWS 95 AND WINDOWS NT SUPPORT**
> *We have attempted to provide versions of all the software tools for both Windows 95 and Windows NT. The CD's root directory contains four main directories: Examples (same for Win95 and NT), VBSSetup (same for Win95 and NT), VBScript95, and VBScriptNT. The rest of this section operates under the assumption that you have selected the directory that applies to your Windows platform.*

The CD is organized into several different parts. You can view the examples directly from the CD, but the CD is a read-only medium. You should use the install program to copy them to your hard disk so that you can work with the examples and save changes to them.

Apart from the example files, which the next section covers, two other directories are of interest (see Figure 3-1). These directories contain the self-extracting executables for the Microsoft tools and the WebEdit program install files, respectively.

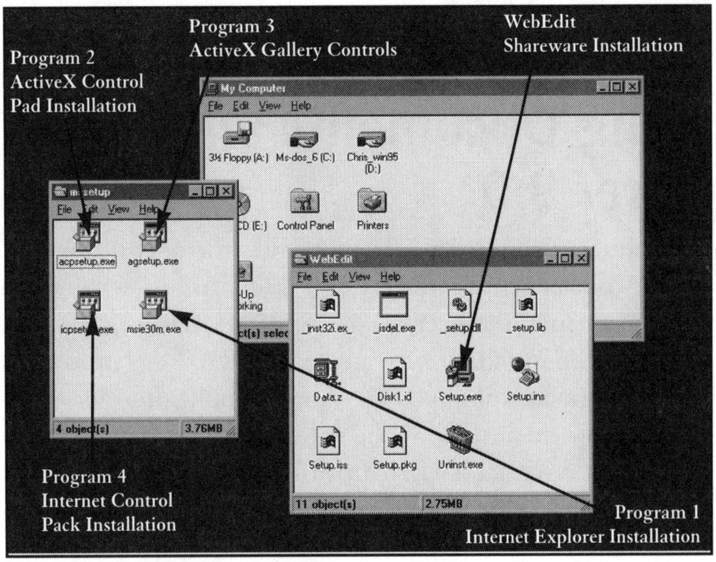

FIGURE 3-1
The contents of the mssetup and WebEdit directories on the VBScript Master's Handbook CD

Installing the Example Files

Most chapters in this book have example documents that you can load and use. Given the quantity of these files, they're organized into a directory structure of their own. You should install these files to your hard disk so you can load and edit them. You can then restore any changes you make simply by copying the relevant file back from the Examples directory on the CD.

Insert the *VBScript Master's Handbook* CD into your drive. Use Windows Explorer or the My Computer folders to examine the contents of the CD. You should see a program called Install.exe. Double-click on the icon to run the automatic installation program. Follow the on-screen instructions to install the example files to your system. You will be prompted for a directory to which to install the files. Besides installing the files, the program creates a program group and adds a Mastering VBScript icon to it. Double-click on that icon whenever you want to load the main Web page for the book, which contains hyperlinks to all the example documents.

NOTE *Remember to install and configure Internet Explorer 3.0 before you load the example documents.*

Loading Documents with Internet Explorer 3.0

Internet Explorer 3.0 currently is the only browser that provides VBScript support, although others are in development. Chapter 2, "Internet Explorer 3.0—The Final Release," discusses how to install it. The installation program for IE 3.0 sets up your computer to use Internet Explorer as the default application for loading HTML documents (identified by the extension HTM or HTML and displayed with a special icon). To run IE 3.0, press the Start menu button and choose the Programs menu, which should contain an entry with the Explorer icon and the text "Internet Explorer." Select the "Internet Explorer" item to load the browser application. If you have set up a dial-up account for accessing the Internet, IE 3.0 attempts to connect you and loads your default start page; for example, `http://www.microsoft.com/`. After IE 3.0 makes the connection, you can navigate the Net.

If you want to load HTML documents stored on your local system, you have two options.

1. Use Windows Explorer or the My Computer directory folders to find the document you want to load, and then double-click on the file's icon to load the browser and display the document.
2. Otherwise, you can use the browser itself to find the document you seek. From the IE menu bar, choose File [->] Open to open a file selection dialog box. Navigate your system until you find the file, and then press the Open button.

You can load the examples provided with the book in either of the preceding two ways. Simply find the directory called *Location*\Examples on your computer, where *Location* is the drive and directory you specified as the place to which to save the VBScript files when you ran the install program of the last section. The Examples directory contains one main file, Default.htm, which contains links to all the examples. The examples themselves are stored in separate subdirectories, named according to chapter number. Some of the example files have cryptic names (eight letters isn't much to express yourself), so you should use the main Web page to link to the examples. Remember: You can access this page from the Start button's Programs menu (this shortcut is set up by the examples' install program).

Setting Up the ActiveX Control Pad and HTML Layout Control

The ActiveX Control Pad is a free product from Microsoft that helps you to insert ActiveX controls, write script functions, and edit HTML Layouts. The tool is invaluable when you enter these areas of VBScript development. Chapter 13, "Using the ActiveX Control Pad and HTML Layout Control," contains instructions and examples for using these items.

The HTML Layout Control is an ActiveX control that you can use to place items at specific x,y coordinates on the Web page. It ships as part of the ActiveX Control Pad's installation and running the setup program installs it for you.

To install this package, insert the CD and select the directory that applies to your Windows platform, such as VBScript95 or VBScriptNT. Next, open the directory called *mssetup*. The ActiveX Control Pad is supplied as a self-extracting executable that automatically starts the install process. Double-click on the Program 2 icon, as shown in Figure 3-1, to install the Control Pad. The install program will ask you to name a program group in which to include the ActiveX Control Pad program icon.

Installing Kenn Nesbitt's WebEdit

Kenn Nesbitt's WebEdit is a special editor that's aware of HTML tags (more about these later in the chapter). It helps you design Web pages more quickly by letting you insert tags, forms, and images simply by administering a few button clicks. It also means you don't have to know (or remember) all the HTML tags.

WebEdit is a shareware program, so after the evaluation period expires, you should register your copy. When you register, you receive a software key with which you can unlock the editor's advanced features. The registered version of the editor was used for creating many of the examples for this book.

Installing WebEdit is simple. Insert the CD and select the directory that applies to your Windows platform. Next, open the WebEdit directory. Figure 3-1 shows the directory listing you should see. Run the program Setup.exe to install the editor to your computer. The setup program will ask you to specify a program group to which to assign the WebEdit program icon.

Registering the ActiveX Controls on Your System

The CD contains two sets of ActiveX controls from Microsoft. These controls, once installed, allow you to add all sorts of new and interesting features to Web pages, including real-time data acquisition, timers, fancy labels, menus, preview windows, and connections to other information servers.

The first of these packs is known as the ActiveX Component Gallery. You can download the controls that it contains from the Microsoft Web site at `http://www.microsoft.com/activex/gallery/`, but they have been placed on the CD for your convenience. The second set is known as the Internet Control pack and you can download it at `http://www.microsoft.com/msdownload/`. These controls are also included on the CD.

To install these packages, insert the CD and select the directory that applies to your Windows platform, such as VBScript95 or VBScriptNT. Next, open the mssetup directory. The control packs are supplied as self-extracting executables. Double-click on the Program 3 icon (see Figure 3-1) to install the ActiveX Control Gallery. Double-click on the Program 4 icon (also shown in Figure 3-1) to install the Internet Control Pack. No executable files will be installed to your system; instead, the new controls will be registered for use on your system. Chapter 12, "ActiveX Controls and VBScript," covers the ActiveX Gallery, while Chapter 14, "Using the Internet Control Pack and Java Applets with VBScript," covers the Internet Control Pack.

An Introduction to HTML and HTML Tags

This section introduces the key points of the HTML language and shows how to compose an HTML document. The reason to start with HTML commands rather than VBScript commands is that you need to set up an HTML document to contain the script before you start writing the actual script.

The key to the HTML cross-platform language is its use of standardized tags to mark sections of text with different styles. Because the tags are standardized within the language, any browser that can interpret HTML can display the document in a format the author intended.

NOTE

One caveat: Browser vendors constantly try to maintain a technological advantage over their competitors, and one of the most visible ways to do so is to extend the HTML language using proprietary tags. Just because any popular tag is sure to become a de jur standard doesn't necessarily mean you should go ahead and use it. It depends entirely on your perceived audience. If you can rely on no users with incompatible browsers viewing your site (very unlikely unless you're on a private intranet), you should plan to support as many fundamental browser features as possible.

So What Do These Tags Look Like, and How Do You Use Them?

All tags look the same—a pair of angled brackets surrounding an instruction. In the past, instructions were all related to formatting text, but now that HTML has expanded to include graphics, sound, and animation, many new options are available. We will now have a look at the simple text HTML commands.

You format a block of text using a pair of *container* tags. One tag marks the beginning of the section, and the other the end. Suppose you want to make a line of text bold. You would include the following line in the HTML document:

```
<B>Welcome to Mastering VBScript</B>
```

Most tags are container tags, but a few tags are exceptions, and are known as *empty tags*. They stand alone in a document because they perform only single event operations and thus don't require both opening and closing tags. Examples of single events are formatting tags like horizontal rules and paragraph breaks.

More advanced tags exist for working with image maps, bulleted lists, tables, and frames. For a tutorial on advanced HTML, several good books are available. When HTML features are used in the example programs, they are explained in more detail.

TIP *If you want to find out some more information about a specific tag without having to buy a new book, the Help on the ActiveX Control Pad provides a comprehensive online reference.*

Now you're ready to view the first HTML document from the CD. Load the main Mastering VBScript Web page (called Default.htm) into your browser, then load the examples by clicking on the relevant hyperlinks. Select `Simple HTML Tags to Create the Basic Document` from the Tutorial section of the main Web page to load the example into the browser and run it. The source code for this example is listed here and contains only a few lines. It has been kept simple by design, and will expand as you learn more commands. See Figure 3-2 to make sure that your document has loaded correctly.

```
<HTML>

<HEAD>
<TITLE>First HTML Document</TITLE>
</HEAD>

<BODY>
<H3>This is an HTML Heading</H3>
</BODY>

</HTML>
```

The best way to learn what the tags do is to work through the code, line by line, and read about each tag in turn. They have been listed below in the order they appear in the above code snippet.

The <HTML> Tag

The <HTML> tag is a container tag for the document, and is *always* the first line in any code. It signals to the browser that the subsequent text should be treated as an HTML document. Because HTML documents are just one of the many items that modern browsers load, the <HTML> tag must be included to let the browser know how to interpret what follows.

The terminating container tag (</HTML>) goes at the end of the document to indicate that the whole document has been received.

The <HEAD> Tag

The next tag in the sample listing is the <HEAD> tag. You can think of it as a cover page for the document, holding information such as the title of the page, keywords for search engines, and any VBScript code.

The HEAD section in this example uses only the <TITLE> and </TITLE> tags. Explorer 3.0 (and most other Web browsers) displays the text between the tags at the top of the page in the Title Bar. The purpose of this text is to make the page easily identifiable, as well as to furnish a default description for the file in the Favorites folder. Later in the chapter, you place some VBScript code in this section. The HEAD section concludes with the </HEAD> tag.

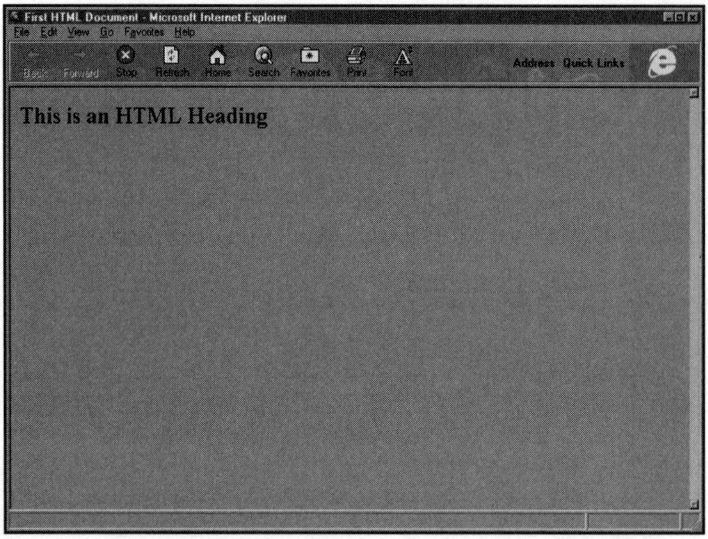

FIGURE 3-2
A basic HTML document

The <BODY> Tag

Following the <HEAD> tag, you see another major feature of any document: the <BODY> tag. As the name suggests, it marks the start of the main body of the HTML document. All the text, images, buttons, forms, sound tracks, frames, and other objects belong in the <BODY> section. It controls how the document appears onscreen.

The body also has an important role in scripting applications, because it creates a framework on which scripting can be built. Most of the active content of a document uses the objects or controls that the <BODY> section contains. Before you can use VBScript to create active content, the scripts must be somehow associated with items on the Web page. You achieve this linking by using events that are generated by form controls and OLE automation objects defined in the BODY section of the document. The <BODY> section serves the crucial role of tying together the scripting and the objects because it names everything to which the scripts will need access. You can insert controls into a document without naming them, but doing so precludes the possibility of using them in your scripts.

Now you know what the <BODY> tag does and what elements are necessary in the <BODY> section to create active content. Figure 3-3 summarizes the different sections of an HTML document and the sort of tags that they contain.

NOTE

For more information on current HTML standards, refer to Chapter 1, "VBScript—What's All the Hype About?" which overviews the latest developments. For the most up-to-date HTML specifications, visit the Web site of the World Wide Web standards body (W3C):

```
http://www.w3.org/
```

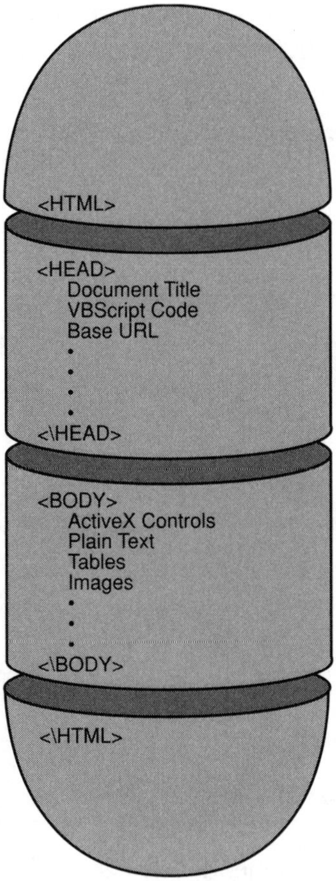

FIGURE 3-3
The concept of an HTML container, with HEAD and BODY sections

Your First Interactive HTML Document

The next step is to incorporate some scripting into your Web pages to make them interactive. The VBScript engine in your browser controls active content, so it's important to make sure that Internet Explorer 3.0 is installed on your computer (see Chapter 2, "Internet

Explorer 3.0—The Final Release"). Explorer 3.0 not only contains a script engine for handling VBScript, but also supports the latest HTML tags and ActiveX controls used in this book. Older versions of Explorer and other browsers might not support these features, so you really should install IE 3.0 to view the examples.

After you successfully install Explorer 3.0 and have the basic HTML commands impressed on your mind, you're ready to take a look at an example containing some Visual Basic script.

Load the script example into Explorer 3.0 from the Web page on the CD Tutorial, by clicking on the `Hello World` hyperlink.

Inside the Explorer window, you should see a Press Me button. Click on it to bring up a dialog box that presents a "Hello World" greeting, as in Figure 3-4.

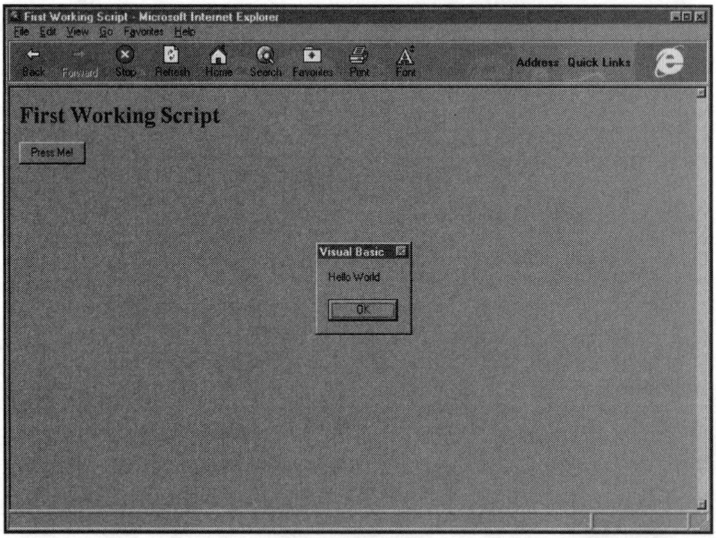

FIGURE 3-4
A familiar "Hello World" greeting with your first VBScript document

Although it might not look tremendously exciting, it does show that your browser is set up correctly and that it recognizes VBScript. It also gives you your first taste of event handling.

Now take a look at the code for this introductory program. In Explorer, just select View [->] Source from the menu bar or right-click the mouse and select View Source from the pop-up menu.

```
<HTML>

<HEAD>
<TITLE>First Working Script</TITLE>

<SCRIPT LANGUAGE="VBScript">
<!—
Sub Button1_OnClick
    MsgBox "Hello World"
End Sub
—>
</SCRIPT>
</HEAD>

<BODY>
<H3>First Working Script</H3>
<FORM><INPUT NAME="Button1" TYPE="button" VALUE="Press Me!"></FORM>
</BODY>

</HTML>
```

The code is fairly short (by design), but builds on what you learned in the last example. The following discussion skips over the basic tags and moves on to the new features.

The New <SCRIPT> Tag

As mentioned in Chapter 1, "VBScript—What's All the Hype About?" the <SCRIPT> tag is a recent addition to the HTML standard and serves to signal the presence of a script to the Web browser. Those chapters didn't cover any of the implementation details—that's how you, as a programmer, actually write scripts. The most important item in integrating script code into a document is the <SCRIPT> tag. Before going any further, it's important to see why such a distinction exists between methods of creating user-interaction within Web pages and the new scripting technology.

The distinction between a client-side scripted application and a server-based application is important, and an example will serve to illustrate why you might want to use a scripting language. Imagine that you need a home page to generate a set of lottery numbers for filling out a lottery form. You design a Web page that has a button that users can press to generate six random numbers onscreen. After the user presses the button, you have two ways to generate the numbers.

The first is the method you had to employ before the advent of scripting. You had to communicate directly with the server and use it to run a program for generating numbers. The problem that using this method presents is that it involves extra network traffic as the client communicates with the server. Besides that, the server needs to use its resources running a number generator when the client could easily perform the same task.

The second, more elegant method, is to generate the numbers in a script on the host computer. When the user clicks on the button, a VBScript procedure in the HEAD section is called and executed. The procedure is written in Visual Basic and carries out the number generation and verification.

Thus, VBScript provides a powerful way to exploit the resources of the host computer to make Web pages interactive, and also minimizes network and server communications, which often are unreliable and slow.

All examples in this book use Microsoft's Visual Basic Scripting Edition for the scripting language. VBScript offers an advantage over JavaScript, in that it retains much of the functionality and style of the Visual Basic programming language. Both languages also can take full advantage of Microsoft's latest range of powerful ActiveX controls for HTML authoring (see Chapter 13, "Using the ActiveX Control Pad and HTML Layout Control").

The browser needs to know which scripting language to use, so you add a language clause to the <SCRIPT> tag in the HEAD section. For VBScript, the tag format is

```
<SCRIPT LANGUAGE="VBScript">
   VBScript code goes here
</SCRIPT>
```

CAUTION

The alpha release of Internet Explorer 3.0 allowed the following syntax for the <SCRIPT> tag:

```
<SCRIPT LANGUAGE="VBS">
```

It's no longer supported, however. As of the beta 1 release of Explorer 3.0, you must use the format

```
LANGUAGE="VBScript"
```

In addition to VBScript, IE 3.0 also supports JavaScript. If you're writing a JavaScript program, you would indicate that in the <SCRIPT LANGUAGE="JavaScript"> tag. If a browser that doesn't support the scripting language tries to run a document that contains VBScript, it tries to display the code on the page and could well run into trouble. To prevent such potential problems, you should envelope the script section of code in HTML comment tags so that the browser knows to ignore it. The <!– and –> tags indicate the beginning and end of a comment block.

Explorer 3.0 currently is the only browser that supports VBScript, so you should include comment tags if you think any users might use older browsers to view your documents.

TIP

We recommend that you insert comment tags whenever you write scripts, to ensure that there are no problems with displaying pages.

Comment tags are included in the preceding sample document. Try loading the same file using Netscape Navigator 2.0. The code doesn't show up, and pressing the button elicits no response.

Where to Place Your Script

Before you get too involved in the content of the sample listings, think about how a good programmer would lay out a document. If you follow good formatting practices, you or others can fix your code more easily if something goes wrong, as well as incorporate it into different pages more easily.

TIP

Programming Tip: It's a good programming practice to keep similar blocks of code together. Sectioning the code into blocks that serve similar functions and putting them in one place keeps everything in order and makes finding the functions with which you need to work easy.

You can place VBScript procedures and functions anywhere in HTML documents. Your code could get messy quickly, however, if you scatter procedures willy nilly. You really should group all scripting together and place it in the HEAD section of a document. One of the main reasons for advocating the HEAD location is that *general* procedures and functions must reside in the HEAD section for easy reference. If you have to put one type of procedure in the HEAD section, you might as well place all of them in it for consistency.

General functions or procedures perform tasks and can be called from anywhere within a script. Suppose a form asks for several date inputs, all of which must fall within one year of today's date. Rather than create a procedure to verify each date on its own, you would write a general procedure to perform date verification, which could be used repeatedly. Using general functions streamlines the code, making it easier to follow. Sticking to layout conventions keeps it neat. As you deal with increasingly complicated scripts in later chapters, you can expect these concepts to become more concrete.

Creating the Button Control

One of the simplest ways to make a page interactive is to use standard controls, such as buttons. You can easily incorporate buttons into scripts and use them to trigger different procedures.

Putting a button on a page is relatively easy. Just include the following line of code in the document:

```
<FORM><INPUT NAME="Button1" TYPE="button" VALUE="Press Me!"></FORM>
```

This line of HTML creates what is known as a form; in this case, an exceedingly simple form that consists of only one element—a button control.

Forms serve to obtain information from the user for a myriad of reasons, including taking customer orders, composing search requests, and so on. Until the introduction of VBScript and JavaScript, this information was basically useless until it was submitted to a server (see Chapter 15, "CGI and ISAPI—What about Web Servers?"). Now the situation is different; you can script client-side validation of data, calculations, and processing user input, eliminating the need to send information back to the server.

Forms can contain style tags, text, and recent HTML extensions known as *intrinsic controls*. The W3C consortium has agreed on these controls as part of the HTML 3.0 standards, and include the following:

- Button 

- Text 

- Password 
- Check box 

- Radio 

- Reset 

- Submit 

This example uses the button control. You can expect to encounter many other controls later in the book.

You must supply the <INPUT> tag with a control type. The TYPE="button" clause specifies this control type, and inserts a button in the form. You then give the control a name so that you can reference it from scripts.

Responding to the Mouse Click

An event handler is a procedure that is called when a particular event takes place. An event can be generated in all sorts of ways, including through user actions. When a user clicks on Button1, the control triggers an event. Certain objects on a Web page can generate events when they're interacted with, but unless you define a specific handler to respond to the event, the user's interactions may be ignored.

The VBScript handler in the Hello World example is defined by the following code:

```
Sub Button1_OnClick
    MsgBox "Hello World"
End Sub
```

One of the first things to note is that programmers use naming conventions for event handlers (known as *event procedures*) in VBScript. First, you write the object name, and follow it with the event to be handled. You then join these two words together with an underscore. Chapters 10 through 14 contain all the events that you can use on the various controls, and explains how to use them.

In this case, the event procedure is Button1_OnClick, and is executed whenever Button1 is clicked. It displays a standard message box.

Onward and Upward

Now you have successfully installed Explorer 3.0 on your computer, have a grounding in basic HTML, and have seen the beginnings of a VBScript document. You have been introduced to the <SCRIPT> tag and some of the simple scripting features, such as the button control. The first sample program has put these together in a no-frills demonstration of the most basic elements of scripting. As you work through the chapters and add new commands to your armory, you will see many more dynamic and exciting applications of scripting. Right now, the Web page is simple, gray, and just about (but not quite) interactive. You have so much more to look forward to, including image maps, animated buttons, sound files, ActiveX controls, forms, frames, spinning labels, and more.

Before you can exploit these advanced features, however, you need to understand how to use more elements of the VBScript language. Chapter 4, "Variables, Arrays, and Data Types." provides the next step.

PART II

Language Structure

CHAPTER 4

Variables, Arrays, and Data Types

All computer languages use variables to store information during execution because they provide an easy way to refer to memory locations and pass information between routines.

The variable concept may be global, but each language has its own distinct way to declare and use variables and data types. One of the key differences between VBScript and several other modern languages is that it categorizes all variables under one type—called the *Variant*, in VBScript. This is an important distinction and is discussed in more depth later. Normally compilers (and in some cases, interpreters) need to know the exact data specifications of each variable well before the variable is used. VBScript deals with variables in a unified, simple way, so read on to discover more.

This chapter covers the following points:

- What variables are and how to declare and assign values to them.
- Variable scope and how this affects your scripts.
- Data types and the Variant data type in particular.
- How and why to convert values to different data types.
- Array variables, including multidimensional and dynamic arrays.
- Resizing array variables to store different amounts of information.

By the end of this section, you should feel comfortable enough with variables and arrays to easily add them to your scripts. Get started now by looking at variables and learning how to use them.

Variables, Are They Really Useful?

A program without variables is like a plane without wings. Variables give you a way to store information, carry out calculations, and make dynamic and interactive inputs and outputs. Two hypothetical examples of variables could be:

- **todays_date** might store the current date as a number
- **company_name** could be used to store data such as a name of a company in the form of a string

Different programming languages treat variables differently and you could assume that variables are also treated the same way in different programming languages. This isn't the case, however. Languages such as C, Pascal, and Java require that variables be *strongly typed*, meaning that they must be declared as a particular kind of variable *before* being used. Strong typing is useful when code needs to be compiled because the compiler can allocate exactly the right amount of space for each variable. Often interpreted languages, such as VBScript, are loosely typed because it makes the language easier to use. The interpreter manages the memory and variables.

Now that you know that variables are important and that VBScript does most of the variable management for you, it's time to take a closer look at what a variable actually is.

What Is a Variable?

One of the best ways to think about variables is to ignore the formal computer definition and imagine that they are boxes that store information. To make this scenario more realistic, and more relevant to variables, think of these boxes as numbered lockers at a railway station. We can now draw parallels to explain the properties of variables.

NOTE *The formal definition of a variable is "a named placeholder referring to a particular memory address."*

The first parallel is that the lockers have numbers for identification whereas variables have names. No two lockers can have the same number and no two variables can share the same name—they must be uniquely identifiable. VBScript variables aren't limited to numbers. Variables can have almost any name, as long as they follow a proscribed naming scheme (covered later).

The second analogy to the rail-station locker system is that you can store whatever you want in a locker, as long as you have the key. When you have the key, you have exclusive access to the locker and don't even have to store anything in it. Obtaining the key for a locker is identical to declaring a variable in VBScript. The declaration tells the interpreter that a memory location should be reserved to store information for future use.

When you relinquish the key, the locker is cleared and ready for reuse. Variables generally are cleared at the end of their associated procedure. If you declare a variable at the beginning of a document, however, it lasts through all procedures.

Naming and Declaring Variables

Before you can use a variable, you must first give it a name. Several rules apply to naming variables, as follows:

- Names must start with a letter of the alphabet.
- A variable name cannot include a period.
- A single name must not exceed 255 characters.
- Variable names must be unique within the scope in which they are defined.
- Names must not be one of the VBScript keywords, such as Set.

You must follow these rules for your code to work properly. In most cases, an error message generates if a name is invalid, but in the case of keywords, the interpreter treats the name as a keyword and not as a variable. No error message generates, but the code won't work as expected. The Table of Contents entries for Appendixes A, B, and C list some of the VBScript keywords that form the language. Don't use any of the identifiers found in the language reference pages as names for your variables.

NOTE

VBScript isn't case-sensitive. Cases can be mixed, but care should be taken not to duplicate variable names by forgetting that the browser interprets lower and upper case characters in an identical manner. The following line of code is invalid, because the same name is effectively being used twice:

```
Dim CJGoddard, CJGODDARD
```

For more information on programming tips, especially relating to variable naming conventions, see Chapter 9, "Writing Well-Organized and Coherent VBScript."

Examples of variable names are:

VARIABLE NAME	VALID NAME	REASON IT'S INVALID
Counter	Yes	
If	No	If is a VBScript keyword
Message_21	Yes	
Sam.Smith	No	Contains an embedded period
Level42	Yes	
5thAvenue	No	Starts with a digit

You're now ready to write the VBScript code for a variable declaration. First, you choose the method you're going to use:

- **Explicit**—when the variable is declared before use
- **Implicit**—when the interpreter automatically detects the need for a new variable when a new name is used

Declaring Variables Explicitly

To make sure memory is set aside for a variable, use explicit declarations. The Dim statement defines a variable explicitly. The new name is placed after the Dim statement as follows

```
Dim MyVariable
```

After you declare MyVariable, it remains empty until a value is assigned to it. You may want to declare several variables at once by chaining the variable names together, separated by commas. The following, for example, declares three variables called Ant, Fly, and Beetle, respectively:

```
Dim Ant, Fly, Beetle
```

After you define variables, you can use them in any subsequent VBScript statements within the scope of the declaration (see Section on "Variable Scope" later in this chapter).

After you declare a variable, some programming languages, such as C++, allow you to check the declaration's success. You can use these checks to warn of system resource shortages, such as (most importantly) running out of memory. VBScript doesn't have such a facility, so you should assume that the browser will make sure that the VBScript engine has enough memory to function properly.

The Other Option—Declaring Variables Implicitly

When you declare something implicitly, you don't declare it separately from the rest of the script. Instead, you let the interpreter allocate space for the variable.

When the VBScript interpreter encounters an identifier (or variable name) that it hasn't already met, it assigns a new storage space in memory to that variable. The variable exists only inside the procedure in which it's first used. If it's created outside a procedure but within the <SCRIPT> tags, then it's accessible from anywhere in the script.

```
<SCRIPT LANGUAGE="VBScript">
Dim a,b
a = 10
b = 15
NewVar = a + b
</SCRIPT>
```

Implicit declaration works well in simple scripts, but as the code grows in complexity, so too grows the chance for user input errors. Because VBScript's error reporting facilities are more limited than other programming languages, the use of explicit declarations is strongly recommended, where possible.

Consider the following section of code, which demonstrates how implicit declaration can create problems if not used with care.

```
Dim Result,a
a = 10
Result = a + b
```

This time b has been declared implicitly in the calculation, `a + b`. However, b is valueless, so using it in any calculation until it has been given a value would be meaningless. The result of this calculation should be considered useless.

When working with anything other than the simplest of scripts, the implicit declaration can create havoc. Even something as small as a single typo can lead to a well-hidden bug. This is because the interpreter creates a new variable to cope with an unrecognized variable name, and then tries to use it. Tracking down bugs like this can be an extremely frustrating and difficult chore, and so explicit declaration is recommended. To prevent implicit declarations being made, you can include the Option Explicit statement at the beginning of the script to force declaration of all variables before use.

Option Explicit—Not an Adult TV Channel

Option Explicit forces all variables to be defined explicitly. You should define variables explicitly as a matter of course, to avoid the kinds of bugs that implicitly declared variables create.

Adding an Option Explicit command to the previous example and running the script would generate an error message because it contains an implicit declaration (which is now forbidden).

```
<SCRIPT LANGUAGE="VBScript" >
Option Explicit
Dim Result,a
a = 10
Result = a + b
</SCRIPT>
```

Using Your Variables—Simple Assignments

You saw in the previous section how (and how not) to declare variables, and are now interested in using them. Declaring a variable is only part of the story. Assigning a value to a variable is easy. Place the variable name to the left of the equals sign and the value to which you want to assign the variable on the right.

```
VariableName = Expression
```

Expressions are explained in more detail in the next chapter. In brief, they can be other variable names, mathematical expressions, strings, or calls to functions, among others.

NOTE

The simple form of assignment described here actually evaluates the expression on the right-hand side and stores the resulting value in the variable. Sometimes when dealing with forms, for example, you need to set up a reference to an object that links the variable to some object on the page. You can't do this using simple assignments—rather, you must use the Set statement. To see the Set statement in action, turn to Chapter 11, "Using Forms with VBScript," or if you want to check out its syntax, check Appendix B, "VBScript Language Reference—Statements."

The next listing shows some assignments to variables and you can load it from the main Web page from the CD. Choose the `Declaring Variables and Assigning Values to Them` link from the Tutorial page to load the example, which should look like Figure 4-1.

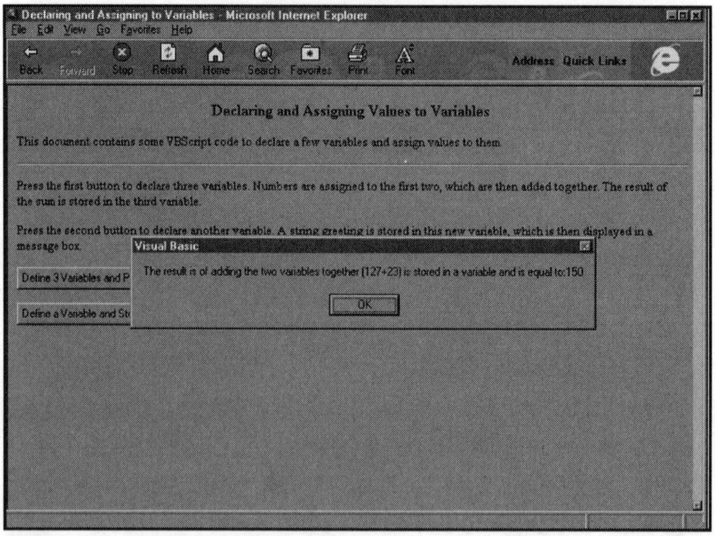

FIGURE 4-1
The Declaring and Assigning Values to Variables example page

This file demonstrates how to assign integer values and strings to variables and how to output them to the screen when users click on buttons. Working through the code, line by line, makes it easier to follow. The comments should help.

If it seems clear, change a few lines of the source code and see the effect it has on the page. View the source code and alter the lines of text. After you make the alterations, save the new file over the original HTML file. Saving it over the old file lets you reload the document into the browser by clicking on the Internet Explorer Refresh button (or pressing F5). Otherwise, you have to use the Open command from the Explorer menu to open the file manually.

```
<HTML>
<HEAD>
<TITLE>Declaring and Assigning to Variables</TITLE>
<SCRIPT LANGUAGE="VBScript">
<!-
Sub Button1_OnClick
```

```
    Rem ***Define three variables to be used as integers
    Dim intVal1, intVal2, intResult

    Rem ***Now assign some values to these variables
    intVal1 = 127
    intVal2 = 23
    intResult = intVal1 + intVal2

    Rem ***Now output the values
    MsgBox "The result is of adding the two variables together
(127+23) is stored in a variable and is equal to:" & intResult
End Sub

Sub Button2_OnClick
    Rem ***Define a variable to be used as a string
    Dim strGreeting

    strGreeting = "Hello from Chris & Mark!"

    MsgBox "The string variable contains: " & strGreeting
End Sub
->
</SCRIPT>
</HEAD>

<BODY>
<CENTER>
<H3>Declaring and Assigning Values to Variables</H3>
</CENTER>
This document contains some VBScript code to declare a few variables
and assign values to
them.
<HR>
Press the first button to declare three variables. Numbers are assigned
to the first two,
```

```
which are then added together. The result of the sum is stored in the
third variable.<P>
Press the second button to declare another variable. A string greeting
is stored in this
new variable, which is then displayed in a message box.<P>
<FORM>
<INPUT TYPE="button" NAME="Button1" VALUE="Define 3 Variables and
Perform a Calculation"><P>
<INPUT TYPE="button" NAME="Button2" VALUE="Define a Variable and Store
a String To It">
</FORM>
</BODY>
</HTML>
```

What's Happening Here?

If you look back at the "Hello World" document in Chapter 3, "Writing Your First VBScript Document," and compare it to this example, you can probably spot several similarities. The basic <HTML>, <HEAD>, <BODY>, and <SCRIPT> tags are all present, plus a form has been defined with two button controls, called Button1 and Button2. Notice the <CENTER> container tags, which center the enclosed items on the page.

Two event procedures for the button controls are in the HEAD section. The Sub command names the procedures. In this case, the variables are declared within the procedures which limit their scope. Four different variables are declared explicitly using the Dim statement and are given values. intVal1 and intVal2 store two numbers and these are added together to give intResult. A text string is stored in strGreeting. The example finishes by displaying message dialog boxes after each button is pressed and displays the values stored in the variables.

Comments Can Help

One other point of interest in this example is the use of the Rem statement. The Rem statement indicates that the rest of the line is a comment and that the VBScript interpreter should ignore it. Comments can help other readers understand your code as well remind you why you did something in the first place. For tips on how to make the most of comments and organizing your script code, see Chapter 9, "Writing Well-Organized and Coherent VBScript."

NOTE

One more way can put a comment, which is more readable than the Rem statement, into the script. The interpreter will ignore any text that follows a single quote symbol ('); for example:

```
dblCirc = pi * dblDiam     ' Calculate the circumference
```

Strings and Numbers—Is This Magic?

You may be wondering how you can use variables to store both numbers and text strings. After all, numbers and characters are as different as apples and pears. Well, there's more to it than that; variables can store times, dates, or manage several values at once; for example, data types and array variables.

Data Types—Giving Variables a Sense of Identity

Now that variables have been introduced and some examples given, it's time to describe exactly what type of information you can store using them. Notice in the previous example that numbers and text strings are declared and values assigned to the variables in an identical manner. VBScript doesn't have to know what kind of data type or value you're storing because the interpreter does it automatically by looking at the value being stored. It then tries to decide whether it's a number, string, date, time, or some other type and bases its internal representation of the value on the result of the decision. In some instances, this can cause problems, when you want to store a value that looks like another type. VBScript will store the value "January 31, 1976" as a date, for example, when you might want it to store the value as a string. Certain special functions, called *conversion functions* (discussed later in this chapter) can solve these difficulties. For the most part, you don't have to worry about the internal distinctions—there's only one data type in VBScript, and it's called *Variant*.

One and Only—The Variant Data Type

Other programming languages, such as C and Pascal, have distinct categories (or *types*) of variables. In these languages, a variable defined as an integer stores only integers and the same applies to strings and so on. The *Variant* data type is more flexible because it behaves as a number when used in a numeric context and as a string when used in a string context.

When the data you are working with looks like a number, VBScript acts on it in a way that is most suitable for numbers. When the data you're working with could only be a string, it's treated as string data. If you want to force VBScript to consider numeric values to be strings, you need to surround them with quotation marks.

```
StrMessage = "400532"
```

This value will be treated as a string containing the characters 400532 rather than the number 400,532. This is important when you want to display numbers. The kinds of values that a Variant can hold actually are more specific than the elementary string versus numeric distinction, which is where subtypes come in.

Subtypes—It's Not That Simple

Generally, you can simply place your data into variables and the interpreter treats them in the most suitable way. Sometimes, though, you want to display your data in a specific format, and you use subtypes for that purpose. Different subtype categories include Boolean values (`True` or `False`), large floating point numbers, and date or time information.

> Dates and times usually are represented in computers by *magic numbers* rather than mm/dd/yyyy structures. The magic number represents the number of days or seconds that have elapsed since a fixed date. You can carry out date calculations with these values, such as addition and subtraction. These values are much easier to work with than weeks, months, hours, and so on. Obviously, a user expects to see a date or time appear in the normal way, so conversion functions do this for you.

Table 4–1 Subtypes of Data That a Variant Can Contain

SUBTYPE	DEFINITION
Empty	Uninitialized. No value has been assigned to the Variant yet. Value is 0 for numeric values or "" (zero length string) for string variables
Null	Variant intentionally contains no valid information
Boolean	One of two values—contains True or False
Byte	Integer in the range 0 to 255
Integer	Integer in the range -32,768 to 32,767
Long	Integer in the range -2,147,483,648 to 2,147,483,647
Single	Single-precision, floating-point number. Negative values in the range -3.402823E38 to -1.401298E-45. Positive values in the range 1.401298E-45 to 3.402823E38.
Double	Double-precision, floating-point number. Negative values in the range -1.79769313486232E308 to -4.94065645841247E-324. Positive values in the range 4.94065645841246E-324 to 1.79769313486232E308.
Date/Time	Holds a number that represents a date between January 1, 100 to December 31, 9999
String	Variable length string that can contain up to 2 billion characters
Object	Contains an OLE Automation object
Error	Holds an error number

Table 4-1 contains a list of all the possible subtypes that a Variant may contain. Although this list is quite comprehensive, for the most part you don't need to worry about the exact distinctions between some of the subtypes. The VBScript interpreter treats your data in the most appropriate way when you store it in a variable. Figure 4-2 is a visual representation of the Variant type and shows how it consists of several subtypes.

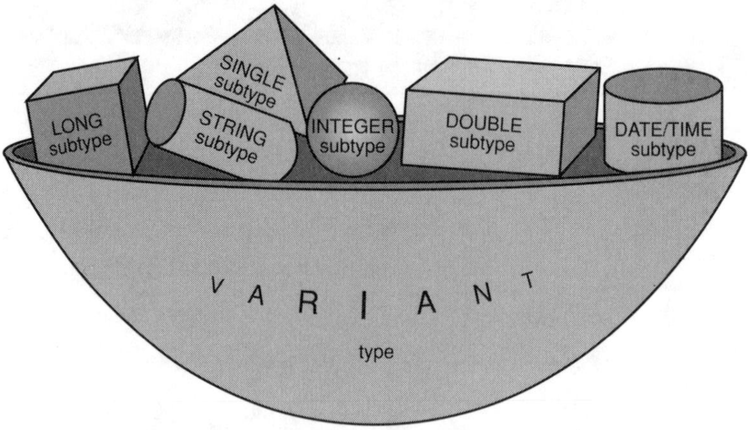

FIGURE 4-2
The Variant data type encompasses all of the subtypes.

If you want to find out how your data is stored within a *Variant*, use the Vartype function (see Appendix A, "VBScript Language Reference—Functions"). This function returns information in the form of a numeric code indicating how data is stored within a Variant. Consider the following lines of script for a demonstration of the Vartype function. You can access the working script on the Tutorial section of the main Web page from the CD by choosing the `Variant Datatype and Subtypes` hyperlink.

Using the Vartype Function

You can find the complete details for using the Vartype function in Appendix A, but here are some example calls to illustrate its use:

Vartype(156) returns 2, which stands for the Integer subtype

Vartype("Hello World!") returns 8, which stands for the String subtype.

Vartype("Jan 24, 1991") returns 7, which stands for the Date subtype.

```
<HTML>
<HEAD>
<TITLE>The Variant Data Type and Its Subtypes</TITLE>
<SCRIPT LANGUAGE="VBScript">
<!-
```

```
Dim svarValue                'script variable

Sub boolButton_OnClick       'Called when boolButton is pressed.
 svarValue = True            'Assign a boolean value to the variable
 Update()                    'Update the Subtype display
End Sub

Sub nullButton_OnClick
 svarValue = Null
 Update()
End Sub

Sub byteButton_OnClick
 svarValue = CByte(10)       'Conversion function forces the Byte
Subtype to be used

                              'By default VB Script would treat this

as an Integer
 Update()
End Sub

Sub intButton_OnClick
 svarValue = 3500
 Update()
End Sub

Sub realButton_OnClick
 svarValue = 3.142
 Update()
End Sub

Sub strButton_OnClick
 svarValue = "soup"
 Update()
End Sub
```

```
Sub Update                   'Displays the current Subtype of the
svarValue variable
 Form1.Text1.Value = Vartype(svarValue) 'Update text box contents
End Sub
->
</SCRIPT>
</HEAD>

<BODY>
<CENTER><H3>The Variant Data Type and Its Subtypes</H3></CENTER >
Click a button to assign different values to a variable.  The Subtype
reported by the Vartype()
function will be displayed in the text box.<P>
<FORM NAME="Form1">
    <INPUT TYPE="Button" NAME="boolButton" VALUE="True" >
    <INPUT TYPE="Button" NAME="nullButton" VALUE="Null" >
    <INPUT TYPE="Button" NAME="byteButton" VALUE="10" >
    <INPUT TYPE="Button" NAME="intButton" VALUE="3,500" >
    <INPUT TYPE="Button" NAME="realButton" VALUE="3.142" >
    <INPUT TYPE="Button" NAME="strButton" VALUE="'Soup'" ><P>
Variant Subtype Reported by Vartype() function:-
    <INPUT TYPE="Text" SIZE=15 NAME="Text1"><P>
0  = Empty<P>
1  = Null<P>
2  = Integer<P>
5  = Double precision floating point<P>
8  = String<P>
11 = Boolean<P>
17 = Byte<P>
</FORM>
</BODY>
</HTML>
```

If you load the document, a number of pushbuttons present with different values written on them, as shown in Figure 4-3. To display the subtype code of one of these samples, click on the desired button. The event procedure for that button then sets the value of a variable to that displayed on the button. The Update procedure is then called to display the subtype that VBScript uses to store the data. The code shown here is the complete HTML source for the document including the VBScript functions which provide the interactive behavior of the document. Notice the standard HTML tags which we have already looked at and the six button controls defined with the <INPUT> tags. The following sections elaborate on several points that this example illustrates.

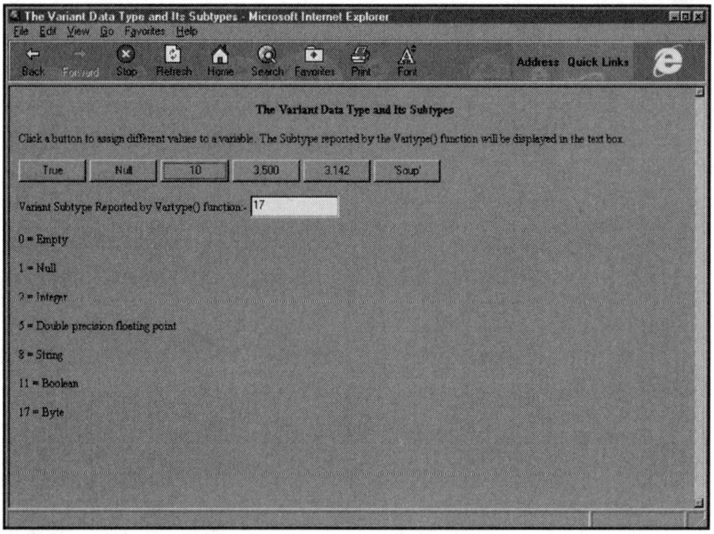

FIGURE 4-3
Using the Variant data type and its subtypes in a script

Ambiguous Subtypes

This example uses several subtypes, which can cause confusion if a value falls within several ranges. As Table 4-1 shows, some ranges of allowed values overlap each other. In such cases, VBScript selects a default subtype for that variable. Any integer automatically then stores as an Integer subtype unless it falls outside this range (-32,768 to 32,767), in which case, the Long subtype is used. Floating point numbers are stored as Double subtype by default.

Conversion functions can cast variables into a specific subtype when required. The following section discusses these type-casting procedures, but you can see how they work by looking at some code.

Consider the following line:

```
svarValue = CByte(10)       'Conversion function forces the Byte
Subtype to be used
```

This forces the number 10 to be stored as a Byte subtype using the Cbyte( ) conversion function. Other conversions are possible for the remaining subtypes and have a similar syntax. Figure 4-4 is a cartoon of how subtype conversion works. If you must have single precision numbers, you just use the CSng( ) function.

FIGURE 4-4
Conversion between integer and byte subtypes using the CByte function.

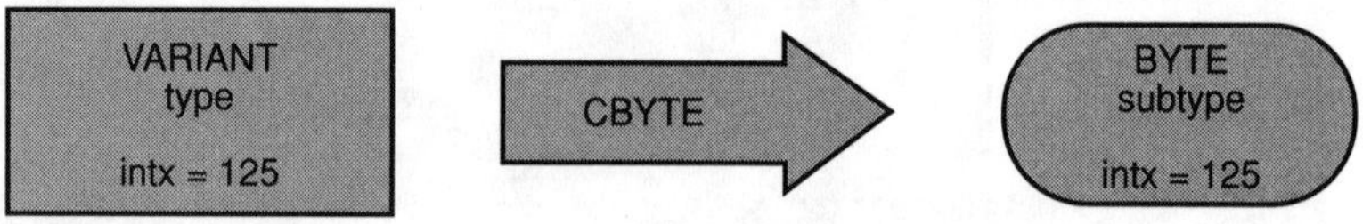

Forms and Textboxes

The script changes the text displayed in the textbox by executing this line:

```
Form1.Text1.Value = Vartype(svarValue)     'Update text box contents
```

The HTML code defines a <FORM> named Form1. A textbox object (or control) is inserted into this form, called Text1. You can access object properties using the object syntax shown here. You signify a property of an object by writing the object name, a period, and the property name (and you can nest to several levels). Here, you're accessing the Value property of the Text1 object. The Value property also is a property of the Form1 object. The value that Vartype( ) returns then is assigned to this property—in this case, the text that appears in the textbox.

Chapter 12, "ActiveX Controls and VBScript," explains forms and controls, such as text boxes, and Chapter 7, "Grouping Statements in Procedures and Functions," discusses functions and return values.

Defining and Calling Procedures

You have already seen an example of an event procedure in the "Hello World" script in Chapter 3, "Creating Your First VBScript Document." This example used a Button1_OnClick procedure to handle an event. The example shown here includes a general function that isn't attached to any particular event. It's called Update and can be used from any other scripts in this document. It executes by the command Update( ). See Chapter 7, "Grouping Statements in Procedures and Functions," for more details.

Converting Values between Subtypes

To discover how to convert between various subtypes, see Table 4-2. This table lists the available conversion functions for typecasting variables. For exact details, see the language reference in Appendix A.

Table 4–2 Conversion Functions for Typecasting Variables

FUNCTION NAME	CONVERTS EXPRESSION TO SUBTYPE
CBool	Boolean
CByte	Byte
CDate	Date
CInt	Integer
CLng	Long
CSng	Single
CStr	String
CVErr	Error

The actual conversion is simple. You place any expression you want to be converted within the parentheses that follow the function name. The result can then be assigned to another variable or used right away.

For example,

```
intA = Cint("1234")                      'String "1234"
converted to subtype Integer

dblB = CDbl(20) * CDbl("31.42E-1")       'Integer and a string converted
to Doubles
```

Many more instances of conversion occur throughout this book and, when necessary, receive commentary.

TIP

The conversion functions are very important if you are writing documents that are likely to be viewed in different locales. Currency symbols, date, and thousand separators are different all over the world. By using the conversion functions for values used in calculations (like CDbl( ), CLng( ), and so on), you will ensure that the numbers are interpreted correctly according to the user's locale settings. For example, if you wanted to represent the number ten thousand in several places around the world, the people in the United States prefer it written as 10,000, whereas a French person, 10.000.

Variable Scope—How Visible Is Your Data?

After you declare a variable, it's visible in other sections of your script. Scope rules govern where variables can be accessed. A variable's scope defines the extent of code where its value is available. There are two different levels:

- **Script level scope**
- **Procedure level scope**

The next section explains the advantages and disadvantages of using both kinds of variables.

An Example Document to Demonstrate Variable Scope

An example document to demonstrate scope can be found on the main Web page installed from the CD, by clicking the "Variable Scope—Global and Procedure Variables" link in the tutorial section. The code reproduced here and the principles behind the example are explained. It should load up looking something like Figure 4-5.

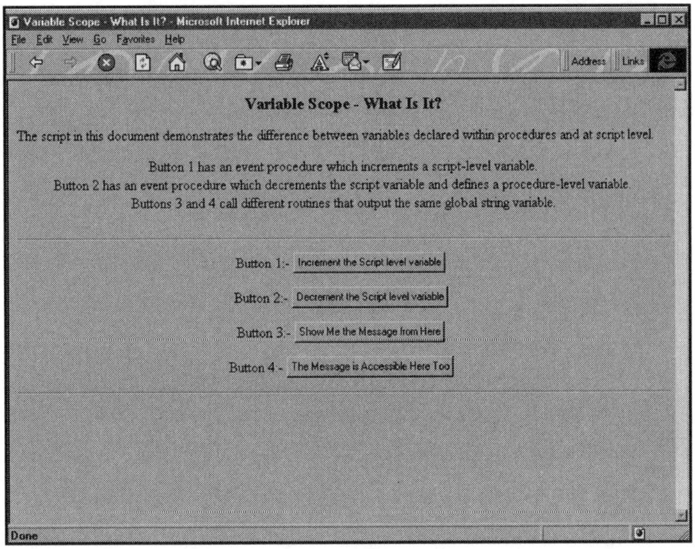

FIGURE 4-5
The difference between variables defined in the script section and those in procedures

```
<HTML>
<HEAD>
<TITLE>Variable Scope—What Is It?</TITLE>
<SCRIPT LANGUAGE="VBScript">
<!–
Dim sstrMessage, sintCount

sintCount = 0
sstrMessage = "A Script Level String"

Sub Button1_OnClick
```

```
    Rem ***sintCount is declared at script level, so we can access it
    Rem ***from anywhere in the document
    sintCount = sintCount + 1
    MsgBox "Script level variable is now = " & sintCount & ". No
➥procedure variables in this routine."
End Sub


Sub Button2_OnClick
    Dim intLocal

    Rem ***This variable has procedure level scope and is only
    ➥accessible from
    Rem ***within this procedure
    intLocal = 999

    Rem ***Declared at script level—We can access it from anywhere
    ➥in the document
    sintCount = sintCount-1
    MsgBox "Script level variable is now = " & sintCount & " and
➥procedure variable = " & intLocal
End Sub


Sub Button3_OnClick
    MsgBox "Script level string is: '" & sstrMessage & "'"
End Sub


Sub Button4_OnClick
    MsgBox "Script level string is still: '" & sstrMessage & "',
➥but it's called from a different procedure"
End Sub
-->
```

```
</SCRIPT>
</HEAD>

<BODY>
<CENTER>
<H3>Variable Scope—What Is It?</H3>
</CENTER>
The script in this document demonstrates the difference between
➥variables declared within procedures and at script level.<P>
<CENTER>
Button 1 has an event procedure which increments a script-level
➥variable.<BR>
Button 2 has an event procedure which decrements the script variable
➥and defines a procedure-level variable.<BR>
Buttons 3 and 4 call different routines that output the same global
➥string variable.<P>
</CENTER>
<FORM NAME="Form1">
<HR>
<CENTER>
Button 1:-    <INPUT TYPE="button" NAME="Button1" VALUE="Increment the
➥Script level variable"> <P>
Button 2:-    <INPUT TYPE="button" NAME="Button2" VALUE="Decrement the
➥Script level variable"> <P>
Button 3:-    <INPUT TYPE="button" NAME="Button3" VALUE="Show Me the
➥Message from Here"> <P>
Button 4:-    <INPUT TYPE="button" NAME="Button4" VALUE="The Message is
➥Accessible Here Too">
</CENTER>
<HR>
</FORM>
</FORM>
</BODY>

</HTML>
```

The HTML source for this document defines a form with four button controls, named Button1 to Button4. Each of the buttons has an event procedure associated with its OnClick event.

Pressing the first button increments the value of a script-level variable which is accessible throughout the script (see the next section "Script Level Variables—Naked Data"). The second event procedure decrements the same variable and also declares a procedure level variable which is only visible inside the event procedure Button2_OnClick (see the section "Procedure Variables—Keep It Neat").

The last buttons have event procedures that display a script-level string variable and demonstrate that you can access such variables from more than one different procedure.

Script Level Variables—Naked Data

Variables can be declared anywhere inside the <SCRIPT> tags. If the declaration falls outside the boundaries of a procedure, it becomes a script level, or *global*, variable. The following declarations are taken from the example document printed above.

```
<SCRIPT LANGUAGE="VBScript">
<!-
Dim sstrMessage, sintCount

sintCount = 0
sstrMessage = "A Script Level String"
```

The variables *sstrMessage* and *sintCount* become global variables because they are not declared within procedures. Any code within <SCRIPT> tags in the document may alter the values stored by these variables. This can be useful if you have some information that several procedures need to modify, such as a running total. It can also cause problems, especially with larger scripts, when the value could be changed accidentally. This leads to mysterious and unexpected errors—nasty bugs. Please note that if you have more than one <SCRIPT> </SCRIPT> section in a document, your global variables are visible in any of the script sections. You cannot declare two variables with the same name simply because they reside in different script blocks.

> **TIP**
>
> *The variable names used in the code snippet may seem a bit strange at first. This is because coding conventions are being used to name items in the script. These conventions are discussed in Chapter 8, "Handling Errors with VBScript." You should prefix all script level variables with the letter "s."*

Procedure Variables—Keep It Neat

A *local* variable is a variable that is declared within a procedure or function and is accessible only by commands within that particular procedure or function. As scripts get longer and more complicated, using *local* variables can be advantageous for two reasons:

- Other sections of code cannot overwrite the values in those variables.
- You do not have to think of different names for variables.

You can declare two variables with the same name only if they have different scopes (that is, are in different procedures or functions).

Figure 4-6 shows the difference between script and procedure scope. The variable lifetime is displayed along the top, and shows that procedure variables vanish once the end of the routine comes up. Script level variables are accessible from any procedure.

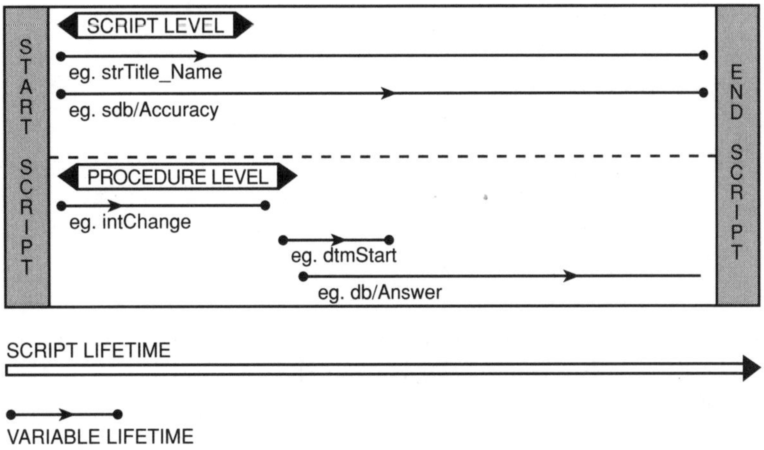

FIGURE 4-6
The lifetime of variables—script and procedure scope

The Static Keyword—Giving Procedures a Memory

The problem with procedure variables is that they lose their values when the procedure finishes executing. Each time the procedure or function is called, all of its variables are defined again. If we want to retain the data over many procedure calls, the first thing that we would think of using are script level variables. However, there is an alternative. The Static statement (see Appendix B, "VBScript Language Reference—Statements") forces VBScript to preserve the values of variable over procedure calls. This can be very useful in certain circumstances, such as keeping visit counts to a section of the script.

The Static keyword affects the lifetime of variables declared with it instead of the Dim keyword. Usually a procedure allocates space for its variables every time it is called and deallocates this memory when the procedure finishes. If Static is used, the variables will not clear when the procedure exits but will retain their values until the next time the procedure is called.

For example

```
Sub MyProc()
    Static intCount, strMessage
    Dim intLoop
    ...
    ***POINT 1
    ...
    intCount = someValue
    strMessage = someMessage
    ...
End Sub
```

This procedure contains a declaration for two static variables, *intCount* and *strMessage*. Whenever the procedure is called and execution reaches "*** POINT 1", these two variables retain the same values from the last finished procedure. In contrast, the variable *intLoop* (declared normally with Dim) redefines every time the procedure is called.

You also can use the Static keyword in front of a function or procedure declaration (see Chapter 7, "Grouping Statements in Procedures and

Functions"). This causes the procedure to treat all its variables as static, even if they are declared using Dim. This means all the procedure's variables will have their old values each time it is invoked. For example,

```
Static Sub MySpecialProc()
```

Arrays—Pigeonholes for Information

Until now, this book has considered only simple *scalar* variables (meaning, each variable refers only to a single data item). Using arrays, you can store a series of values in one place. Array variables are declared similarly to scalar ones, the only difference being the addition of a pair of parentheses following the variable name. The parentheses enclose a number that indicates how many elements the array can contain. For example:

```
Dim intList(15)
```

This line declares an array variable containing 16 elements. Arrays in VBScript are zero-based. To see what this means, see the following caution.

CAUTION

VBScript, along with most other modern programming languages, uses zero-based arrays. The elements of such arrays are numbered beginning at zero. Thus, a declaration such as Dim intList(15) creates an array with 15 + 1 elements. This is not very intuitive for novice programmers and care must be taken to begin accessing arrays from position 0, and *not* from position 1. This is most often an issue when writing loops to carry out an operation on each member of the array, where the zeroth element might be overlooked.

The C language uses zero-based arrays but declares them slightly differently. A C declaration like

```
int a[5];
```

declares an array variable called `a`, which contains *five* elements, numbered from 0 to 4. A VBScript declaration such as

```
Dim a(5)
```

declares an array with *six* elements numbered from 0 to 5. Existing C programmers should be aware of this difference.

You can change and retrieve the values contained in arrays quite easily. You can load the example from the Tutorial section of the main page installed from the CD, using the hyperlink `Introduction to Array Variables`, and review it to see how array variables are handled.

The source code for the document is shown here and once again there are some new features to look at. Figure 4-7 shows the layout of the document as it appears when loaded in Explorer 3.0.

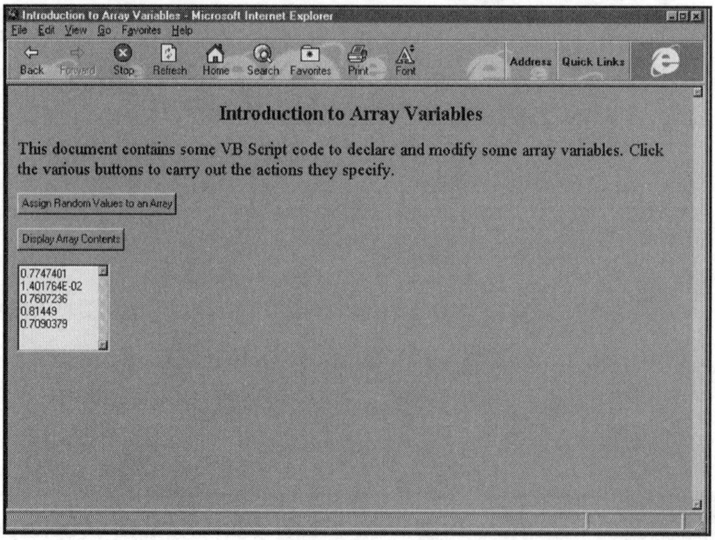

FIGURE 4-7
Assigning random values to the cells of an empty array

Press the top button to place random values in the global array called sngArray1, then press the second button to display the values stored in the array in a multiple line textbox.

```
<HTML>
<HEAD>
<TITLE>Introduction to Array Variables</TITLE>
<SCRIPT LANGUAGE="VBScript">
<!–
Option Explicit
Dim sngArray1(4)        'Declare a global array with 5 elements
```

```
Sub Button1_OnClick      'Assign 5 random values to the array—could use
➥a loop, see Chp 6
 sngArray1(0) = Rnd() : sngArray1(1) = Rnd()
 sngArray1(2) = Rnd() : sngArray1(3) = Rnd()
 sngArray1(4) = Rnd()
End Sub

Sub Button2_OnClick      'Display the contents of the array ina text
➥area control
 Document.Form1.Text1.Value = sngArray1(0) & " " & sngArray1(1) & " "
➥& sngArray1(2) & " " & sngArray1(3) & " " & sngArray1(4)
End Sub
—>
</SCRIPT>
</HEAD>

<BODY>
<CENTER>
<H3>Introduction to Array Variables</H3>
</CENTER><P>
This document contains some VB Script code to declare and modify some
➥array variables.
Click the various buttons to carry out the actions they specify.<P>
<FORM NAME="Form1">
    <INPUT TYPE="Button" NAME="Button1" VALUE="Assign Random Values to
➥an Array"><P>
    <INPUT TYPE="Button" NAME="Button2" VALUE="Display Array
Contents"><P>
<TEXTAREA  NAME="Text1" ROWS=5  COLS=20>Empty
</TEXTAREA>
</FORM>
</BODY>
</HTML>
```

Accessing Array Data Members

To assign a value to an item in an array, write the array name followed by the index of the desired item in parentheses on the left-hand side of an assignment statement, such as

```
sngArray1(3) = expr
```

expr is any valid expression and is stored in the *fourth* element of the array. Data may be retrieved from an array in a similar fashion. For example,

```
SomeVariable = sngArray(3)
```

NOTE *Always remember that array indices start from 0. So* `sngArray(3)` *is the fourth element of the array.*

In addition to assigning and retrieving values from an array, several additional elements in this example require further discussion.

Chaining Multiple Statements Together

You can write several statements on one line by placing colons between them. This can be useful for short statements because it can make the code look neater and takes up less space onscreen. This technique can be seen in the event procedure Button1_OnClick of the array example just discussed. The lines in question are reprinted here.

```
    sngArray1(0) = Rnd() : sngArray1(1) = Rnd()
    sngArray1(2) = Rnd() : sngArray1(3) = Rnd()
```

The TEXTAREA Control—Another Form Goodie

The script you have just looked at uses a TEXTAREA control. This is another form control, originally introduced by Netscape, and will be explained in detail in Chapter 12, "ActiveX Controls and VBScript." The TEXTAREA control itself is created by these lines of HTML

```
<TEXTAREA  NAME="Text1" ROWS=5  COLS=20>
```

```
Text to be displayed
</TEXTAREA>
```

The VBScript engine exposes these HTML elements as objects to scripts so that the text they contain can be accessed. In the case of the random array example, the textbox item is altered using the following line of code:

```
Form1.Text1.Value = Some Expression
```

where the control was named as Text1 in the BODY section. Note that the Form object is accessed using the name given in the BODY section. The Form object in turn holds a textbox object, which itself has a member variable named *Value* that holds the *String* displayed in the textbox.

Multi-Dimensional Arrays

So far we have only considered arrays with one dimension. Array variables can have as many as 60 dimensions. Two dimensional arrays can be thought of as tables with rows and columns, three dimensional as a 3-D grid, and so on. Figure 4-8 shows a visual representation of one, two, and three dimensional arrays. To declare a multidimensional array, separate the array's size parameters with commas, such as

```
Dim MyArray(6,10)
```

which declares an array with 7 rows and 11 columns, or

```
Dim OtherArray(3,4,5)
```

which has 4 slices of 5 rows and 6 columns. For most applications, three dimensions will be enough—it is hard to visualize many more than that. To access a particular item within the array, identify it by writing its position indices within parentheses. To set the item in the third row and second column of MyArray, you would write the following

```
MyArray(2, 1) = Some Expression
```

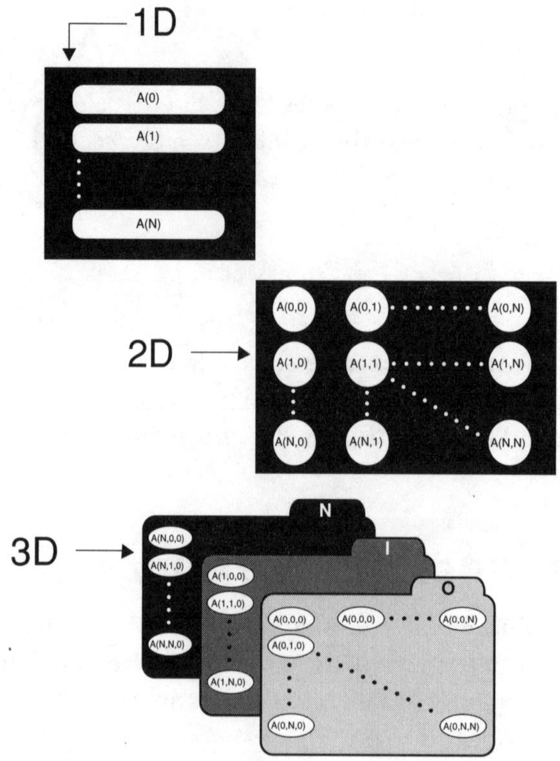

FIGURE 4-8. *A visual representation of 1-D, 2-D, and 3-D array variables*

Fixed-Size Arrays

All the arrays so far have had a fixed number of elements. This can be a severe limitation to the programmer. For example, you could be storing a matrix of figures in your array but don't know how many items there will be when the script is written. Using fixed-size arrays, the script would have to be written to allocate space for the maximum number of values considered possible.

Dynamic, Resizable Arrays

Certain arrays can change their size while the script is running. These arrays are known as dynamic arrays. The form of declaration for a dynamic array is different because no numbers appear between the parentheses. Both the Dim or the ReDim statement (explained shortly) can be used, as shown here:

```
Dim FlexibleArray()

ReDim StretchyArray()
```

Before a dynamic array can be used, space must be allocated for it by using the ReDim statement. This is used in the same way as the Dim statement introduced earlier. An example of this can be seen in the dynamic arrays example listing shown here. You can also access this code from the Tutorial section of the main document installed from the CD, by choosing the `Taking It Further - Dynamic Arrays` hyperlink.

TIP

Dynamic arrays come into their own when the parameters used to resize them are variables themselves. This means the size of the array is not hard-coded *into the script. User input or results from calculations can therefore influence the size of the array.*

```
<HTML>
<HEAD>
<TITLE>Taking It Further—Dynamic Arrays</TITLE>
<SCRIPT LANGUAGE="VBScript">
<!—
Dim dynArray1()              'Declare a dynamic array

Sub Button1_OnClick          'Redimension the array, place some values
in it, and display
 ReDim dynArray1(4)
 dynArray1(0) = "Item 0" : dynArray1(1) = "Item 1"
 dynArray1(2) = "Item 2" : dynArray1(3) = "Item 3"
 dynArray1(4) = "Item 4"
 Document.Form1.Text1.Value = dynArray1(0) & " " & dynArray1(1) & " "
& dynArray1(2) & " " & dynArray1(3) & " " & dynArray1(4)
End Sub

Sub Button2_OnClick
 ReDim Preserve dynArray1(6)  'Make the array larger by 2 items,
keeping existing contents
```

```
 dynArray1(5) = "New 1"        'A new value
 dynArray1(6) = "New 2"
Document.Form1.Text1.Value = dynArray1(0) & " " & dynArray1(1) & " " &
dynArray1(2) & " " & dynArray1(3) & " " & dynArray1(4) & " " &
dynArray1(5) & " " & dynArray1(6)
End Sub
->
</SCRIPT>
</HEAD>

<BODY>
<CENTER>
<H3>Taking It Further—Dynamic Arrays</H3>
</CENTER><P>
This document contains some VB Script code to declare and modify a
dynamic array.<P>
<HR>
Press this button to declare an array to hold 5 items. Some strings
will be placed
into the array, and will be displayed in the text box.<P>
<FORM NAME="Form1">
<INPUT TYPE="Button" NAME="Button1" VALUE="Place Values in Dynamic
Array"><P>
Press this button to make the array larger by 2 items. The contents of
the whole array
will then be displayed in the text box.<P>
<INPUT TYPE="Button" NAME="Button2" VALUE="Redimension the Dynamic
Array"><P>
<TEXTAREA  NAME="Text1" ROWS=7  COLS=12>Empty
</TEXTAREA>
</FORM>
</BODY>
</HTML>
```

The dynamic array example, as shown in Figure 4-8, declares a global dynamic array. By clicking the first button, the number of dimensions and size of the array is determined. In this case, it is one dimensional with 5 elements. The event procedure for Button2 resizes the array to contain 7 elements and then displays these. You use the Preserve keyword to retain the contents of the array as the resizing transpires. You can resize arrays an unlimited number of times.

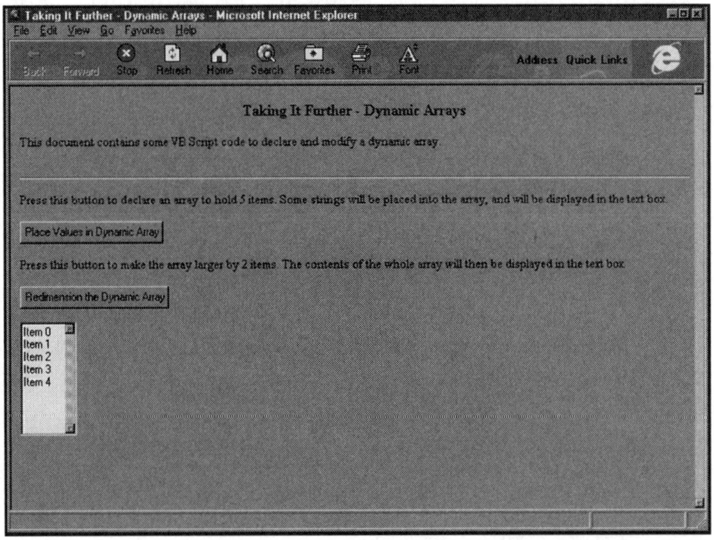

FIGURE 4-9
Resizing dynamic arrays and preserving array contents

CAUTION **By inserting the Preserve keyword between the ReDim statement and array name, you can preserve the contents of the array. This is safe when increasing the size of an array, but you need to be careful about reducing the array's size because you will lose any data in the eliminated elements.**

Conclusions

This chapter covered many of the features and uses of variables in VBScript. It presented the Variant datatype and discussed how it differs distinctly from variables in other languages. You should also have noted the amazing power of the interpreter to predict what type of subtype to assign to a general variable. Although this capability can prove useful under many circumstances, you should be alert to situations in which the interpreter can get confused—remember the addition of two numbers giving a string. This chapter explained how to cope with such situations. You should now feel comfortable using variables in your code.

Scope was another issue that the chapter touched upon. It described the two-tier system of script and procedure level, both graphically and in words, and showed that procedure level variables exist only for a limited period of time and so could not be used to pass information between routines. To maintain variables between procedure calls, you must use global, or script level, variables. Additionally, you can directly transfer data between routines, which are covered in later chapters on procedures and functions (see Chapter 7, "Grouping Statements in Procedures and Functions").

Finally, the chapter examined arrays and using them to store several pieces of information under the one variable name. Arrays are commonly used in many codes and let the programmer file large amounts of information away neatly and compactly in many dimensions.

The next chapter looks at commands that give variables the power to take part in operations—the theme of expressions, operators, and constants.

CHAPTER 5

Expressions, Operators and Constants

Chapter 3, "Creating Your First VBScript Document," covered the essential elements of HTML and scripting and Chapter 4, "Variables, Arrays, and Data Types," told about variables. Now you're ready to study more of the language syntax. This chapter focuses on the way in which VBScript deals with expressions, operators, and constants. You need to grasp these issues before you move on to the structural aspects of the language, such as control flow and procedures.

After you read this chapter, you should be familiar with the following:

- Understanding expressions
- Dealing with dates and times
- Understanding operators
- Using the different operators
- Evaluating expressions
- Defining and using constants in VBScript

Most of this chapter targets the novice programmer, and explains the principles of expressions and operators, along with some basic examples. Experienced programmers who want to become familiar with the features that VBScript offers should pay most attention to the sections on dates, times, and string manipulation, as this element perhaps differs most from what you see in other programming languages. If you need a quick and comprehensive guide to any particular function, the language reference at the back of the book is the best place to look for technical details. Appendixes A, B, and C cover the functions, statements, and operators that VBScript uses.

What Is an Operator?

Before getting carried away with introducing the vast range of operators that VBScript supports, the first matter at hand is to define *operator*. An operator is a symbol that instructs the compiler to perform specific mathematical or logical operations on some value(s).

Values in this case refers to *operands*, and can be constants, variables, or expressions. Some operators are known as *unary* operators and have only one operand. Placing an exclamation mark in front of a variable of subtype boolean, for example, changes it to the opposite state.

For example, if *variable1* holds the value *True* then the value of *Not variable1* is *False*. The unary operator *Not* has been applied to the operand *variable1*. The operators which take one argument are the simplest, but there aren't many operations which only use one operand (think mathematical calculations for instance).

The remaining operators are usually *binary* (they have two operands, that is). A familiar example of a binary operation would be simple addition that returns the sum of two variables

```
( a + b )
```

In this case, the operator (+) acts on both the a and b variables.
The three main categories of operator are as follows:

- **Arithmetic** Arithmetic operators are the ones with which everybody is familiar: simple mathematical symbols such as +, –, *, and /. These are explained in their own section.

- **Comparison** Comparison operators are used to compare values and objects. They're crucial for holding together the constituents of most *condition expressions* (explained using the If ... Then ... Else construct in Chapter 6, "Controlling Program Flow in VBScript").
- **Logical** Logical operators rely on the underlying concepts of True and False and allow the expression of complex conditions using a simple set of operators.

Arithmetic Operators

The most commonly known operators are those used for standard arithmetic, and VBScript supplies a full complement of these. Table 5-1 lists these operators and makes some special observations of note.

Table 5–1 VBScript Arithmetic Operators

SYMBOL	DESCRIPTION
+	Addition (or string concatenation)
–	Subtraction
*	Multiplication
/	Standard division
\	Integer division
Mod	Modulo Arithmetic
^	Exponentiation
–	Unary negation
&	String concatenation

The +, – (binary subtraction and unary negation), *, and / operators are the ones everybody knows and loves from hand-held calculators. They don't require further explanation, but you might not have come across some of the others.

Integer division (\) returns the integer part of the result of a division; for example, 16\3 equals 5. The operands are rounded to integers before the division is carried out. The result is an integer, rounded down to the nearest value.

Modulo arithmetic (Mod) returns the remainder of a division. The modulo of an expression is the remainder of the first operand divided by the second operand; for example, (21-16) mod 3 equals 2 (the remainder of 5\3, that is, 2).

Exponentiation (^) raises any numeric expression to a power; for example 2^3 equals 8, and 25^0.5 equals 5.

String concatenation technically isn't an arithmetic operator, but is evaluated before the comparison and logical operators (see the section, "Order of Evaluation," later in this chapter), so is placed with the other arithmetic operators. The result of the concatenation of two strings, x and y, is the string xy. For example, "Hello" & "World!" is the single string "Hello World!."

CAUTION **When the operation a + b is performed on two string values, the VBScript interpreter carries out a string concatenation rather than an addition—a definite problem if you're adding values that a user has typed into controls on the page. These controls have string type properties for the text they contain (even if a number has been typed), so an explicit typecast must be used to force the interpreter to treat the values a and b as numbers for addition. For example, as follows:**

```
result = CInt(a) + CInt(b)
```

Comparison Operators

To refresh your memory, the comparison operators enable the VBScript programmer to make comparisons between various expressions or values. Most of these operators are self-explanatory and Table 5-2 presents a comprehensive list. The important element of the comparison operator is the *return value*. The comparison operators return a value that depends on whether a statement is true or false. If the comparison statement is true, then a Boolean True is returned. If the comparison statement is false, then it returns a Boolean False.

Table 5-2 VBScript Comparison Operators

SYMBOL	DESCRIPTION
=	Equality
<>	Not equal to
<	Less than
<=	Less than or equal to
>	Greater than
>=	Greater than or equal to
Is	Object equivalence

The comparison operators are almost exclusively used in control flow statements that test the state of variables to determine which code to execute next. Comparison operators become much more relevant in Chapter 6, "Controlling Program Flow in VBScript," and in understanding control flow statements.

The only operator that needs further explanation is the Is operator, which is used to test whether two variables contain a reference to the *same* object. Object references can be set up using the Set statement (see sidebar, "Setting Up and Testing Object References"), and they let variable names serve to reference objects like the current window or document. Sometimes the script needs to check whether two references point to the same object, hence the importance of the Is statement.

Setting Up and Testing Object References

You can assign values to normal variables (integers, strings, floating-point numbers) simply using the equals sign (=); for example:

```
intPosition = 3 * intHeight - HANDICAP
```

This form of assignment isn't good enough when dealing with objects. These are items such as text boxes, buttons, drop-down lists, and the Explorer window itself. These items are much more complicated than simple variables, because they can consist of many properties (such as name, current value, maximum allowed length, and so on) and support methods (functions or procedures that carry out tasks relating to the object). Objects can even generate their own events.

You can store references to an actual object in a variable by using the Set statement, which lets you use a variable to refer to the object instead of using the object's name. This presents two advantages: One, some objects have long names, such as Window.Forms(0).Elements(3), and using a shorter (or more descriptive) variable name can lead to more readable code. Two, using a variable to refer to an object means you can write configurable code, maybe in a function, which can operate on any object. To set up a reference to an object, write something like the following

```
Dim myObject
Set myObject = Window.Forms(0).Elements(3)
```

You can now use this variable in place of the object name, to modify the object itself. Remember, the Set statement only sets up a reference to the object, it does *not* make a separate copy.

```
MyObject.Value = "New Button Caption"
```

After setting up a reference to an object, you might need to test the variable to determine the object to which it refers. You can use the Is operator to serve this purpose. If two items refer to exactly the same object (not just the same kind of object), the Is operator returns True; otherwise, it returns False. Using the most recent Set definition as an example, you could use the following line of code to check that *myObject* still referred to the object to which it was assigned.

```
If myObject Is Window.Forms(0).Elements(3) Then MsgBox "The object
➥reference still holds"
```

Logical Operators

The Logical operators are powerful, but need a short preamble to introduce the system of values with which they work.

In logical terms, any number other than zero is considered True, and zero is considered False. VBScript also uses the Boolean subtype, which can store either True or False values. The *Boolean subtype* is how the results of the logical operators are returned. These operators can be used to formulate condition expressions that express quite complex criteria, such as:

If x is true and y is true, or z is not true, and a is not equal to b Then ...

which could be written as:

```
If ((x And y) Or (Not z)) And (a Xor b) Then ...
```

Table 5-3 lists the available logical operators, and then the following text presents some examples of their uses.

Table 5–3 VBScript Logical Operators

SYMBOL	DESCRIPTION
And	Conjunction
Or	Disjunction
Xor	Logical Inequality
Not	Negation
Eqv	Logical Equivalence
Imp	Logical Implication

Rather than discuss each operator in turn, Table 5-4 presents a truth table for their operations. The number 1 stands for True, and 0 for False.

Table 5–4 VBScript Logical Operators Truth Table

P	Q	NOT P	P AND Q	P OR Q	P XOR Q	P EQV Q	P IMP Q
0	0	1	0	0	0	1	1
0	1	1	0	1	1	0	1
1	0	0	0	1	1	0	0
1	1	0	1	1	0	1	1

These operators work as well applied to numbers as they do applied to Boolean expressions. Used on numbers, the logical operators perform their function on each bit of the operands in turn. Used on Boolean expressions, the items are treated as True or False (thought of as 1 and 0).

The operator Not is a unary operator and applies only to one operand. It negates the value to which it is applied. So *Not True* evaluates to *False* and vice versa. The number 5 is represented in binary by 00000101 (with 8 bits). The value of *Not 5* in binary is 11111010—note that each bit has been negated.

The And operator is used to check for two values being True at once. It's a binary operator and takes two arguments. Only if both of the operands evaluate to True is the result of *p And q* True. An example of its use is:

```
If intYes And intUserConfirmed Then MsgBox "You have
➥confirmed the operation"
```

If either intYes or intUserConfirmed are False (contain a zero), the And operation yields a False value. The message box appears only if both values are True (non-zero).

The Or operator complements And. It too is a binary operator and requires two arguments, but it yields True if either one of its operands are True. The value of *p Or q* is False only if both *p* and *q* are False (contain a zero)—useful when you want to perform an operation if one condition or another condition (or both) hold.

Xor, Eqv, and Imp aren't so simple. Xor, which stands for exclusive or, is the logical equivalent of <> (not equal to). It's True only if the two operands are different, as opposed to the regular Or, where if either, or both, of the variables are True (non zero), the whole statement is True. Use Xor if you want to carry out an operation if only one expression is True, but NOT both.

Eqv is the exact opposite of Xor, and is known as the equivalence operator. It's True only if the two operands are identical. In this case, they can either both be True, or both be False. This operator can be used rather than the equals sign (=) to check for two expressions being equal to each other. It checks for bit equality, rather than string equality, so is reserved for use with Boolean values. There are no clear cases where the Eqv operator is superior to the = operator, so it boils down to a matter of style.

```
If blnFlagA Eqv blnFlagB Then MsgBox "They are equal"
```

has the same effect as writing

```
If blnFlagA = blnFlagB Then MsgBox "They are equal"
```

Imp is known as the implication operator, and is a somewhat abstract concept. It's True if the first operand's truth or falsity does in fact imply that the second operand holds; otherwise, it's False. Most VBScript programmers don't have call to use implication, but if the operation you want to perform matches the truth table (see Table 5-4) for Eqv, feel free to use it.

The operator lists covered in the previous sections contain all the operators that VBScript implements. You are responsible for choosing the best operator to satisfy your requirements. The combinations of these operators allow programs to react to user and data input, as well as provide the computational mechanics behind the guts of any program. All but the most trivial of applications require some form of expressions and operators.

What Is an Expression?

An *expression* may be defined officially as any valid combination of operators, constants, and variables. This definition doesn't really offer much meaning for the novice programmer, for whom the questions "What is a 'valid combination' for instance?" remains unanswered.

A *valid combination* is one that obeys VBScript's rules for using each operator that the expression contains. The following sections furnish examples of all sorts of expressions and technical details, showing what you can and can't do. First, a few simple examples are introduced, leading to more specific discussions dealing with such matters as dates, times, and strings.

Table 5-5 shows a list of expressions; some are valid, some aren't. The table's purpose is just to give you an idea about valid expressions. The range of possibilities for different expressions is huge; however, they all are comprised of a finite set of operators acting on variables and literal values. The operators available for use in expressions are covered in this chapter.

Table 5–5 Example Expressions

EXPRESSION	VALID	REASON IF INVALID
x+y-z	Yes	
+x-y	No	Addition needs two operands, one each side
(16*x)+5	Yes	
((12*x)-z	No	Closing bracket,), is missing
32*Celsius(z)	Yes	
x And 255	Yes	
Or z	No	Or needs an operand on either side
1345	Yes	
#03-13-96#	Yes	

The examples in Table 5-5 should give you some idea of the range of subjects that expressions can cover. Some kinds of expression require special handling, most notably, those that deal with dates and times.

Writing a Valid Expression

An expression can be a combination of operators, variable names, function calls, literal values, and constants. The key when you compose an expression is to follow the rules for the operators you use to join the different elements together. Some operators are binary, which means they take one operand on either side, while others (Not and unary –) are unary and lie on the left-hand side of the value to which they apply.

The most important form of expression is the assignment expression, which takes the following form:

```
varname = expression
```

The item on the left-hand side can only be a variable name. It cannot be a constant value, such as 156 or a "Hello World!." Neither can it be a function call. You have much more freedom when formulating the right-hand side of the assignment expression. It can consist of function calls (see Chapter 7, "Grouping Statements in Procedures and Functions"), literal values (76, 1.45, #July 16, 1945#, or "Wow"), other variable names, object properties (Form1.Button1.Value), and constants. Constants in VBScript are covered near the end of this chapter.

The main point when you write an expression is that you must follow the rules for combining operators—if you don't, you get a syntax error message. You also need to be aware of *precedence rules*, which govern how the interpreter calculates an expression. These are dealt with later in this chapter under the heading "Order of Evaluation of Expressions."

String and Numeric Expressions

The VBScript interpreter deals with strings without much special attention. It automatically displays date values as strings when necessary, and even concatenates two strings together when the addition (+)

operator is applied to two strings. The explicit string concatenation operator (&) has also been introduced.

Other times, you have more complex situations in which you might want to manipulate strings, to get at specific parts of them or convert them into other types. You can carry out type conversions using functions listed in the Chapter 4, yes, but what about string manipulation? Table 5-6 lists the functions available. Chapter 14, "Using the Internet Control Pack and Java Applets with VBScript," provides an example document that uses several of these functions to split a string into various components.

Table 5–6 VBScript String Manipulation Functions

FUNCTION NAME	PURPOSE
CStr	Converts the expression supplied to a String subtype
Str	Returns a string representation of a number
Val	Returns the numbers contained in a string expression
StrComp	Performs string comparisons
String	Creates a repeating character string of a specified length
Len	Finds the length of a string
Left	Returns the left portion of a string
Mid	Returns a section from the middle of a string
Right	Returns the right portion of a string
LTrim	Creates a copy of a string without leading spaces
RTrim	Creates a copy of a string without trailing blanks
Trim	Removes both leading and trailing spaces from a string

Date Expressions

Dates and times are notoriously difficult to handle when programming. Different languages and platforms treat them in different ways and have different built-in capabilities for handling them. A sidebar in

Chapter 4, "Variables, Arrays, and Data Types," discusses how most systems use *magic numbers* to represent a date or time by the number of seconds or days that has elapsed since some predetermined date.

Part of the reason for dwelling so much on date formats is that Web pages should be consistent in their content across international boundaries. Different countries use different formats for currency, dates, and so on, which raises a problem. VBScript programmers should be aware that values such as dates and times display differently on client PCs in different countries. By planning with care, you can ensure that dates and times you use are written unambiguously. This matter is of even greater import given the advent of active content on the WWW, where dates are an important element of pages that can alter appearances according to the current time or date. VBScript provides a whole range of functions for converting dates and extracting values from them (documented in full in the Appendix A, "VBScript Language Reference—Functions"). Careful use of these facilities can ensure that your scripts work properly with dates all over the world.

How VBScript Stores Dates

VBScript can store any date value between January 1, 100 AD, and December 31, 9999—quite a large range. Most languages have different ways of storing dates in magic numbers. VBScript uses real numbers to store both dates and times. The integer part of the number represents the date and the fractional part holds the time of day (see Figure 5-1 for a graphical representation). Any date falling before December 30, 1899 is represented by a negative number.

It would be completely unreasonable to expect users, or programmers for that matter, to use the internal representation for dates and times, so VBScript supports several ways of writing these values (explained in the next section).

Writing Date Values

There are three main ways to specify a date using VBScript, each of which has its own advantages and disadvantages:

- Writing string literals containing date information

- Writing special date literals
- Using built-in functions to return date information

A *string literal* is any set of characters enclosed by double quotes; for example, "Hello World!". String expressions are discussed more later in the chapter.

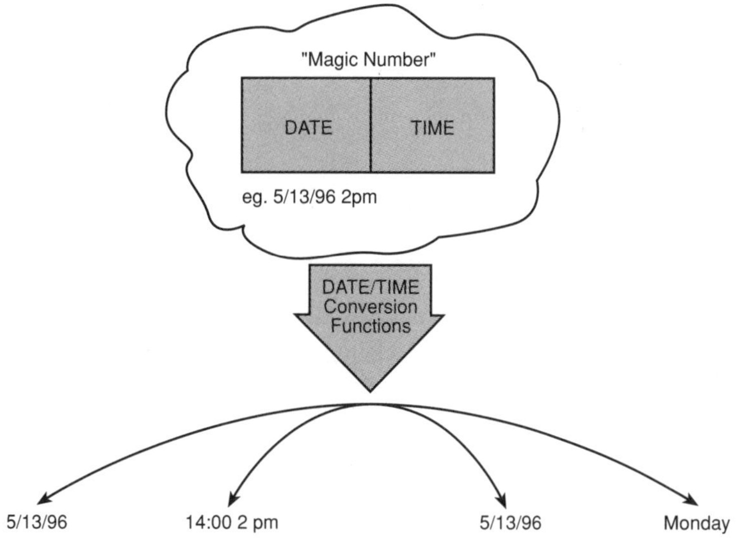

FIGURE 5-1
An overview of date and time handling using VBScript

String Literals Containing Dates

VBScript interprets any string that contains valid date information as a Date subtype when it's used in the correct context. Meaning, you can hard-code dates into your scripts, or users can type them into text boxes on the page, as string variables.

Valid date strings are ones that contain only numbers separated by *date separators* (usually /) and fall within allowed ranges, for example, July can have only 31 days, no more, no less. VBScript recognizes the order for month, day, and year according to the Short Date format in your system settings; in the U.S., it's MM/DD/YY and in the UK, it's DD/MM/YY. Additionally, VBScript can recognize unambiguous dates containing month names, either abbreviated or in long form.

> The current year from your computer's settings is used if the year part of any date is omitted. If a date is written as numbers and is unambiguous, for example, 24/08/1997, it's recognized correctly even if the locale settings specify a different date format, in this case, MM/DD/YYYY.

Some valid string literals containing dates are

- "15/07/1996"
- "25/12/95"
- "Jan 31, 1995"
- "May 17"
- "13:00 February 29, 1996"

TIP

To ensure that your code functions correctly in all locales, you should use an unambiguous format to specify dates that are written into your source code. The best method is to write dates using abbreviated month names; for example, "Mar 20, 1997". When the date you are writing can only be one day, for example, "25/12/1995" versus "12/25/1995", it doesn't matter how you write it.

Special Date Literals

To signal clearly to anyone reading your code, and to the interpreter, that you're using a date or time, you can use the special date/time literal symbol. Enclose the value you're writing in number symbols (#). For example:

```
Dim specialDate
specialDate = #11/07/1974#
...
specialDate = #Nov 7, 1974#
```

Generating Date Information with Functions

VBScript offers a collection of functions for generating and manipulating dates (described in detail in the Function Reference in Appendix A). For now, Table 5-7 is a complete list of functions and what they do, some of which you can see in action in the Dates example that follows.

Table 5-7 VBScript Date Manipulation Functions

FUNCTION NAME	PURPOSE
CDate	Converts values to Date subtype
IsDate	Checks to see if expression supplied is a valid date
Date	Returns current system date
DateSerial	Returns a Date subtype for the specified day, month, and year
DateValue	Returns a Date subtype representing the expression supplied
Day	Extracts the day of the month from a date expression
Month	Extracts the month of the year
Year	Extracts the year from a date expression
WeekDay	Returns an integer that represents the day of the week

Working with Dates: An Example

This section contains quite a bit of information on handling date information because it's one of the aspects of programming that even experienced users can easily mess up. To that end, you can load a prepared example from the Tutorial section of the main Web page as an introduction to date processing. Just select the '`Dates - How to Handle Them`' hyperlink . You will find the full document source code printed here; if you want to edit the HTML, choose View|Source from the Explorer 3.0 menu bar.

See Figure 5-2 for a screen capture of the example in action. Make sure that you have the same document loaded in your browser, and try it out. Try entering your date of birth in the text box and pressing the Calculate button—you might get a nasty shock!

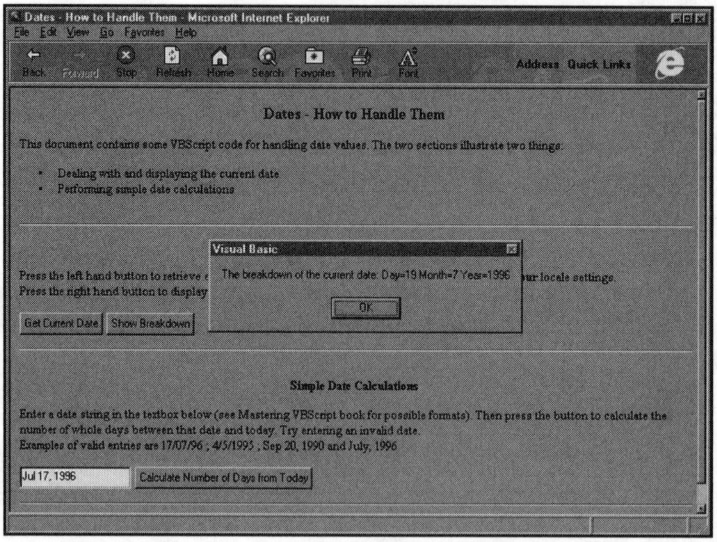

FIGURE 5-2
Breaking down today's date into days, months, and years

```
<HTML>
<HEAD>
<TITLE>Dates - How to Handle Them</TITLE>
<SCRIPT LANGUAGE="VBScript">
<!-
Sub DateButton_OnClick                          'Display the current system
➥date
    Dim dtToday
    dtToday = Date()
    MsgBox "Today's date is: " & dtToday    'Date variable
➥automatically converted to a string
End Sub

Sub BreakButton_OnClick                         'Display the current date as
➥day, month and year
    Dim dtToday
    dtToday = Date()
    MsgBox "The breakdown of the current date: Day=" & Day(dtToday) &
➥" Month=" & Month(dtToday) & " Year=" & Year(dtToday)
End Sub
```

```
Sub CalcButton_OnClick                  'Calculate the difference
➥between current date and some
    Dim dtToday, dblDifference          'user defined value
    dtToday = Date()
    If IsDate(Form1.DateText.Value) Then
        dblDifference = CDate(Form1.DateText.Value) - dtToday
        MsgBox "There are " & CInt(dblDifference) & " days between " &
➥Form1.DateText.Value & " and today."
    Else
        MsgBox "An invalid date has been entered.  Please try again!"
    End If
End Sub
->
</SCRIPT>
</HEAD>

<BODY>
<CENTER><H3>Dates - How to Handle Them</H3></CENTER>
This document contains some VBScript code for handling date values. The
➥two sections
illustrate two things:
<UL TYPE="circle">
<LI>Dealing with and displaying the current date
<LI>Performing simple date calculations
</UL>
<HR>
<FORM NAME="Form1">
<CENTER><H4>Retrieving the Current Date</H4></CENTER>
Press the left hand button to retrieve and display the current system
➥date in the
format specified by <B>your</B> locale settings.<BR>
Press the right hand button to display a breakdown by Day, Month and
➥Year of the current
date
<P>
```

```
    <INPUT NAME="DateButton" TYPE="button" VALUE="Get Current Date">
    <INPUT NAME="BreakButton" TYPE="button" VALUE="Show Breakdown">
<HR>
<CENTER><H4>Simple Date Calculations</H4></CENTER>
Enter a date string in the textbox below (see Mastering VBScript book
➥for possible formats).
Then press the button to calculate the number of whole days between
➥that date and today.
Try entering an invalid date.<BR>
Examples of valid entries are 17/07/96 ; 4/5/1995 ; Sep 20, 1990 and
➥July, 1996<P>
    <INPUT NAME="DateText" TYPE="text" VALUE="Jul 17, 1996">
    <INPUT NAME="CalcButton" TYPE="button" VALUE="Calculate Number of
➥Days from Today">
<HR>
</FORM>
</BODY>
</HTML>
```

There are a few points to note from this example.

Automatic Date Display

The DateButton_OnClick procedure gets the current system date into the variable named dtToday and displays it in a message box. The value in dtToday automatically appears in the format specified by your computer's settings, not as the interpreter's own internal representation (see Figure 5-2).

Breaking the Date into Pieces

Sometimes you might need to access the different components of a date. These may include payroll calculations, where the date entered has to be checked to see whether it falls before or after the 15th of the month, and so on. The event procedure for BreakButton shows how to do this, and breaks the current system date into its component parts using the Day( ), Month( ), and Year( ) functions.

Validating User Input

If dates are hard for programmers to work with when designing a script, then imagine the users, who are the most likely to be in a hurry or concentrating on several things at once. They can easily make mistakes when entering structured values such as dates and times, and giving them all the help you can makes for good design practice.

To this end, you should always validate values the user enters before trying to use them. The CalcButton_OnClick event procedure performs some date validation. The following line,

```
If IsDate(Form1.DateText.Value) Then
```

uses the VBScript function IsDate to see whether the value is a proper date expression. IsDate( ) returns True if the result is a proper date, which in turn allows the calculation to proceed; otherwise a message appears to tell the user that an invalid date was entered. See Chapter 6, “Controlling Program Flow in VBScript,” for more details about the If ... Then ... Else construct.

Time Expressions

You can apply most of the discussion so far to time expressions. This section covers the details specific to dealing with times. VBScript has several functions you can use on times, as detailed in the Language Reference Appendixes (and summarized in Table 5-8).

Table 5-8 VBScript Time Manipulation Functions

FUNCTION NAME	PURPOSE
Time	Returns current sytem time
Now	Returns current system date and time
CDate	Converts value to Date subtype, including time information
IsDate	Checks to see whether expression supplied is a valid date/time

continues

Table 5-8 Continued

FUNCTION NAME	PURPOSE
TimeSerial	Returns a Date subtype for the specified hour, minute, and second
TimeValue	Returns a Date subtype that represents the time expression supplied
Hour	Returns a Date subtype for the specified day, month, and year
Minute	Returns a Date subtype that represents the expression supplied
Second	Returns an integer that represents the day of the week

You can use these functions for much the same purposes as those in Table 5-7, including validating user input, arithmetic on time values, separating the time components, and retrieving system information.

You can use twenty-four hour values and the usual time separator is the colon (:). The following table presents some sample valid and invalid time literals:

TIME LITERAL	VALID REASON IF INVALID
"12:05:32 AM"	Yes
"31:00"	NoTimes are almost always hh:mm or hh:mm:ss
#2:24PM#	Yes
#1:30PM 12/12/96#	Yes
#1:30PM 34/04/96#	NoInvalid date section
"22:00"	Yes

Figure 5-3 shows how you can easily calculate the number of days between two dates by performing a simple subtraction. Note also the number of date formats that you can use as inputs. As an exercise, try modifying the Date example to carry out a similar function with times. Then you might be able to find out how many seconds you've been alive!

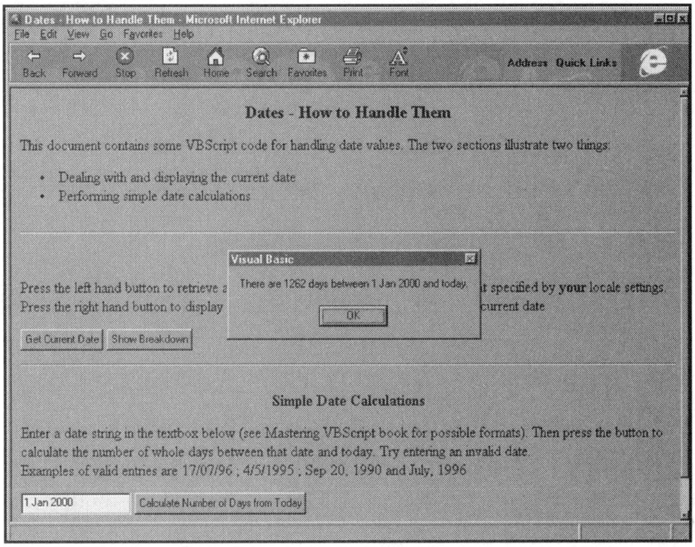

FIGURE 5-3
Dates can be input in any format, and treated just like real numbers with VBScript's magic number format.

Order of Evaluation of Expressions

Before the VBScript interpreter can execute the code that you write, it must parse it. It breaks down all the statements in the script into tokens that represent variables, keywords, literal values, operators, and so on. The expressions that you write, using the operators described here, must be translated into some form of internal representation. As well as deciphering the tokens that make up your script, the interpreter also must be able to determine the order in which statements should be executed.

Operator precedence enters the picture now. The rules are similar to those operator precedence in algebra, but there are a few more operators to consider.

The operators are evaluated in the following order of precedence, with the topmost having highest precedence:

I Arithmetic operators

1. ^ Exponentiation
2. – Unary negation
3. * Multiplication

4. / Division
5. \ Integer Division
6. Mod Modulo Arithmetic
7. + Addition
8. – Subtraction
9. & String concatenation

II Comparison operators

Evaluated from left to right in the order they appear; they have equal precedence.

III Logical operators

1. Not Negation
2. And Conjunction
3. Or Disjunction
4. Xor Exclusion
5. Eqv Equivalence
6. Imp Implication

Arithmetic operators are evaluated first, followed by comparison operators, and logical operators come last.

If addition and subtraction occur together in an expression they are evaluated in order of appearance from left to right. The same applies for multiplication and division.

You can use parentheses to override the default precedence settings; for example, as follows:

```
(x+y)*37      'Force the x+y to be calculated before the
➥multiplication
```

or

```
If  (Not x)=y Then ...        'Force "Not x" to be compared with y
```

Any operations within parentheses are performed before those outside, but the sections within the actual parentheses still retain the normal precedence rules.

Defining and Using Constants

Constants are a feature of most programming languages and are often treated as different kinds of values from anything else discussed thus far. The C language, for instance, lets you define constant values in several ways, including the *#define* statement or the *const* keyword. Those of you who aren't familiar with C don't need to worry about how it handles constants, we are merely using the language as a comparison tool. VBScript, however, has no built-in support for constants. Read on.

What Is a Constant—Is It Cast in Stone?

In programming, a *constant* is a name that never changes and that is given to a value (number, string, date or time). Constants used to refer to special values and to make code clearer. For example, you might use a constant to represent the number of ounces in a pound—something that never changes, even by accident.

As well as to clarify code, you can use constants when a special value may change later in the development cycle. The constant is defined in one place in the code, usually near the beginning. Whenever the special value is used in the script, the constant name is used instead of the actual literal value. The advantage of this method is that the value can be changed in one place in the script, but the change will be reflected throughout.

That said, VBScript's support for constants actually is the same as its handling of ordinary variables—the language has no constants defined separately by the language. They are implemented as literal values assigned to normal variables. Constants are useful for making code clearer. So how are they defined using VBScript?

Defining Constants—Make Your Mark on the World

Constants are created in VBScript in the same way that variables are declared. The Dim statement is used to define the constant name, after the declaration a literal number, string, date, or time can be assigned to this new storage space.

There actually isn't a functional difference between constants defined like this and normal VBScript variables. You can overwrite the values stored in your constants by assigning different values to them. Therefore, you should use a naming scheme to differentiate between constants and ordinary variables. The coding conventions recommended by the VBScript development team (see Chapter 9, "Writing Well-Organized and Coherent VBScript") suggest that you use capital letters for constant names. Here are some examples of constant declarations:

```
<SCRIPT LANGUAGE="VBScript">
Dim SIZE_OF_DOZEN, MY_BIRTHDAY, ERROR_MSG
SIZE_OF_DOZEN = 12
MY_BIRTHDAY = #September 14, 1973#
ERROR_MSG = "That was completely wrong!"
...
...
intApples = intBaskets * SIZE_OF_DOZEN            'Using the constant
...
MsgBox ERROR_MSG            'Display an error message
...
intAge = Date() - MY_BIRTHDAY            'Use the date constant in a
➥calculation
...
</SCRIPT>
```

As you can see, the meaning of the code is much clearer when using constants. Also, if the size of a dozen were to change overnight you would only have to change one line of code to reflect this throughout the script.

Conclusions—Where to Now?

This chapter has presented quite a varied collection of information. You should now be familiar with all sorts of expressions, operators, and some new ways of dealing with special values. The sections on dates and times should prove to be invaluable sources of information when you start writing some more complex scripts.

Until now, this book has dealt only with syntactical details of the VBScript language, rather than structural ones. Having now laid the foundations for further work, the next two chapters tell you how to repeat sections of code using loops and control flow constructs, make choices, and write procedures and functions.

CHAPTER 6

Controlling Program Flow in VBScript

This chapter concentrates on two powerful means to control the flow of a script and add an active dimension to your documents: conditional expressions and loop constructs. Using these comparison tools, you can repeat actions and make decisions about what part of code you want to execute next. This is the basis of a truly active environment and gives users flexibility rather than forcing them to follow fixed routes. Being able to control program flow is like taking the car to work rather than going by bus. One takes you exactly where you want to go, the other sticks to its route.

Interspersed among these conditional commands are more information about forms and also an introduction to using the password control in your documents.

Once again, those of you who have used Visual Basic may find that you already know most of what this chapter has to say. Even so, skim over the code examples to become familiar yourself with any differences that may exist between these two language varieties.

After you complete this chapter, you should know how to do the following:

- Make decisions about what sections of code to execute
- Write loops to carry out operations a fixed number of times
- Run statements until a condition is True
- Run statements while a condition is True

These constructs give you the freedom and power to write scripts that are far superior to the examples seen in the last chapters. With only a modest amount of code, you can see the potential for real applications in a scripting environment.

Making Decisions—If...Then...Else

Conditional execution is an important aspect of any programming language because it introduces a way to control the sequence of procedure execution. Specific conditions direct what actions should follow what, giving your programs a great degree of flexibility. To control this flow, you use logical operators and Boolean expressions to determine how an event status should be treated and what portion of code should be called next.

The If...Then...Else construct is based on the logical comparison of a set of statements or condition that yields a result that is either True or False. You can use each of these possibilities to execute one or many statements of code that performs a function. If only one statement is run, it's called a single-line syntax. To run many statements, you need several lines of code (multiple-line syntax terminology) to execute, depending on the outcome of the conditional statement.

Most of the conditions are expressed using the comparison operators that Chapter 5, "Expressions, Operators, and Constants" discusses, like the greater than, less than operators, or logical conditions like NOT and OR.

Simple Conditionals—Using the Single-Line Syntax

You can only use the single-line syntax in your code if the conditional statement runs a single command. Single-line means that all the code must be placed on one line, so you can't use any "" symbols for multiple entries, which limits the number of commands that can be run to one.

If you need to carry out two or more actions—for example, increment a register *and* call a procedure—you have to use a multiple statement and follow the instructions given in the next section.

For conditions that give True results and run only single commands, you would use the following syntax.

```
If (Condition Expression) Then Statement
```

The parentheses are not essential but helps make code more readable.

You often want to carry out one action if the condition is True, another if it's False. When that's the case, you can use a slightly longer version of the same command, as shown here:

```
If (Condition Expression) Then Statement1 Else Statement2
```

Using these constructs is best illustrated by example. Like the other examples, you can find an appropriate example on the main *VBScript Master's Handbook* Web page in the Tutorial section. Choose the Decisions, Decisions – If...Then...Else hyperlink.

In the first section, you enter a password into a textbox control called a PASSWORD control. The PASSWORD control is identical to the standard textbox control, except that instead of displaying the characters the user types, it replaces them all with asterisks. This allows you to create standard password-style controls similar to those used to log in to Microsoft Windows NT or Windows 95 with a password. You can see how the password control looks in Figure 6-1. The password control will be discussed in more detail in Chapter 12, "ActiveX Controls and VBScript." Clicking on the Open button in the example invokes a VBScript event procedure, OpenButton_OnClick, which uses an If...Then condition to check the password against the correct word. If you enter the letters correctly, a message appears. If you get it wrong, nothing happens because the If…Then syntax has room enough for only one command. The If…Then…Else statement gives the program another option to execute when the wrong password is entered. The code for checking the password is as follow:

```
If (Form1.Passwd.Value = strPassword) Then MsgBox "Hello, Ali Baba!"
```

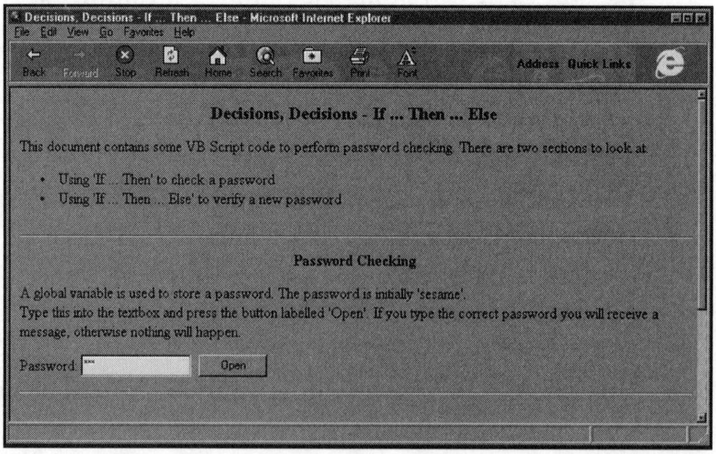

FIGURE 6-1
Using If…Then to check a password entered in a password control

The second section uses an If…Then…Else construct that allows the user to change the password required for the PASSWORD control at the top of the window. Two PASSWORD controls and a button enable you to enter a new password to store as the *strPassword* variable. See Figure 6-2 to see how it works. The If…Then command makes sure that both entries are identical. If they match, the password is stored; if not, a help message appears. This last condition is written into the code using the Else statement:

```
If (Form2.Passwd1.Value = Form2.Passwd2.Value) Then
➥strPassword=Form2.Passwd1.Value Else MsgBox "Try again!"
```

You may be wondering why there isn't a message saying something like "Your password has been changed." Because you're using the single-line syntax (change the password), there is no room for another command to output a confirmation message. You have to wait for the multiple-command syntax before you can add greater functionality to the If…Then…Else construct.

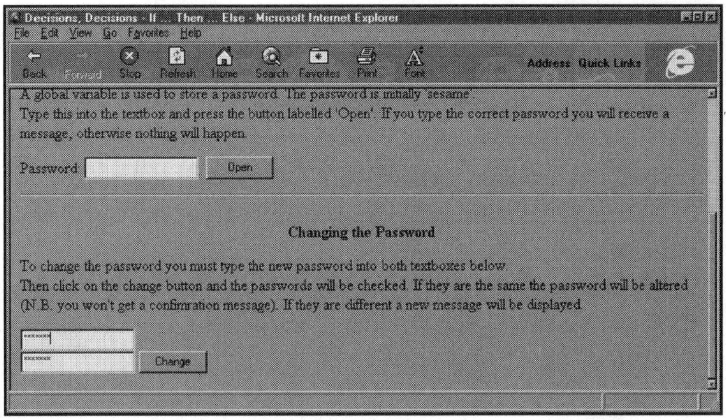

FIGURE 6-2. *Using If… Then…Else to change a password.*

Here's the HTML source for the document:

```
<HTML>
<HEAD>
<TITLE>Decisions, Decisions - If…Then ... Else</TITLE>
<SCRIPT LANGUAGE="VBScript">
<!–
Dim strPassword                              'Define a script-level
➥variable to store the password
strPassword = "sesame"

Sub OpenButton_OnClick
    If (Form1.Passwd.Value = strPassword) Then MsgBox "Hello, Ali
➥Baba!"
End Sub

Sub ChangeButton_OnClick
    If (Form2.Passwd1.Value = Form2.Passwd2.Value) Then
➥strPassword=Form2.Passwd1.Value Else MsgBox "Try again!"
End Sub
–>
</SCRIPT>
</HEAD>
```

```
<BODY>
<CENTER>
<H3>Decisions, Decisions - If…Then ... Else</H3>
</CENTER><P>
This document contains some VB Script code to perform password
➥checking.  There are
two sections to look at.
<UL TYPE="circle">
<LI>Using 'If…Then' to check a password
<LI>Using 'If…Then ... Else' to verify a new password
</UL>
<HR>
<CENTER><H4>Password Checking</H4></CENTER>
A global variable is used to store a password.  The password is
➥initially 'sesame'.<BR>
Type this into the textbox and press the button labelled 'Open'.  If
➥you type the correct password
you will receive a message, otherwise nothing will happen.<P>

<FORM NAME="Form1">
Password:
    <INPUT TYPE="password" NAME="Passwd"     VALUE="">
    <INPUT TYPE="button"   NAME="OpenButton" VALUE="Open">
</FORM>
<HR>
<CENTER><H4>Changing the Password</H4></CENTER>
To change the password you must type the new password into both
➥textboxes below.<BR>
Then click on the change button and the passwords will be checked.  If
➥they are the same
the password will be altered (N.B. you won't get a confirmation
➥message).  If they are different a new message
will be displayed.<P>

<FORM NAME="Form2">
```

```
    <INPUT TYPE="password" NAME="Passwd1"   VALUE=""><BR>
    <INPUT TYPE="password" NAME="Passwd2"   VALUE="">
    <INPUT TYPE="button"   NAME="ChangeButton" VALUE="Change">
</FORM>
</BODY>
</HTML>
```

As always, this example brings up a couple new noteworthy points, which the following sections discuss.

More Than One Form—Getting Greedy

Look at the code for both the event procedures in the last example. Notice the references to two different forms, Form1 and Form2. These have been set up with different names using following HTML code snippet. The definitions consist of a <FORM> container tag plus a NAME= entry, which enables the interpreter to distinguish the forms. Programmers often want to use more than one form in a document to place text in separate areas.

```
<FORM NAME="Form1">
    ...
    Form elements
    ....
<FORM>
```

and

```
<FORM NAME="Form2">
...
    Form elements
    ....
<FORM>
```

> **CAUTION** Many forms can contain several controls in a complex HTML document, which is why you need to name forms. If you have more than one form and forget to name them, the VBScript interpreter doesn't know which controls your event procedures are referring, and the scripts aren't invoked when events occur.

The PASSWORD Control

This control is a variant of the textbox control you encountered in Chapter 5. The only difference is that it hides the text with asterisks. Chapter 12, "ActiveX Controls and VBScript," covers passwords in greater detail, but if you can't wait, here's the HTML line:

```
<INPUT TYPE="password" NAME="Passwd" VALUE="sesame">
```

Multiple-Line Syntax

Up to the present, you have been restricted by the number of statements that can follow a conditional expression because we have only been using the single-line syntax. The multi-line syntax allows you to place several commands after an If or Else condition, improving the control capabilities of the decisions.

Now look at the second part of the password example and see how you could enhance ut by using the many line syntax. You could improve the code by placing two commands after the If statement: one to change the password and the other to display a message that says "Your password has now been changed." This makes the routine more realistic and also gives more the user more information. The possibilities for such improvements are myriad, and the preference for multiple-line syntax over the single-line becomes clear.

The first essential element that the multiple-line syntax adds is the new keyword End If, which must be included at the end of the If...Then...Else block. The second new element is the ElseIf keyword, which lets you check for additional conditions within one conditional block. The format of the extended conditional statement is:

```
If (Condition Expression) Then
    Statments
    ...
    ...
ElseIf (Condition Expression N) Then          ' This block is
➥optional
    Statements
```

```
    ...                                                     ' There can be an
➥arbitrary number of ElseIf blocks
    ...
Else                                                        ' This part of
➥the construct is also optional
    Statements                                              '
    ...                                                     ' There can only
➥be one Else clause
    ...
End If
```

As in the single-line syntax, the Else section is optional, but the End If keyword must always be present. Minus the End If statement, the interpreter can't distinguish where the conditional statements end and normal program flow resumes. Adding the ElseIf keyword enables you to use one conditional block to check several conditions—if none of them are True, the interpreter executes the statements in the Else section. To demonstrate the multiple-line syntax format for If...Else statements, you can load another example from the Tutorial section of the main Web page. Select the `More Decisions - Multiple Line Syntax` link to load the document. The complete document source is printed at the of the following section on nesting conditionals.

Nesting Conditionals

Another way to add more flexibility to conditionals in VBScript is *nesting*. Nesting is a general concept that applies to the If...Then...Else statement as well as other constructs discussed later in this chapter. This means that you can place a conditional statement such as If...Then...Else block anywhere within a script or even within another conditional. In the case of the If...Then...Else statement, as long as each multiple-line conditional ends with End If, everything will work. The nested conditional exists within the outer conditional just like any other multi-line code segment.

```
<HTML>
<HEAD>
<TITLE>More Decisions - Multiple Line Syntax</TITLE>
<SCRIPT LANGUAGE="VBScript">
<!-
Sub PlayButton_OnClick
    If Form1.Text1.Value = "roadrunner" Then
        Window.location.href = "file:MeepMeep.wav"
        MsgBox "Here You Go!"
        Form1.Text1.Value = "Now try anything else"
    Else
        Window.location.href = "file:Ahhhhh.wav"
        MsgBox "Unlucky - Wrong Choice"
        Form1.Text1.Value = "You're Dead !"
    End If
End Sub
```

Section One: Multiple Line Syntax

```
Sub SelectButton_OnClick
    If Form2.Text2.Value = "arnie" Then
        MsgBox "Are You Sure You Wanted To Do That?"
        Window.location.href = "file:terminat.wav"
    ElseIf Form2.Text2.Value = "mccoy" Then
        MsgBox "Beam me up Scottie!"
        Window.location.href = "file:Doctor1.wav"
    ElseIf Form2.Text2.Value = "blues" Then
        MsgBox "It's Dark and You're Wearing Sunglasses"
        Window.location.href = "file:Mission.wav"
    ElseIf Form2.Text2.Value = "funk" Then
        MsgBox "Dance On"
        Window.location.href = "file:Wild1.wav"
    Else
        MsgBox "Try Again"
        Window.location.href = "file:Gong.wav"
    End If
End Sub
```

Section Two: Nested Conditionals

```
->
</SCRIPT>
</HEAD>
<BODY>
<CENTER>
<H3>More Decisions - Multiple Line Syntax</H3>
</CENTER><P>
This document contains some VB Script code which uses the multiple-line
➥syntax of
the If…Then ... Else construct.  There are two sections to look at.

<UL TYPE="circle">
<LI>Using 'If…Then ... Else' to carry out several operations
<LI>Nesting conditionals
</UL>
N.B. The example makes use of the sound playing facilities of Explorer
➥3.0, you need
a sound card or driver installed to hear them.
<HR>

<CENTER><H4>Multiple Line Syntax</H4></CENTER><P>
Type a word into the text box, then click the button marked Play.
➥Typing 'roadrunner' will
execute three statements in an If…Then block to play a sound, display
➥a message and
change the text in the text box. Anything else will execute the three
➥statements in the
Else ... End If block<P>
<FORM NAME="Form1">
Sound Clip:
    <INPUT TYPE="text" NAME="Text1">
    <INPUT TYPE="button" VALUE="Play" NAME="PlayButton">
</FORM>
<HR>
```

```
<CENTER><H4>Nested Conditionals</H4></CENTER><P>
Type one of the following words in the textbox to play its sound
➥sample: 'arnie' 'mccoy'
'blues' or 'funk'. Nested conditionals determine which of the four
➥options you picked and calls
the sound file accordingly<P>
<FORM NAME="Form2">
    <INPUT TYPE="text" NAME="Text2">
    <INPUT TYPE="button" NAME="SelectButton" VALUE="Select">
</FORM>
</BODY>
</HTML>
```

The example you load has two sections: one is the multiple-line syntax (see Figure 6-3), and the other, `ElseIf` keyword conditionals (see Figure 6-4). The first section asks you to type the word **roadrunner** in the textbox. Doing so executes a series of commands in a block: a message box flashes up onscreen, a sound sample plays, and the text inside the textbox changes to say, "Now try anything else." Anything other than **roadrunner** causes the If statement to jump to the Else option to execute a different set of instructions. Note the End If statement at the end of the blocks of code in Section One.

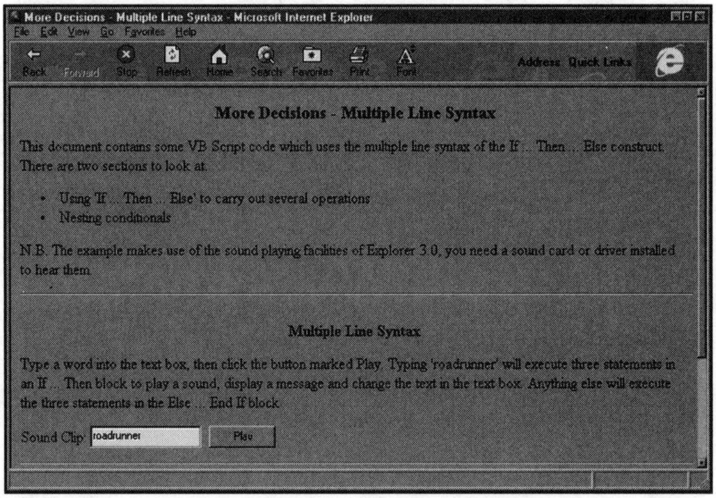

FIGURE 6-3
Using the multiple-line syntax to play a tune, display a message, and change a text entry

The second part of the code demonstrates how to use ElseIf to check an entry against a set of options. Typing one of the words on the list into the textbox runs some code that plays a sound sample. This is controlled by the various ElseIf blocks that check to see whether they recognize the entry. If the entry isn't recognized, you are instructed to try again.

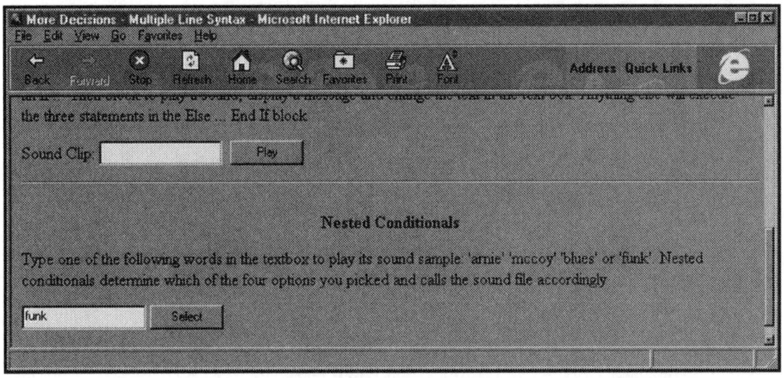

FIGURE 6-4
Multiple line conditionals allow one of several sound samples to be selected and played by using the ElseIf keyword.

TIP *Try to indent each nested If statement clearly so you make sure that you always have a corresponding End If. This is an easy way to stop bugs from creeping in.*

The following section discuss the various points of interest from this example.

Simple Use of the Multiple-Line Syntax

Section One is a straightforward example of how to use the multiple-line syntax discussed earlier. You place the commands after the If...Then statement in the order in which you want them to run. You end the block with either an Else statement or End If, depending on what follows.

Conditionals With ElseIf—What Happens If There's No Match?

The second section of code uses both multiple-line syntax and the ElseIf keyword. A True result anywhere in the chain causes the code that follows it to run. If there is no match, the code in the Else...End

If block executes. You will be instructed to try again and a gong sound will play.

TIP

If an expression could take several values and you want to test for these conditions, use the Select Case statement rather than the multiple-line version of If...Then...Else.

How Are the Sounds Being Played?

Playing sounds in Explorer 3.0 is an easy, one-step process. The following line of code controls the whole event.

```
Window.location.href = "some WAV file URL"
```

The preceding line uses the Window object to load the wave (WAV) file into the Explorer's audio player application. The location and href objects together point to the URL address of the WAV file, and then the browser automatically loads the audio player to output the sound byte. After the sound plays, you must close the audio player yourself.

You can also use the Window object to load new pages into the browser. This uses the same construction as sound files but allows the programmer to cause Explorer to change the page it is currently displaying. Running a sound file uses the audio player as its host and leaves the page setup unaltered. Chapter 10, "The Object Model for Scripting," explains the Window object in more detail.

The Select Case Statement—Different Decisions

The Select Case statement enables you to perform the equivalent of an If...Then...ElseIf...Else...End If block, but with less typing. The format of the Select Case statement is as follows:

```
Select Case TestExpression
    Case ExpressionList1
        ...
        Statements
```

```
        ...
    Case ExpressionListN
        ...
        Statements
        ...
    Case Else
        ...
        Statements
        ...
End Select
```

The *TestExpression* is any VBScript expression that evaluates to give a single result. The result can be a string, number, date, or time—but not an object. You usually use a variable name as the item you're going to test. The *ExpressionList* parts of the statement are comma-delimited lists of values for which you're testing. You don't need to have more than one value. Usually only one value is used in each expression list. If the test expression evaluates to one of the values after a `Case` keyword, the statements in that block execute and control passes to the next line after the `End Select` keywords. This is best illustrated with an example:

```
Select Case intFlag
    Case 1, 4, 5
        MsgBox "You're out of gas"
        StopEngine()
    Case 3
        MsgBox "The engine's just blown up"
        CrashCar()
    Case Else
        MsgBox "Everything's fine"
        ArriveHome()
End Select
```

The first block of statements executes if the variable *intFlag* holds the value 1, 4, or 5. Notice the separation of the values with commas. The value 3 causes another block of statements to execute. You can have as many of these Case clauses as you like and can even nest other conditionals or other Select Case statements within a single Case block. The

Case Else block traps any remaining conditions and must be the last entry in the list and is good programming practice. Figure 6-5 shows a flow chart of the Select Case statement in operation.

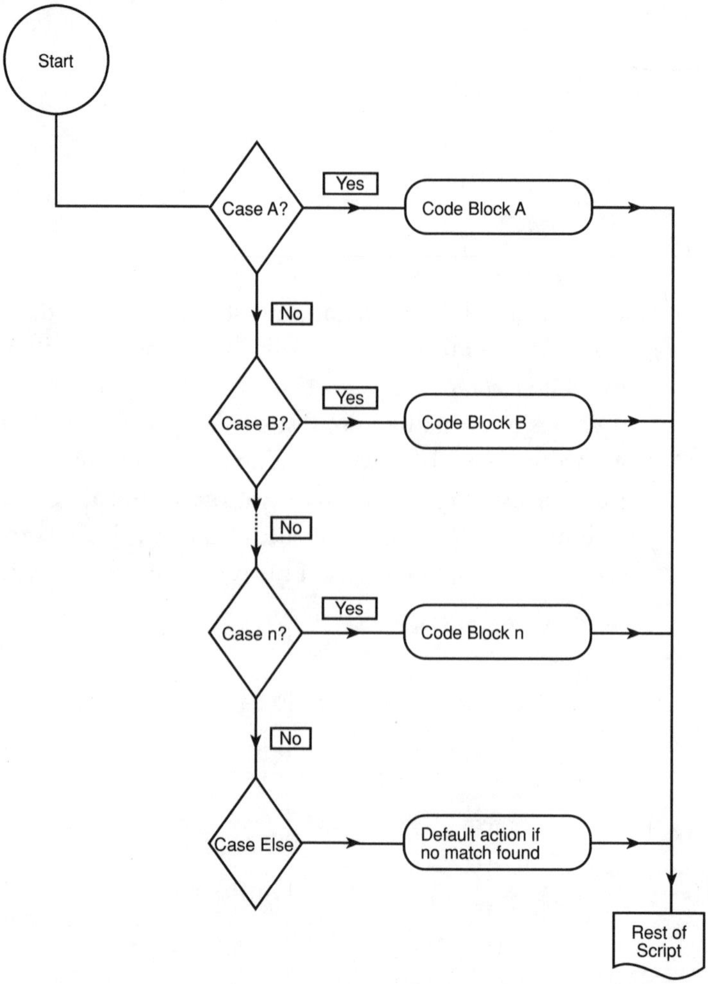

FIGURE 6-5
A flow chart showing the operation of the Select Case statement

NOTE *Try rewriting the sound byte example, "More Decisions—Multiple-Line Syntax," using the Select Case Statement.*

Now that you understand conditional execution, you're ready to expand your VBScript arsenal to include loops and repeated execution.

Repeating Code a Set Number of Times—For ... Next

Repeating a set of operations a fixed number of times—executing algorithms, processing elements in an array, and creating desired visual effects, for example—is often useful. VBScript provides this capability in the form of the For...Next construct.

For...Next uses a counter variable whose value increments or decrements with each iteration of the loop. The structure of the For loop is as follows

```
For var = StartVal To EndVal
     Statements
     ...
     ...
Next
```

The For statement specifies which variable to use as the counter variable; in this case, *var*. *StartVal* and *EndVal* then give the starting and ending values for the counter.

Three points that are worth noting about For...Next are:

- All statements between the For and Next are executed on each iteration.
- Next signifies the end of the loop and increments the counter variable by one each time. The execution then loops back to the top and starts again.
- When *var* exceeds the value of *EndVal*, the loop finishes.

CAUTION **If you're using the For loop to modify the contents of an array, make sure that the counter variable starts at zero. Arrays in VBScript are zero-based, as explained in Chapter 4, "Variables, Arrays, and Data Types."**

This VBScript procedure would cause *TheProc* to be called 100 times.

```
<SCRIPT LANGUAGE="VBScript">
<!-
Sub DoTheLoop
     Dim Count
     For Count = 1 to 100
          TheProc()
     Next
->
</SCRIPT>
```

You can use two extra keywords with the For construct, as discussed in the following two section, respectively.

The Step Keyword—Skipping Values and Counting Backwards

The Step keyword increases the flexibility of the For loop and allows the counter variable to increment or decrement by a specified value. This is useful in two ways: for counting backwards (the Step is set to -1) and for skipping values as the loop iterates; for example, 2,4,6,8.

The format of the loop is now

```
For var = StartVal To EndVal Step StepVal
    Statements
    ...
    ...
Next
```

StepVal can be any nonzero integer. If a negative value is being used, the end value for the counter must be less than the starting value. Even if the step value means the counter variable never takes on the actual value specified for *EndVal*, the loop will terminate as soon as the counter is equal to, or exceeds, *EndVal*.

The looping constructs discussed so far are demonstrated in an example from the CD. It can be accessed in the same way as the others by choosing the `Loops, Loops, Loops, Loops` hyperlink from the

Tutorial section. The example is split into two, with the first part using a simple loop and the second adding the use of the Step keyword. The code is reproduced here:

```
<HTML>
<HEAD>
<TITLE>Loops, Loops, Loops, Loops</TITLE>
</HEAD>

<BODY>
<CENTER>
<H3>Loops, Loops, Loops, Loops</H3>
</CENTER><P>
This document contains some VBScript code which uses loops to modify
➥the HTML of the
document itself. No event procedures have been written. The scripts are
➥interpreted as
the HTML is parsed by the browser, and so must be placed where the
➥modification is to
take place
There are two sections to look at.

<UL TYPE="circle">
<LI>Using a simple For ... Next loop to display a triangle
<LI>Introducing the Step keyword to make a 'parabolic' shape
</UL>
<HR>
<SCRIPT LANGUAGE="VBScript">
<!—
Dim x,y
For x = 1 to 20                     'Outer loop - repeats for 20 lines
    For y = 1 to x                  'Inner loop displays x *-symbols on
➥the page
        Document.Write("*")
    Next
    Document.Write("<BR>")         'Insert a line break tag
```

```
Next
->
</SCRIPT>
<HR>
<SCRIPT LANGUAGE="VBScript">
<!-
Dim x,y
For x = 1 to 16                    'Repeat for 16 lines
    For y = 1 to x*x Step 6
        Document.Write("*")
    Next
    Document.Write("<BR>")
Next
For x = 15 to 1 Step -1            'Repeat the same pattern backwards
    For y = x*x to 1 Step -6       'Note the negative step values
        Document.Write("*")
    Next
    Document.Write("<BR>")
Next
->
</SCRIPT>
<HR>
</BODY>
</HTML>
```

Two patterns appear on the page when you load the document, both of which are generated by sections of VBScript. Notice the use of the Step keyword in the second part to skip some values or to count backwards. A For...Next loop generates a triangle (see Figure 6-6). A Step is then added to change the shape to an inverted parabola (see Figure 6-7).

As usual, this example brings up several interesting details to note, which are explained in the following paragraphs.

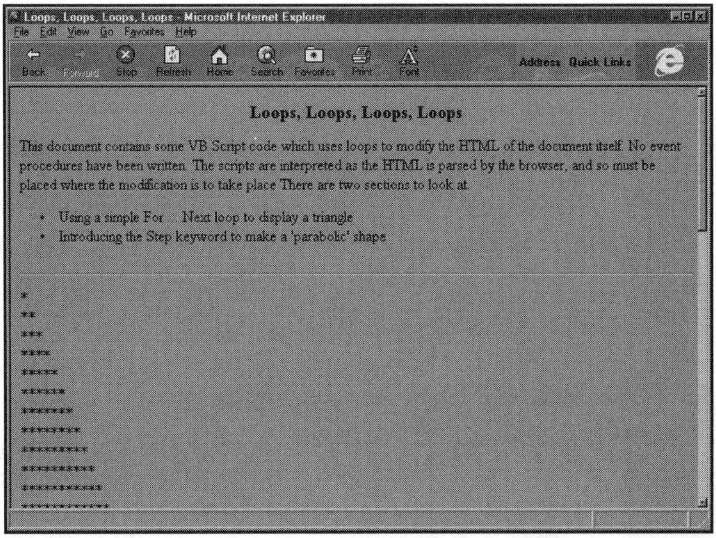

FIGURE 6-6
Single step increments generate a triangle.

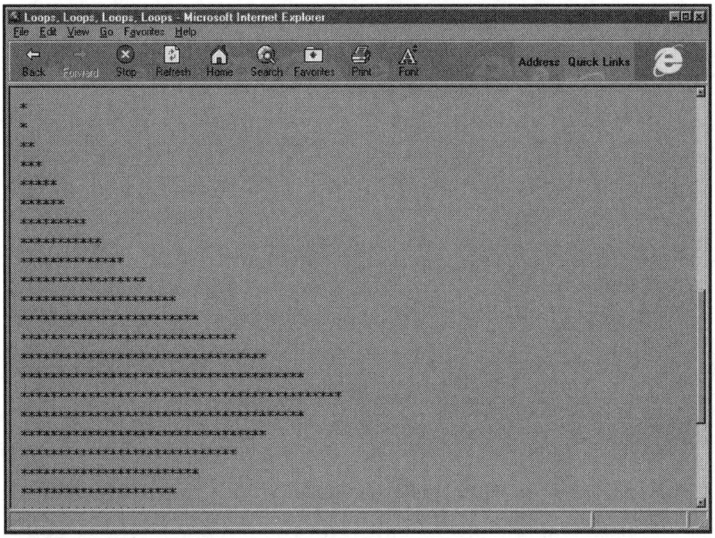

FIGURE 6-7
Adjusting the Step between loops creates a weird pattern.

Immediate Execution of VBScript Code

We have written the code in sections of VBScript instead of using any procedures in this example. As the browser comes across these scripts, it executes them immediately. Therefore, any changes they make to the document happen from the spot where the scripts are placed. This is known as *immediate execution*.

CAUTION

Anything that modifies the actual HTML contents of a document, such as the text on the page, must be called during HTML parse time; that is, before the document finishes loading and displays onscreen. The code to make these changes, therefore, must reside in a script block that will execute as the document is parsed (as in the loop example). You can use form control and object properties and methods anytime *after* definition of the object. The immediate execution restriction applies only to changes that affect the HTML source.

This runs counter to earlier advice that you keep all code in the <HEAD> tags. Place code in the BODY section *only* if you're using it to modify the HTML content of the page; for example, inserting a current visit count or a "last modified" date.

The Document.Write() Method

You use the Document.Write() method in the loop example to modify the HTML content during parsing of the document. The Document object provides access to the properties of the currently active document in the window and is explained in more detail in Chapter 10, "The Object Model for Scripting."

Exit For—Quitting the Loop Early

You may want to terminate a loop before all its iterations have been completed; for example, when an error is detected. Use the keyword Exit For and you can place it anywhere in the loop. Because you would not want to exit a loop early every time, you usually would place Exit For within a conditional block that is tested during every iteration. If the interpreter encounters the Exit For keyword, execution jumps to the first line of code following Next. For example:

```
<SCRIPT LANGUAGE="VBScript">
<!—
```

```
Sub DoTheLoop
     Dim Count, errorVal
     For Count = 1 to 100
          errorVal = TheProc()
          If errorVal = "Error" Then
               MsgBox "An error occurred, quitting the loop now!"
               Exit For
          End If
     Next
->
</SCRIPT>
```

Repeating Code Using Do...Loop

The Do loop is similar to the For loop, in that it allows a group of statements to run indefinitely until a condition is met. The difference is that the Do...Loop can be controlled so that it repeats only while or until a condition is True.

The basic Do loop uses the keywords Do and Loop to delimit the block of code you want to repeat. The Do loop isn't particularly useful on its own because the code within the block gets repeated forever and the script becomes stuck in an infinite loop. The next example is a contrived event procedure for a button called Loop that shows this effect. If you try running this script, be ready to use the Task Manager to close down Explorer 3.0 after you get bored of clicking on the OK button. Do this by pressing Ctrl+Alt+Del.

```
<SCRIPT LANGUAGE="VBScript">
<!-
Sub Loop_OnClick
 Do
    MsgBox "You're stuck"
 Loop
End Sub
->
</SCRIPT>
```

NOTE *The simple Do ... Loop construct can be used in this way when combined with the Exit Do statement. See the section that follows. But as you will see it is better to use the* While *or* Until *keywords, because it makes the loop's dependencies clearer.*

Repeating Statements While a Condition Is True

You use the While keyword to check a condition in a Do loop. You can put it at the beginning or at the end of the loop (these are different cases of the While command).

As its name suggests, the While keyword means that the loop will continue *while* the condition expression still evaluates to True. The two forms of the While loop are written as follows:

```
Do While (Condition Expression)
    Statements
    ...
    ...
Loop
```

or, with the check at the end of the loop:

```
Do
    Statements
    ...
    ...
Loop While (Condition Expression)
```

The distinction between these two is made clearer by considering the diagrams in Figure 6-8.

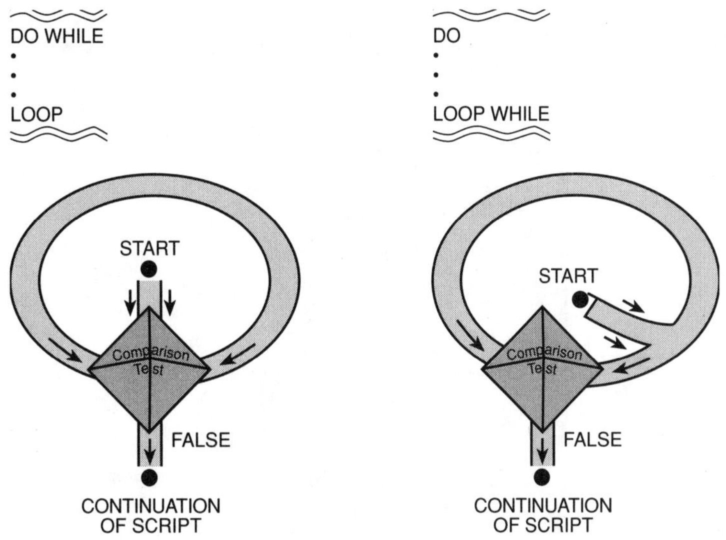

FIGURE 6-8
The difference between placing the While command at the beginning of the loop and the end of the loop.

When the check comes at the beginning of the block, the condition may be False right from the get-go. This condition would prevent the block of code from running. On the other hand, if the check comes at the end, you can guarantee that the loop statements will execute before the condition is ever evaluated. Now look at some examples.

Load up the Web page by clicking on the `Conditional Loops` hyperlink on the Tutorial CD. You should see three buttons that demonstrate the use of the Do...While commands (see Figure 6-9). Each button invokes an event procedure to run one of the Do loops. There are three different examples of loops: one that uses the Do While command with the condition being True for several iterations; one Loop While routine with repeats; and one Do While command where the condition is never True so the loop instructions never execute. These different loops show how the positioning of the command that tests the condition affects the number of times a loop executes.

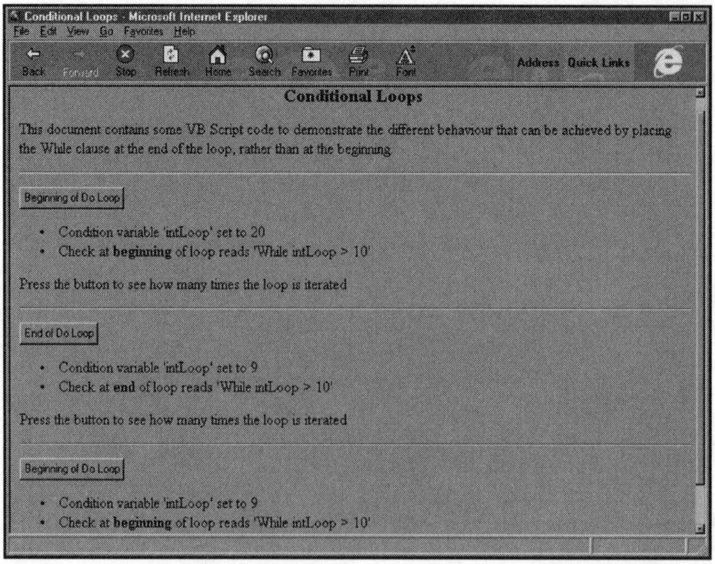

FIGURE 6-9
The importance of the positioning of the While part of the Do…Loop

All the examples use a message box to display how many passes were made through the loop. Look at the code now to see what you would expect to happen, and then run the script.

```
<HTML>
<HEAD>
<TITLE>Conditional Loops</TITLE>
<SCRIPT LANGUAGE="VBScript">
<!-
Sub StartButton_OnClick
    Dim intCount, intLoop
    intCount = 0
    intLoop = 20
    Do While intLoop > 10              'The loop condition is checked
➥before the loop body
        intLoop = intLoop - 1
        intCount = intCount +1
    Loop
    MsgBox intCount & " iterations of the loop were made"
End Sub
```

```
Sub EndButton_OnClick
    Dim intCount, intLoop
    intCount = 0
    intLoop = 9
    Do
        intLoop = intLoop - 1
        intCount = intCount +1
    Loop While intLoop > 10          'The loop condition is checked
➥after the loop body
    MsgBox intCount & " iterations of the loop were made"
End Sub

Sub StartButton2_OnClick
    Dim intCount, intLoop
    intCount = 0
    intLoop = 9
    Do While intLoop > 10            'The loop condition is checked
➥before the loop body
        intLoop = intLoop - 1
        intCount = intCount +1
    Loop
    MsgBox intCount & " iterations of the loop were made"
End Sub
->
</SCRIPT>
</HEAD>

<BODY>
<CENTER>
<H3>Conditional Loops</H3>
</CENTER><P>
This document contains some VB Script code to demonstrate the different
➥behaviour
that can be achieved by placing the While clause at the end of the
➥loop, rather than at the
```

```
beginning.
<HR>
<FORM NAME="Form1">
    <INPUT TYPE="button" NAME="StartButton" VALUE="Beginning of Do
➥Loop">
    <UL TYPE="circle">
        <LI>Condition variable 'intLoop' set to 20
        <LI>Check at <B>beginning</B> of loop reads 'While intLoop >
➥10'
    </UL>
Press the button to see how many times the loop is iterated
    <HR>
    <INPUT TYPE="button" NAME="EndButton" VALUE="End of Do Loop">
    <UL TYPE="circle">
        <LI>Condition variable 'intLoop' set to 9
        <LI>Check at <B>end</B> of loop reads 'While intLoop > 10'
    </UL>
Press the button to see how many times the loop is iterated
    <HR>
    <INPUT TYPE="button" NAME="StartButton2" VALUE="Beginning of Do
➥Loop">
    <UL TYPE="circle">
        <LI>Condition variable 'intLoop' set to 9
        <LI>Check at <B>beginning</B> of loop reads 'While intLoop >
➥10'
    </UL>
Press the button to see how many times the loop is iterated (or NOT
➥iterated)
</FORM>
</BODY>
</HTML>
```

The code for StartButton_OnClick is straightforward; the loop iterates 10 times and then control passes to the line after the keyword Loop. Even though the condition is never True, the

EndButton_OnClick section executes the loop once because the check comes at the end of the loop and isn't reached until the statement block has already executed once.

> **CAUTION** Be wary of using the Do...Loop While form in certain circumstances. If the condition expression is checking for some error condition, for example, the end of an array, it might already exist even before the loop begins. In this case, executing the loop even once can cause a run-time error by trying to access past the end of an array.

Compare the result of the EndButton_OnClick procedure with that of StartButton2_OnClick. This time there are no passes through the loop because the check is carried out at the beginning of the block.

Repeating Statements Until a Condition Is True

The While keyword allows a set of statements to run as long as a particular condition is True. If you need to execute a block *until* a condition becomes True, you can do it in VBScript by using the Until keyword. You use Until similarly to how you use `While`, placing it at the beginning or at the end of the `Do Loop`:

```
Do Until (Condition Expression)
    Statements
    ...
    ...
Loop
```

or, with the check at the end of the loop:

```
Do
    Statements
    ...
    ...
Loop Until (Condition Expression)
```

NOTE

You can achieve the Until effect by using the While keyword and slightly modifying the condition expression. Prefixing the entire condition with the Not operator (see Chapter 5, "Expressions, Operators, and Constants") has the same meaning as using Until. The reason to use the second form is that it makes code more readable and intuitive.

The next example ties together some of the controls you have seen in this chapter. Remember, the ideas behind them also apply to the more exciting ActiveX controls and other objects. Try to improve these examples after you read the sections later on in the book. Load the script into your browser by selecting the `Looping Until a Condition is Satisfied` hyperlink from the *VBScript Master's Handbook* Web page.

```
<HTML>
<HEAD>
<TITLE>Looping Until a Condition is Satisfied</TITLE>
<SCRIPT LANGUAGE="VBScript">
<!-
Sub EnterButton_OnClick
    Dim arrL(3), arrR(3), i, Countdown, Timer
    arrL(0)="->            " : arrL(1)="     ->        "
    arrL(2)="        ->    " : arrL(3)="             ->"
    arrR(0)="           <-" : arrR(1)="        <-    "
    arrR(2)="    <-        " : arrR(3)="<-            "
    Countdown=50
    Do
        Form1.LeftButton.Value = arrL(i)
        Form1.RightButton.Value = arrR(i)
        i = (i + 1) Mod 4
        Countdown = Countdown - 1
     Timer = 0
     Do
     Timer = Timer + 1
     Loop Until Timer > 8000
```

```
    Loop Until Countdown=0
End Sub
-->
</SCRIPT>
</HEAD>
<BODY>
<CENTER>
<H3>Looping Until a Condition is Satisfied</H3>
</CENTER><P>
This document contains some VB Script code to that executes a loop
➥Until a countdown
variable reaches a certain value. The effect is not stunning but using
➥ActiveX controls
from the examples later in the book some compelling effects can be
➥designed.<BR>
Press the button labeled 'Enter the Cave'.
<HR>
<CENTER>
    <FORM NAME="Form1">
        <INPUT TYPE=button NAME="LeftButton" VALUE="->             ">
        <INPUT TYPE=button VALUE="Enter the Cave" NAME="EnterButton">
        <INPUT TYPE=button NAME="RightButton" VALUE = "            <-
">
    </FORM>
</CENTER>
</BODY>
</HTML>
```

After you load up, you should see three buttons in a row: one labeled `Enter the Cave` and two others with flanking arrows. The arrows are for decoration and won't do anything if you click on them. Pressing the `Enter` button invokes the event procedure listed above and the Do loop executes until Countdown equals zero. Then the arrows run along the buttons. See Figure 6-10 for a static shot of the screen.

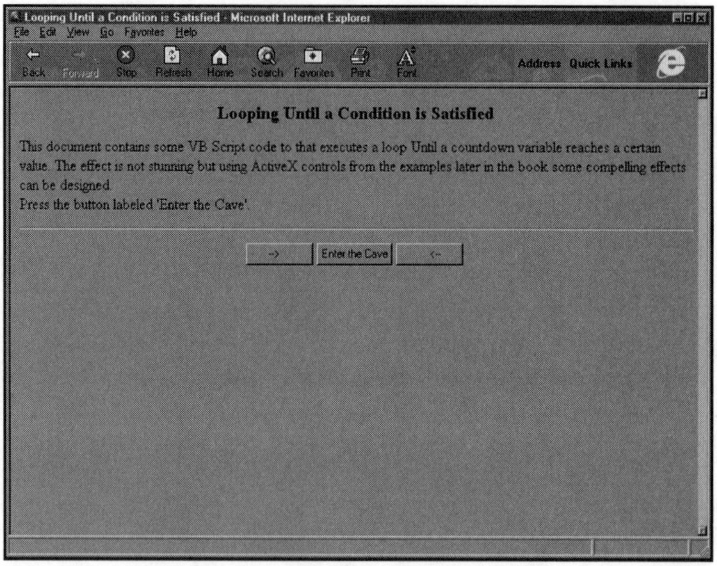

FIGURE 6-10
Simple animation using Do...Loop Until

The following three sections address three areas of import from this sample program.

Use of Modulo Arithmetic and the Mod Operator

Here, the modulo command is used to loop through the contents of the array in the example. We use modulo arithmetic because it always gives the same pattern for `i` (the array index), as we increment the value of `i`. Thus `i = (i + 1)` mod 4 causes the variable `i` to cycle through 0,1,2,3,0,1,2,3,0.... This may not be very intuitive and you should look in Chapter 5, "Expressions, Operators, and Constants," for a more detailed explanation of modulo arithmetic. In this case, it prevents the program from trying to access something outside the array boundaries. Basically, when you divide by the number four, you know you'll never get a remainder greater than three.

Getting a Move on with Arrays

Here, two arrays store the positions of the arrows as string variables. You set them up by equating the array member with the string you want. When the user clicks on the middle button, the arrays cycle through and the effect is a brief animation sequence. Notice the use of colons to put many commands on one line.

Slowing Things Down with a Delay Loop

Without a delay loop between arrow sequences, the arrows race along the buttons faster than your eyes can track them. To slow it down, the example contains a short sequence of code using an empty loop to cycle a few thousand times. It adds a few milliseconds between the arrow's movements and makes the animation easier to follow.

Exiting a Do...Loop from within the Loop

Sometimes you have to leave the Do loop in the middle of the statement block. Just as in the For...Next case, you use a certain method to handle encountering an error or meeting some extra condition. You can place the keyword Exit Do anywhere within the block, usually within a conditional statement, and execution jumps to the first line after Loop. The VBScript for this looks like this:

```
Do While (Condition Expression)
    Statements
    ...
    If (Error Condition) Then Exit Do
    ...
Loop
```

This applies to all four forms of the Do loop discussed so far.

TIP *Exit Do can avoid endless loops by placing a check for conditions that might result in the While or Until clause never being met. For example, if a value used in the loop condition is already greater than the one against which it's being checked you can avoid program crashes.*

While...Wend—For Existing VB Programmers

VBScript supports one more looping construct, but it's intended only for existing Visual Basic programmers. It's not as flexible as the Do...Loop and eventually will be phased out—Microsoft recommends using the Do...Loop instead. For reference, While...Wend is written like this:

```
While (Condition Expression)
    Statements
    ...
    ...
Wend
```

Conclusions—Where to Go from Here

You've seen how conditional structures and loops control the flow of a script and have used them in examples such as password controls, nested conditionals, and simple animated buttons. Loops will appear again and again and are a useful asset in many different cases. You also saw sound files in one of the examples in a multiple-syntax statement and observed how easily the browser coped with playing them.

The next chapter looks at program flow and introduces procedures and functions, including calling them, passing variables to them, and receiving values back from them (functions only). It's essential information and will help you write useful and exciting scripts.

CHAPTER 7

Grouping Statements in Procedures and Functions

The first six chapters lay the foundations of VBScript; you see how the language deals with variables, types, expressions, operators, and program flow constructs. Now it's time to tie sections of code that contain those concepts into procedures and functions, which allows repeated reuse of the code. You've already seen them in action in some of the script examples. This chapter explains what procedures and functions are and how to write them.

This chapter addresses the following topics:

- Distinguishing between functions and procedures
- Understanding the necessity of functions and procedures
- Writing procedures
- Writing functions
- Passing parameters to your functions and procedures

- Returning values from a function
- Calling conventions
- Placing functions and procedures in a document

Why Are Procedures and Functions Needed?

Functions and procedures are the best way to group language commands into blocks of code for easy execution. You might use many procedures in a single program and can call them in turn from the main body section of the document. Two simple procedures in a section of code, for example, might be a password check and a welcome message display. Before you can differentiate these procedures, you need to give each one a name so you can execute them in any order you want. To run a procedure or function, you simply call the name. Functions and procedures are useful for a variety of reasons, some more important than others. The main benefit of using these facilities for grouping code are:

- **Code reuse**—not having to rewrite sections of code you use regularly
- **Code modularity**—keeping logically distinct sections of code separate from each other.
- **Code readability**—by naming functions and procedures sensibly, the calls to them can make the intended meaning of your code clear to the reader.

Grouping Statements Together in a Named Function

The first benefit of procedures and functions isn't new; you've seen often in earlier examples. It is simply that you can refer to a series of statements that may consist of several lines of code by using a single name. Until now, this has been important when dealing with event procedures, such as button clicks and menu selections, in which you want to run a section of code when an event happens. Minus the grouping that naming provides, you couldn't associate particular commands with script events, which would seriously limit the scripting language's usefulness.

NOTE *Throughout the rest of the book, the word* routine *is used whenever the discussion refers to functions and procedures in the same context, simply for the sake of efficiency. The differences between the two entities still apply, however.*

Parameter Passing

Routines are far more important than just naming a series of statements; they allow you to process data by passing parameters (otherwise known as *arguments*) to them when they are called. These arguments bring an additional degree of flexibility to procedures. Later in the chapter, you begin to use arguments to direct the actions of a routine, or to have the routine act on a set of data. You almost always pass a routine *some* form of an argument, unless it's a fairly trivial routine.

Returning Values

You can pass arguments to both procedures and functions, but only functions can return values—and that is the distinguishing feature between the two types of routine. When a function returns a value, it essentially replaces the function call with the return value in the script. This return value can then be stored by the calling code and used as necessary. Return values can result from calculations, error values, or basically anything that you can store in a variable.

Code Reuse and Modularity

Imagine writing a script that has to sort lots of lists of information without being able to use procedures. Each time a new list is encountered, you would have to reproduce the block of sorting code at that point in the document—which is completely unwieldy. Code reuse is one way to overcome this problem, and is a major benefit of writing routines. You put the code into the script just once, and then can call it from anywhere in the script, eliminating the need to rewrite it again and again.

> **NOTE** *The* modular *approach to writing code has been common practice for years, but only in the last few years has object-oriented programming (OOP)become mainstream. OOP extends the ideas of code reuse and modularity to objects themselves, which have properties and methods that are accessed through published interfaces. Languages like C++ and Java are object-oriented languages (OOLs) and operating systems like Windows 95 and NT are using more and more object-oriented code and design methods; for example, OLE Automation.*

The fact that you write the routine only once lets you make changes to it without having to alter every location to which a routine is called. This idea has been extended to object-oriented programming as well.

Now that you have learned about the benefits afforded by using routines, you need to gain an understanding of the rules for writing them. Procedures and functions are discussed separately, owing to some significant differences between them.

Writing Procedures

You can put procedures anywhere in a script because they're executed only when they specifically are called. To put it formally, they are *declarations*—you *declare* what would happen if the procedure were invoked.

A procedure declaration must contain the following elements:

- A procedure name
- A reference to any arguments that are required
- A body section for the code
- A procedure end

The beginning and end of a procedure are labeled with the keywords Sub (followed by the procedure's name) and End Sub, respectively. A procedure that lacks parameters looks something like this:

```
Sub MyProc()
    Statements
    ...
    ...
End Sub
```

You've seen declarations of this nature in most of the examples, so the following should look familiar:

```
Sub Button1_OnClick
    If Form1.Text1.Value = "sesame" Then MsgBox "Welcome Ali Baba!"
    Form1.Text1.Value = ""
End Sub
```

The preceding code defines an *event procedure* (a specialized form of procedure) that's called whenever the OnClick event is generated by the Button1 control. The browser program automatically takes care of calling the procedure, and the call doesn't take any arguments.

In the following example, you can see the code for a procedure that has some arguments. You can load the example into Explorer 3.0 by choosing the `Writing Procedures` link in the Tutorial section of the main Web page installed from the CD.

TIP

Remember to surround all script code and routines with HTML comment tags (<!– and –>). Doing so tells browsers that don't support VBScript to skip over these sections. Explorer 3.0 recognizes the comment tags and executes the code between them.

On loading the document, you see two textbox controls and four buttons (see Figure 7-1). The script in this page implements a *very* simple calculator that calls a procedure to process the numbers and operations. Each button activates event procedures that call SimpleMathProc to calculate and display the results of the sums. Try out the script and have a look at the code reproduced here. Several elements of this example serve well to illustrate good procedure declaration.

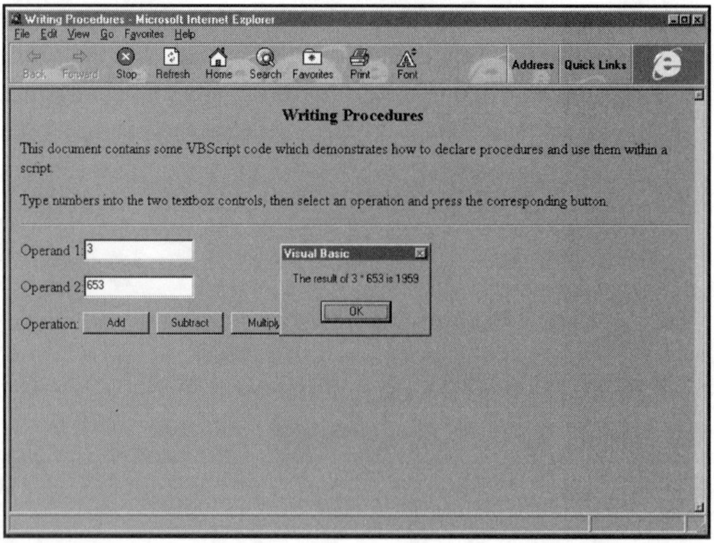

FIGURE 7-1
A simple calculator program that uses procedures to calculate the result.

```
<HTML>
<HEAD>
<TITLE>Writing Procedures</TITLE>
<SCRIPT LANGUAGE="VBScript">
<!–
Sub SimpleMathProc(x, y, intOp)          'User defined procedure
' Parameters:-  x - 1st operand for calculation
'                y - 2nd operand
'                intOp - operation code, 1:+  2:-  3:*  4:/
    Dim result, strSymbol
    If intOp = 1 Then
        result = CDbl(x) + CDbl(y)
        strSymbol = " + "
    Else
        If intOp = 2 Then
            result = x - y
            strSymbol = " - "
        Else
            If intOp = 3 Then
                result = x * y
```

```
                strSymbol = " * "
            Else
                result = x / y
                strSymbol = " / "
            End If
        End If
    End If                  'Now display the result
    MsgBox "The result of " & x & strSymbol & y & " is " & result
End Sub

Sub AddButton_OnClick
 SimpleMathProc Form1.NumText1.Value, Form1.NumText2.Value, 1
End Sub

Sub SubButton_OnClick
 SimpleMathProc Form1.NumText1.Value, Form1.NumText2.Value, 2
End Sub

Sub MulButton_OnClick
 SimpleMathProc Form1.NumText1.Value, Form1.NumText2.Value, 3
End Sub

Sub DivButton_OnClick
 SimpleMathProc Form1.NumText1.Value, Form1.NumText2.Value, 4
End Sub
-->
</SCRIPT>
</HEAD>

<BODY>
<CENTER><H3>Writing Procedures</H3></CENTER><P>
This document contains some VBScript code which demonstrates how to
➥declare procedures
and use them within a script.<P>
Type numbers into the two textbox controls, then select an operation
```

```
➥and press the
corresponding button.
<HR>

<FORM NAME="Form1">
Operand 1:<INPUT NAME="NumText1" TYPE="text" VALUE="0">
<P>
Operand 2:<INPUT NAME="NumText2" TYPE="text" VALUE="0">
<P>
Operation:  <INPUT NAME="AddButton" TYPE="button" VALUE="Add">
          <INPUT NAME="SubButton" TYPE="button" VALUE="Subtract">
          <INPUT NAME="MulButton" TYPE="button" VALUE="Multiply">
          <INPUT NAME="DivButton" TYPE="button" VALUE="Divide">
</BODY>
</HTML>
```

Defining Argument Names

The following line declares a procedure that takes three arguments:

```
Sub SimpleMathProc(x, y, intOp)          'User defined procedure
```

The three arguments are assigned the names *x*, *y*, and *intOp* and they take the Variant type. When the main body of the code calls SimpleMathProc, it passes values into *x*, *y*, and *intOp* and the procedure then uses them. All procedure variables vanish at the end of the routine because they weren't declared using the *Static* keyword (see Chapter 4, "Variables, Arrays and Data Types"). Here, *x* and *y* are the operand variables, and *intOp* defines the operation—1 for addition, 2 for subtraction, and so on.

Argument names are placed within parentheses after the procedure name; for example, SampleProc (x,y,z). The order of the arguments in the parentheses is important. See Figure 7-2 to see how arguments are passed.

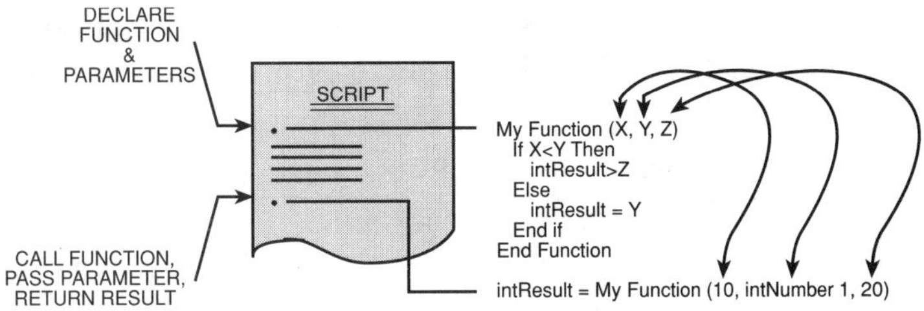

FIGURE 7-2
You can pass arguments to functions or procedures by placing them in parentheses.

TIP

Choose argument names that relate to the context in which you use them. In the simple calculator example, the variable names x *and* y *were chosen because of mathematical convention.* intOp *took its name from the fact that it's an integer and specifies the operation to perform. You would do well to place comment lines at the start of a routine indicating the purposes of the various arguments. See Chapter 9, "Writing Well-Organized and Coherent VBScript," for more tips on programming conventions.*

Calling the New Procedure

After you write a routine, you need some way to invoke it (normally referred to as *calling a procedure*). In this example, calling a procedure is done using the following line:

```
SimpleMathProc Form1.NumText1.Value, Form1.NumText2.Value, 3
```

The preceding line invokes SimpleMathProc with its arguments, taking the values Form1.NumText1.Value, Form1.NumText2.Value, and 3, respectively. Read the section "Calling Conventions and Examples," later in this chapter for more information.

String Concatenation and the CDbl() Typecast

The message box for displaying the results is passed a concatenated String variable—*strSymbol* & *result*. The string concatenation operator (&) acts to join the strings together (see Chapter 5, "Expressions, Operators, and Constants").

You may have noticed the use of the CDbl() function to typecast *x* and *y* for the addition:

```
result = CDbl(x) + CDbl(y)
```

Using CDbl() forces the interpreter to treat *x* and *y* as numeric values. Form1.NumText1.Value and ...NumText2... are interpreted as String subtypes because they're the contents of a text box. The operators -, *, and / obviously are operators on numeric subtypes, so VBScript automatically interprets the values of x and y as such. When you try to carry out the operation x + y, however, the interpreter treats it as a string concatenation (alter the HTML source and try it) giving the string xy rather than the numerical sum of x and y. If you typed 1.23 in one text box and 4.56 in another, for example, the result of x + y would be the string "1.234.56" rather than the number 5.79. In this situation, calls to CDbl() serve to explicitly change x and y to numeric values.

Writing Functions

A *function* is a series of statements grouped together under one name, just like a VBScript procedure. Like procedures, functions can accept arguments, but unlike procedures, they can return a single value to the main body of the script—a highly significant feature.

So how would you approach passing back a value from a function? Well, you would incorporate a line into the script that equates the function name with the value of the variable you want to return, as follows:

```
myFunction = returnResult
```

Here the function is called myFunction. You can place this line of code anywhere in the function section, but should note that the value isn't returned until the function finishes executing. Generally, execution terminates if an End Function keyword is reached or if the function has to finish early (see the section "Exiting a Procedure or Function Early").

NOTE *The return type of any function is* always *a Variant. The result may contain values of some other subtype, such as Integer or String, but the result is always a Variant value.*

Sometimes you want to use a function to see whether an item fulfills certain conditions. In this case, each condition may have different return values. To avoid overwriting the correct return value later in the function, you would use nested If constructs to separate out the possible values. The following example shows a typical function structure:

```
Function CalcSomething(arguments)
    If (Trivial Arguments)
        CalcSomething = 0
    Else
        Statements
        ...
        CalcSomething = result
    End If
End Function
```

You can find another example document using functions and procedures on the CD. You can load it by choosing the `Functions and Procedures - The Whole Picture` hyperlink. You can load the file and look at it now, but a few extra points await coverage to complete the example.

Exiting a Procedure or Function Early

The return result of a function isn't passed back to the calling code until the End Function keyword is reached. Many occasions occur in programming in which a programmer would like a function to terminate without executing to the end, including in the following situations:

- Exiting on an error condition
- Conditional execution depending on arguments
- User interaction interrupts the function

You can use two keywords to leave a routine early: Exit Sub and Exit Function. Exit Sub applies to procedures and Exit Function applies to functions. Whenever the interpreter encounters one of these statements, control returns to the calling code. In order to pass the function's result back successfully, the return value must have been set *before* the Exit Sub or Exit Function.

You can now rewrite the function CalcSomething as follows:

```
Function CalcSomething(arguments)
    If (Trivial Arguments)
        CalcSomething = 0
        Exit Function
    End If

    Statements
    ...
    CalcSomething = result
End Function
```

TIP

You can write code (even complex code) that doesn't use Exit Sub or Exit Function keywords by carefully placing conditionals and loops. Purists argue against ever using a goto in a program, as well as against using more than one exit route from a routine. Refusing to use goto statements and insisting on having just one exit route, however, can overcomplicate the code structure. You are better off to go ahead and use the Exit keywords available to you.

Placing Procedures and Functions within HTML

Any routines that you write must be defined before they can be used, so that the VBScript engine knows what you're referring to when it encounters a procedure or function call. Given this requirement, you should write all procedures and functions within the HEAD section of the document. You also should write all subsequent code between the <HEAD> tags. The chapter on programming conventions (Chapter 9) should offer some help in this area. Figure 7-3 shows you format in which you should set an HTML document.

TIP *For more information on the* VBScript Master's Handbook *CD, turn to Appendix D, "What's on the CD."*

Calling Conventions and Examples

Despite several examples of defining and calling routines, you still deserve a clear explanation of the rules for calling VBScript functions and procedures (known as *calling conventions*). This section deals with functions and procedures separately.

Two Ways of Calling a Procedure

You actually have two ways to call a procedure, both of which are equally valid. The first is simplest but can make scripts look quite confusing if they contain many arguments and/or complicated argument expressions. This calling method is written as the procedure name followed by the arguments, which must be separated by commas; for example:

```
MyProc "message", 67, "Ball"
```

The other way is to use the Call statement (see Appendix B, "VBScript Language Reference—Statements"), only with the Call statement, you put parentheses around the arguments. Then it would look like this:

```
Call MyProc("message", 67, "Ball")
```

Both calls to MyProc do exactly the same thing, but if the arguments are complex expressions, using the Call syntax is clearer because the parentheses mark the beginning and end of your argument section.

How to Call a Function

You already know how to write a function and get back a value, so now you are ready to tackle the calling method. To call a function, type the name followed by parentheses that contain the values for any arguments. These values can consist of any valid VBScript expression, variable name, or constant. Functions that don't take any arguments should be called by following the name with an empty set of brackets. Examples of function calls:

```
dblFourier = FourierTransform(x, y, 16 * arrPoints(4), arrPoints)
```

or

```
MsgBox "The result of Project(x,y,z) is " & Project(x, y, z)
```

In the first line, the result of FourierTransform is stored to a variable, and in the second line, Project's result appears in a message box.

NOTE

You have encountered calls to functions like CDbl() and procedures like MsgBox throughout this book. All of these routines, and those described in Appendix A, "VBScript Language Reference—Functions", are known as intrinsic *(or built-in) functions and can be called using the same conventions as those routines defined by the programmer. If you wonder what functions are built-in to the VBScript engine, just peruse Appendix A, "VBScript Language Reference—Functions." You may find functions that will reduce the amount of code you have to write. Take for example the Left and Right functions that return the left- and right-hand sections of strings in one simple operation.*

Functions and Procedures—The Whole Picture: An Example

Function or procedure—which one should you use? The rule of thumb is that if a function doesn't return a useful value, use a procedure. Easy enough.

All the points that this chapter raises are now tied together into a working example. You can load it from the `Functions and Procedures - The Whole Picture` hyperlink in the Tutorial section of the main *VBScript Master's Handbook* Web page. Take some time to use the script before you examine the code.

The HTML and VBScript code implements a simple perimeter-and-area calculator for some basic shapes. Choose the shape with which you want to work, enter the length of one of its sides (or the radius, if it's a circle) and press one of the buttons to carry out the calculation. Figure 7-3 shows the Web page for the perimeter of a square of side 10. The script contains two functions, Perimeter and Area, and two event procedures for the button controls. The script has been written out in full below, and the ensuing paragraphs describe some of the useful features of the script.

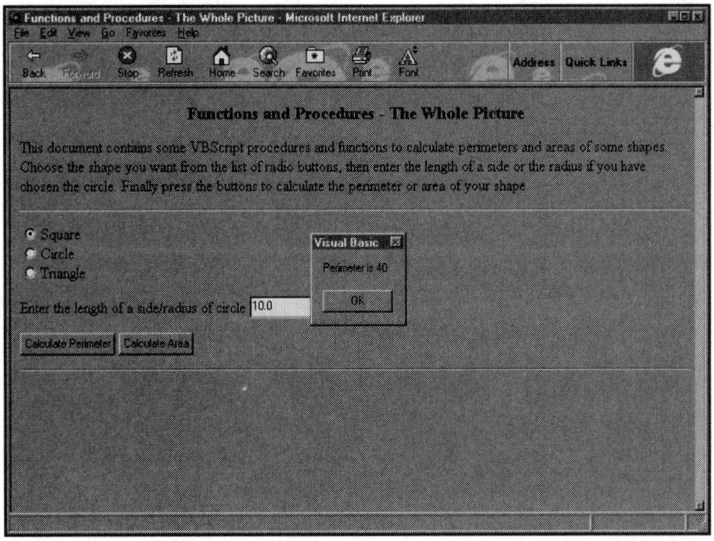

FIGURE 7-3
Combining functions and procedures together to create a working program.

```
<HTML>
<HEAD>
<TITLE>Functions and Procedures - The Whole Picture</TITLE>
<SCRIPT LANGUAGE="VBScript">
Dim ShapeIndex                                 'Stores which radio
➥button is checked
ShapeIndex=1

Function Perimeter(Shape, dblLength)          'Calculate perimeters of
➥shapes
    If (not IsNumeric(dblLength)) Then        'Make sure a numeric value
➥has been entered
        Perimeter = -999
        Exit Function                          'Exit with error value
➥returned
    End If
    If Shape = 1 Then
        Perimeter = 4 * dblLength             'Square
    Else
        If Shape = 2 Then
            Perimeter = 2 * 3.14157 * dblLength     'Circle
        Else
            If Shape = 3 Then
                Perimeter = 3 * dblLength   'Triangle
            Else
                Perimeter = -999              'None of the above -
➥error
                Exit Function
            End If
        End If
    End If
End Function

Function Area(Shape, dblLength)               'Calculate areas of shapes
    If (not IsNumeric(dblLength)) Then        'Check for a valid length
```

```
        Area = -999
        Exit Function
    End If
    If Shape = 1 Then
        Area = dblLength * dblLength
    Else
        If Shape = 2 Then
            Area = 3.14157 * dblLength * dblLength
        Else
            If Shape = 3 Then
                Area = 0.5 * dblLength * dblLength * Sqr(3)/2.0
            Else
                Area = -999
                Exit Function
            End If
        End If
    End If
End Function

Sub PerimButton_OnClick
    Dim dblPerim
    dblPerim = Perimeter(ShapeIndex, Form1.LengthText.Value)
➥'Call Perimeter
    If dblPerim = -999 Then
        MsgBox "Bad input value for length"
    Else
        MsgBox "Perimeter is " & dblPerim        'Simple calling
➥convention
    End If
End Sub

Sub AreaButton_OnClick
    Dim dblArea
    dblArea = Area(ShapeIndex, Form1.LengthText.Value)
➥'Call area
```

```
    If dblArea = -999 Then
        Call MsgBox("Bad input value for length")
    Else
        Call MsgBox("Area is " & dblArea)        'Note the use of Call
➥statement
    End If
End Sub
</SCRIPT>
</HEAD>

<BODY>
<CENTER>
<H3>Functions and Procedures - The Whole Picture</H3>
</CENTER><P>
This document contains some VBScript procedures and functions to
➥calculate perimeters and
areas of some shapes. Choose the shape you want from the list of radio
➥buttons, then enter
the length of a side or the radius if you have chosen the circle.
➥Finally press the buttons
to calculate the perimeter or area of your shape.
<HR>
<FORM NAME="Form1">
<INPUT NAME="ShapeRadio" TYPE="radio" CHECKED
➥OnClick='ShapeIndex=1'>Square<BR>
<INPUT NAME="ShapeRadio" TYPE="radio"
OnClick='ShapeIndex=2'>Circle<BR>
<INPUT NAME="ShapeRadio" TYPE="radio"
OnClick='ShapeIndex=3'>Triangle<P>
Enter the length of a side/radius of circle
<INPUT NAME="LengthText" TYPE="text" VALUE="10.0"><P>
             <INPUT NAME="PerimButton" TYPE="button" VALUE="Calculate
➥Perimeter">
             <INPUT NAME="AreaButton" TYPE="button" VALUE="Calculate
➥Area">
```

```
</FORM>
<HR>
</BODY>
</HTML>
```

Different Ways To Call MsgBox

This example uses two different calling conventions to initiate the intrinsic MsgBox routine. The first method makes use of the routine name followed by the text that is to appear in the box, whereas the second method involves using the Call keyword followed by the routine name. Both methods work in exactly the same way, and it is personal preference on which style you choose to adopt when calling routines.

Setting the Value for the Radio Group

The group of radio buttons are new to the examples used so far. They too are intrinsic form controls, like the text box, and generate an OnClick event when pressed. The radio controls are mutually exclusive, selecting one deselects the others. They are grouped by giving each control the same name. See Chapter 11, "Using Forms with VBScript," for more information on the radio control. For now, just observe how this example discovers which radio button is checked (see the gray box).

Each radio control has a *Checked* property. In the HTML source code, all three <INPUT> tags that declare radio buttons use the same value for the control name—that's to group the them together so the browser knows which ones to deselect when the other member of the group is selected. This means you cannot write an event procedure in the <SCRIPT> section of the document to handle the radio button OnClick events. You can overcome this limitation by using a script-level variable to track which control is selected. In the following example, each control has an associated scriplet that changes the value of ShapeIndex with each radio button. The HTML for the form in this document is:

```
<FORM NAME="Form1">
```

```
<INPUT NAME="ShapeRadio" TYPE="radio" CHECKED
➥OnClick='ShapeIndex=1'>Square<BR>
<INPUT NAME="ShapeRadio" TYPE="radio"
➥OnClick='ShapeIndex=2'>Circle<BR>
<INPUT NAME="ShapeRadio" TYPE="radio"
➥OnClick='ShapeIndex=3'>Triangle<P>
Enter the length of a side/radius of circle
<INPUT NAME="LengthText" TYPE="text" VALUE="10.0"><P>
             <INPUT NAME="PerimButton" TYPE="button"
➥VALUE="Calculate Perimeter">
             <INPUT NAME="AreaButton" TYPE="button"
➥VALUE="Calculate Area">
</FORM>
```

Each radio control contains an entry like this one:

```
OnClick='ShapeIndex=?'
```

When another event procedure is invoked, ShapeIndex will already store the value of the currently checked radio control.

Error Values

Given invalid arguments (such as a string when a number is expected), both functions return the error value of -999 . Returning an error value means that the calling code can interact with errors, and try to resolve the problem. In this case if the length is input incorrectly, an error message is displayed and the user can try again. You may be writing functions that can be used in many circumstances, so structuring them so that they test for errors and return appropriate codes is advisable.

Conclusions

This chapter should have improved your programming skills significantly, allowing you to move on from basic HTML documents to fully featured programs with control flow, stored data, and a modular structure. You may have noticed that the examples are becoming more practically useful, and that this chapter began to pay considerably more attention to the host environment for which scripting was designed. Procedures and functions play a key role in writing scripts for Web pages, so they were given fairly in-depth coverage. Now that you've finished this chapter, you can build sections of code that you can reuse in other scripts.

The next two chapters deal with some advanced VBScript topics, including error handling, forms, objects, and true active content. Chapter 9, "Writing Well-Organized and Coherent VBScript," covers coding conventions and you should get a handle on these issues before you start writing your own examples.

CHAPTER 8

Handling Errors with VBScript

The previous four chapters cover the essential features of the VBScript language. Declaring variables, handling data types, defining constants, controlling program flow, and writing procedures are among the many things you should be familiar with by this point. But what if things go wrong? Every computer user encounters errors, so why not write scripts with the idea in mind of minimizing the impact of these errors? VBScript's designers have included some special capabilities for detecting and dealing with run-time errors. The next few pages tell you about them, and concentrate on these topics:

- Understanding error handling
- Using the On Error statement
- Using the Err object

- Generating your own error conditions
- Responding to and recovering from errors

This is a relatively brief chapter, but the techniques that it discusses can make a world of difference to your scripts; by keeping run-time errors under control, you can make *your* active Web pages look more professional than the competition's. Good programming practices such as these can give your Web site a crucial advantage over the rest.

What Is Error Handling?

The question may seem like an obvious one, but in the context of computer programming, error handling has a specific meaning. It refers to the techniques used to trap and handle errors that may occur as a program executes. These errors are run-time errors, not *logical* errors.

Logical errors are problems with the design of a program, such as failure to validate data input by a user, using an incorrect sorting algorithm, or simply poor system design that makes a program hard to use. Unfortunately, you can't do much to help resolve logical errors automatically. You just have to work through the script until you identify weaknesses in the code.

Run-time errors, on the other hand, are situations that cause the interpreter to signal an error condition, meaning it cannot continue processing the script normally. Examples of run-time errors include division by zero, accessing past the final element of an array, or referring to a nonexistent property of some object. Left unattended, these problems cause the VBScript interpreter to display an error message and halt execution of the script. So what can a programmer do in these situations?

You can follow two basic procedures to keep these errors in check. The first method involves inserting checks (usually conditional statements that check variable values) for specific conditions within your code. To check for division by zero, for example, you might use the following code:

```
...
<> 0 Then
    dblResult = dblX / dblY
```

```
Else
    MsgBox "Cannot divide by zero. Please re-enter number and try
again!"
    Exit Function
End If
...
```

Placing sections of code like this within scripts can handle possible error conditions quite adequately, but this technique has two shortcomings. You first must consider every possible error that could occur (in this example the calculation might overflow) to render the operation error-proof. Conditional statements also cannot be used to check for every kind of error—for example, accessing a nonexistent member of an object.

The other option for dealing with error conditions is to use VBScript's built-in capabilities for error handling. The core elements of the language for dealing with errors are the On Error statement and the Err object. By combining these elements, you can ensure that your script continues to execute even if a run-time error occurs. The rest of the chapter deals with this form of error handling, followed by two practical examples illustrating the ideas presented here.

Using the On Error Statement

The Visual Basic language supports a statement that enables an error handling routine with which existing Visual Basic programmers may be familiar. VBScript supports a limited form of the On Error statement that is slightly less flexible. In order to enable error handling within a VBScript routine, place the following line of code near the beginning of the body of the routine:

```
On Error Resume Next
```

Without the above line of code, any operation that causes a run-time error is fatal. Fatal means a standard error message displays and execution of the script stops immediately. As well as being annoying to a user, these unhandled errors make your active document look unprofessional. Inserting the On Error statement instructs the interpreter to transfer control to the line immediately following the statement that caused the error. The statements following the occurrence of the error can do one of two things: ignore the error and continue processing, or check for the occurrence of an error and respond accordingly.

Ignoring an error condition would be inadvisable because it gives the user a false impression that everything is working fine. One thing going wrong in a script may cause the rest of the algorithm to produce incorrect results. In some ways, this is worse than halting the script with a system error message. The recommended course of action is to check for the error condition and inform the user and retry the operation or execute some code to recover from the error.

NOTE

Each On Error Resume Next statement is only active within the procedure where it occurs. Any routine requiring error handling to be enabled, must contain this statement. If error detection is enabled in a procedure or function that calls another routine with no On Error statement, an error occuring in the called routine passes control immediately to the statement following the procedure or function call. See the section "Detecting and Handling Errors with Mathematical Calculations" for an example.

How do you check for the occurrence of an error? This is where the Err object mentioned earlier comes into play. The Err object is a system object that can contain information about run-time errors and can identify the problem.

Using the Err Object

This object is an important entity when it comes to handling run-time errors, so you should be familiar with its properties and methods if you want to add comprehensive support for error handling to your scripts. Table 8-1 shows a complete list of its properties and methods.

Some of the entries in Table 8-1 require a little more explanation before you move on to some example scripts—the next two sections contribute some additional information.

Table 8-1 The Err Object

PROPERTIES	DESCRIPTION
Description	Property for setting or retrieving a string that descibes the most recent error. You should use this property to identify what has gone wrong—a number conveys little meaning to a user.
Number	Specifies a number for the most recent run-time error. These numbers can be system defined errors or errors made up by the programmer. This is the Err object's default property—referring simply to Err in your code will access Err.Number.
Source	Property for setting or retrieving the name of the object or application that generates the most recent error.
HelpContext	Property for setting or retrieving a help context ID for a topic in a Windows Help file. This ID (if used) should point to an explanation of the error.
HelpFile	String expression that sets or retrieves the fully qualified path name of a Windows help file. The help topic identified by *HelpContext* should be contained within this file.
METHODS	**DESCRIPTION**
Clear	Clears all the property settings of the `Err` object. You should use this method once an error has been handled.
Raise	Signature is Raise Number, Source, Description, HelpFile, and HelpContext. This method generates a run-time error with the specified arguments being assigned to the properties of the same name. All the arguments are optional, apart from Number.

Properties of the Err Object

A single statement could generate a whole host of different errors. Consider a function call to an ActiveX control (see Chapters 12 through 14). The authors of the control could have designed the control to respond to problems by generating run-time errors. These errors could cover anything from invalid arguments to problems executing the requested method. The properties of the Err object can be used to describe the error to a user or programmer in a standard way.

When handling errors (stored in the Err object) within a script, the programmer has two options.

- Check for specific errors and respond in a different way for each one
- Inform the user that an error has occured and use the Description property to describe the error to them.

Checking for specific errors usually involves checking the `Number` property, rather than the `Description`, with a `Select Case` statement (see Chapter 6, "Controlling Program Flow in VBScript"). To identify errors to somebody reading your scripts, you should declare constants for error numbers you want to handle. The following portion from an imaginary script could check for specific errors.

```
Sub DoSomeErrorChecking()
    Dim FAIL_CONNECT, LOSE_CONTACT, CORRUPT_DATA
    FAIL_CONNECT = 1001  :  LOSE_CONTACT = 1002  :  CORRUPT_DATA =
➥1003
    ....
    On Error Resume Next
    ...
    FTPObject.FetchData(strBuffer, intSize)
    If Err.Number <> 0 Then
        Select Case Err.Number
            Case FAIL_CONNECT
                FTPObject.Connect()
                ....
            Case CORRUPT_DATA
                FTPObject.ReRead(strBuffer, intSize)
                ...
            Case LOSE_CONTACT
                MsgBox "The remote host appears to have gone
➥off-line. Please try again later"
            Case Else
                MsgBox "An unexpected error occured while fetching
➥the data"
        End Select
        Err.Clear
        Exit Sub
```

```
    End If
    ...
     Other code
    ...
End Sub
```

Note the use of the Select Case statement to check the various possibilities. You should try to deal with any expected errors seamlessly. This may involve trying an operation again or some kind of recovery to get the code causing the error to work correctly. There will always be some unexpected errors that either cannot be recovered from or happen very infrequently. In these cases, it is probably best to report the error to the user and let them try the operation again (or get in touch with the technical support department!).

We just mentioned that the second option for dealing with errors is to use the `Description` property to inform the user about the error. The description usually contains a meaningful message (to a programmer at least) such as

```
"Division by Zero" or "Object does not support that property or
method"
```

When an error occurs, you can call a specific error handling routine you have written or deal with the error where it happens. The following section of code shows both of these methods.

```
...
Sub SomeRoutine()
    On Error Resume Next
    ...
    dblResult = dblX / dblY
    If Err.Number <> 0 Then
        MsgBox "An error occured while dividing the quantities. The
➥error was " & Err.Description
        Err.Clear
        Exit Sub
    End If
    ...
    MyObject.Calculate(dblResult)
```

```
    If Err.Number <> 0 Then Handle_Error()

End Sub

Function Handle_Error()
    MsgBox "Run-time error caused by " & Err.Source & ". Error was
➥" & Err.Description
    Err.Clear
End Function
```

Calling a function to inform the user of the error makes the script look less cluttered and means the code to print the error message and reset the Err object only needs to be written once. The only problem with this is the error message does not convey quite as much information. For instance, an error Description like Type Mismatch is much less helpful to a user than a message which reads, "Please make sure you enter a numeric quantity and press the button again."

The method you choose for dealing with run-time errors is entirely up to you and may be different in different circumstances. An important consideration is not to get too tied up looking for errors. Unnecessary code complexity can easily introduce new bugs into scripts, so use error handlers only in places you consider important. Stopping the error from occurring in the first place is far better than having to deal with it later. Therefore, always insert code to validate data values that the user enters before using these values in sensitive operations.

TIP

The Err object is an intrinsic object that is automatically declared when the document loads. Because it can be accessed from any section of script in the document, passing its properties to an error handling function is unnecessary. Unless the properties are passed ByVal (see Sub statement in Language Reference), the Err object doesn't reflect the changes to them. You can just refer to it directly within the error handler.

Methods of the Err Object

The two code samples in the previous section both use the Clear method of the Err object to reset the error. After an error is detected and handled, be sure to call this method. If you don't, any subsequent code in the same routine that checks for errors still detects the earlier error condition.

NOTE

The VBScript interpreter invokes the Clear method automatically when encountering any of the following statements:

- *On Error Resume Next*
- *Exit Sub*
- *Exit Function*

Clear sets the Description property to an empty string and the error number to zero. The simplest way to check for an error is to examine the Number property. If it's nonzero, an error has occurred or the last error hasn't been cleared yet.

What about generating your own run-time errors? You can do this using the Raise method introduced in Table 8-1. The Raise method generates a run-time error with properties that the programmer defines. The method's complete signature is Raise Number, Source, Description, HelpFile, HelpContext. The only compulsory argument is Number. Some examples of calls to this method follow.

```
Raise 1024
```

The above generates an error with error number 1024. Any other properties of the error, such as its description, retain their existing values. It is not advisable to generate errors like this because the user will not know what the error is, or worse still, the Description may refer to an earlier error.

```
Raise 2000, "HawkEye Call Logger", "Cannot connect to the phone server"
```

This one generates an error with a number, source, and description. These details fully describe the error and can be cleared with a call to Err.Clear.

```
Raise 2001, "HawkEye Call Logger", "Invalid Host Address",
➥"C:\VB_Script\HawkEye\Trouble.hlp", 156
```

And this one generates a run-time error complete with a reference to a topic within a help file. You could use it to refer the user to some help material describing the error.

TIP

Avoid using small error numbers because they may refer to system errors and cause confusion. For example, "6" is the number for an overflow error. The allowable range for the Number property extends up to 65,535, so try using larger numbers for user-defined errors.

Deferred Error Handling

Up until now, each line of code causing a run-time error has been followed immediately with a check for an error condition. If many operations may cause errors, checking for them after every line of code is a major hassle. All that extra work would cause all but the most hardened programmers to ignore the errors altogether. However, a compromise is reachable. Because the On Error Resume Next statement stops the interpreter from displaying messages and halting execution, errors can essentially be ignored until later in the procedure or function.

Of course, one error may lead to others, but in certain circumstances (such as preparing a TCP connection) you would have to repeat the whole operation anyway. Consequently, you can place the error handling code at the end of a block of related statements. Structuring code in this way means a routine that previously had ten or twenty separate error checks, now has three or four. The following block of pseudo-code illustrates the principle.

```
Function DoSomeComms(ByRef blnSuccess)
    ...
    Operations to open a TCP connection
    ...
    If Err.Number <> 0 Then
        Select Case Err.Number
            Deal with various errors
```

```
            End Select
            blnSuccess = False
            Exit Function
        End If
        ...
        Operations to transfer some data
        ...
        If Err.Number <> 0 Then
            Select Case Err.Number
                Deal with various other errors
            End Select
            blnSuccess = False
            Exit Function
        End If
        ...
        Operations to close a TCP connection
        ...
        If Err.Number <> 0 Then
            Select Case Err.Number
                Deal with any other errors
            End Select
            blnSuccess = False
            Exit Function
        End If
        blnSuccess = True
        DoSomeComms = strDataRetrieved
    End Function
```

Two Practical Examples

Before concluding this chapter, there are two example documents on the CD that demonstrate error handling. The first of these examples deals with detecting and handling errors and the second shows how to raise your own errors.

Detecting and Handling Errors with Mathematical Calculations

One of the most common causes of run-time errors are mathematical calculations, which can have problems like overflow or divide by zero. If you have some complex calculation that involves many variables, checking each one before using it can prove difficult. Even then, the calculation might overflow. In these cases, your best bet is to use an error handler to deal with all the possibilities. The CD contains an example that detects errors using a simple division operation (although the principle applies to much more complex calculations). You can load the example from the main Web page by selecting the `Detecting and Handling Errors with Mathematical Calculations` hyperlink from the Tutorial section.

Figure 8-1 shows a screen capture of the document after a divide by zero error has been generated. Follow the on-screen instructions to generate various errors. In addition to those suggested, you could try some other values to cause an error that hasn't been listed.

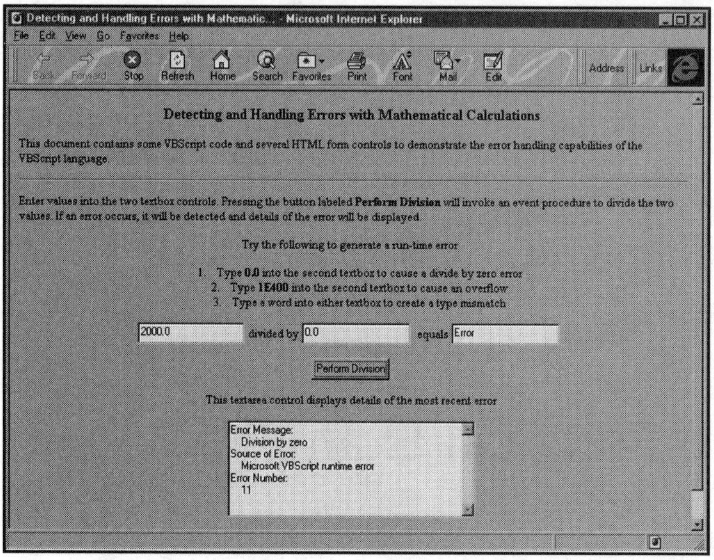

FIGURE 8-1
An example document showing an error handler in action

The HTML source for the document is listed below for you to study. Notice that the division operation that causes the run-time errors actually is contained in a separate routine to the error handling code. This is a perfectly legal way to detect errors—if a procedure doesn't contain an On Error statement, but the calling procedure does, control jumps back to the calling code when an error occurs.

```
<HTML>
<HEAD>
<TITLE>Detecting and Handling Errors with Mathematical
➥Calculations</TITLE>
<SCRIPT LANGUAGE="VBScript">
<!-
'*********************************************
' Purpose:
'  Calls a function to divide the two numbers entered by the user
' Comments:
'  Contains an error handler to detect any run-time errors with
'  the calculation. The details of any error are displayed in the
'  ErrorText control.
'*********************************************
Sub DivideButton_OnClick()
    Dim dblResult
    On Error Resume Next               'Enable error-handling routine

    dblResult = DoCalc()               'Perform the actual division
    If Err.Number <> 0 Then            'Only True if an error has
➥occured
        ErrorText.Value = "Error Message:" & Chr(13) & Chr(10) & "
➥" & Err.Description
        ErrorText.Value = ErrorText.Value & Chr(13) & Chr(10) &
➥"Source of Error:"
     ErrorText.Value = ErrorText.Value & Chr(13) & Chr(10) & "    " &
➥Err.Source
     ErrorText.Value = ErrorText.Value & Chr(13) & Chr(10) & "Error
➥Number:"
```

```
        ErrorText.Value = ErrorText.Value & Chr(13) & Chr(10) & "     " &
➥Err.Number
        Err.Clear
            ResultText.Value = "Error"
            Exit Sub
    End If
    ResultText.Value = dblResult        'The calculation was successful
End Sub


'********************************************
' Purpose:
'  Divides the two numbers entered in the textboxes & returns the
➥result
' Comments:
'  Any error which occurs here will be trapped in the calling
➥procedure
'********************************************
Function DoCalc()
    DoCalc = NumberText.Value / DivisorText.Value
End Function
->
</SCRIPT>
</HEAD>

<BODY>
<CENTER><H3>Detecting and Handling Errors with Mathematical
➥Calculations</H3></CENTER>
This document contains some VBScript code and several HTML form
➥controls to demonstrate
the error handling capabilities of the VBScript language.
     <HR>
Enter values into the two textbox controls. Pressing the button labeled
➥<B>Perform Division</B>
```

```
will invoke an event procedure to divide the two values. If an error
➥occurs, it will be
detected and details of the error will be displayed.<P>
<CENTER>Try the following to generate a run-time error
<OL>
<LI>Type <B>0.0</B> into the second textbox to cause a divide by zero
➥error
<LI>Type <B>1E400</B> into the second textbox to cause an overflow
<LI>Type a word into either textbox to create a type mismatch
</OL>
</CENTER>
<CENTER>
    <INPUT TYPE="Text" VALUE="2000.0" NAME="NumberText"> divided by
    <INPUT TYPE="Text" VALUE="100.0" NAME="DivisorText"> equals
    <INPUT TYPE="Text" VALUE="" NAME="ResultText"> <P>
    <INPUT TYPE="Button" VALUE="Perform Division" NAME="DivideButton">
➥<P>
This textarea control displays details of the most recent error<P>
<TEXTAREA NAME="ErrorText" ROWS=6 COLS=55>No error....yet!
</TEXTAREA>

</CENTER>
<HR>
</BODY>
</HTML>
```

TIP

If you experience problems working out what an error is, or why it's happening, try inserting some error handling code to display all the details of the error. This form of debugging allows you to continue execution of your script even if an error occurs. After you figure out the cause of the problem, the error detection can either remain in place or be removed to reduce the size of the script.

Raising Your Own Errors

What about generating your own errors? You may want to do this for several reasons, especially when you write a block of code to be used many times and to interact with other entities, such as ActiveX controls or the network. Generating run-time errors is an effective way to return status information to the calling code—the errors can then be dealt with in whatever way seems fit.

This example document simulates a TCP connection and data transfer over the network. You can load it by selecting the `Raising Your Own Errors` hyperlink from the Tutorial section of the CD's main Web page. Rather than use an ActiveX control to connect to another computer (see Chapter 14, "Using the Internet Control Pack and Java Applets with VBScript"), the script pretends to connect to a remote host and has a random chance of encountering an error. The source code follows, and includes comments that explain the purpose of each function or procedure. Figure 8-2 shows what the document should look like after one of the user-defined errors is raised.

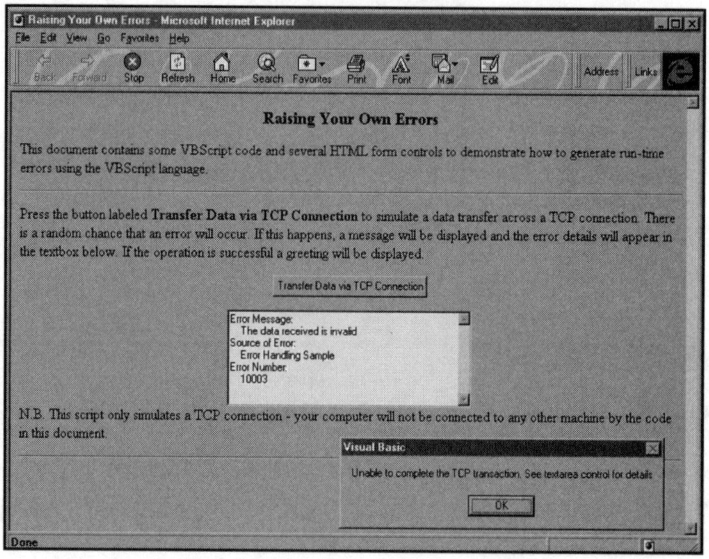

FIGURE 8-2
An example document after a user-defined error has occurred

```
<HTML>
<HEAD>
<TITLE>Raising Your Own Errors</TITLE>
<SCRIPT LANGUAGE="VBScript">
<!-
Dim TCP_REFUSED, TCP_NOHOST, TCP_CORRUPT, TCP_NODATA      'Define some
➥error constants
TCP_REFUSED = 10001 : TCP_NOHOST = 10002 : TCP_CORRUPT = 10003 :
➥TCP_NODATA = 10004

Randomize              'Initialize the random number generator

'**************************************************
' Purpose:
'  Simulates opening a TCP connection.
     ' Comments:
'  One of two errors can randomly occur.
'**************************************************
Function Sim_TCPOpen(strHost, intPort)
    Dim intWhatToDo
    intWhatToDo = Int(10 * Rnd())
    If intWhatToDo = 1 Then Err.Raise TCP_REFUSED, "Error Handling
➥Sample", "The connection was refused by the host machine"
    If intWhatToDo = 2 Then Err.Raise TCP_NOHOST, "Error Handling
➥Sample", "The host machine could not be found"
End Function


'**************************************************
' Purpose:
'  Simulates transferring some data over a TCP connection.
     ' Comments:
'  One of two errors can randomly occur. If neither error
'  is generated, a string of text is returned by this function
'**************************************************
```

```
Function Sim_TCPTransfer()
    Dim intWhatToDo
    intWhatToDo = Int(10 * Rnd())
    If intWhatToDo = 3 Then
        Err.Raise TCP_CORRUPT, "Error Handling Sample", "The data
➥received is invalid"
    ElseIf intWhatToDo = 4 Then
        Err.Raise TCP_NODATA, "Error Handling Sample", "There is no
➥data to transfer"
    Else
        Sim_TCPTransfer = "Happy Birthday to You!"
    End If
End Function


'*************************************************
' Purpose:
'  Simulates closing a TCP connection.
    ' Comments:
'  Procedure does nothing-  it is here to complete the example
'*************************************************
Function Sim_TCPClose()
End Function


'*************************************************
' Purpose:
'  Reports an error to the user by diplaying diagnostic messages
' Comments:
'  A message dialog alerts the user to the error, while the details
'  are displayed in a textarea control within the document.
'*************************************************
Sub Report_Error()
    ErrorText.Value = "Error Message:" & Chr(13) & Chr(10) & "     " &
```

```
➥Err.Description
    ErrorText.Value = ErrorText.Value & Chr(13) & Chr(10) & "Source of
➥Error:"
    ErrorText.Value = ErrorText.Value & Chr(13) & Chr(10) & "    " &
➥Err.Source
    ErrorText.Value = ErrorText.Value & Chr(13) & Chr(10) & "Error
➥Number:"
    ErrorText.Value = ErrorText.Value & Chr(13) & Chr(10) & "    " &
➥Err.Number
    MsgBox "Unable to complete the TCP transaction. See textarea
➥control for details"
End Sub


'**************************************************
' Purpose:
'  Performs a transaction, with error checking, over a simluated
'  TCP connection.
     ' Comments:
'  Errors are checked for after opening the connection, and after
'  transferring some data. If no errors are encountered, the
'  function returns the data 'received' over the connection
'**************************************************
Function DoSomeComms()
    Dim strDataReceived
    On Error Resume Next                        'Enable error handling

    Sim_TCPOpen "253.123.22.12", 102         'Open a TCP connnection

    If Err.Number <> 0 Then
        Report_Error()                          'Report the error and
➥quit
        DoSomeComms = ""
        Exit Function
    End If
```

```
    strDataReceived = Sim_TCPTransfer()       'Fetch some data from the
➥TCP socket

    If Err.Number <> 0 Then
        Report_Error()                         'Report the error and
➥quit
        DoSomeComms = ""
        Exit Function
    End If

    Sim_TCPClose()
    DoSomeComms = strDataReceived             'Return the data
➥received
End Function



Sub TransferButton_OnClick()
    Dim strData

    strData = DoSomeComms()                   'Call main function of
➥script
    If strData <> "" Then MsgBox "Data received is: " & strData
End Sub
-->
</SCRIPT>
</HEAD>

<BODY>
<CENTER><H3>Raising Your Own Errors</H3></CENTER>
This document contains some VBScript code and several HTML form
➥controls to demonstrate
how to generate run-time errors using the VBScript language.
    <HR>
Press the button labeled <B>Transfer Data via TCP Connection</B> to
```

```
➥simulate a data
transfer across a TCP connection. There is a random chance that an
➥error will occur. If this
happens, a message will be displayed and the error details will appear
➥in the textbox below.
     If the operation is successful a greeting will be displayed.<P>

<CENTER>
<INPUT TYPE="Button" VALUE="Transfer Data via TCP Connection"
➥NAME="TransferButton">
<P>
<TEXTAREA ROWS=6 COLS=55 NAME="ErrorText">No Error Yet!
</TEXTAREA>
</CENTER>
N.B. This script only simulates a TCP connection-  your computer will
➥not be connected to
any other machine by the code in this document.
<HR>

</BODY>
</HTML>
```

NOTE *Both of the examples in this chapter have used HTML form elements—the BUTTON, TEXTBOX, and TEXTAREA controls. You can find out more about these and other form controls in Chapter 11, "Using Forms with VBScript."*

That's All for Now

Now that you've come to the end of this chapter, you should be well-equipped to deal with those nasty problems that are bound to arise from time to time. The skills presented in the last few pages can make all the difference to the impression conveyed by an active document.

One thing this book hasn't covered yet is when to write the error handling code in a script. Adding it in as you build the first test is pretty much pointless—iron out the bugs in the design first. The best time to add the bulk of the error handling is when you think the design is nearing completion. This should make the code more robust. Remember, users will undoubtedly use your documents differently than you envisioned.

Now that the VBScript language has been explained, what other topics remain? The syntax of the scripting language is only part of the whole picture. Chapter 9, "Writing Well-Organized and Coherent VBScript," covers programming conventions and tips for debugging your scripts. Chapters 10 through 15 cover some of the most exciting developments in active content on the Web—the Object Model for Scripting and ActiveX technology.

CHAPTER 9

Writing Well-Organized and Coherent VBScript

Every programmer should master the ability to stick to coding conventions. The reason for bothering with conventions in the first place is to standardize script writing and help others (but mainly yourself) understand how your code works. Conventions may concern such matters as naming variables in a certain way or putting procedures in a certain place. You may have your own conventions that you like to use, and these are fine for documents with a small circulation; but if you plan to write applications for the Web where others may use your code, you really should hold to standard conventions. This chapter covers Microsoft's standard methods for writing VBScript code, which apply to all Visual Basic incarnations. By the end of it, you should sense a marked difference in the clarity and intelligibility of your scripts. Remember: coding conventions aren't just about being neat. They dramatically assist in debugging your scripts, and can decrease the amount of time you spend chasing after erroneous variables or finding an unpaired If...End If statement.

This chapter takes you through the following areas of programming style:

- Understanding conventions for naming variables and objects
- Making your code more readable using comments and remarks
- Conserving screen space and structuring code logically
- Structuring your scripts properly
- Previewing some extra VBScript functions that you may find useful
- Reviewing the document prologue you should use with HTML 3.2
- Debugging, or, getting your scripts up and running

Each language has its own particular set of conventions, so even if you're familiar with another language, skimming through this chapter would be well worth the effort.

Naming Conventions for Variables, Objects, and Procedures

The main reason to have a consistent set of coding conventions is to render scripts precise, reliable, and easy to follow. Computers don't care what scripts are called, so naming conventions exist to benefit the *humans*. One of the simplest ways to write good code is to use names that are relevant and meaningful to individuals reading the scripts.

There are several different types of naming conventions, and these can be broken down into the following categories:

- Naming constants
- Naming variables, including all subtypes
- Conventions for procedures and functions
- What to call objects such as ActiveX controls and intrinsic controls

> **NOTE** *Names that belong to the following categories cause major problems, because they're part of the scripting language. Avoid them at all costs:*
>
> - ***VBScript keywords*** *for example, Call, Dim*
> - ***VBScript functions*** *for example, Date(), Cos()*

How to Name Constants

Constants have the simplest labeling structure of all. They're just names written in uppercase letters with underscores between the words; for example:

```
CLOSING_DATE
MAXIMUM_CAPACITY
```

They have a robust appearance, reflecting their constant nature in the script, and are easy to tell apart from variables. Although VBScript actually is case-insensitive, the capitalization makes constants stand out from the rest of the script to the human eye. In addition to basic readability, using all uppercase letters to denote constants is common practice in many other languages, especially C and C++. Even readers who aren't completely familiar with VBScript but are more familiar with another language can quickly recognize the constant construct. HTML also is case-insensitive, but you should use case to enhance the readability of your code; for example, objMyCalendar is more readable than objmycalendar.

Deciding What to Call Your Variables and Labeling Their Scope

Chapter 4, "Variables, Arrays, and Data Types," discussed the complete range of variable subtypes, so you shouldn't be surprised to discover that there is a recommended way of naming them. The convention governing naming variable subtypes is to use a prefix for each subtype, followed by the variable name; the purpose being to assist with keeping the code consistent and readable. Table 9-1 lists the prefixes and furnishes an example for each one.

Table 9-1 Variable Naming Conventions		
SUBTYPE	PREFIX	EXAMPLE
Byte	byt	bytCOM1flags
Integer	int	intCounter
Long	lng	lngStellar_Dist
Single	sng	sngAverage
Double	dbl	dblAtomic_Diameter
String	str	strCoffee_Type
Object	obj	objButton
Boolean	bln	blnFemale
Date (Time)	dtm	dtmBirthday
Error	err	errFail_Setup

You should always define variables with the smallest possible scope. If use of a variable is necessary only in a certain procedure, you should declare it as such, not at the script level. You label script variables with an additional *s* prefix, and you need to declare them in the HEAD section of an HTML page, outside any procedures. Procedure-level variables don't require any further prefixes than those listed in Table 9-1.

An example of a script-level variable is sintNumPeople—the *s* prefix increases the length of the variable name slightly, but conveys more information.

The one question that invariably arises in discussions about variable naming concerns the preferred length of name. Ultimately, you must achieve a balance between errors that crop up from using names that are too short, and therefore misunderstood, and errors that result from names that are too long, and incorrectly typed (not to mention the waste of time typing them in). Research suggests that you obtain the least amount of error and shortest debug time by using variable names that fall between 10 and 16 characters in length. Now, if you're the type of person who will try to make sure every single one of your variables falls within this preferred length range, a word of advice: Don't get obsessive about it, my friend. The point is to provide them with meaning. If a short name works, don't use a needlessly long one.

Procedure Names—Making Them Meaningful

Almost every useful script contains a significant number of procedures and functions, choosing distinguishable names as the script grows in complexity and length is important. A procedure name should use mixed case, and should be long enough to describe its purpose. They should always begin with a verb, because they perform actions; for example, OpenFile.

TIP *If you decide to use abbreviations in your script, make sure they are consistent throughout the document. Random switching between abbreviations tends to be extremely misleading. If you use two variables for counting operations, you should label them Count1 and Count2, for example, rather than Cnt1 and Count2.*

Naming Your Objects

The ActiveX controls (also known as objects) introduced in Chapters 10 through 13 require special labeling (see Table 9-2).

As the number of scripting objects evolve over time, you should consult the Microsoft Web site to find out the recommended syntax for the new items as they appear:

```
http://www.microsoft.com/vbscript/
```

Code Commenting Conventions

Some people consider adding comments to code one of the most singularly boring and utterly pointless tasks on Earth—hmmm, wonder why! Okay, so a thrill a minute, it ain't, but taking the time to add some meaningful and illustrative comments hasn't ever killed anybody, and

Table 9-2 Object Naming Conventions in VBScript

OBJECT	PREFIX	EXAMPLE
3-D Panel	pnl	pnlButtons
Animated Button	ani	aniMoving_Arrow
Check Box	chk	chkSmall_Medium_Large
Combo Box	cbo	cboCar_Make
Command Button	cmd	cmdExit
Common Dialog	dlg	dlgPrint
Frame	fra	fraPicture
Horizontal Scroll Bar	hsb	hsbVolume
Image	img	imgBackground
Label	lbl	lblWarning
Line	lin	linHorizontal
List Box	lst	lstDays_of_Week
Spin	spn	spnPages
Text Box	txt	txtWelcome
Vertical Scroll Bar	vsb	vsbPage_Scroll
Slider	sld	sldScale

even tends to make scripts readable (especially if you follow a standard format for commenting with each script).

You can consistently add annotations to several common sections of your script to make the code more understandable. The first place to add a comment is the head of the script and the comment basically entails a fairly extensive description of what the script does (see the Script Comments section in the following script sample). The second is to label each procedure with a short section of code to make it clear what is happening in that routine. You generally want to add a few lines that can jog your memory of what the procedure does and the variables that it uses. Finally, you can put individual comments on lines of code that might be difficult to follow and require further explanation.

The commenting structures described in this section may seem over the top. If your scripts are small and uncomplicated, they probably would be—but as you get up to speed and take advantage of VBScript to power your Web site, your scripts will get much longer and more complex. Then good comments can really make a difference.

Script Comments

Putting script comments into code for documentation purposes is the behavior of a wise programmer. You place script comments at the top of the script to summarize the entire script, including what it does, the author, the version, and any bugs known to exist at the time. You can then follow these comments with a list of all the procedures and functions used in the script, including a brief commentary for each one. To round off the script comment, you should define all of the global variables you use during the course of the script, along with an indications of their uses. Here is an example of a script comment:

```
'
**********************************************************************
➥************
'                               MORTGAGE CALCULATOR
' Purpose:   Performs repayment calculations for a standard capital
➥repayment or endowment
'            mortgage.
' Author:    M.D. White
' Modified:  14th September 1996
' Bugs:      None at present
' Functions:
'    Mortgage_Init - Setup the calculator
'    Capital_Calc  - Calculates a capital repayment mortgage
'    Endowment_Calc-      "      an endowment           "
'    Various event procedures
```

Procedure Comments

To make your scripts more intelligible to others, one thing that you can do is to put a brief comment before each procedure to describe what it does. The statement ought to be short and shouldn't describe exactly how the routine works, but rather, should concentrate on concisely stating what it does. The actual implementation of a routine may well change over time, so you should save comments about how it works for the function body itself. For example, a procedure that sorts an array may have a comment such as the following:

```
'*****************************************************************
➥***
' Purpose:        Procedure to sort an array in alphabetical order
' Arguments:      sortlist: array containing items to be sorted
'                 ascend_descend: 1 = ascending ; -1 = descending
' Assumptions: None - no global variables used.
' Other info:     Currently uses Quicksort - may change in future
➥versions
'*****************************************************************
➥***

Sub Sorting(sortlist, ascend_descend)
```

If you're passing arguments to the procedure and their purpose isn't obvious, adding a comment into the script to label the argument is pretty important. Not only does it serve to remind you of the argument's raison d'etre, but it also helps during debugging. You also should insert comments when a procedure expects the argument to fall within a specific range. Table 9-3 summarizes of the procedure header comments that you should try to include in your scripts.

Table 9-3 How to Structure Procedure Comments—The Overview

SECTION HEADING	COMMENTS
Purpose	What the procedure does
Assumptions	List of any external variables or controls that are passed into the procedure.
Effects	List of the procedure's effect on each external variable or control.
Inputs	Any arguments. Each argument should be on a separate line of the comment text.
Return values	Explanation of the value returned.

In addition to these comments, you should remember the following points:

1. Each important variable you use inside the procedure should have an inline comment that describes its use.
2. Straightforward variables, controls, procedures, and functions should have meaningful names, such as strGreeting, so that no inline reference is required.
3. You should place the overview of your script at the beginning of the code, enumerating objects, procedures, algorithms, dialog boxes, and other system dependencies. Sometimes including a piece of pseudocode to describe a particular algorithm can be useful.

Individual Comments

Sometimes you can disentangle the complexity of a line of code by reading the short inline comment that the author has added. These inline comments may seem insignificant at the time of writing, but if others are going to use your code, such details are gold dust.

To add a comment to a line of code, all you have to do is to put the ' symbol before your comment—by far the neatest way to attach an annotation to a line, and preferable to the REM statement, which you have to place on a line by itself or incorporate into a multiple-line statement. Most of the examples in this book include inline comments to make it easier to work through the code of the examples. Imagine how unintelligible you might find them minus comments or meaningful variable, object, and procedure names!

Often, if you're working on a larger project, you must write a detailed description of the sections of code you will write before you put down a single line of code. If you organize your description with the previous comments in mind, you can use them as the template for your code, and have your comments finished before you start. This is a much different scenario than waiting until the very end, and trying to quickly document the code to finish it off. Even if you're working alone, creating program descriptions ahead of the game not only allows easier commenting later on, but is a powerful tool in software design. Although covering software design and programming description languages doesn't fit within the scope of this book, several good books on the market explain code construction, principally, Steve McConnell's *Code Complete* (Microsoft Press).

So, that's it for comments. Now on to a few tips on making your document layout neat and professional.

Tips for Formatting Your Code Layout

The secret of producing a well-formatted document is to conserve screen space as much as possible. Not to say you should shove all your code on one line with colons galore, but rather, that you include a sensible amount of information on each line and indent code blocks to make the information legible.

Here are a few pointers to help you get optimal results:

- Indent standard nested blocks four spaces.
- Indent the overview comments of a procedure one space and enclose them between two lines of asterisks (*).
- Indent statements that make up the procedure body four spaces and indent each nested block another four spaces.

The example layout shown here simply demonstrates the points that this section aims to make.

```
'*********************************************************************
➥*****************
 ' Purpose: Calculates some important value
 ' Inputs:
'      intCount - Number of loop iterations to make
'      blnFast  - Boolean flag indicating whether or not to perform
➥fast algorithm
'      dblX     - Parameter X for 'Magic Number' formula
'      dblY     - Parameter Y for 'Magic Number' formula
' Returns:
'      Function return value is the 'Magic Number' (see printed
➥documentation for algorithm)
'      It is a Double subtype value.
'*********************************************************************
➥*****************
Function Calculate_Magic()
    Dim intTemp             'Loop counter variable
    Dim dblIntemediate, dblDiff     'Intermediate values for the
➥algorithm

    For intTemp = 1 To intCount
        If (blnFast = True) Then        'Fast algorithm
             dblIntermediate = SOME CALCULATION WITH DblX and DblY
        Else                              'Accurate, slower algorithm
             dblDiff = DblX
             Do While Abs(dblIntermediate-dblDiff) > 0.00456
                 dblDiff = SOME HEFTY CALCULATION
                 dblIntermediate = ANOTHER CALCULATION
             Loop
        End If
    Next
    Calculate_Magic = dblIntermediate    'Set the return result
End Function
```

The Standard Document Template

When you embark on a large document or Internet application, deciding on a layout format before you start is good thinking. The following sections take you through the standard format that Microsoft recommends and offer a few tips for keeping things structured.

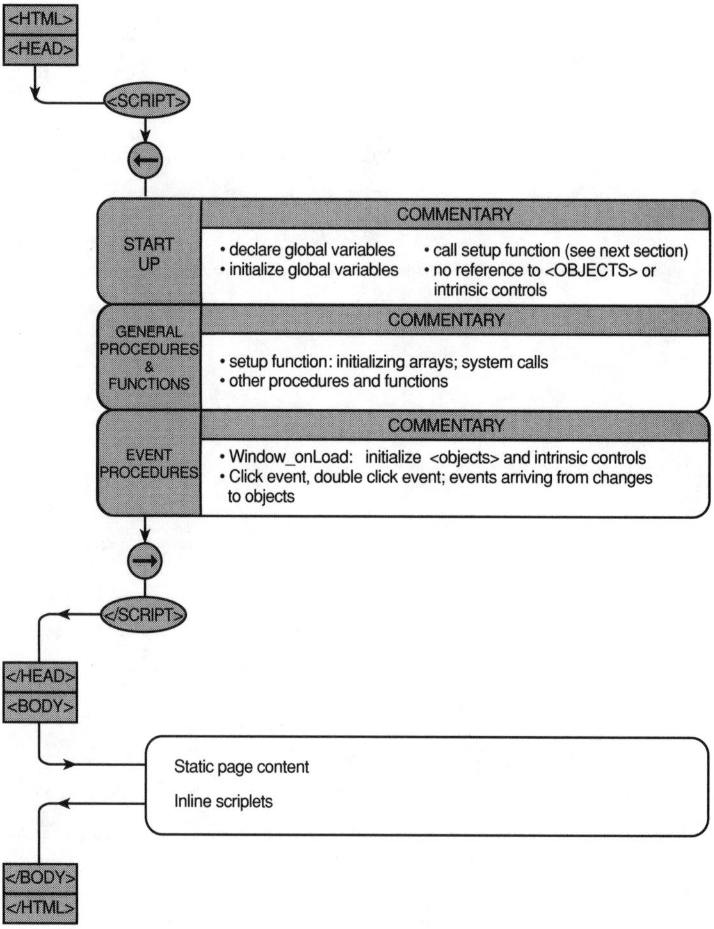

FIGURE 9-1
The recommended template for Visual Basic scripting-enabled pages

Figure 9-1 shows the different stages of laying out a document. The following sections take a closer look at the sections to which Figure 9-1 refers.

The Startup Section in the Document Template

Every good document deserves a decent startup section. Here, you declare the global variables (and include a commentary on their purposes) and initialize their values. You include the script comments discussed earlier (like author, version, and so on), and any other information you think might help others who may work with the code. You may not make any reference to <OBJECTS> or intrinsic controls, because these will not have been defined yet. See below for more information on this.

TIP *Instead of putting tons of initializations in the Startup Section, write a separate setup-function for initializing arrays and system calls, then put it in the general procedures and functions section and call it from the Startup section. In this way, you prevent cluttering and streamline your code.*

General Procedures and Functions

When writing your procedures and functions, group them together in a section called General Procedures and Functions. You should include a commentary for each routine, explaining what it does, and reference any variables associated with it.

You also should develop a habit of including a setup function in this section (see previous tip) to initialize all your variables and system attributes. For short scripts, you can do this in the Startup section, but as the number of variables grows, initializing them elsewhere works better. Although you must place declarations of global variables in the Startup section, you can initialize from anywhere in the script.

Event Procedures

You should place event procedures in the last section of the script, just before the </SCRIPT> tag—not just for style points, but because it's affected by the way the browser interprets the script. Explorer 3.0

performs a one-pass-parse on each page, meaning, it first loads the entire document into memory, then parses it, and finally displays it onscreen as a complete page. Because the browser proceeds through the code from top to bottom, the rule of thumb is to locate general procedures and functions above event procedures. The same goes for a general procedure that calls another. The idea is to be sure to define any procedure *before* it may be needed.

The following example would generate an error, because the browser would not have encountered the ReserveBooking routine at the Call statement, and consequently, wouldn't know where to find it. For all the scripting engine knows, the routine may not even exist.

```
<SCRIPT LANGUAGE="VBScript">
<!-
'**********************************************************************
➥*****
' Trying to call a procedure that hasn't yet been encountered
' The following code extract would generate an error
'**********************************************************************
➥*****

...
    Call ReserveBooking (dtmArrival)
...

Sub ReserveBooking (dtmArrival)
    ...
    ...
End Sub
->
</SCRIPT>
```

If you follow the suggested code layout that Figure 9-1 illustrates, you can avoid these types of errors.

The Window_onLoad Event Procedure

You cannot refer to objects or intrinsic controls in the startup section of a script, because when the browser encounters script code in the HEAD section, it parses it immediately. The browser executes any code that falls outside a procedure immediately, which is fine as long as you're declaring and initializing global variables, but any attempts to initialize an undeclared object will cause a run-time error. What you want to determine is how you can adjust an object's attributes before the user sees it onscreen but after it has been declared?

The OnLoad event that the Window object generates lets the programmer do just this. After the document finishes loading, but just before it appears on-screen, the Window object generates this event. An event handler for this event can configure any of the HTML controls or objects in the document, because they now have all been defined (but not yet displayed). Chapter 10, "The Object Model for Scripting," covers this event and the other features of the Window object in greater detail.

One example use of the OnLoad event is to fill a combobox control with options.

```
Sub Window_OnLoad()
    ComboBox1.AddItem("Brazil")
    ComboBox1.AddItem("Spain")
    ComboBox1.AddItem("Yugoslavia")
    ComboBox1.AddItem("Norway")
End Sub
```

Handy VBScript Extras

Several useful VBScript functions are tucked away in the VBScript Language Reference Appendixes at the back of the book. Some of them deserve an airing, so this section now looks at a few examples of how you can use them to good effect.

MsgBox Function

The idea of using a message box to display a message isn't new. You've seen it in action in many of the examples, and now want to take advantage of its other properties. The message box syntax is as follows:

```
MsgBox (prompt[,buttons][,title][,helpfile, context])
```

The prompt is the message that appears, and needs no further explanation. You can add buttons to the box by using the values described in Appendix A, "VBScript Language Reference—Functions." You insert these in place of the buttons argument, and you can add a title by inserting a string. You don't use the *helpfile* and *context* options much in scripting applications—they're more pertinent to Visual Basic programming. Here's an example of the MsgBox function:

```
intAnswer = MsgBox("The video failed to load. Do you wish to retry?",
➥4, "Web Video Player")
```

The above code would display an information message box with two buttons.

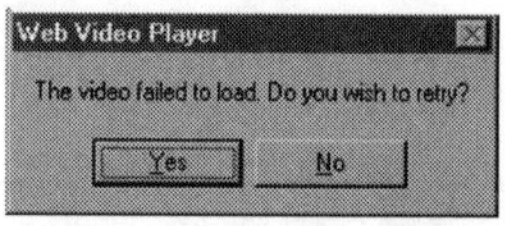

Pressing the Yes button would return a value of 6, which would then be stored in intAnswer. Pressing the No button would return the value 7. A script could then carry out some action based on this result.

InputBox Function

You should use the InputBox function when you want to get an input into a dialog box. Its syntax is:

```
InputBox(prompt[,title][,default][,xpos][,ypos][,helpfile, context])
```

The message appears in a message box located at (xpos, ypos) from the corner of the screen. *xpos* and *ypos* have units of twips (1/1440 inch). You can use the *title* option and the default text value for the dialog box passed to the function with the *default* argument to add titles. For example, the following would place an input box at the top center of the screen, requesting an e-mail address:

```
strEmail_Address = InputBox("Enter email address", "Request for Email
Address", "mark@msn.com")
```

The user can enter a new address or press Enter to submit the default value.

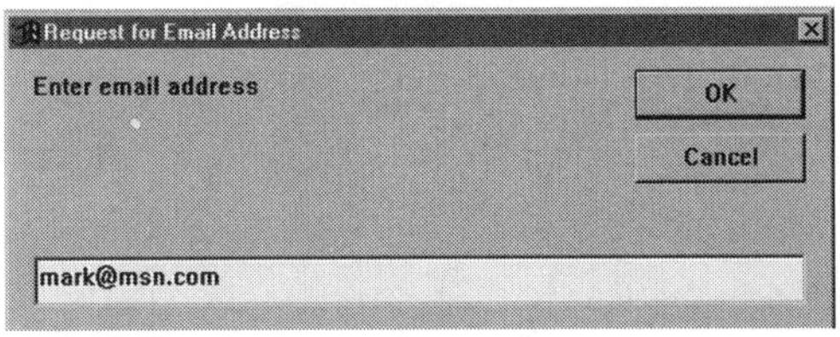

LBound and UBound Functions

You use these functions to identify the size of an unknown array. The syntaxes for these commands are identical:

```
LBound(arrayname[,dimension])
```

```
UBound(arrayname[,dimension])
```

The value of the array's upper or lower bound is returned as an integer, and the total size of the array dimension can be calculated by performing a subtraction. Don't forget that most arrays include a zeroth element, so you will have to add one to your result.

```
Dim A(-3 To 2)
...
Number_elements_in_A = UBound(A) - LBound(A) + 1
```

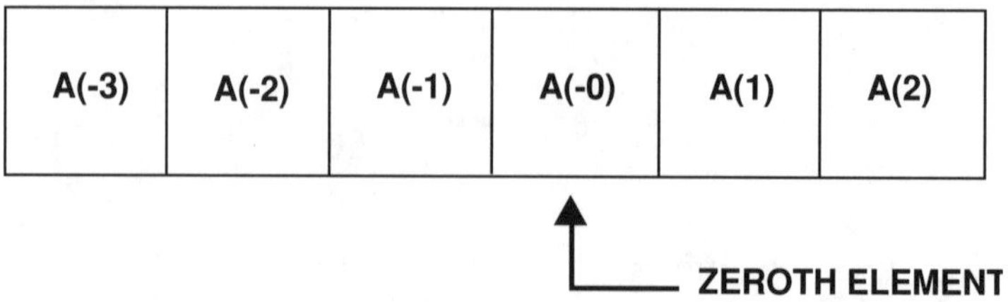

In the illustration above, UBound(A) gives the value 2. LBound(A) gives -3. The number of elements in the array A is therefore 6. These two functions also provide an easy way to cycle through all the elements of an array. Suppose you wanted to increase the value of each cell of a numerical array by 10 percent. You could write a loop that started at LBound and ran to UBound and performed a simple calculation.

The use of these functions can be best illustrated by an example. This sample code cycles through all the elements of a one-dimensional array and multiplies each one by 12.5 percent.

```
Function InflateArray(arrData)
    Dim intLoop
    For intLoop = LBound(arrData) To Ubound(arrData)
        arrData(intLoop) = arrData(intLoop) * 1.125
    Next
End Function
```

Arrays can have up to sixty dimensions, and you use the Dim option to single out which one you want to consider. The following example selects the second dimension and calculates the size of that dimension of Array1:

```
intNo_of_Elements = UBound(Array1,2) - LBound(Array1,2) + 1
```

You should also note that array elements can have labels that are non-positive. This means that intA(-3) is a valid element of an array, and would be the first element in the following declaration:

```
Dim intA(-3 To 4)
```

This array has eight elements. LBound would give the value -3, and UBound the value 4.

LTrim, RTrim, and Trim Functions

Sometimes you have to remove the blank spaces from the beginning or end of a string variable. The LTrim, RTrim, and Trim functions serve exactly that purpose. LTrim returns the string argument minus the leading spaces; RTrim removes the trailing spaces; and Trim removes both leading and trailing spaces.

You would use them as follows:

```
strFilename_Without_Trailing_Spaces = RTrim(strFilename)
```

StrComp Function

You use the StrComp function to compare two strings, using the following syntax:

```
StrComp(string1, string2[,compare])
```

It returns one of four values:

1. If string1 comes before string2 in the alphabet, **-1** is returned.
2. If string1 comes after string2, **+1** is returned.
3. Identical strings give a **zero** value.
4. If either string has a Null value, a **Null** result is returned.

The compare option allows you to perform an alphabetic or a binary sort (default: alphabetic). If you choose to do a binary comparison, an eight bit binary code represents each character in the string, and the binary value of the whole word is calculated. The sort takes place on the size of the compounded binary numbers. Say, for example, that you used CAB and ZZ as your two strings. CAB has more letters, and thus has a higher binary value, than ZZ, even though the Zs are further down the alphabet. You probably wouldn't have much call for doing binary sorts on strings, so don't worry about them too much.

HTML 3.2 Document Prologue

Because several versions of HTML now are widely used, the W3C has defined a document prologue that should occur at the beginning of any HTML 3.2 document. This prologue is used to tell browsers that support more than one implementation of the markup language which version the current document is written in. Include the following line at the start of any HTML 3.2 files you create:

```
<!DOCTYPE HTML PUBLIC "-//W3O/DTD HTML//EN">
```

You should include this header when your documents use the HTML 3.2 language extensions. If you omit this header line, browsers may have trouble identifying the version of HTML the document uses. You should place this tag even before the opening <HTML> tag.

New applications, such as Microsoft's FrontPage, are aware of this header line and insert it automatically for you when you generate a new Web page.

Debugging Tips

The VBScript engine's debugging and error reporting facilities aren't exactly legendary for a good reason: the engine was designed as a lightweight addition to a Web browser. Knowing this incidental tidbit of information probably doesn't provide much comfort when your script isn't working right, or even worse, isn't working at all. You may well have turned here precisely because your script isn't in great working order, so this section compiles a list of points and tips that may help.

If you're new to programming, the reality of debugging a program may come as a bit of a shock. It is commonly quoted in the software writing world that 90 percent of the development time is spent working on the last 10 percent of the program; that is, on debugging and fine-tuning a module. Adhering to good programming practices can help you cut your debugging days and hours down to a minimum.

The golden rule when searching for a bug, or problem: *Be methodical and thorough.* It's too easy to skim over something and assume that it's correct. It's the same as reading a letter or report you write—you hardly ever notice your own spelling mistakes. First of all, if a bug really stumps you, take a break and work on something else for a while, even just fifteen minutes. When you return to it with a fresh perspective, the problem often reveals itself right away.

When you check through code, be sure to look out for the following points.

- Make sure that you have not accidentally used a VBScript keyword, function, or constant name in your script. Try to avoid ambiguity when you name your items. Placing a standard prefix on all your procedure and variable names can help.
- Use the Option Explicit keyword as the first statement inside the <SCRIPT> tags (see Chapter 4) to force you to use Dim to declare all variables before they can be used. Without the Option Explicit statement, the interpreter simply creates a new variable when it encounters a new identifier. Simple typing errors can introduce bugs if you fail to use the explicit keyword.
- Declare all your variables at the beginning of a procedure or section and assign known values to them so you can be sure of the state in which your script procedures start.
- Make sure that you have indented any statement blocks contained in loops or conditionals, then check carefully that each block has a terminating statement. Verify that each If has an End If, each Do has a matching Loop and that each routine has an End Sub or End Function.

- If a function you have written appears to not be working correctly, make sure that you're setting the return value properly, and that it's set before every possible exit route from the function.
- When loops seem to get stuck and repeat indefinitely, several causes can be the culprit. The most common cause is when the loop's controlling variable is not updated. If you're using a Do loop to repeat some statements and the condition depends on a counter variable, make sure that the counter is incremented (or decremented) within the loop body. If not, the loop condition is never satisfied. Another cause of infinite loops arises when the checks are too exact. If a While clause says something like `Do While (intCount <> 567)`, the loop will terminate only if this exact value is reached. You're better off checking for ranges of values, such as `Do While (intCount < 567)`. Then if the controlling variable overshoots the cut-off value, the loop terminates correctly. Try to formulate conditions in this way whenever possible.
- If code written within event procedures doesn't seem to work right, the event actually may not even be firing. To see if that's the case, place a visible cue within the event handler, such as a call to the MsgBox function. If the event handler is being called, a message dialog will confirm it. If the dialog box appears, you know you've written faulty code, and if it doesn't, you need to determine whether you have set the object up properly. See Chapter 13 for information on the events and attributes of objects.
- When you write function calls incorrectly, the VBScript interpreter often displays a Type Mismatch error. Make sure that the function name and arguments are correct and that you're using the correct calling convention. Chapter 7 covers calling procedures and functions. Make sure that you use the Call statement when using parentheses in procedure calls. Also check to make sure that you have closed any opening brackets of a function call.

There is a certain technique you can use to simulate the interactive debuggers that ship with products like Visual C++ and Visual Basic. It provides only simple feedback about the values of your variables, but can give you vital clues to the source of a problem. There may be variables in whose values you're interested, such as a loop counter or a condition flag. You can't stop the script and query the values the way you would with an official debugger, but you still can discover their values. Place several simple HTML elements, such as buttons or text boxes, in your document (see Chapter 11) and set their Value properties to the value you're interested in whenever that variable changes. Mark these extra lines of code with comments, so that you can find and remove them after you fix the bug. Now you have a visual display of the internal workings of the script built into your document.

Imagine that the following example document contained two button controls, called Button1 and Button2. The loop counter and running total both are displayed as the code segment executes. Sometimes the values change too quickly onscreen, so you may want to introduce some kind of delay. Simply add a call to the MsgBox function (although this doesn't help much when the loop performs many iterations before the problem arises, it's still useful).

```
Do While (intCount > CUTOFF_VALUE)
    dblTotal = SomeFuntion()
    Button1.Value = dblTotal
    intCount = intCount - StepFunction()
    Button2.Value = intCount
    MsgBox "Paused"                 'Used to pause processing if the
display changes too fast
Loop
```

Wrapping It Up

You've completed coding conventions and are ready to move on to the scripting object model in Chapter 10, and forms processing in Chapter 11. The next chapter covers the methods, properties, and events available to scripting engines in Internet Explorer. Internet Explorer 3.0

provides the programmer with a fully scriptable model to control the browser and the document it contains. Now that you have covered the essential features of VBScript itself, you're armed and ready to combine your knowledge of the language with the new features offered by the browser, including the Object Model, HTML 3.2 standards, and ActiveX technology.

PART III

Integrating VBScript and HTML

CHAPTER 10

The Object Model for Scripting

The previous chapters introduced you to the VBScript language, and by now you should be ready to put your newly acquired knowledge to work. If you're an experienced Visual Basic programmer, you may well have turned straight to this section and want to get started with scripting on the World Wide Web. Whatever your situation, the next five chapters cover a large amount of new and exciting material. Chapters 10 and 11 thoroughly discuss the Object Model for Scripting and HTML forms, and Chapters 12 through 15 cover one of the Web's newest developments—Microsoft's ActiveX technology.

This chapter covers the following topics:

- Defining the Object Model for scripting
- Identifying the eleven components of the Explorer Object Model

- Dealing with windows and frames
- Setting and clearing browser timeouts
- Navigating the Web with a script
- Modifying a document at run-time
- Using cookies to store important values
- Using links as active entities

Also this chapter provides you with two kinds of information:

- Reference information for the components of the Object Model
- Tips and examples for using these new objects in your scripting applications

Before delving into the information this chapter has to offer, you should have a solid operating definition of the Object Model. The following section addresses that introductory need.

What Is the Object Model?

Any good modern application program is designed modularly, defining different modules for different tasks. The modular design methodology has been extended in recent years, and now is called *object-oriented design*. Object-oriented design specifies particular *classes* of object which have a public *interface*. These interfaces tell the outside world what properties, methods, and events the object supports. The person who uses the object doesn't have to know exactly how the class implements this behavior—the user simply uses the externally published interface.

Besides defining classes that contain normal data types (such as Integers and Strings), OOP design allows existing classes to serve as members of a new class. This is known as *inheritance*, and leads to highly structured object hierarchies.

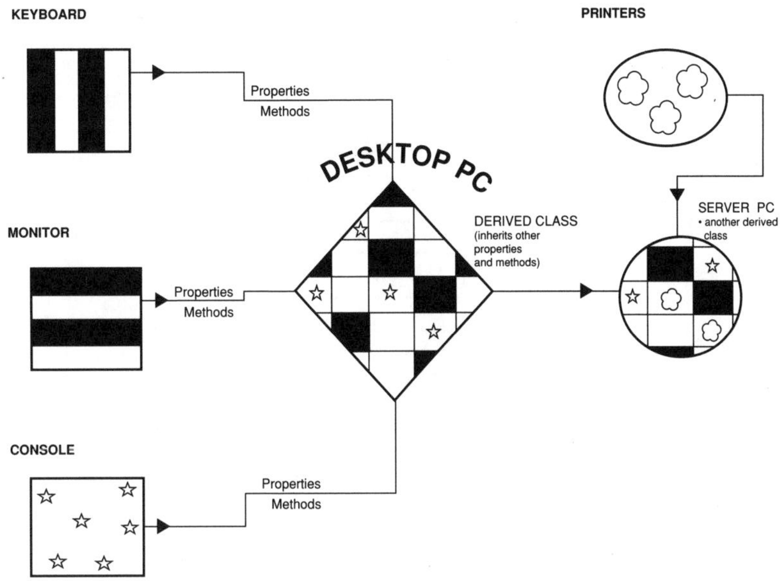

FIGURE 10-1
An example of an object hierarchy, showing inheritance.

Internet Explorer 3.0's design is based on an object hierarchy, and it makes a large amount of this structure accessible to scripting applications. The *Object Model for Scripting* is the official specification of the objects that have been exposed for scripts to use. This model defines the objects, and the properties, methods, and events they support, that can be used to control the browser itself. This chapter looks at the eleven separate components, some of which are more complicated (or useful) than others, but before dealing with the specific details, it's important to understand the fundamental structure of the object model.

Figure 10-2 shows a graphical outline of the Object Model for Scripting. Notice that this hierarchy consists of four levels, ranging from the Window object at the top level to the Elements array at the bottom level. The following sections explain the elements of, and uses for, each of these objects.

NOTE *The Internet Explorer Object Model has been designed for compatibility with the model of the JavaScript language that the Netscape Navigator browser uses. It's available to any scripting engine that is plugged into the ActiveX scripting framework, such as Visual Basic Scripting Edition.*

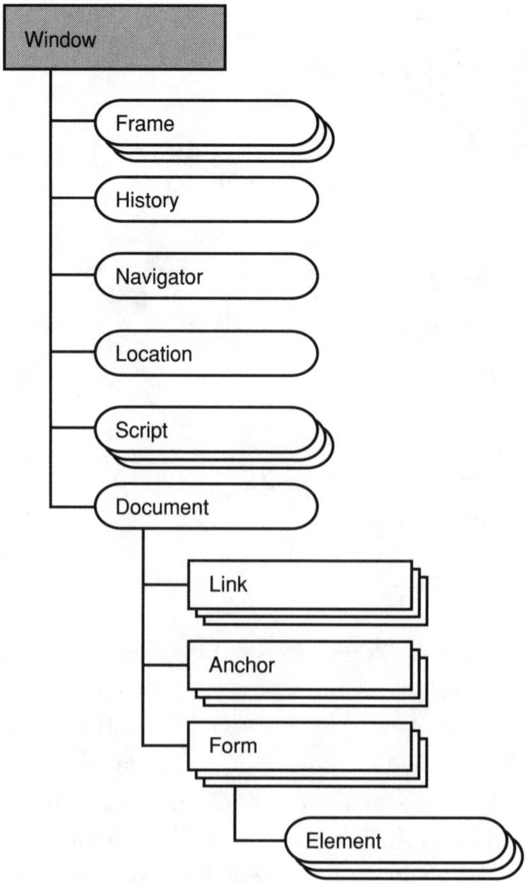

FIGURE 10-2
The Object Model for Scripting hierarchy

The Eleven Entities

You know that Internet Explorer implements a model that scripting engines can use to control the browser. The model is broken down into distinct parts, each of which provides access to certain features of the browser. The first of these items is the most important of all, because it contains all the others—the Window object.

The Window Object—Starting from the Top

The Window object is the top level object in the scripting model and contains all the other items this chapter discusses. The Window actually represents the Internet Explorer application window, including its methods and properties. Programmers using C++ to control Explorer would access the same properties and methods that a VBScript engine can use. What exactly are these properties, methods, and events? Table 10-1 lists them.

Using Objects in VBScript

Figure 10-1 shows an example object hierarchy in which the Desktop PC object inherits all the properties, methods, and events of the Keyboard, Monitor, and Unit objects. Objects in VBScript also can contain properties and methods and generate events. But, how do you refer to them in a script?

If an object contains a item to which you want to refer, simply write the object name, a period (.), and the item's name. For instance, the button elements you have seen in several examples before now have a property called Value. To access the Value propety from a script, you would use the following code:

```
ButtonName.Value = "New Caption"
```

The same approach also applies to method names, such as

```
Form1.Gradient1.Repaint()
```

Notice that there are two object references within the same line of code. An object can contain other objects, which are referred to using the dot-syntax (Object.Item). You can nest along this course to as many levels as necessary. The following line of code is a somewhat unrealistic, but possible scenario:

```
Window1.Frame1.Document1.Form1.Textbox1.Value = "New text"
```

Table 10-1 The Window Object

	PROPERTIES
Name	String containing the current window name. This property cannot be changed at run-time and is read-only
Parent	Returns the Window object that is the current window's parent. The parent of any window is the frame that contains that window, and if there is no such frame *Parent* returns the current Window object. This property is also read-only.
Self	This property is read-only and returns the Window object of the current window.
Top	The window containing all frames in the current browser instance is the topmost frame. Top returns this Window object and is read-only.
Location	Returns the Location object for the current window—see relevant section later in the chapter.
DefaultStatus	Sets the default string to be displayed on the status bar on the bottom left of the Explorer window.
Status	Sets the string to display in the status bar at the bottom of the Explorer window.
Frames	Returns the array of frames contained by the current window—see Frames section.
History	Returns the current History object of the window—see History section.
Document	Returns the Document object of the current window—see Document section.
Navigator	Returns the current window's Navigator object—see the Navigator Object section.
	METHODS
Alert	Signature is *Alert strMessage*. Displays an alert dialog with the message stored in *strMessage*.
Confirm	Signature is *Confirm strMessage*. Displays a confirmation dialog with Yes and No buttons containing the string *strMessage*. Returns a boolean value indicating the user's response.
Prompt	Signature is *Prompt strMessage, strDefault*. Prompts the user for input. The dialog box displays the prompt stored in *strMessage*, and the default value in the textbox is *strDefault*.

	METHODS
Open	Signature is *Open URL, strTarget, WindowProperties, intWidth, intHeight*. Creates a new instance of the Internet Explorer window. Returns a Window object representing a window named *strTarget*, displaying the *URL* of the specified height and width. See under Opening and Closing Windows.
Close	Closes the current Window.
FireOnLoad	Triggers the *OnLoad* event.
FireOnUnload	Triggers the *OnUnload* event.
SetTimeout	Signature is *SetTimeout Expression, intMsec, strLanguage*. Sets a timer to call a function after a specified number of milliseconds. The code or function to execute is specified by *Expression* and the *strLanguage* argument indicates the scripting language, i.e. "VBScript" or "Javascript." Returns an ID for the timer object.
ClearTimeout	Signature is *ClearTimeout intID*. Cancels the timer indicated by *intID*.
Navigate	Signature is *Navigate URL*. Navigates the current window to the specified *URL*.
	EVENTS
OnLoad	Event fires once the contents of the window have been successfully loaded. See "Using the Window Events."
OnUnload	Fires after the contents of the window are unloaded. See "Using the Window Events."

Refer back to Figure 10-1: notice that the Window object also contains an item named Script. Script isn't actually a single item; it represents any script code, or script routines, in the document currently displayed onscreen. Any script code, therefore, is stored at the same level in the object hierarchy as the Window object, meaning, script routines can be accessed directly, without placing the text "Window." before their names. For example, the following two lines serve identical roles:

```
Window.MyProcedure(arg1, arg2)

MyProcedure(arg1, arg2)
```

NOTE *To refer to an item that is a member of some object, use the* dot *syntax. Place a period (.) between the object to which you refer and the item that it contains. This can nest to several levels, for example:*

```
Document.Button1.Value = "Press Me"
```

One consequence of the script routines being on the same level as the Window object is that all of its properties, methods, and events become reserved words in whatever scripting language you use. Hence, you cannot use the names of any of the Window elements to name your variables or routines.

If you use Explorer's frame capabilities, you may well want to access script functions or controls in documents held by other frames. The Top and Parent properties of the Window object enable you to gain access to these frames without having to refer explicitly to their names (see the section "The Frames Array—Lots of Little Windows" for more details).

Navigation is simple using the object model. For simple navigation, use the Navigate method to load a different URL into the browser window. The Location object is also available.

A handy way to customize the browser, and display context-sensitive messages is to use the Explorer window's status bar. Assign your message string to the Status property after loading the document. You can use the status bar to display help messages when the user moves over ActiveX controls or links. Alternatively, you could scroll a greeting or advertising message across the status bar by using it in conjunction with timers. See the section, "Setting and Clearing Timeouts," in this chapter.

Naming a Window

Window names are most important when you use frames, because they enable you to identify each part of your document more easily. Before you can access a window using frames, you must assign it a Name, in one of three ways:

- Naming the window using the <FRAMSET> tag

  Example (creates two windows, named *Banner* and *Main*, as part of a frame-set):

```
<FRAMESET rows = "40%, 60%">
    <FRAME Name="Banner" src="banner.htm">
    <FRAME Name="Main" src="main.htm">
</FRAMSET>
```

- Opening a new window using Window.Open

  Example (opens a window, named TOCWindow, that has the default properties and default size, and contains the file contents.htm):

```
<SCRIPT Language="VBScript">
Sub Button1_OnClick
    Open "contents.htm", "TOCWindow"
End Sub
</SCRIPT>
```

- Creating the window using a TARGET attribute

  Example (opens a window, InfoWin, that contains the file other.htm):

```
<A HREF="other.htm" TARGET="InfoWin">Select his link for more
➥information</A>
```

Opening and Closing Windows

The Window object supports two methods, Open and Close, which you use to open and close instances of the Explorer window. The simplest of the two is the Close method, which you use simply by typing the following (where *WindowName* is the name of the window you want to close):

```
WindowName.Close
```

Opening a window is a little more complicated (refer to Table 10-1 for the Open function's signature). The URL and Target parameters are quite straightforward, specifying a correctly parsed URL string and the name of the new window, respectively. The intHeight and intWidth parameters specify the size of the new window. The only argument that requires further explanation is WindowProperties, which indicates the features required of the new window. This is a list of item names and Boolean values separated by commas, and can contain entries for the following:

- Toolbar
- Location
- Directories
- Status
- Menu bar
- Scroll bars
- Resizeable

Boolean values that are acceptable include Yes, No, True, and False. To create a window without scroll bars or a menu bar, you would use the following line of code:

```
NewWindow = Window.Open "http://www.site.com/page.htm", "WindowName",
➥"toolbar=yes, scrollbars=no, menubar=no, status=yes", 800, 600
```

TIP

When you use the Open method to create a new window, make sure that the file or location you try to access exists on the target machine. If it doesn't, the open operation cannot complete successfully and the original copy of Internet Explorer hangs, which doesn't exactly benefit your Web site's corporate image.

Using the Window Dialogs

All the examples in the previous chapters have used VBScript's MsgBox function to display message boxes. Alternative methods for displaying message boxes are available using the Window object: you can use the Alert, Confirm, and Prompt methods to inform the user of certain conditions or to retrieve information.

The Alert method displays the message string passed to the procedure in a dialog box on the screen. The alert message box shown here was generated by this line of code:

```
Alert "A new Video has been downloaded and can be viewed now"
```

The Alert method doesn't provide as much flexibility as the MsgBox function, but it's easier to use. The two functions seem to behave slightly differently, and caused some trouble with the ViewTracker control example in Chapter 12, "ActiveX Controls and VBScript," (see that example for an explanation).

The Confirm method displays a message box that contains OK and Cancel buttons, and which you can use to ask yes or no questions. The function returns a Boolean value regardless of which button the user chooses. When the user presses OK, Confirm returns True, and vice versa. You usually use confirmation dialog boxes to ask whether the user wants to continue. The following example dialog was the result of this line of VBScript:

```
blnAnswer = Confirm "This will submit data to a server. Do you wish to
➥continue?"
```

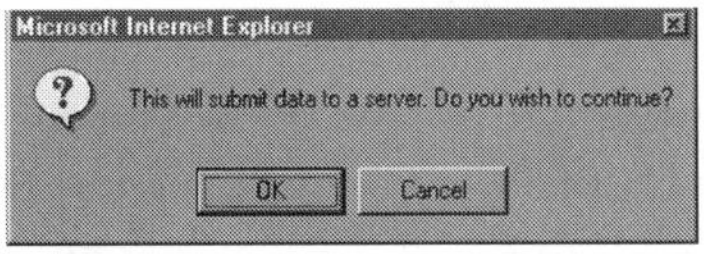

Last, but not least, you can use the Prompt method to get input from the user. You can provide a prompt string and a default reply to the function. Prompt returns the string that the user types. The picture below is a sample prompt dialog box generated by this line of code:

```
strAddress1 = Prompt "Please enter Address Line 1", "10 Church Close"
```

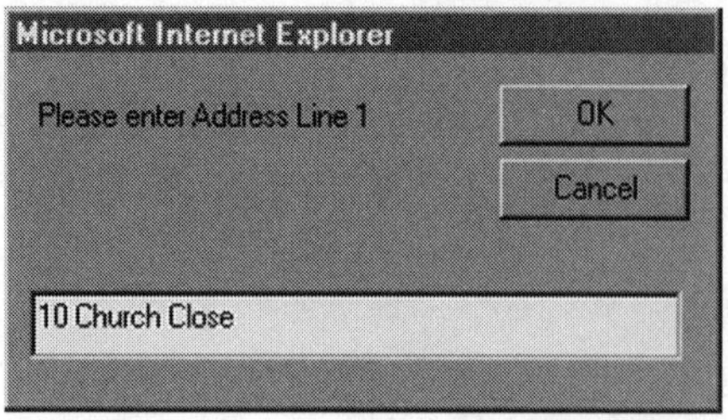

Setting and Clearing Timeouts

Two methods of the Window object make setting and using timers in your scripts blissfully simple. You use the SetTimeout and ClearTimeout methods in conjunction to set up and cancel these timers. You can use a timer to call a function or execute a line of code after an interval specified in milliseconds.

The timer fires only once, so to repeat an action, you must reset the timer each time it expires. Table 10-1 gave the syntax for the SetTimeout and ClearTimeout methods, but this section illustrates their use. You can load the sample document by using the `Setting and Clearing Timeouts` link on the book's main Web page.

The document consists of some text and two HTML button controls (discussed in Chapter 11, "Using Forms with VBScript"). When you press the first button, an event handler sets a timer to fire after 100 milliseconds. After 100 milliseconds elapse, the timer fires and calls the procedure Timer_Proc(). This procedure changes the background color of the document to a random color and sets another timer to fire after another 100 milliseconds. The process continues indefinitely until the user presses the second button. The event procedure for this button clears the current timer using the ClearTimeout method. Figure 10-3 shows what the document should look like after you load it into your browser.

This example introduces some new items, including the document color attributes (described later in this chapter) and the BUTTON element (covered in Chapter 11, "Using Forms with VBScript").

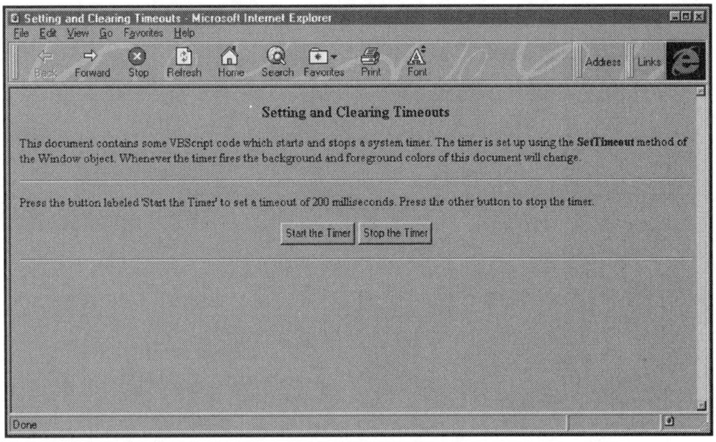

FIGURE 10-3
The example document, Setting and Clearing Timeouts

```
<HTML>
<HEAD>
<TITLE>Setting and Clearing Timeouts</TITLE>
<SCRIPT LANGUAGE="VBScript">
<!—
'********************************
' Script to make the document background flash in different colors
➥using system timers.
'********************************
Dim intTimerID                        'ID of the current timer
intTimerID = 0

'********************************
' Sets the first timer
'********************************
Sub StartButton_OnClick
    Randomize()                        'Set up the random number seed
    'Now set a 100 ms timeout and call Timer_Proc after that time
    intTimerID = SetTimeout ("Call Timer_Proc()", 100, "VBScript")
End Sub

'********************************
' Stops the current timer
```

```
'******************************
Sub StopButton_OnClick
    If intTimerID <> 0 Then       'Only stops an active timer
        ClearTimeout (intTimerID)
        intTimerID = 0
        Document.bgColor="gray"   'Reset document colors to sensible
➥values
        Document.fgColor="black"
    End If
End Sub

'******************************
' Timer procedure - changes colors and resets the timer
'******************************
Sub Timer_Proc
    Document.bgColor = Rnd * 255 * 255 * 255
    Document.fgColor = "#ffff00"
    intTimerID = SetTimeout ("Call Timer_Proc()", 100, "VBScript")
End Sub
->
</SCRIPT>
</HEAD>
<BODY>
<CENTER><H3>Setting and Clearing Timeouts</H3></CENTER>
This document contains some VBScript code which starts and stops a
➥system timer. The timer is set up using
the <B>SetTimeout</B> method of the Window object. Whenever the timer
➥fires the background and foreground
colors of this document will change.
<HR>
Press the button labeled 'Start the Timer' to set a timeout of 200
➥milliseconds. Press the other button to stop the timer.
<P>
<CENTER>
<INPUT TYPE="Button" NAME="StartButton" VALUE="Start the Timer">
```

```
<INPUT TYPE="Button" NAME="StopButton" VALUE="Stop the Timer">
</CENTER>
<HR>
</BODY>
</HTML>
```

Using the Window Events

Before concluding the discussion of the Window object, one topic remains—the Window events. The Window object supports only two events namely, OnLoad and OnUnload. You probably wonder just when exactly these events are generated.

The OnLoad event is triggered after the browser has loaded and parsed the entire HTML contents of the document. It fires before the document appears and preempts any user interaction. Therefore, the *Window_OnLoad* event handler is the perfect place for initializing object attributes and other dynamic items—which you can't do using code in the HEAD section of the document, because the browser would not have created the objects being initialized at that point. Chapters 11 and 12 both contain examples that utilize the OnLoad event.

The OnUnload event is triggered when the contents of the current document are unloaded from the browser, such as when the user exits the Explorer program or loads another document. You can use the Window_OnUnload event handler to stop tasks that have been repeating in the background or to provide a farewell message or fanfare. Consider the previous timer example. Instead of using a button to stop the timers from running, you could have used the *OnUnload* event to clear the system timer when the document was unloaded.

The Frames Array—Lots of Little Windows

The *Frames* array is not an object with its own properties and methods, but rather, is an array of Window objects that represent any frames that the current document contains. Frames are a relatively new addition to the HTML standard, and enable you to produce much more interesting documents. HTML 3.2 includes the <FRAMESET> and <FRAME> tags, but you should be aware that the specifications may change slightly, or expand, in the future. Explorer 3.0 and Netscape's new Navigator support frames (as do some other browsers), so most users will be able to use documents with frames after they obtain current versions of their software.Frames can be named, and the objects and script routines they contain can be accessed from other frame windows using these names.

The Frames array has one property, which is available to all array objects in VBScript. The number of frames that a particular document contains is stored in the Length property of the Frames array. If the document doesn't contain any frames, the length is zero. You can use the Length property, and the Frames array itself, to perform an operation on all the frames that a particular document contains. For example, you might set the document colors in each frame. You could use a section of code like this:

```
<SCRIPT LANGUAGE="VBScript">
<!-
Sub Change_Frames()
    Dim intLoop
    For intLoop = 0 to Frames.Length-1
        Frames(intLoop).Document.bgColor = "#000080"        'Set frame
➥background to dark blue
        Frames(intLoop).Document.fgColor = "#ffff00"        'Set frame
➥foreground to yellow
    Next
End Sub
->
</SCRIPT>
```

NOTE *The loop variable, intLoop, is set to count from zero to the length of the array minus one, because VBScript arrays are zero-based.*

Setting Up Frames

Frames work by displaying different HTML files in separate areas of the browser window. These frame windows can have scroll bars and can be resized by the user. You also can define borderless frames that users cannot resize. Internet Explorer 3.0 also introduces floating frames, which you can position anywhere within a document.

The frames must be organized by using <FRAMESET> tags in the parent document. The parent document usually is fairly simple, containing only the essential HTML tags and some <FRAMESET> definitions. The real content of the Web page(s) is in the HTML files that are loaded into each frame.

You can use the <FRAMESET> tag to set up a frame document, which separates the window vertically or horizontally. If you need some column windows and some row windows, you can nest the frameset definitions because <FRAMESET> is a container tag. You use percentages (%), pixels, or a wild card (*) to specify the sizes of the windows. If you use a wild card character, it instructs the browser to use whatever space is left over for that row or column. Here are some example framesets:

```
<FRAMESET COLS="120,300,*">
```

The above frameset defines a frame document with three columns of 120 pixels, 300 pixels, and whatever is left as the column widths.

```
<FRAMSET ROWS="*,27%"
```

This one results in a document with two frames, the larger one being the top frame.

The HawkEye phone call logging program developed later in Chapter 14, "Using the Internet Control Pack and Java Applets with VBScript," uses frames. Figure 10-4 shows an early version of the document with three frames, and includes the HTML source code that defines the frame windows. Note also, two framesets are defined; the first separates the window into two rows and the second splits the larger section into two columns. Several items can appear within the <FRAMESET> and </FRAMESET> tags, including the <FRAME>

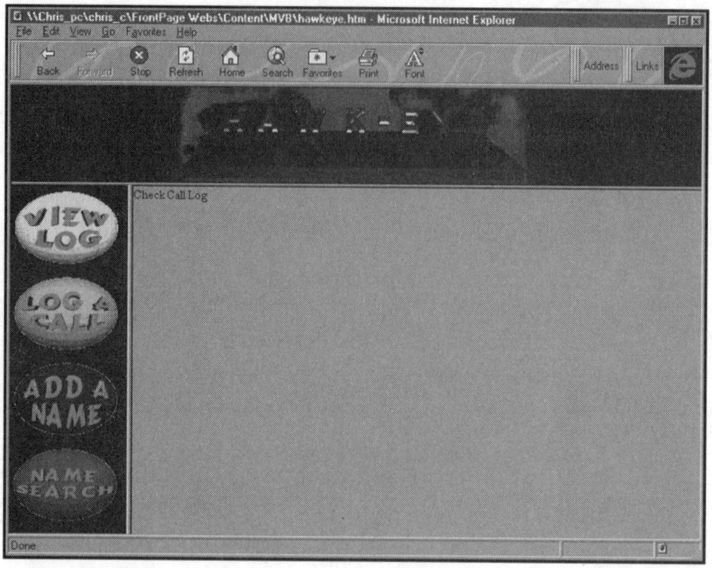

FIGURE 10-4
Frame windows—an early version of the HawkEye call logging system

and <NOFRAMES> tags. You don't need to study the HawkEye program right now, it's simply another example of using frames.

The <FRAME> tag defines the name, contents, and attributes for a particular frame in a frameset. You can use the <FRAME> tag to specify the margin sizes, frame spacing, resizing options, and URL. Visit `http://www.microsoft.com/ie` to find the complete details for the frame support in Internet Explorer. Otherwise, experiment with the source code shown below to see what effect the different options have.

Finally, you can use the <NOFRAMES> tag to provide information for browsers that don't support frames. The best use for this tag is to inform the user that they need to update their browser (politely!), or to provide a link to a non-frames version of the document that they can use. <NOFRAMES> is a container tag, so you just place any content you want to appear between the <NOFRAMES> and </NOFRAMES> tags. The HawkEye example includes such an entry.

TIP

If you declare a frame document to have N frames, you should have a total of N <FRAME> or further <FRAMESET> entries in that set. If you don't have enough frames, the browser has every right to misbehave and parse your document incorrectly.

```
<!DOCTYPE HTML PUBLIC "-//W3O/DTD HTML//EN">

<html>
<head>
<title>HawkEye Phone Center</title>
</head>
<frameset rows="102,*">
    <frame frameborder="NO" src="frbanner.htm" name="banner"
➥marginwidth="1"
    marginheight="1" NORESIZE>
    <frameset cols="130,*">
        <frame src="frconten.htm" name="contents" marginwidth="1"
        marginheight="1">
        <frame src="frmain.htm" name="main" marginwidth="1"
        marginheight="1">
    </frameset>
    <noframes>
    <body>
    <p> </p>
    <p>This Web page uses frames, but your browser doesn't
    support them.</p>
    </body>
    </noframes>
</frameset>
</html>
```

NOTE

The HTML source code for the phone call logging system contains this line of text, which is the header you should include when your documents use the HTML 3.2 language extensions:

```
<!DOCTYPE HTML PUBLIC "-//W3O/DTD HTML//EN">
```

Without this header line, browsers may have trouble identifying the version of HTML that the document uses. The <!DOCTYPE> tag is explained in Chapter 9 "Writing Well-Organized and Coherent VBScript."

Accessing Other Frame Members

An important thing to remember when creating frame documents is that scripts must be able to interact *across* frames. To the viewer of a framed document, it appears as a single entity. The fact that it consists of three separate documents doesn't matter to the viewer. To develop scripts for these pages, however, it matters very much to the programmer. With that in mind, this section looks at how to access different frames from your scripts.

You have already seen that frame windows are accessible through the Frames array, but you know that referring to frames by name is more advisable whenever possible. You, and anybody who may need to alter you scripts, can then quickly gather to which window a certain command is referring. You name frames by including the NAME="FrameName" clause inside the defining <FRAME> tag. Examples are

```
<FRAME SRC="frconten.htm" NAME="contents">
```

and

```
<FRAME SRC="frmain.htm" NAME="main" MARGINWIDTH="1" MARGINHEIGHT="1">
```

After you define a frame window with a name, accessing the items that window contains is relatively simple. For example, the following displays the name of the window *contents* in a message dialog:

```
MsgBox "Title is " & contents.Name
```

Although perhaps rather trivial, you also can access the ActiveX controls and HTML form elements that another window contains. You can then place all the script code for an application in the main frame window, leaving your designers free to work on the textual and graphical content of the frames themselves.

Handling the interactions between frames can be tricky. The HawkEye Phone Center application in Chapter 14, "Using the Internet Control Pack and Java Applets with VBScript," is written using frames and its source code contains several references to different frame windows that make up the whole example.

The History Object—Backward and Forward

That concludes the discussion of the top level of the scripting model. Several other objects are members of the Window object (refer to Figure 10-1). The first of these is the History object, which gives the script writer access to the Explorer history list, (that is, the URLs of any pages that have been loaded in the current session). The History object doesn't actually give the full URL—you access items according to their position in the history list, meaning, the History object isn't exceptionally useful. The history list is different every time someone uses the browser.

The History object does have its uses, though, especially when writing scripts that deal with several documents linked in a particular way. You may want to provide buttons, or use timers to move backward and forward through a selection of Web pages. The Location object or HTML client-pull both are better suited for this task, however. Table 10-2 lists the properties and methods available.

Table 10-2 The History Object

	PROPERTIES
Length	Returns the length of the browser's history list.
	METHODS
Back	Signature is *Back n*. Moves back through the history list by *n* items. This has exactly the same effect as clicking on the Back button on the toolbar *n* times.
Forward	Signature is *Forward n*. Moves forward through the history list by *n* items. This has exactly the same effect as clicking on the Forward button on the toolbar *n* times.
Go	Signature is *Go n*. Moves to the item at position *n* in the History list. The first item is item number 1.
	EVENTS
None	

Here a couple examples of using the History object.

This one moves the browser to the last item in the history list:

```
History.Go History.Length
```

This one moves the browser to the first item in the history list:

```
History.Go 1
```

If the argument specified for the position is beyond the end of the list, nothing happens.

> CAUTION **One reason to stay away from using the history list is that people might worry that sites can track their Web browsing. By revisting the sites in somebody's history list, you can discover their browsing habits. Visitors to your site might be concerned about you finding out about their visits to *Playboy*, and so on. So, Web page developers may want to be cautious about using the History object.**

The Navigator Object—Browser Information

This object provides information about the browser application itself. The name may seem strange, but it reflects the fact that Netscape designed the original object model for scripting applications. Table 10-3 shows the details of this object.

You can load an example file to determine exactly which version of your browser you're using. Choose the `Browser Information - Using the Navigator Object` link on the main Web page. The Document object's Write method is used to modify the contents of the HTML file as it loads. See the section on the Document object later in this chapter for further details.

Table 10-3 The Navigator Object

	PROPERTIES
AppCodeName	Returns the current application code name
AppName	Returns the current application name
AppVersion	Returns the current application version
UserAgent	Returns the current application user agent
	METHODS
None	
	EVENTS
None	

```
<HTML>
<HEAD>
<TITLE>Browser Information - Using the Navigator Object</TITLE>
</HEAD>
<BODY>
<CENTER><H3>Browser Information - Using the Navigator Object</H3>
➥<CENTER>
<HR>
<CENTER>
<B>Application Code Name:-</B>
<SCRIPT LANGUAGE="VBScript">
    Document.Write(" " &  Navigator.AppCodeName)
</SCRIPT><P>
<B>Application Name:-</B>
<SCRIPT LANGUAGE="VBScript">
    Document.Write(" " &  Navigator.AppName)
</SCRIPT><P>
<B>Application Version:-</B>
<SCRIPT LANGUAGE="VBScript">
    Document.Write(" " &  Navigator.AppVersion)
```

```
</SCRIPT><P>
<B>Application User Agent:-</B>
<SCRIPT LANGUAGE="VBScript">
    Document.Write(" " &  Navigator.UserAgent)
</SCRIPT><P>
</CENTER>
<HR>
</BODY>
</HTML>
```

The sections of script have been inserted inline in the document, because they have an immediate effect. To position the text the scriptlets produce correctly, you must place the script code where you need it, rather than in the HEAD section. Figure 10-5 shows a sample of this document's output.

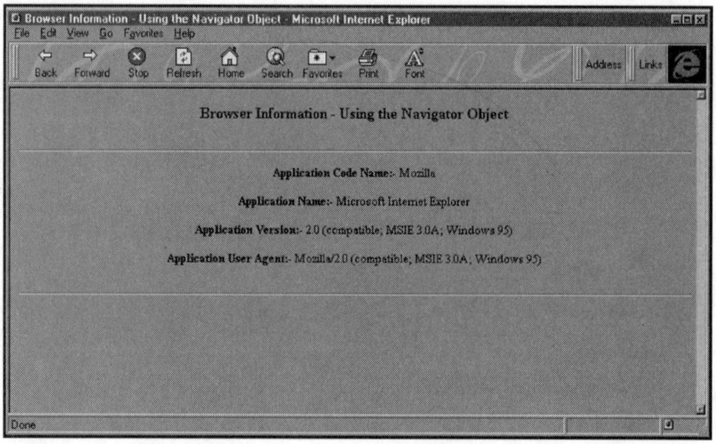

FIGURE 10-5
Using the Navigator Object to determine browser statistics

The Location Object—Moving through Cyberspace

The Location object represents the current URL displayed in the window. It breaks the URL down into its constituent parts, as well as allowing the programmer to read/write the entire URL at once. Assigning values to any of the members of the Location object causes the browser to load the document specified by the newly constructed URL.

Table 10-4	The Location Object
	PROPERTIES
HRef	This property is used to retrieve or set the complete URL for the document.
Protocol	Retrieves or stores the protocol section of the URL.
Host	Retrieves or stores the host and port section of the URL (host-name:port).
Hostname	Retrieves or stores the host section of the URL. This can written as an IP address or a domain name. For file protocols this property is always "".
Port	Retrieves or stores the port section of the URL. For file protocols this property is always "".
Pathname	Retrieves or stores the pathname section of the URL. This is the portion of the URL that specifies the actual directory and file on the Web site, e.g. /ie/activex/default.htm.
Search	Retrieves or stores the search section of the URL. The search portion starts with a question mark (?). If there is no search portion, this property will be return Null.
Hash	Retrieves or stores the protocol section of the URL. If there is no hash section this will simply return "#". The hash portion of an URL refers to internal anchors in the document.
	METHODS
None	
	EVENTS
None	

You generally use the Location object to set a complete URL. Assigning a value to the Href property causes the browser to try to load the document specified by that string. For example, the following line will navigate the browser to Microsoft's Web site, and load the document default.htm from the VBScript part of the site:

```
Location.HRef = "http://www.microsoft.com/vbscript/"
```

Another use for the Location object is to navigate within a document, using the Hash property, an example of which is presented in the next section.

Navigating within a Document

The Hash property refers to the hash portion of an URL. In the following example, it's the part of the URL printed in a bold typeface.

```
http://www.vbscript.com/docs/reference.htm#function_list
```

The #function_list instructs the browser to navigate to the anchor named "function_list" in the file reference.htm. Anchors are defined in a similar way to links, using the <A> tag. The difference is an absence of a HREF="someURL" clause when defining an anchor. Anchors need to be named, however, before they can be useful—the anchor name is used in the hash portion of the URL.

To name an anchor, use the NAME="AnchorName" clause, as follows:

```
<A NAME="Link1" >This is an anchor called Link1</A>
```

This line of HTML defines an anchor called Link1.

NOTE *The <A> tag is a container tag. Anything that appears between the <A> and </A> tags becomes part of the link or anchor. This means you can use images, or even ActiveX controls, as links.*

The CD contains an example that uses script routines to navigate around a document. You can load it by choosing the `Internal Navigation - Using the Location Object` link on the main Web page. Figure 10-6 shows the example in action.

The document contains three buttons and three anchors. Pressing each of the buttons calls a different event procedure. These procedures then assign values to the Hash property of the window's Location object to move around the file. Although this is just a simple example, you could use it to great effect on a more complicated Web site.

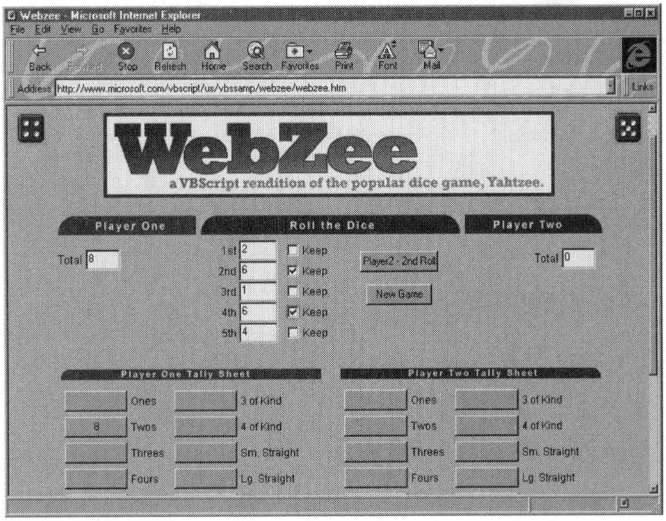

FIGURE 10-6 *Using the Location object to navigate within a document*

```
<HTML>
<HEAD>
<TITLE>Internal Navigation - Using the Location Object</TITLE>
<SCRIPT LANGUAGE="VBScript">
<!—
Sub Button1_OnClick
    Location.hash = "Link1"
    MsgBox "Now moving to Link1"
End Sub

Sub Button2_OnClick
    Location.hash = "Link2"
    MsgBox "Now moving to Link2"
End Sub

Sub Button3_OnClick
    Location.hash = "Link3"
    MsgBox "Now moving to Link3"
End Sub
—>
</SCRIPT>
</HEAD>
```

```
<BODY>
<CENTER><H3>Internal Navigation - Using the Location Object</H3>
➥</CENTER>
This document contains three anchors, which are used to mark specific
➥points on
a page. These points are usually section headings. <P>
Using the Location object script routines can move the user to a
➥particular part of a
document. This would be most useful as part of a search engine - the
➥user would be
navigated to the relevant section of a reference document after
➥performing a search.
<HR>
There are three anchors defined in this document, called <B>Link1</B>,
➥<B>Link2</B>,
and <B>Link3</B> respectively. Press the buttons at the top of the
➥page to navigate to
the different positions.<P>
<CENTER>
<INPUT TYPE="Button" Name="Button1" VALUE="Move to Link1">
<INPUT TYPE="Button" Name="Button2" VALUE="Move to Link2">
<INPUT TYPE="Button" Name="Button3" VALUE="Move to Link3"><P>
<HR>
<A NAME="Link1" >This is an anchor called Link1</A>
<P>-<P>-<P>-<P>-<P>-<P>-<P>-<P>-<P>
<A NAME="Link2">This is an anchor called Link2</A>
<P>-<P>-<P>-<P>-<P>-<P>-<P>-<P>-<P>
<A NAME="Link3">This is an anchor called Link3</A>
</CENTER>
<HR>
</BODY>
</HTML>
```

Script Elements—Putting the Puzzle Together

Any script code written in an HTML file resides at the same level in the hierarchy as the Window object itself. This means that all of the Window properties, methods, and events become reserved words in the scripting language.

All the current script functions, code, and so on, become part of the Object Model instance of the running copy of the browser. You already know how to define and name frame windows. You can access the scripts that these windows contain from other frames, using the same method as for accessing the built-in items.

Imagine that the HawkEye example had a script function called Validate_Call() stored in the file frmain.htm. To access this from one of the other frame windows (not the file that contains the <FRAMESET> tags), you would use the following line of code:

```
Top.Main.Validate_Call()
```

Main is the name given to the frame, and is a child window of the topmost document. The essential point is that naming is important in scripting. After you give an item a name, it is almost always accessible to a section of script code, even when it's in another document.

The Document Object—Links, Anchors, Forms and More

The Document object sits just below the Window in the Object Model hierarchy. It's important because it provides access to the HTML elements on the page being displayed. These elements include the links, anchors, and forms in the current document. Forms have an important role in scripting (see Chapter 11, "Using Forms with VBScript").

Figure 10-7 shows the Object Model for Scripting hierarchy, for convenient reference as the discussion picks it back up.

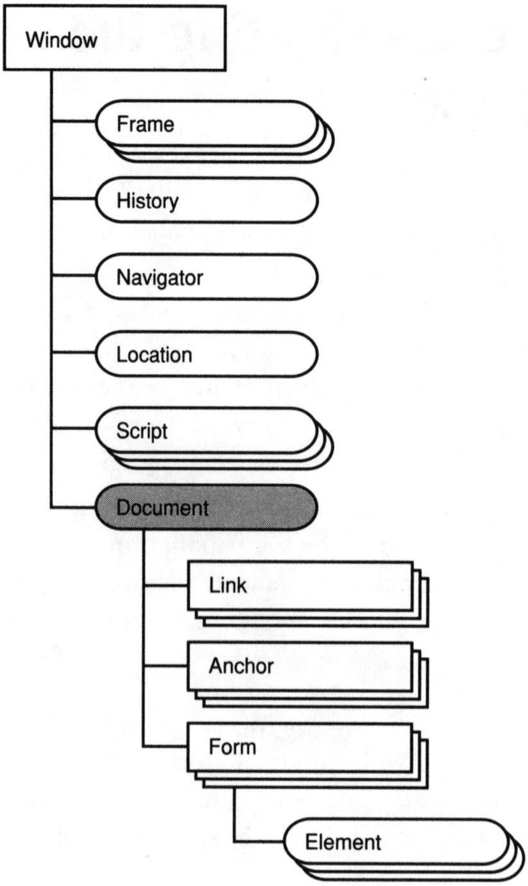

FIGURE 10-7
The Object Model for scripting hierarchy, revisited

You can use the Document object to modify the actual HTML content of a document, although only at parse time. It's quite useful for generating context-sensitive information, such as dates and times, visit counts, or query results. See the section "Modifying the Document at Run-time" for more details. Before discussing the Document any further, Table 10-5 provides a complete list of its features.

Table 10-5 The Document Object	
	PROPERTIES
LinkColor	Sets or retrieves the color of links in a document.
ALinkColor	Sets or retrieves the color of active links in a document. Active links are currently not supported by Internet Explorer.
VLinkColor	Sets or retrieves the color of visited links in a document.
bgColor	Sets or retrieves the background color of a document.
fgColor	Sets or retrieves the foreground color of a document.
LastModified	Returns the date when the document was last modified.
Title	Returns a string containing the document's title. This property is read-only.
Cookie	Sets or retrieves the document's current cookie. Cookies are explained in the section "Using the Cookie Property—It's Not Edible."
Referrer	Returns the URL of the referring document.
Location	Returns a read-only copy of the Window's Location object.
Links	Returns the array of links for the document.
Anchors	Returns the array of anchors for the document.
Forms	Returns the array of HTML forms for the document.
	METHODS
Write	Signature is *Write strText.* Writes the text stored in *strText* into the current document. This can only be used at parse time.
WriteLn	Signature is *WriteLn strText.* Writes the text stored in *strText* into the current document. This can only be used at parse time. This method is the same as *Write*, except for the addition of a newline character at the end of the line being written.

Table 10-5 The Document Object

	METHODS
Open	Signature is *Open [mimetype]*. Opens the document stream for output. The mime type is an optional parameter and can be used to specifiy any valid mime type supported by your browser.
Close	Closes the document stream and updates the screen to display all the data that has been written since the last invokation of the *Open* method.
Clear	Clears the current document. See the section "Modifying the Document at Run-time" for more details on all these methods.
	EVENTS
None	

This section takes a detailed look at some of the Document object's components, but first, a few of its properties deserve mention.

The HTML 3.2 standards stipulate that the title of a document must be set using the <TITLE> tags. The W3C has set this requirement to ensure that users can identify documents at a glance.

TIP *After a document loads, its title cannot change, but the Title property can be used in scripts to customize messages. Use the Document's Title as the dialog box title for the MsgBox function—this makes your Web applications look much more professional.*

Most documents on the WWW are reached by navigating from another document. The URL of the referring document is stored in the Referrer property. This property is likely to be different each time the document loads, but can serve navigation purposes.

Information on the WWW can age quickly, so you should include the last modification date somewhere on a document; especially when you're talking about software releases, bugs, and products in development. You don't have to edit this section by hand every time you make a modification—you can use the LastModified property instead. A section of HTML and VBScript like this does the trick:

```
...
...
<CENTER>Last Updated :-
<SCRIPT LANGUAGE="VBScript">
<!—
    Document.Write(" " & Document.LastModified)
—>
</SCRIPT>
</CENTER>
...
...
```

You should place the preceding fragment exactly where you want the date to appear, because it's parsed and output as soon as the browser encounters it.

Using the Cookie Property—It's Not Edible

The Cookie property is effectively a text file that you can attach to a particular document. It can contain a string of different values separated by semi-colons and is one solution to a common problem when writing WWW applications—saving values across documents. The VBScript samples page on Microsoft's Web site has an example that uses cookies to store and retrieve user-defined variables.

The Cookie property is set to contain items in the following format:

```
"varname1=value1;varname2=value2;...;varnameN=valueN"
```

A VBScript function written by Microsoft uses string manipulation to look for a variable name and return the value associated with that variable from the Cookie property. By default, cookies expire at the end of a user's session. If you want to preserve values longer than that, you can insert a particular extra clause, the *expires* clause, which sets an expiration date for the cookie:

```
"varname1=value1;expires=01-Jul-96 GMT;...;varnameN=valueN;expires=20-
Aug-96 GMT"
```

If you want to use cookies in your document, you definitely should take a look at the sample on Microsoft's Web site:

```
http://www.microsoft.com/vbscript/us/vbssamp/cookies/extcookie.htm
```

You also can access a complete explanation of cookies on Yahoo's Web site at

```
http://www.yahoo.com/computers_and_internet/internet/world_wide_Web/http
/protocol_specification/persistent_cookies/
```

VBScript is a safe language and provides no access to the user's hard disk, so writing applications that save any data is difficult. The data could range from preferred color schemes to personal details to calculation values. Using cookies is about the only way to store such information, and with a little thought and some experimentation, most modestly ambitious applications are possible.

Modifying the Document at Run-time

Ideally, a script writer would be able to modify a document at any time. This complete flexibility would impose a large processing overhead on a browser—it would have to reinterpret and display the document after each individual change. Consequently, any changes to the HTML content of a document must be made during loading of the document.

Making changes to HTML content during loading is achieved by inserting sections of inline code in the relevant positions throughout a document. You have just seen how to use this technique to insert a modification date. You also can create whole documents using script code and the methods of the Document object.

The Write method places the given string at the current position in a document. It only has an effect during parsing of a document, including the time when a document is loading and any point between calls to the Document.Open method and the Document.Close method. A slightly different method is WriteLn, which outputs the given string and a new-line character.

NOTE *Be aware that an HTML interpreter ignores new-line characters unless they appear between <PRE> and </PRE> tags. Usually, but not always, Write and WriteLn behave identically.*

If you want or need to create a document from scratch, you can use the Open, Write, Close, and Clear methods.

Open usually is followed by a set of calls to Write or WriteLn that provides the content for the new page. If the Open method is called from an existing document, the current contents are cleared. Note that VBScript is a safe language and doesn't overwrite the file itself, it simply clears the browser's page. Pressing the Refresh button (F5) brings back the original document contents.

Clear simply clears the current contents of a document, and is equivalent to this sequence:

```
Document.Open()
Document.Close()
```

Call the Close method after inserting the set of new lines into the document. Be careful not to call Close during parsing of the document, because it could cause the browser to behave unpredictably. Don't call Close in a line of code that doesn't lie within an event procedure or function.

You can load an example that uses these capabilities by choosing the `Modifying a Document at Run-time` link on the main Web page on the CD. It inserts a modification date into the page as it loads. There is also an HTML button which when pressed, opens a new page, and writes a message to it. Figure 10-8 shows the document as it should appear after you load it.

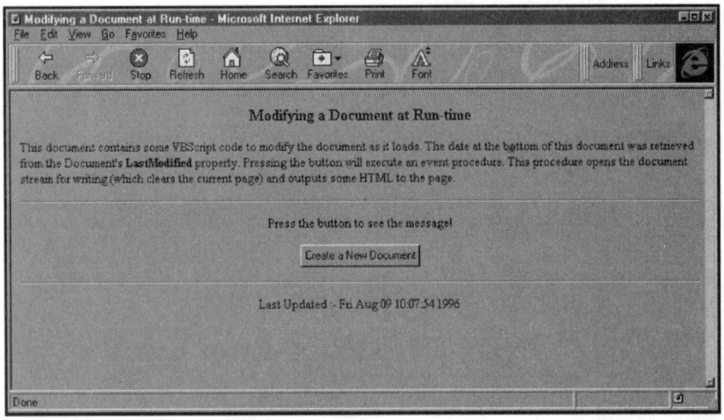

FIGURE 10-8
Using Document object methods to alter a document at parse-time

```
<HTML>
<HEAD>
<TITLE>Modifying a Document at Run-time</TITLE>
<SCRIPT LANGUAGE="VBScript">
<!-
Sub WriteButton_OnClick
    Document.Open()
    Document.Write("<CENTER><H2>Welcome to VBScript</H2></CENTER><P>")
    Document.Write("You will now have to reload the original docu-
ment!")
    Document.Close()
End Sub
->
</SCRIPT>
</HEAD>

<BODY>
<CENTER><H3>Modifying a Document at Run-time</H3></CENTER>
This document contains some VBScript code to modify the document as it
loads. The date at the bottom of this
document was retrieved from the Document's <B>LastModified</B> proper-
ty. Pressing the button will execute
an event procedure. This procedure opens the document stream for writ-
ing (which clears the current page) and
outputs some HTML to the page.
<HR>
<CENTER>
Press the button to see the message!<P>
<INPUT TYPE="Button" NAME="WriteButton" VALUE="Create a New Document">
</CENTER>
<HR>
<CENTER>Last Updated :-
<SCRIPT LANGUAGE="VBScript">
<!-
    Document.Write(" " & Document.LastModified)
->
```

```
</SCRIPT>
</CENTER>
</BODY>
</HTML>
```

Setting Document Colors

The Document object supports different colors for the links in a document. The object model further subdivides this into normal, active, and visited links. You can set these colors only at parse time, because the VBScript designers considered the performance hit of redrawing all the links in a document too great.

NOTE

An active link *is one in which you hold the mouse button over the link without releasing. If you then release the mouse button over the link, the browser navigates to the link's target; if not, the link goes back to its normal color. Internet Explorer doesn't currently support active links, but has included them in the Object Model for compatibility.*

One possible use for the link colors (LinkColor, ALinkColor, VLinkColor) would be in conjunction with the Cookie property. The user's preferred color scheme could be stored in the Cookie and retrieved during reload of the document. The colors could be set at parse time, giving the user some fine-grained control over their document. The effort involved in this would be justified only on frequently accessed pages; for example, a home page on an Intranet.

Foreground and background colors of the document can be set at any time, and the screen is updated immediately. You probably have seen several examples of this already in the book (see the section "Setting and Clearing Timeouts" earlier in this chapter).

The Links Array—Where to Go from Here

What is the Links array? Most documents contain links to other pages on your Web site, or the WWW as a whole, and the Links array stores data on each of these links.

A link is defined by an anchor tag which contains an HREF="someURL" clause, such as

```
<A HREF="http://www.epic.com">Click here to move somewhere</A>
```

Whenever the browser encounters such a declaration, it adds an entry to the Links array. These entries are in fact read-only versions of the Location object. Table 10-6 lists and summarizes the properties of each item in the array.

Table 10-6 The Link Object

	PROPERTIES
HRef	This property returns the complete URL for the document.
Protocol	Returns the protocol section of the URL.
Host	Returns the host and port section of the URL. (hostname:port).
Hostname	Returns the host section of the URL. This can written as an IP address or a domain name. For file protocols this property is always "".
Port	Returns the port section of the URL. For file protocols this property is always "".
Pathname	Returns the pathname section of the URL. This is the portion of the URL that specifies the actual directory and file on the Web site, e.g. /ie/activex/default.htm.
Search	Returns the search section of the URL. The search portion starts with a question mark (?). If there is no search portion, this property will be return Null.
Hash	Returns the protocol section of the URL. If there is no hash section this will simply return "#". The hash portion of an URL refers to internal anchors in the document.
	METHODS
None	

	EVENTS
MouseMove	Signature is *MouseMove(shift, button, x, y)*. Fires any time the the mouse pointer moves over a link. See the section on 'Responding to Link Events'.
OnMouseOver	Fires any time the mouse moves over a link, but does not have any further status information. See the section on 'Responding to Link Events'.
OnClick.	Fires any time a mouse button is pressed over a link. See the section on "Responding to Link Events."

The Links array actually has an extra property. The number of links in a document is stored in the *Length* property of the array. The following line of code would print the number of links in the current document:

```
MsgBox "Number of links is " & Document.Links.Length
```

The locations pointed to by links cannot be changed after the document loads, which is the reason for the items in this array being read-only. If you do need to access any of the links in an array, you can do so in two ways. One, the indexed array can be used (remember, the first link is stored in the zeroth entry), and two, the name of the link can be used. For example, the following defines a link called MyLink and sets the window status bar equal to its URL:

```
<A NAME="MyLink" HREF="http://www.epic.com">Click here to move some-
where</A>
<SCRIPT LANGUAGE="VBScript">
    Window.Status = Document.Links(0).HRef
    Window.Status = MyLink.HRef
</SCRIPT>
```

Both lines of code within the script tags have the same effect. Using the Links array is better for writing loops, while naming individual links makes code more understandable.

Responding to Link Events

The Links array supports three events. Each individual link in the array can generate these events, so you should name your links if you want to write event handlers for them.

MouseMove is an event with four parameters. Shift indicates the status of the shift keys. A value of 1 means that it is held down, while a 0 means that it is not being pressed. Button indicates which button is being pressed, if any. A zero value means that no buttons are being pressed, while a 1 or 2 (or 3) indicates that one of the buttons is currently depressed. The X and Y parameters hold the current pointer position in pixels, and can be used to respond in different ways when the user moves (or clicks) over different parts of the link. If you don't require as much detail, then use the other two events (MouseOver and OnClick), which have no parameters.

MouseOver and OnClick are quite straightforward, and you can use them in the same way as the other events you have encountered.

One of the main uses for the link events is to set a message on the status bar as the pointer moves over a link, although as you develop more complex documents, you probably will want to use them to script custom actions. Consider the following code sample:

```
<A NAME="MyLink" HREF="http://www.epic.com">Click here to move some-
where</A>
...
...
<SCRIPT LANGUAGE="VBScript">
Sub MyLink_OnClick
    Window.Status = "Now loading document at " & MyLink.HRef & ".
Please Wait!"
End Sub
</SCRIPT>
...
...
<SCRIPT LANGUAGE="VBScript" FOR="MyLink" EVENT="MouseOver">
    MsgBox "You should visit this site for the latest stock prices!"
</SCRIPT>
```

The script shown here demonstrates two different ways of responding to events. The first uses the procedure name, MyLink_OnClick, to identify the event and object in question, while the second is a complete script section for one object only, `<SCRIPT LANGUAGE="VBScript" FOR="MyLink" EVENT="MouseOver">`.

The Anchors Array

Anchors basically are links, but with a significant essential difference—they don't refer to a separate document, but rather, to another point within the current document. The Anchors array stores the names of each anchor, and not much else.

You can use the Name property of each anchor to set or retrieve the name of the anchor. You initially set a name using the NAME="AnchorName" clause of the <A> tag. For example, you might use the following to define the Index heading of a document as an anchor called DocIndex:

```
<A NAME="DocIndex"><H3>Index</H3></A>
```

You could then change this name in the following two ways:

```
Document.Anchors(0).Name = "NewAnchor"
```

or

```
DocIndex.Name = "NewAnchor"
```

As with most of the object arrays that this book has covered, the Anchors array has a Length element that stores the number of anchors in the current document (it's read-only). The following line of VBScript displays a message dialog box showing the number of anchors in the current document:

```
MsgBox "Number of anchors is " & Document.Anchors.Length
```

Form Processing and the Object Model

Check Figure 10-6 now and see if you can find two items this chapter hasn't yet examined. The Form and Element objects represent the forms and HTML elements that a document contains. This is a large and important topic, and Chapter 11, "Using Forms with VBScript," deals solely with these two parts of the Object Model. Form processing is much more specific than the various items that this chapter covers and the next chapter includes examples of all the different form elements.

What Next?

This chapter has dealt with the major structural details of the Object Model for Scripting. By now, you should have a good idea of what the Object Model is and the possibilities for controlling Internet Explorer with VBScript. This chapter should prove useful as a reference to the individual components that make up the model. Now it's time to take another step and move into forms processing with VBScript.

Chapter 11, "Using Forms with VBScript," builds on the topics covered so far by giving examples of the HTML elements available for use in forms, and also provides details of the properties, methods, and events that each one supports. The chapters following Chapter 11 move on to some new technologies for using objects on the World Wide Web—most notably, Microsoft's new ActiveX technology.

CHAPTER 11

Using Forms with VBScript

The last chapter introduced the Internet Explorer Object Model for Scripting and discussed the objects that the browser provides. One essential element was left out of that discussion—how to use forms with VBScript. This chapter covers placing and using HTML form controls within your documents.

This area of the HTML standards continues to evolve, and this book tries to provide the most accurate and up-to-date information so that the documents you produce use these features of the language effectively.

This chapter covers the following topics:

- History and background of form processing using HTML
- New standards for scripting using form controls
- Applications of forms and VBScript
- Creating all the standard form controls
- Accessing forms elements from scripts
- Submitting forms to the server and what happens to them next

We will begin by discussing form processing, including historical and current developments. The chapter focuses primarily on providing examples that guide you through using each form element, and it finishes by explaining how to perform validation before submitting the form.

Background to Form Processing

In its infancy, HTML provided a crude mechanism for sending keywords to an HTTP server and returning query results. As time progressed,the protocols and HTML language were extended with the development of the Mosaic browser by the National Center for Supercomputing Applications (NCSA). Mosaic added the capability to display graphics files and text, as well as basic form fields such as radio buttons, check boxes, text fields and select menus. There was no client-side processing to deal with these forms. The contents of the form were simply converted into a list of attribute/value pairs and sent to the server when the Submit button was pressed. It was then up to the server to process the form and send back the results in the form of an HTML document.

TIP

To find out more about CGI and server-side scripting, turn to Chapter 15, "CGI and ISAPI—What about Web Servers?."

This approach to interactive behavior on the Web has its limitations, including the following:

- Data must travel back and forth between client and server, introducing delays.
- There is no scope for client-side validation of the form data before it transmits.
- The server has more work to do, which has implications for the performance of the Web site dealing with the forms—mainly that all the other programs running on the server have to compete for the limited resources such as memory and disk space.

These limitations are now overcome with the advent of new scripting technology on the client computer. Using VBScript, you can write code to perform complex validation, help the user to fill in the form, and generally make the document more interactive.

Client-Side Scripting with Forms—Closer to Home

The introduction of scripting required some changes to the HTML standards for creating forms. Netscape was the first developer to extend the forms specification to allow for scripting. It produced the JavaScript Object Model, which quickly became the accepted standard and the Internet Explorer object model is compatible with it. This model provides a specification for the events and properties of form controls that are accessible to a script. For example, the OnClick event that you see so often in this book, didn't exist before the introduction of this object.

The main benefits associated with this new model for form processing are as follows:

- Forms become much more interactive with immediate feedback for the user.
- The extra processing and network delays caused by communication with the server are minimized. This leads to much better performance.
- Fields that require special handling; for example, calculations based on values entered by the user, can be dealt with by a script.

To demonstrate the essential difference between the server-based approach and scripting, take a look at Figures 11-1, 11-2, and 11-3.

The first two show what happens when an *invalid* value is entered in a field using the old server-based methods. Figure 11-1 shows the user submitting the form to the server, unaware that they have entered an erroneous value of "Visa" instead of the Visa credit card number itself. The server checks the form to see if the values are valid and finds that there is an invalid quantity. It generates an HTML document (see Figure 11-2) and returns it to the user's browser. The user must correct the form and resubmit it to the server.

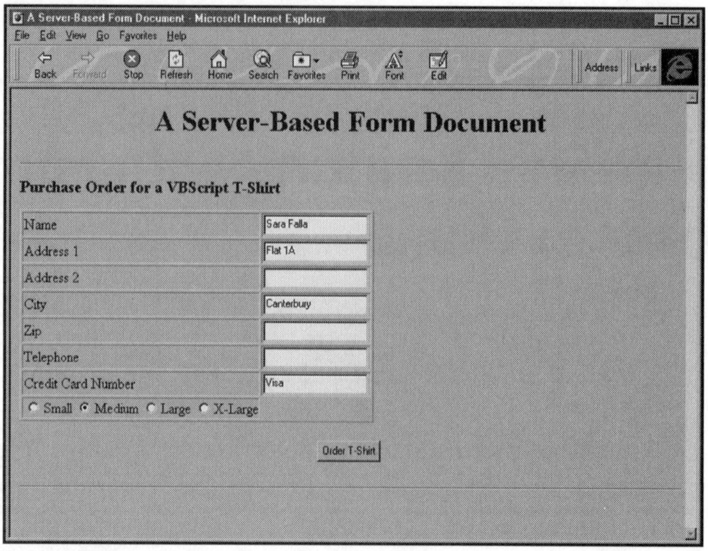

FIGURE 11-1
An HTML form ready to be submitted to a server

Using scripting, you write validation procedures to check all the values as you enter them. You can let the user deal with an incorrect value immediately or you can write script code to automatically adjust the information without informing the user at all. Figure 11-3 shows such a script in action.

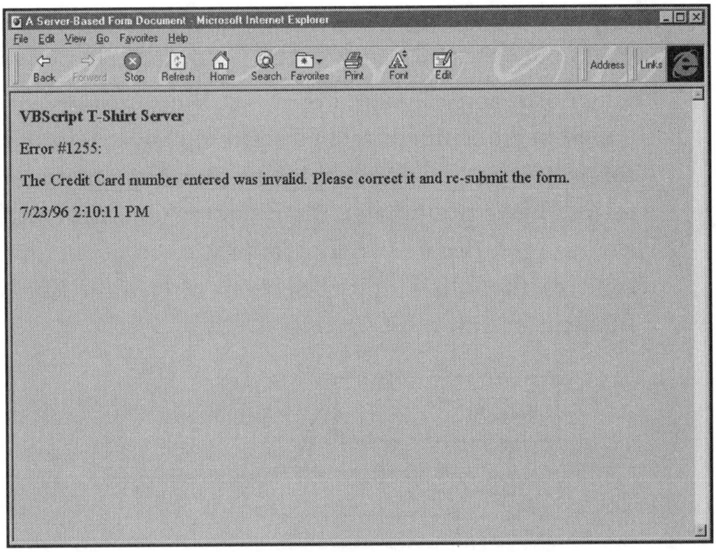

FIGURE 11-2
An example reply from a server, indicating problems with a form

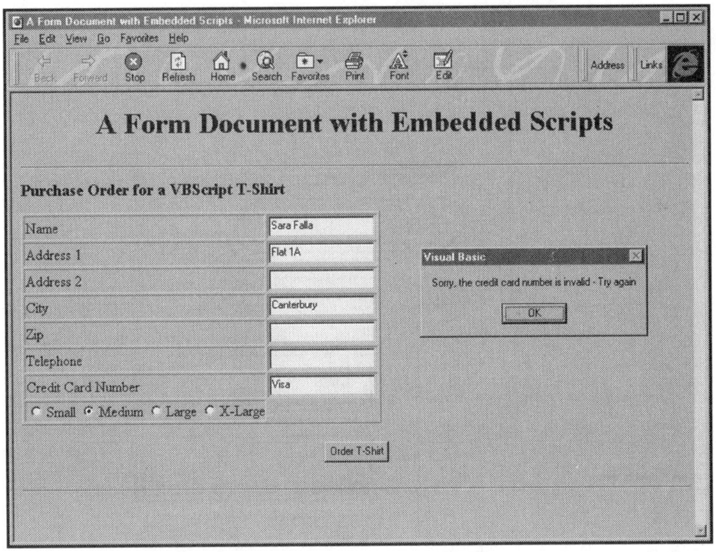

FIGURE 11-3
An HTML form using scripting to perform validation

Putting It All Together—The Scripting Object Model

The Object Model for Scripting implemented by Explorer 3.0 was described in the previous chapter, which covered the Window and

Document objects and all the other objects they contain. The next few pages put the final pieces of the jigsaw puzzle in their places.

The Form and Element objects let Web authors access the forms contained in a document from a scripting engine. Both objects expose useful properties and events which allow the creation of interactive forms. Their positions in the Explorer object hierarchy are shown in Figure 11-4. Before you look at how to create and use the individual controls, the following two sections discuss the Form object and the Element object, respectively.

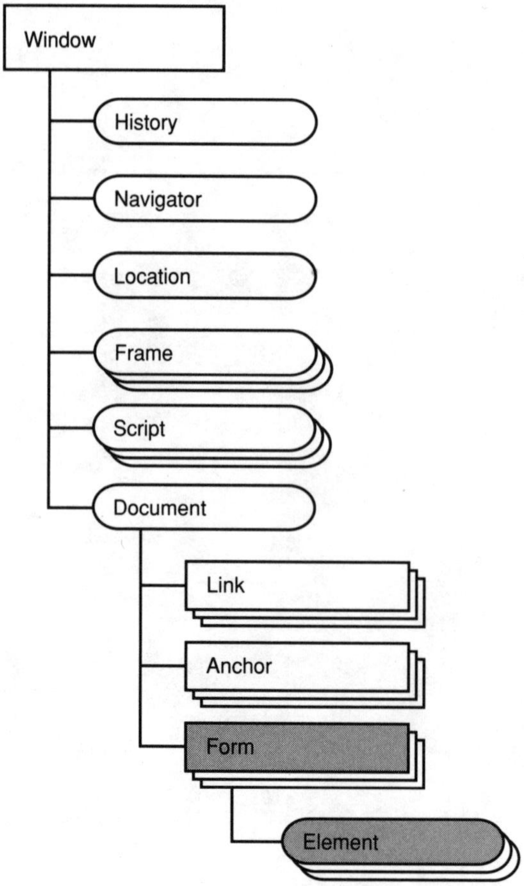

FIGURE 11-4
The Form and Element objects in the Explorer Object Model for Scripting

The Form Object

The Form object, an important component, resides below the document in the object hierarchy. It represents an actual form in the HTML document. The Form object accesses the Element object and the individual controls on the form. There can be multiple *instances* of the Form object, one for each form defined by the HTML source.

NOTE *The Form and Element objects are described in detail in the Object Model for Scripting Reference. The coverage in this chapter highlights important areas and gives ideas for using the objects in scripting applications. For complete lists of properties, methods, and events, look in the reference section.*

Because there can be many forms in a single document, there must be some way to access them and the elements they contain. There are actually two different naming schemes, each with their own benefits.

Accessing Forms by Name

The first way in which forms are stored is by name. After the HTML source defines a form, the NAME="formname" attribute of the <FORM> tag gives the form a name. You have seen this in many of the examples in the Language Structure chapters. For example:

```
<FORM NAME="UserForm">
<INPUT NAME="Button1" TYPE="Button" VALUE="Press Me">
...
...
</FORM>
```

This section of HTML code defines a form called UserForm. This form is now visible to any script within the current window. The Microsoft documentation states that the way to access such a named form is as follows:

```
<SCRIPT LANGUAGE="VBScript">
<!–
Sub SomeProcedure
    Document.UserForm.Action =
```

```
"http://www.vbscript.com/scripts/tshirt.cgi"
End Sub
->
</SCRIPT>
```

This procedure changes the Action property of UserForm to a new URL (see later in this chapter for more details). Referring back to Figure 11-4, you see that the Form object is a child of the Document object. It makes sense then, to access the forms you create by referring to the Document (Document.UserForm). This notation gets clumsy when there are many references to the forms within the script. The Tip explains a simpler way to refer to named forms.

TIP

You may have noticed that all the code samples in previous chapters have omitted the 'Document.' part of the reference. This is because the form names are visible at the Window object level as well; in other words, the same level at which script routines exist. It is perfectly valid to write

```
UserForm.Action = ...
```

instead of

```
Document.UserForm.Action = ...
```

and can save time and space when writing code.

Naming forms not only makes it clear what their purposes are but also makes it easier to modify the elements they contain. You can access forms through the *Forms* array, but this is only recommended in certain circumstances. Details on how to do this are in the next section.

Accessing Forms by Index

The VBScript programmer makes use of the Forms array as well as referring to a form by its name. This array is a member of the Document object and each element refers to a single form. As the browser parses a document, it creates entries in the array for each set of <FORM> tags it encounters. The tags do not have to contain a NAME="formname" clause because this is only necessary when referring to forms by name.

Imagine if the previous example had been defined like this:

```
<FORM>
<INPUT NAME="Button1" TYPE="Button" VALUE="Press Me">
...
...
</FORM>
```

This time the form has no name, but it can be accessed from within a script by the following line of VBScript:

```
Document.Forms(0).Method = ...
```

Note that this is the first form in the document and the array indexes start from zero. (The Method property is explained later).

If there are several forms in a document, you can discover how many there are from the Length property of the Forms array. The VBScript to retrieve the number of forms would be:

```
someVar = Document.Forms.Length
```

At first glance, it may seem unnecessary to use this property—after all, won't you always know how many forms are in a document you have written? The answer to this question can be found in the gray box below.

Why Are There Two Ways of Accessing a Form from a Script?

Currently all the VBScript code you write has to reside within <SCRIPT> tags or is attached to controls in the document. The <SCRIPT> tag was designed to allow for a `SRC="someURL"` attribute to be implemented. This means that you are able to download and run script files that are stored separately from your documents.

Referencing forms explicitly by name is fine for now, but when the `SRC` attribute is implemented, it will pave the way for generic scripts. These scripts are able to examine the `Forms` array to find the number of forms and reference each form by using an index. These scripts would not be able to work with form names alone. General scripts could then be written to perform useful tasks on any script; for example, decent date and time validation routines.

Other Form Attributes

Before moving on to the controls that can appear on forms, there are a few attributes of the Form object to look at. The Length property of the Forms array, the first of these, has already been covered.

The Action Property

Any form needs a destination before being submitted to a server. The Action property's role is to provide this information. A script can read, or set, this property like this:

```
strAction = UserForm.Action

UserForm.Action = "http://www.microsoft.com/scripts/search"
```

The Action is usually an URL which points to a CGI script on the server. If no URL is specified (for example, just a CGI script name), the URL is considered relative and the BASE URL of the document is used instead.

The Method Property

The Method property specifies how the form data should be sent to the server. There are two values which this property has:

- **GET** Appends the arguments to the Action URL and opens it as if it were a normal anchor.
- **POST** Sends the data via an HTTP post transaction. Use this whenever possible. For example:

```
UserForm.Method = "POST"
```

The Target Property

Form results can display in a different window than the current one. The window for displaying the results can be set using the Target property of the Form object. This is just the same as the TARGET attribute of the <FORM> tag (see a current HTML reference).

To display the results in a window named ResultWindow, write:

```
Document.Forms(0).Target = "ResultWindow"
```

or

```
UserForm.Target = "ResultWindow"
```

Elements Array

The *Elements* array allows the programmer to access all of the individual controls contained in each form. A section dedicated to the Element objects which make up the array follows in a moment.

The Submit Method

The Submit method and OnSubmit events go hand-in-hand with each other. The Submit method causes the browser to submit the form to the address specified by the Action property. The OnSubmit event triggers whenever the user presses a SUBMIT button, or IMAGE element. For information on these items and using them to perform extra validation before submission, see the section named 'Validating and Submitting—Check and Sign Please Sir!' in this chapter.

The Element Object

An element is one of two things—an intrinsic HTML control or an object inserted in the HTML with the <OBJECT> tag. This chapter deals with the intrinsic controls that are inserted using the <INPUT> or <SELECT> tags. Objects, and particularly ActiveX controls, are explained in the next three chapters.

There can be many elements in each form so an array is used to store each one. Just like the Forms array, the Elements array is used to access item properties and methods. For instance:

```
Document.Forms(0).Elements(0).Value = "Press Me"
```

would set the Value property of the first element of the first form to "Press Me".

Once again, if you wish to find out how many elements there are in a particular form, use the Length property of the Elements array.

```
IntX = Document.Forms(0).Elements.Length
```

Using the Elements array to get at control properties can be quite unwieldy, and Forms(0).Elements(0) doesn't tell anyone very much about what the control is or what it does. It makes more sense to name the controls and objects you use— and here's how.

Element Names and Scope—Where Are You Hiding?

If an intrinsic control is declared with the NAME="SomeName" attribute, it can be referenced by name in a script. You can define these controls using the <INPUT> or <SELECT> HTML tags (explained later), and place them anywhere within the document body. Examples of named controls have been used throughout the previous chapters and include

```
<INPUT TYPE="Button" NAME="MyButton" VALUE="Press Me">
```

and

```
<INPUT TYPE="Text" NAME="SurnameText">
```

which creates a button named MyButton and a text field named SurnameText.

These declarations can appear anywhere within the BODY section, but can be part of a form or stand alone in the document. Whether or not the declaration appears within a set of <FORM> tags affects how you reference the control from a script.

When you place a control in a form, it becomes a child control of that form and can only be accessed by referring to the form. An example form and section of VBScript would be:

```
<FORM NAME="Form1">
Enter your name
<INPUT TYPE="Text" NAME="NameText">
...
```

```
...
</FORM>
```

and

```
...
strName = Form1.NameText.Value
strName = "Mr. " & strName              'Prefix a title to the name
...
```

On the other hand, a control defined outside form tags becomes a child of the Window object itself. Scripts exist as children of the window object and are at the same level in the hierarchy as the named controls so you can refer to them directly by name. If the text field NameText had not been defined within <FORM> tags, the following would be valid:

```
...
strName = NameText.Value
strName = "Mr. " & strName              'Prefix a title to the name
...
```

TIP *You should always try to place intrinsic controls within a set of <FORM> tags. Even if the form is not going to be submitted to a server, it makes it clear where the control belongs and provides easy access to it from scripts.*

What about Objects?

Remember that elements can be both intrinsic controls and objects. These objects, notably Microsoft's new ActiveX controls, are the most interesting new developments for scripting. If you want to find out more, see Chapters 12, 13, and 14. Form processing is the main way of getting information back from users to the server, so if you need to use forms for any practical applications, just read the rest of this chapter.

The Name and Value Properties

Different types of intrinsic controls are available. There are a couple of properties which apply to almost every one of these controls—the Name and Value properties.

The Name of an element is a string containing the element's name as specified in the NAME= clause. You can change the name of an element once the document loads. The VBScript interpreter updates all references to the object internally to keep up with the change. To see this in action, load the example named "Changing a Control's Name at Run-time" from the Tutorial section of the main Web page.

Most of the HTML source has been included here for you to study. Whenever you click the button control, an OnClick event generates. The event procedure for this event changes the name of the button to Button2 on the first press, Button3 on the second, and so on. Load the document and press the button. You might expect that once the control is renamed Button2, the event procedure Button1_OnClick would not match with the control's name. However VBScript tracks the change of name and updates all the internal references to the control. Figure 11-5 shows a screen shot of the document once the button has been pressed a few times.

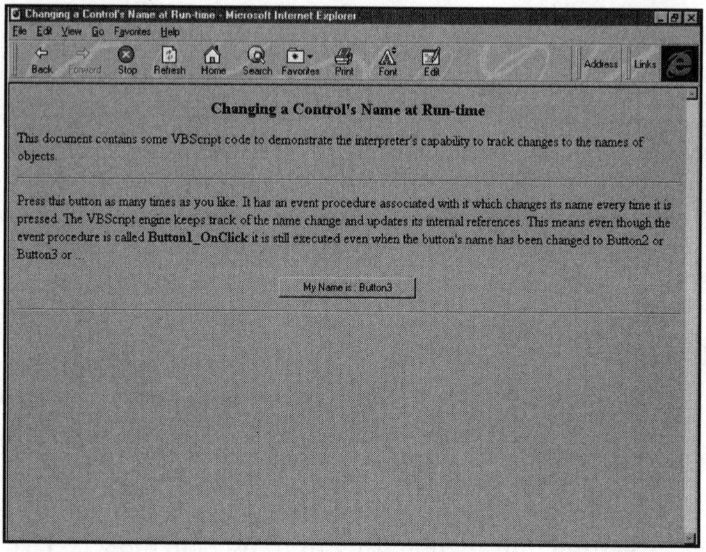

FIGURE 11-5
Changing the name of an intrinsic control at run-time

```
<HTML>
<HEAD>
<TITLE>Changing a Control's Name at Run-time</TITLE>
<SCRIPT LANGUAGE="VBScript">
<!-
```

```
Dim intButtonNumber
intButtonNumber = 2

Sub Button1_OnClick
       Button1.Value = "My Name is : " & Button1.Name
       Button1.Name = "Button" & intButtonNumber
       intButtonNumber = intButtonNumber + 1
End Sub
—>
</SCRIPT>
</HEAD>

<BODY>
<CENTER><H3>Changing a Control's Name at Run-time</H3></CENTER>
This document contains some VBScript code to demonstrate the
interpreter's capability to track changes to the names of objects.
<HR>
************EXPLANATORY TEXT
************
<CENTER>
<INPUT TYPE="Button" NAME="Button1" VALUE="Press Me to Change My
Name!">
</CENTER>
<HR>
</BODY>
</HTML>
```

The <FORM> Tag

The next sections cover how to define forms and controls, what controls are available, and what can be done with them.

The form contains the control elements. You're already familiar with the Form Object and how to access its properties from a script. What about the <FORM> tag itself?

The <FORM> tag is the HTML element that defines the overall attributes for an interactive form. The structure of most form definitions looks somewhat like this:

```
<FORM
    NAME="FormName"
    ACTION="URL"
    METHOD=GET or POST
    TARGET="ResultWindow"
>
Form contents
</FORM>
```

All of these attributes actually are optional, but any form you submit and use in a script needs to include at least the NAME, ACTION, and METHOD attributes.

The <INPUT> Tag

Almost every example you have looked at so far has made use of the <INPUT> tag to define a form control. Until now, there has been no real explanation of the various options available.

The <INPUT> tag specifies a form control and there are several types. You can define all of these controls with the TYPE= clause to specify which kind of control to insert. The sections that follow explain each control in turn.

The different controls to choose from are:

- Buttons
- Single-line text fields
- Multiple-line text fields
- Password fields
- Check boxes
- Radio buttons
- Select lists

- Reset buttons
- Submit buttons

You can load one fairly large example document into your browser to look at all the controls in one go. Do this by selecting the hyperlink labeled "Form Controls Aplenty" from the Tutorial Web page.

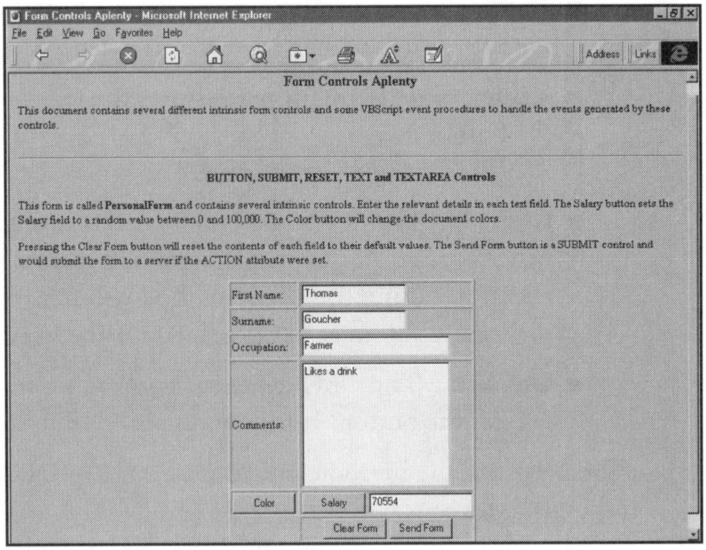

FIGURE 11-6 *The example document, Form Controls Aplenty, shows the different control types used for the form called PersonalForm.*

The BUTTON, RESET, and SUBMIT Elements

All three of these controls look the same when they display in a document. Each one is a standard Windows button but each has a separate function.

The BUTTON Element

General scripting uses buttons for its tasks; for example, starting a timer, calculating a value, and so on. It is defined in the following way:

```
<INPUT
    TYPE="Button"
```

```
    NAME="ButtonName"
    [VALUE="Button Text"]
>
```

The BUTTON control has two properties, one method, and one event.

- **Name** The `Name` property names the button which is set by the `NAME` attribute of the <INPUT> tag.
- **Value** The `Value` property stores the text that displays on the button face. It is set by the NAME= clause of the <INPUT> tag.
- **Click( )** The `Click` method is used to simulate the button being pressed. It does not, however, generate the OnClick event, so calling the Click method will not invoke the event procedure you may have defined for the button.
- **OnClick** The OnClick event generates whenever the user presses the button. It is now discussed in more detail.

When pressed, the button element generates an OnClick event, which responds in three ways:

- Write a specific event procedure called ButtonName_OnClick
- Write a script for that event and button using the notation

```
<SCRIPT LANGUAGE="VBScript" FOR=ButtonName EVENT=OnClick>
```

- Place inline code within the <INPUT> tag, such as

```
<INPUT TYPE="Button" Name="Button1" OnClick='VBScript code'>
```

Different Responses to Events

The last bulleted list mentions three ways of responding to an event, but this book really has dealt with only one of these before now. The programming conventions set out in Chapter 9, "Writing Well-Organized and Coherent VBScript," suggest that you place all VBScript code in the HEAD section of a document. This convention means there is little reason to write script section for a particular object and event.

Instead of writing

```
<SCRIPT LANGUAGE="VBScript">
    ...
    Some procedures and functions
    ....
Sub Button1_OnClick
    MsgBox "I've been pressed"
End Sub
    ....
    Other procedures and functions
    ....
</SCRIPT>
```

you can write

```
<SCRIPT LANGUAGE="VBScript" FOR="Button1" EVENT="OnClick">
    MsgBox "I've been pressed"
</SCRIPT>
```

This notation means you can omit the Sub and End Sub lines, but a new <SCRIPT> tag is needed for every event you wish to handle. It is neater to organize all your script code in one block in the HEAD section.

When you want to carry out a simple action with one code line, you can use another form of event handling. The script code is written within the object definition itself. The event name is written, followed by an equals sign (=), followed by the script code within single quotes. For example,

```
<INPUT NAME="Button1" TYPE="Button" VALUE="Press Me" OnClick='MsgBox
"I've been pressed"'>
```

This format is really only useful when you have just one line of code to execute.

You should use the first method for all but the simplest tasks. The Form Controls Aplenty document contains examples of button controls and event procedures (refer to Figure 11-6).

Finding Out More about a Control

You can find out what methods, properties, and events a particular control or object has by using Microsoft's ActiveX Control Pad. Chapter 13, "Using the ActiveX Control Pad and HTML Layout Control," tells you more about this free product. If you have already read that chapter or just want to take a look:

Load the HTML document containing the form controls you have just defined into ActiveX Control Pad and select Tools|Script Wizard from the menu bar.

Look for the name of the form you have defined and press the + symbol next to it. This should expand the listing to display all the controls in the form. Select the control you want to know more about and more details will display.

The left-hand window shows only events, such as OnClick, while the right-hand window shows properties and methods. This method has proven very useful in exploring the capabilities of the controls and objects used in this book. Turn to Chapter 13, if you want to know more.

The RESET Element

This is a specialized form of the BUTTON which has a very useful function. One press of this control clears all the contents of the form it is a member of, and resets to the initial values. Apart from this, it is treated in the same way as a regular BUTTON element.

The HTML to define it is:

```
<INPUT
    TYPE="Reset"
    NAME="ResetName"
    [VALUE="Reset Text"]
>
```

Like the BUTTON, the RESET element has the following members:

- **Name** Names the control
- **Value** Text that displays on button face

- **Click( )** The `Click` method is used to simulate the user pressing the button from a portion of script code—the user doesn't actually press the button. Once again, the OnClick event does not trigger by invoking this method, but the form clears.
- **OnClick** The `OnClick` method is used in the same way as the BUTTON element.

There is a RESET element in the form *PersonalForm* in the 'Form Controls Aplenty' example (see Figure 11-6).

The SUBMIT Element

This is a specialized form of button with a single function. Pressing this button causes the form contents to be submitted to the address (usually an URL) specified by the ACTION= clause of the defining <FORM> tag. There is much more information on submitting forms later in this chapter. Other than this, the SUBMIT element can be treated much like a BUTTON.

A SUBMIT element is defined by:

```
<INPUT
    TYPE="Submit"
    NAME="SubmitName"
    [VALUE="Submit Text"]
>
```

Like the BUTTON, the RESET element has the following members:

- **Name** Names the control and is set by the `NAME=` attribute of the <INPUT> tag.
- **Value** Text that displays on button face.
- **Click( )** The `Click` method is used to simulate the user pressing the button. Once again, the OnClick event does not trigger by invoking this method, but the form submits.
- **OnClick** The `OnClick` method is used in the same way as the BUTTON element.

There is a SUBMIT element in the form *PersonalForm* in the Form Controls Aplenty example shown in Figure 11-6. The ACTION attribute is not set for this form so it does not actually get sent anywhere.

TEXT and TEXTAREA Elements

HTML provides two kinds of text field, single and multiple line elements. These elements are actually defined in very different ways, and will be discusses separately.

The Single-Line TEXT Element

This control provides a convenient space for a user to enter strings, numbers or dates to be sent back for processing. Like the button element, you have encountered this control on several occasions already, but the full details are given here.

A TEXT element is defined in HTML by:

```
<INPUT
    TYPE="Text"
    NAME="TextName"
    [SIZE=element width]
    [MAXLENGTH=max # of characters to accept]
    [VALUE="Default Text"]
>
```

This control has three properties, three methods, and four events and has the TYPE, NAME, and VALUE attributes. The SIZE and MAXLENGTH attributes are fixed at HTML parse time and are not available to a scripting application.

- **DefaultValue** This property holds the initial value given to the element by the VALUE= clause of the defining HTML. It is *read-only* and changing it does not change the default text held in the field.
- **Name** Equivalent to NAME= clause of the <INPUT> tag
- **Value** Equivalent to VALUE= clause of the <INPUT> tag

- **Select( )** This method highlights the contents of the text field. Pressing Ctrl-C copies the contents to the Clipboard and Ctrl-X cuts the selection from the element.
- **Focus( )** This method makes the element the currently active control in the document window. The control will now accept user input when characters are typed in.
- **Blur( )** The current input focus is directed away from the control by this method. The control now will not accept keyboard input.
- **OnSelect** This event triggers whenever the user selects some, or all, of the contents of the text field.
- **OnBlur** The OnBlur event generates whenever the input focus leaves the control. You can respond to this event to perform validation; for example, making sure a field is not left blank.
- **OnFocus** This event generates whenever the control receives the input focus. You can respond to this event to display tips on filling in the field, for example.
- **OnChange** This event generates when the contents of the text field (the Value property) changes. When the focus leaves the control, perhaps by pressing the Tab key, it implements range validation, and so on.

The Multiple-Line TEXTAREA Element and <TEXTAREA> Tags

You can use this control when larger pieces of information need to be collected from the user. It is useful for items such as comments, messages, or special requirements, and it has its own set of HTML container tags to define it.

A multiple-line text field inserts in a form with:

```
<TEXTAREA
    NAME="TextAreaName"
    ROWS=10
```

```
    COLS=30
>
Text to be displayed initially
</TEXTAREA>
```

NOTE *By specifying the TYPE as "Textarea," a multiple-line text field can be defined using the <INPUT> tags. This control is somewhat more limited than using the <TEXTAREA> container tags because it does not accept newline characters and does not have as many events/methods. You should use the <TEXTAREA> syntax rather than <INPUT TYPE="Textarea">.*

This element has the same three properties, three methods, and four events as the TEXT element.

There is an example TEXTAREA element in the form called PersonalForm of the example in Figure 11-6.

The PASSWORD Element

This element is a refined form of the TEXT control. It provides a single-line text field that hides the characters entered by displaying them all as asterisks (*). It is most commonly used to get a password from a user when they are using a restricted service on the Web; for example, a free download service.

To define a PASSWORD control, add these lines of HTML to the document:

```
<INPUT
    TYPE="Password"
    NAME="PasswordName"
    [VALUE="Password Text"]
>
```

The PASSWORD has no events, three methods, and three properties. The lack of events makes it harder to use than the TEXT control. It would benefit from an OnChange event to perform validation. You can work around this by validating the PASSWORD contents before submitting the form (see the section "Validating and Submitting—Check and Sign Please Sir!").

- **Name** Element name from the `NAME=` attribute
- **Value** String contained by the control
- **DefaultValue** Read-only property which holds the initial value of the element. When the form clears by a RESET element, the password contents resets to this value.
- **Focus( )** This method causes the element to receive the input focus.
- **Blur( )** The Blur( ) method causes the element to lose the current input focus, and no longer accepts user input.
- **Select( )** This method highlights the contents of the control.

The second section of the Form Controls Aplenty example contains two password controls. Try entering two different values and clicking on the Submit image—you will be informed that the new passwords do not match. Figure 11-7 shows the section of the document we are referring to.

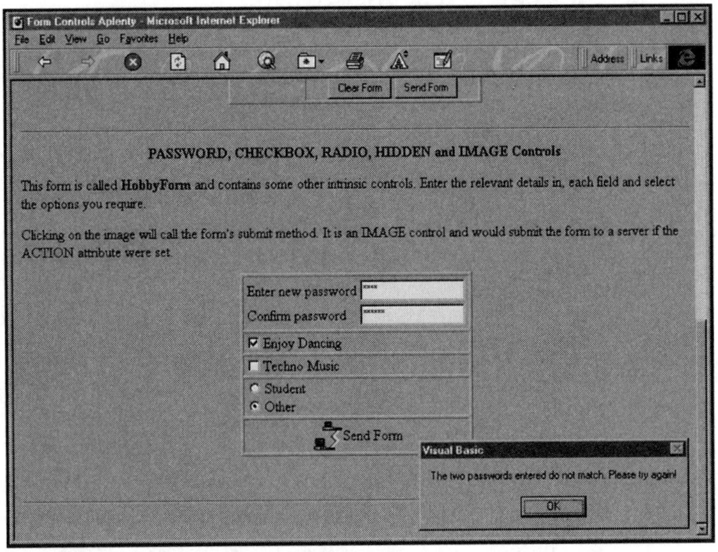

FIGURE 11-7
The example document, Form Controls Aplenty, shows the remaining control types used for the form called HobbyForm.

The CHECKBOX Element

This control provides a square option box which you can select or unselect. It is useful for getting the user to choose particular options.

If you have a set of mutually exclusive options; for example, only one option can be selected at a time, you should use a radio control instead. A check box is declared as follows:

```
<INPUT
    TYPE="Checkbox"
    NAME="CheckboxName"
    [VALUE="Value if checked"]
    [CHECKED]
>
Text to be displayed next to checkbox
```

Check boxes have four properties, one method, and one event. If the check box is to be selected when the form loads, you must include the CHECKED option in the HTML source. The VALUE= clause specifies what value should be returned when the control switches on. The members of this element are:

- **Name** The control name
- **Value** This property is the value of the control when it is checked.
- **Checked** A boolean value which is TRUE if the control is checked, FALSE if it is not.
- **DefaultChecked** A read-only property that specifies the initial value for the `Checked` property.
- **Click( )** This method simulates the user clicking on the check box. It does not, however, invoke the OnClick event. If you have written an OnClick event handler and wish to execute this code, you should call it directly when simulating a click.
- **OnClick** Event triggered whenever the user clicks on the check box. You can respond to this event in the same three ways as in the BUTTON element section.

The form HobbyForm in Figure 11-7 contains two check box elements. You can look at the source code for the document in a few pages to see how they are defined, or select View [->] Source from the browser menu.

RADIO Buttons

These controls allow Web authors to group mutually exclusive options together into sets. Only one of the RADIO elements can be selected at any one time, so these controls are great for Yes/No or multiple choice answers.

There are a few traps to be aware of when using these controls in scripts, but these are explained in this section.

A radio element in a group is defined as follows:

```
<INPUT
    TYPE="Radio"
    NAME="RadioGroupName"
    [VALUE="Value if checked"]
    [CHECKED]
>
Text to be displayed next to RADIO button
```

All the radio elements which are to be grouped together must be given the same name in the NAME= section of the declaration. This is so the browser knows which elements go together, but this can lead to difficulties when writing scripts to deal with clicks on individual radio elements.

Usually when writing an event handler, the procedure name creates from the control name, an underscore and the event name. This does not work with radio groups because there are several controls with the same name. To respond to the OnClick event of an individual button, use the syntax:

```
<INPUT TYPE="Radio" NAME="GroupName" OnClick='VBScript code'>
```

What about finding out which radio button is selected? You can access the individual elements by using the Elements array. In the Form Controls Aplenty example you will see this line of code:

```
MsgBox "The Student radio button is set to: " &
➥Document.Forms(1).Elements(4).Checked
```

where the value of one of the radio buttons is being displayed in a message dialog. You could use this procedure to check each of the radio button elements in turn until you find the one that is selected. By using the Length property of the radio group, and a simple for loop, you can cycle through the elements.

```
For count = 0 To 5          'There are 6 elements in our radio group
    If Document.Forms(0).Elements(count).Checked Then
        intSelected = Document.Forms(0).Elements(count).Value
        Exit For
    End If
Next
```

The RADIO element has five properties, one method, and one event.

- **Name** The radio group name as specified by the NAME= clause
- **Value** The value that returns when the control is selected.
- **Checked** Property indicating whether or not this radio button is currently checked.
- **DefaultChecked** Initial value of the `Checked` property. This is a read-only property.
- **Length** Property which indicates how many items are in the radio group. This property is *only* accessible when referring to the whole group by name; for example, HobbyForm.StudentRadio.Length, and not through the `Elements` array.
- **Click( )** Method to simulate the user clicking on the radio element. The current state of the radio element will toggle to the other possible value. This method does not trigger the OnClick event.
- **OnClick** Event generates whenever the radio element is clicked. See the discussion above about how to handle this event.

There is a group containing two RADIO elements in the form called HobbyForm in the example of Figure 11-7. When the OnSubmit event of the form is triggered, its event handler displays the Checked property of one of the radio buttons.

Send Us YOUR COMMENTS

Dear Reader:

Thank you for buying this book. In order to offer you more quality books on the topics ***you*** would like to see, we need your input. At Prima Publishing, we pride ourselves on timely responsiveness to our readers' needs. If you complete and return this brief questionnaire, ***we will listen!***

Name (First) ____ (M.I.) ____ (Last) ____

Company ____ Type of business ____

Address ____ City ____ State ____ ZIP ____

Phone ____ Fax ____ E-mail address: ____

May we contact you for research purposes? ❑ Yes ❑ No

(If you participate in a research project, we will supply you with the Prima computer book of your choice.)

❶ How would you rate this book, overall?

- ❑ Excellent
- ❑ Very good
- ❑ Good
- ❑ Fair
- ❑ Below average
- ❑ Poor

❷ Why did you buy this book?

- ❑ Price of book
- ❑ Content
- ❑ Author's reputation
- ❑ Prima's reputation
- ❑ CD-ROM/disk included with book
- ❑ Information highlighted on cover
- ❑ Other (please specify): ____

❸ How did you discover this book?

- ❑ Found it on bookstore shelf
- ❑ Saw it in Prima Publishing catalog
- ❑ Recommended by store personnel
- ❑ Recommended by friend or colleague
- ❑ Saw an advertisement in: ____
- ❑ Read book review in: ____
- ❑ Saw it on Web site: ____
- ❑ Other (please specify): ____

❹ Where did you buy this book?

- ❑ Bookstore (name): ____
- ❑ Computer store (name): ____
- ❑ Electronics store (name): ____
- ❑ Wholesale club (name): ____
- ❑ Mail order (name): ____
- ❑ Direct from Prima Publishing
- ❑ Other (please specify): ____

❺ Which computer periodicals do you read regularly? ____

❻ Would you like to see your name in print?

May we use your name and quote you in future Prima Publishing books or promotional materials?

❑ Yes ❑ No

❼ Comments & suggestions: ____

TAPE HERE

❽ I am interested in seeing more computer books on these topics

- ❑ Word processing
- ❑ Databases/spreadsheets
- ❑ Networking
- ❑ Programming
- ❑ Desktop publishing
- ❑ Web site development
- ❑ Internetworking
- ❑ Intranetworking

❾ How do you rate your level of computer skills?

- ❑ Beginner
- ❑ Intermediate
- ❑ Advanced

❿ What is your age?

- ❑ Under 18
- ❑ 18–29
- ❑ 30–39
- ❑ 40–49
- ❑ 50–59
- ❑ 60–over

SAVE A STAMP

Visit our Web site at **http://www.primapublishing.com**

and simply fill out one of our online response forms.

PRIMA PUBLISHING
Computer Products Division
701 Congressional Blvd., Suite 350
Carmel, IN 46032

PLEASE
PLACE
STAMP
HERE

The HIDDEN Element

This is a form control which is not displayed onscreen at all! What use is this? HIDDEN elements are used to store data and pass it back to the server. This data may concern the state of the client/server interaction or hold special calculated values.

The HTML tag to define one of these controls is:

```
<INPUT
    TYPE="Hidden"
    NAME="HiddenName"
    [VALUE="HiddenValue"]
>
```

Because there is no user interaction when using one of these elements, it is quite simple. There are just three properties.

- **Name** The control's name as specified by the NAME= option
- **Value** The current value held by the control
- **DefaultValue** The initial value assigned to the control at load time.

There is a single HIDDEN element in the HobbyForm of the example document. It is not used for much but does show how to define such an element. One feature of form elements in a Web page is that, typically, when you move back and forth between pages in a browser, the information you may have entered into a form remains. For example, if you fill out a questionnaire and leave the page using some link or navigation button (and not exit the browser in the same session), and return later, the data you entered would still be there. Many Web designers used this feature to store information about a session which would maintain itself if the user left the page. However, this is not the most elegant method, and the use of cookies is more flexible and allows you to store information permanently.

The IMAGE Element

Bored of simple buttons? How about using a picture instead of a SUBMIT element to send the form? You can do this with the IMAGE element When the user clicks over the image, the form's OnSubmit event triggers and the form submits.

You can define an IMAGE control like this:

```
<INPUT
    TYPE="Image"
    NAME="ImageName"
    SRC="GraphicFileName"
    ALIGN=TOP or MIDDLE or BOTTOM
>
Text to appear beside the image
```

When the form submits in response to the user clicking on the image, extra pairs of values are sent to the server. The x and y co-ordinates of the mouse click are sent under the field names .x and .y, respectively.

The IMAGE element has only one property.

- **Name** The element's name

Form Controls—An Example

All of the form controls introduced in the previous section are found in this extended example (shown in Figures 11-6 and 11-7). The source code is shown here, giving examples of handling events, setting properties, and calling methods. Load the example by selecting the `Form Controls Aplenty` hyperlink from the Tutorial section of the main Web page and then work through the code.

```
<HTML>
<HEAD>
<TITLE>Form Controls Aplenty</TITLE>
<SCRIPT LANGUAGE="VBScript">
<!-
```

```
'***************************************
' Script procedures for 'PersonalForm'
'***************************************
'****
'Makes sure that a name has been entered when the user leaves the
➥field
'****
Sub NameText_OnBlur
    If PersonalForm.NameText.Value = "" Then
        MsgBox "You must enter a first name"
        PersonalForm.NameText.Focus()
    End If
End Sub

'****
' Sets the Salary field to a Random value between 0 and $100,000
'****
Sub SalaryButton_OnClick
    PersonalForm.SalaryText.Value = Int(100000 * Rnd())
End Sub

'****
' Tests the Salary field whenever it changes and ensures that it is a
➥numeric value
'****
Sub SalaryText_OnChange
    If not IsNumeric(PersonalForm.SalaryText.Value) Then
        MsgBox "Salary must be a numeric value!"
        PersonalForm.SalaryText.Value="10000"
        PersonalForm.SalaryText.Focus
    End If
End Sub

'****
' Changes the document colors in response to a Button click
```

```
'****
Sub ColorButton_OnClick
    Document.fgColor = "#ffff00"
    Document.bgColor = "#002080"
End Sub
->
</SCRIPT>

<SCRIPT LANGUAGE="VBScript">
<!-
'****************************************
' Script procedures for 'HobbyForm'
'****************************************
'****
' Carries out some checks before submitting the form
'****
Sub HobbyForm_OnSubmit
    MsgBox "The Student radio button is set to: " &
➥Document.Forms(1).Elements(4).Checked

    If HobbyForm.PassText1.Value <> HobbyForm.PassText2.Value Then
        MsgBox "The two passwords entered do not match. Please try
➥again!"
        HobbyForm.Target = ""
    Else
        HobbyForm.Target = "http://script target"
    End If
End Sub
</SCRIPT>
</HEAD>

<BODY>
<H2 ALIGN=CENTER>Form Controls Aplenty</H2>
<P>This document contains several different intrinsic form controls and
➥some VBScript event procedures to handle the events generated by
➥these controls. <P>
```

```
<HR>
<H4 ALIGN=CENTER>BUTTON, SUBMIT, RESET, TEXT and TEXTAREA Controls</H4>
This form is called <B>PersonalForm</B> and contains several intrinsic
➥controls. Enter the relevant details in
each text field. The Salary button sets the Salary field to a random
➥value between 0 and 100,000. The Color button
will change the document colors.<P>
Pressing the Clear Form button will reset the contents of each field
➥to their default values. The Send Form button is
a SUBMIT control and would submit the form to a server if the ACTION
➥attribute were set.<P>

<CENTER>
<FORM METHOD="POST" NAME="PersonalForm">

<TABLE BORDER>
<TR><TD>First Name: </TD>
<TD><INPUT TYPE="Text" NAME="NameText" SIZE=20 MAXLENGTH=20></TD>

<TR><TD>Surname:</TD>
<TD><INPUT TYPE="Text" NAME="SurnameText" SIZE=20 MAXLENGTH=20></TD>

<TR><TD>Occupation:</TD>
<TD><INPUT TYPE="Text" NAME="JobText" SIZE=30 MAXLENGTH=30></TD>

<TR><TD>Comments:</TD>
<TD>
<TEXTAREA NAME="CommentText" ROWS=10 COLS=30>
</TEXTAREA>
</TD>

<TR><TD ALIGN=CENTER><INPUT TYPE="Button" NAME="ColorButton"
➥VALUE="Color"></TD>
<TD ALIGN=CENTER><INPUT TYPE="Button" NAME="SalaryButton"
➥VALUE="Salary">
```

```
<INPUT TYPE="Text" NAME="SalaryText" VALUE="100000"></TD>

<TR><TD></TD>
<TD ALIGN=CENTER>
<INPUT TYPE="Reset" NAME="ResetButton" VALUE="Clear Form">
<INPUT TYPE="Submit" NAME="SubmitButton" VALUE="Send Form">
</TD></TABLE></FORM>
</CENTER>
<HR>

<H4 ALIGN=CENTER>PASSWORD, CHECKBOX, RADIO, HIDDEN and IMAGE
Controls</H4>
This form is called <B>HobbyForm</B> and contains some other intrinsic
➥controls. Enter the relevant details in,
each field and select the options you require.<P>
Clicking on the image will call the form's submit method. It is an
➥IMAGE control
and would submit the form to a server if the ACTION attribute were
➥set.<P>
<CENTER>
<FORM NAME="HobbyForm" METHOD="POST">

<TABLE BORDER>
<TR><TD VALIGN=MIDDLE>
<TABLE>
<TR><TD>Enter new password</TD><TD><INPUT TYPE="Password"
➥NAME="PassText1"></TD>
<TR><TD>Confirm password</TD><TD><INPUT TYPE="Password"
➥NAME="PassText2"></TD>
</TABLE></TD>

<TR><TD><INPUT TYPE="Checkbox" NAME="DancingBox" VALUE=True
➥CHECKED>Enjoy Dancing</TD>
```

```
<TR><TD><INPUT TYPE="Checkbox" NAME="TechnoBox" VALUE=True>Techno
➥Music</TD>

<TR><TD><INPUT TYPE="Radio" NAME="StudentRadio" VALUE="Yes"
➥CHECKED>Student<BR>
<INPUT TYPE="Radio" NAME="StudentRadio" VALUE="No">Other</TD>

<TR><TD ALIGN=CENTER>
<INPUT TYPE="Image" SRC="submit.gif" ALIGN=MIDDLE
➥NAME="SubmitImage">Send Form</TD>
</TABLE>
<INPUT TYPE="Hidden" NAME="HiddenValue" VALUE="Staus: OK">
</FORM>

<P><P><HR>
</BODY>
</HTML>
```

There are several points to note from this example.

HTML tables are used to arrange the form fields neatly on the page. Modifying this example should give you some ideas, but the best place to find out more details is the HTML reference for Internet Explorer 3.0. This can be found on Microsoft's Web site

`http://www.microsoft.com/.`

The forms in the example do not have their ACTION attribute set. This is because there is actually no script waiting to service the form data on a server. Once you write your own forms, make sure to set the ACTION attribute to the name of the server script you want to handle the form.

There is an event handler for HobbyForm's OnSubmit event. This performs some validation and displays a message before submitting the form. There is a section later that discusses form submission.

The <SELECT> Tag

There is one type of form control not covered so far—the SELECT element. It is perhaps the most complex of all the intrinsic controls.

The SELECT element allows you to define static or scrolling lists of options from which the user can select one or more items . You can specify what the items are and how many the user can select at a time.

There are special tags for defining these lists. The HTML to define a SELECT object looks something like:

```
<SELECT
    NAME="SelectName"
    [SIZE="Select Height"]
    [MULTIPLE]
>
<OPTION [VALUE="ReturnValue"] [SELECTED]> Option Text
[OPTION [VALUE="ReturnValue"] [SELECTED]> Additional Option Text]
</SELECT>
```

The MULTIPLE option tells the browser to allow the user to select more than one item at a time. Omitting this option limits the user to selecting only one item.

The SIZE option specifies how many lines high the control should be. A value of 1 produces a drop-down list box, whereas any other displays a list box on the page. Scrollbars are added by the browser whenever they are necessary.

You can have as many OPTION items as you wish (each is defined by an <OPTION> tag), followed by the text to appear in the SELECT element. Specifying the SELECTED keyword within the <OPTION> tag sets that item as the default selected item for the list. If MULTIPLE is not set, the last time the browser encounters the SELECTED keyword is the one it selects.

The Select Object is a little more complicated than the others you have seen so far. It has five properties, no methods, and three events.

- **Name** The SELECT element's name
- **Length** Property indicating how many items are in the list

- **DefaultSelected** Property indicating which item is the default selected item in the list. If there are multiple selected items, the first one is returned. If there are no default selections, this may contain random values.
- **SelectedIndex** The index of the first selected item in the `Options` array. If more than one item is selected, it returns the lowest index.
- **Options array** Provides programmatic access to the different items in the list. See below for details.
- **OnFocus** Event triggered when the control receives the input focus.
- **OnBlur** Event triggered when the control loses the input focus.
- **OnChange** Event triggered whenever the user selects, or deselects, any of the options in the list.

The Options Array

The Options array has several properties of its own. This array has one entry for each of the items in the SELECT element. The indices start from zero like all VBScript arrays.

To access the *Text* property of the third item you would write:

```
strVar = Form1.Select1.Options(2).Text
```

The properties contained in each entry in the Options array are:

- **Index.** Specifies which item in the list this is and starts from zero.
- **Text.** Stores the text that displays for that list item.
- **Selected.** Boolean value used to set or discover the selected state of the item. Set it to TRUE (or 1) to highlight the item, FALSE (or 0) to deselect it.
- **Value.** Holds the value returned when this item is selected. It is not currently functioning. See note in previous section.

The next example demonstrates the Select element, so read on to see how to use it.

An Example of Some Form Controls

Select the `SELECT Elements—The Last Intrinsic Control` link from the Tutorial section of the main Web page. This should load a document containing two different SELECT controls, one single and one multiple line.

Figure 11-8 and Figure 11-9 show what the document should look like when you have selected some items from the lists.

The full source is shown here so you can select View|Source from the browser menu to edit it.

```
<HTML>
<HEAD>
<TITLE>SELECT Elements - The Last Intrinsic Control</TITLE>
<SCRIPT LANGUAGE="VBScript">
<!-
Sub DropSelect_OnChange
    Dim Current
    Current = DropSelect.SelectedIndex
    Text1.Value = ""

    Text1.Value = Text1.Value & "I am item #" &
DropSelect.Options(Current).index & "  in the list" & Chr(13) & Chr(10)

    Text1.Value = Text1.Value & "My text is " &
DropSelect.Options(Current).text & Chr(13) &Chr(10)

    Text1.Value = Text1.Value & "The value I return is = " &
➥DropSelect.Options(Current).value & Chr(13) & Chr(10)

    Text1.Value = Text1.Value & "There are " & DropSelect.length & "
➥items in this list" & Chr(13) & Chr(10)
```

```
    Text1.Value = Text1.Value & "The currently selected item is #" &
➥DropSelect.SelectedIndex & Chr(13) & Chr(10)
End Sub

Sub MultiSelect_OnChange
    Dim Current
    Current = MultiSelect.SelectedIndex

    Text2.Value = ""

    Text2.Value = Text2.Value & "I am item #" &
➥MultiSelect.Options(Current).index & "  in the list" & Chr(13) &
➥Chr(10)

    Text2.Value = Text2.Value & "My text is " &
➥MultiSelect.Options(Current).text & Chr(13) &Chr(10)

    Text2.Value = Text2.Value & "There are " & MultiSelect.length & "
➥items in this list" & Chr(13) & Chr(10)

    Text2.Value = Text2.Value & "Selected Items List:" & Chr(13) &
➥Chr(10)

    Text2.Value = Text2.Value & "Item 0 : " &
➥MultiSelect.Options(0).Selected & Chr(13) & Chr(10)
    Text2.Value = Text2.Value & "Item 1 : " &
➥MultiSelect.Options(1).Selected & Chr(13) & Chr(10)
    Text2.Value = Text2.Value & "Item 2 : " &
➥MultiSelect.Options(2).Selected & Chr(13) & Chr(10)
    Text2.Value = Text2.Value & "Item 3 : " &
➥MultiSelect.Options(3).Selected & Chr(13) & Chr(10)
    Text2.Value = Text2.Value & "Item 4 : " &
➥MultiSelect.Options(4).Selected & Chr(13) & Chr(10)
    Text2.Value = Text2.Value & "Item 5 : " &
➥MultiSelect.Options(5).Selected & Chr(13) & Chr(10)
```

```
    Text2.Value = Text2.Value & "Item 6 : " &
➥MultiSelect.Options(6).Selected & Chr(13) & Chr(10)
    Text2.Value = Text2.Value & "Item 7 : " &
➥MultiSelect.Options(7).Selected & Chr(13) & Chr(10)
    Text2.Value = Text2.Value & "Item 8 : " &
➥MultiSelect.Options(8).Selected
End Sub
->
</SCRIPT>
</HEAD>

<BODY>
<CENTER><H3>SELECT Elements - The Last Intrinsic Control</H3></CENTER>
This document contains some VBScript code and HTML to demonstrate how
➥to define and use
SELECT elements.
<HR>
<CENTER><H4>Single-Line Select Elements</H4></CENTER>
Select a continent from the list. An event handler for the OnChange
➥event of the SELECT element will
then display all sorts of information about the control in the text
➥area control below.<P>
<CENTER>
Choose a Continent
<SELECT NAME="DropSelect" SIZE=1>
    <OPTION VALUE="1" SELECTED>Africa
    <OPTION VALUE="2">Asia
    <OPTION VALUE="3">Antarctica
    <OPTION VALUE="4">Australasia
    <OPTION VALUE="5">North America
    <OPTION VALUE="6">South America
    <OPTION VALUE="7">Europe
</SELECT>
<P>
<TEXTAREA NAME="Text1" ROWS=10 COLS=35>Notes appear here
```

```
</TEXTAREA>
</CENTER>

<HR>
<CENTER><H4>Multiple-Line Select Elements</H4></CENTER>
Select some ingredients from the List. The OnChange event handler for
➥the element will then display
some details in the text area control below<P>
N.B. Hold down the Ctrl key when selecting items to add to the list
➥already hilighted<P>
<CENTER>
<B>Choose Some Ingredients</B><P>
<SELECT NAME="MultiSelect" MULTIPLE SIZE=6>
    <OPTION>Flour
    <OPTION>Sugar
    <OPTION>Water
    <OPTION>Milk
    <OPTION>Butter
    <OPTION>Chocolate
    <OPTION>Cherries
    <OPTION>Strawberries
    <OPTION>Cream
</SELECT>
<P>
<TEXTAREA NAME="Text2" ROWS=12 COLS=35>Notes appear here
</TEXTAREA>
<HR>
</BODY>
</HTML>
```

The HTML code to define the single line element starts with:

```
<SELECT NAME="DropSelect" SIZE=1>
    <OPTION VALUE="1" SELECTED>Africa
```

while the HTML definition for the multiple line list begins:

```
<SELECT NAME="MultiSelect" MULTIPLE SIZE=6>
    <OPTION>Flour
```

When you select any items from either of the two lists, comments about your selections display in the TEXTAREA controls below them. This is achieved by responding to the OnChange events generated by the SELECT controls.

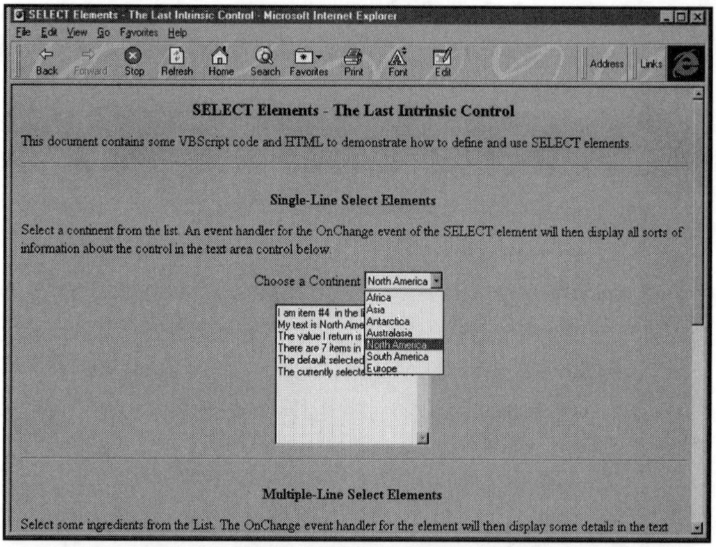

FIGURE 11-8
Example document displaying a single-line SELECT element

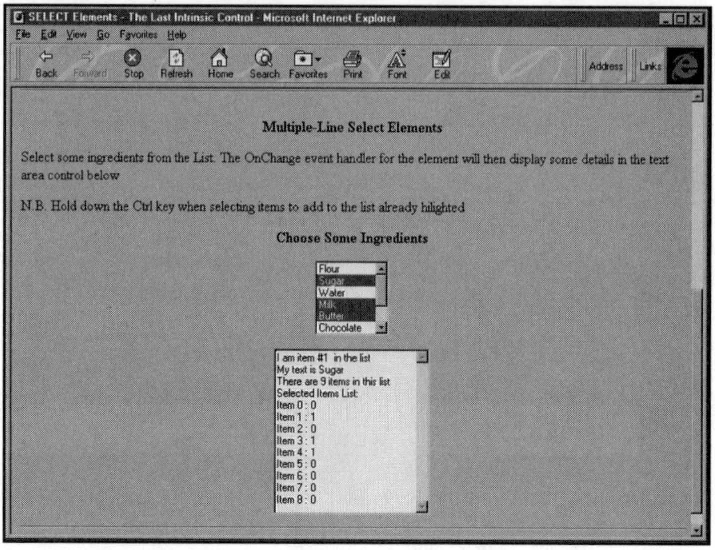

FIGURE 11-9
Example document displaying a multi-line SELECT element

Multiple Selections—Only the First Selection Counts

Select several items from the second list. You will notice that the first few lines of the comment box only apply to the topmost selection. This is because the *SelectedIndex* property of the SELECT element is single-valued. By convention, the VBScript interpreter places the index of the topmost selected item into this variable.

If you want to find out which items are selected, check the Selected property of each item in the Options array. This is done in the event procedure *MultiSelect_OnClick*. Look at the document source to see how this is achieved. The example displays a list for all the items in the list. A value of 1 means that option is selected, and 0 means it is not.

Formatting Text in a TEXTAREA Control

In order to break the text stored in the TEXTAREA controls into separate lines, special characters must be inserted into the string. These consist of carriage return and linefeed combinations. Because these are non-printing characters, you have to use the *Chr()* function (see Appendix A, "VBScript Language Reference—Functions") to add them to the text string. An example of this would be:

```
Text1.Value = Text1.Value & "My text is " &
➥DropSelect.Options(Current).text & Chr(13) &Chr(10)
```

Validating and Submitting—Check and Sign Please Sir!

Now that you know about the SUBMIT, IMAGE, and RESET elements, as well as the rest of the HTML form controls, it's time to tie the details together.

Having designed your form and implemented it, there is still quite a bit of work to do. There may be many checks to perform before submitting the form. Values may need to fall within certain ranges, some fields may require a value to be provided, and calculations may need to be performed. Throughout this chapter there have been example solutions to these problems. A brief run-down of the options open to you as a programmer follows.

Chapter 15, "CGI and ISAPI—What About Web Servers?" contains more information on the processing of form data once the user presses the SUBMIT button.

Checking That Values Fall within Ranges

All these kinds of values may have some restrictions upon them: dates, ages, sizes, quantities. Client-side scripting allows you to perform this kind of validation before submitting the form.

In most cases, the TEXT element would be used to get these values from the user. Providing an OnChange event handler to validate the data is the most effective solution. An example of this was implemented in the event procedure for the SalaryText control of the Form Controls Aplenty document.

Ensuring Values are Provided

Sometimes a value is required in all circumstances as in an e-mail address. The OnBlur event of the TEXT element is very useful in these situations. Whenever the control in question loses the input focus, a script checks to see if a value has been provided. If not, it informs the user and calls the control's Focus( ) method to return focus to the control. An example of this is seen in the name element of PersonalForm in the form controls example.

Performing Calculations

You may need to calculate values based on other fields in the form or provide values that change over time. The form's OnSubmit event handler is used to good effect here. This event triggers just before the form data submits to the server.

Write some VBScript code in this event handler to calculate the necessary values. These values can then return to the server by including HIDDEN elements in the form and setting their Value properties to the calculation results before submission.

Performing calculations on the client machine has two advantages. The processing resources of the server computer are not taken up and the calculation may fail and require the user to enter new values.

Delaying Submission of a Form

Once the OnSubmit event triggers, the form is bound to be submitted. What if the form doesn't pass validation? The simplest way of preventing it from being sent to the server is to change the Action property.

This was done in the HobbyForm_OnSubmit event procedure earlier in the chapter. By setting the form's Action property to "" on failure, or some CGI script on success, you control whether or not the form reaches the server.

Conclusions

If you've made it this far, you should have a sound knowledge of intrinsic controls. This chapter covered all you will need to know to write effective, interactive forms with client-side validation and many added extras.

Feel free to use the examples from this chapter to create some forms of your own. After you write a useful procedure or function, say to validate customer ID's or check ranges, be sure to keep the code somewhere. Reusing code is one of the most time saving practices when programming—why reinvent the wheel every time you write a script?

That's about it for the standard HTML constructs and the Object Model for Scripting. The next few chapters will introduce you to, and reveal the secrets of, the most exciting development in WWW scripting technology to date—*ActiveX Controls*.

You will see how to use lots of free objects from Microsoft, learn about the ActiveX Control pad, encounter the <OBJECT> tag, and much more. Go on, turn the page!

CHAPTER 12

ActiveX Controls and VBScript

This chapter may well contain the secrets of interactive Web content you have been searching for. Up until now, this book has dealt with the VBScript language itself, the Scripting Object Model, and HTML form controls. Now it's time to introduce some cutting edge technologies and objects.

This and the following chapters reveal what ActiveX controls are, how to insert them into your documents, and how to get the most out of them. The discussion includes numerous examples that demonstrate the essential features of these brand new controls. This chapter covers the following topics:

- Understanding objects
- Inserting objects into HTML with the <OBJECT> tag
- Setting object attributes with the <PARAM> element
- An introduction to Microsoft's new ActiveX technology
- Licensing and redistribution of ActiveX controls
- Examples of all the ActiveX controls in the ActiveX Gallery on Microsoft's Web site

If you are using this book in conjunction with the software on the CD, make sure that you install all the software on your system (see Chapter 3, "Creating Your First VBScript Document"). All of the examples can be accessed from the main Web page. Even without the software installed, you will find this chapter an invaluable resource. Each example has full source code listings and screen captures that display the controls themselves.

This is a fast expanding area of Web authoring and anybody involved in leading edge development in this field should know about ActiveX controls. Effective use of ActiveX technology alongside Java applets and the new HTML standards for frames and tables will make *your* Web site stand out from the crowd. If you want to know more, this is the place to start.

What Are Objects?

In the context of HTML, the term object refers to a very broad range of different items. It covers things such as images, videos, sounds, plug-ins, Java applets—and now ActiveX controls. Before delving into the specific details of the <OBJECT> tag and ActiveX, you need some background information.

HTML 2.0 had a very limited provision for inserting different media into documents. The <IMG> tag allowed authors to include images in their Web pages. Although this tag has proved very useful, many different kinds of media have been developed for the World Wide Web (W3C). These new items have emerged from many sections of the development world and up until recently, there was no standard way of inserting these objects into HTML documents.

Different developers experimented with different means of inserting nonstandard elements—Microsoft introduced the DYNSRC attribute for loading audio and video, Sun used the <APP> and <APPLET> tags for inserting Java applets, while Netscape proposed the <EMBED> tag for embedding documents within others. All of these new proposals had limitations and particular applications, but what was needed was a worldwide standard for embedding different media within HTML.

The W3C proposed the <OBJECT> tag that became part of the HTML 3.2 standards. This single tag is designed to provide backwards compatibility for existing browsers, while providing developers with a means of developing new media for incorporating into Web documents. The <OBJECT> tag is general purpose and allows object attributes (such as size on the screen) to be defined, location of data to be specified, and alternative representations to be specified for unknown objects. This last capability is important in providing backwards compatibility for older browsers. For example, a browser that does not support video can display an image instead—thus preserving some of the document's intended content.

The <OBJECT> Tag

The <OBJECT> tag is designed to support many different kinds of media, so it has many options. Not all of these are applicable to the discussion in this chapter. This book deals only with the details you need to insert ActiveX controls into HTML, so if you require a broader explanation, look at an HTML 3.2 reference. These references can be found quite easily on the Web:

`http://www.microsoft.com/` or `http://www.w3.org/`

The <OBJECT> tag is a container tag, just like the familiar <BODY> or <HEAD> tags. In order to provide the flexibility required, the designers included another new element. The <PARAM> tag resides within the body of an object definition and provides extra information about the object. In the case of ActiveX controls, the <PARAM> tags are used to set object properties, such as background color.

Inserting Objects into HTML

Before looking at the details in turn, here is a sample of an object definition:

```
<OBJECT ID="iegrad1"
     WIDTH=100
     HEIGHT=70
     CLASSID="clsid:017C99A0-8637-11CF-A3A9-00A0C9034920"
     TYPE="application/x-oleobject"
>
     <PARAM NAME="StartColor" VALUE="#66ff00">
     <PARAM NAME="EndColor" VALUE="#0000ff">
Your browser does not support ActiveX controls, or cannot find the
➥Gradient control.
</OBJECT>
```

You may already have seen definitions like this if you looked at the HTML source code for some of the book's examples. This instance of the <OBJECT> tag inserts an ActiveX control called the Gradient control (see later in the chapter). There are several different parts to the definition.

Notice the opening <OBJECT> and closing </OBJECT> tags. Each opening tag must be followed at some point by a terminating tag. This indicates to the browser that the object definition is complete. Another important feature is the list of attributes that appears within the initial <OBJECT> tag. These are described in detail in the next section, and specify the size, type, and class of the object.

There are two PARAM entries inside the object body. These are used to define the values of the properties, *StartColor* and *EndColor*, of the

Gradient control. Different objects have different properties, and the <PARAM> tag provides a simple way of initializing these to the values necessary for each instance of a control.

Just in case a browser does not support a particular kind of object, there is provision for an alternative representation. This can be any other valid HTML segment and is placed within the <OBJECT> tags. In this example, the following line of text will be displayed if the Gradient control is not supported or cannot be found.

```
"Your browser does not support ActiveX controls, or cannot find the
Gradient control."
```

<OBJECT> Tag Parameters

In order to load and present the different kinds of media correctly, the browser needs to be provided with detailed information about the object. This information is conveyed to your browser via the extra attributes of the <OBJECT> tag. The attributes relevant to inserting ActiveX controls are explained in this section. All of these extra options appear within the opening <OBJECT> tag. For instance

```
<OBJECT
    OPTION1="value1"
    OPTION2="value2"
    ...
    OPTIONn="valueN"
>
```

Even though the <OBJECT> tag has many options, you do not need to provide all of them. The following section covers all of the possible object tags.

TIP

The HTML standards do not require a new line for each optional clause within the <OBJECT> tag. However, because HTML does not pay attention to carriage returns, it can make your document source much easier to follow and debug because the attribute/value pairs do not get lost in a sea of text.

Object Identification

Active content relies heavily on scripting and event procedures. This was evident in Chapters 10 and 11, which dealt with the Object Model for Scripting. An object cannot be referred to from script code (VBScript or JavaScript) without some form of a name. Many examples were given for the intrinsic HTML form elements; for example, TextArea1 or DateText.

Objects require names for exactly the same reasons and the <OBJECT> tag includes this facility. There are, in fact, two options which concern object names and both are covered here.

An object is given a document wide name by the following clause

```
ID="MyObject"
```

The scope of this name is the current document and it can be used to refer to the object itself or indirectly to access the object's attributes. For example,

```
intColor = MyObject.fgColor
```

would store the fgColor attribute of MyObject to a variable.

NOTE *Objects can also be inserted within <FORM> tags. Forms should be given names to make them accessible from script routines. Any objects placed within a form become children of that form, and must be referred to by using a form name. An object named MyObject, within a form named MyForm, will be accessed by*

```
MyForm.MyObject.SomeAttribute = SomeValue
```

The NAME attribute names an object for inclusion in a form submission. The clause to name an object in this way would be

```
NAME="MyFormObject"
```

This may look very similar to ID="MyObject", but it causes the browser to handle the object differently when it appears within form tags. If the NAME tag is present, the browser submits the object's name and attribute values along with the values of the other form controls at submit time. Exactly how the attribute/value pairs are encoded depends on the object system being used.

HEIGHT and WIDTH

Now that you can identify objects, what about specifying their size? This is quite simple, the HEIGHT and WIDTH attributes can be set for an object which will direct the browser to display the object using the specified dimensions. The Gradient control example made use of these tags, specifying that the control should be 100 pixels wide and 70 pixels high.

The size of an object is specified by

```
HEIGHT="HeightValue"
WIDTH="WidthValue"
```

TIP *Some objects provide functionality rather than visual feedback and do not actually display onscreen. An example of such a control is the ActiveX Timer Object. Set the HEIGHT and WIDTH of such objects equal to 1 and they will not interfere with the rest of the document.*

The size of an object can actually be specified in several different ways, and is *only* a suggestion to the browser about how to display the item in question. Almost always, the size of the object will conform to the suggestion, but there's a small chance that the browser may resize the object to fit into a page. The options are:

- **Pixels.** An integer value for the number of screen pixels required, such as HEIGHT="768"
- **Relative Sizes.** A percentage of the current window or table cell height, or current space between the left and right margins. For example, WIDTH="65%"
- **Inches.** Fixed unit of length. Inches are specified using the abbreviation *in*, for example HEIGHT="3.56in."
- **Points.** Size in font points, specified using the abbreviation *pt*. An example is HEIGHT="18pt."
- **Picas.** Size in standard windows unit, suffixed by the letters *pi*. An example would be WIDTH="12pi."
- **Centimeters.** Finally, metric units can be used, indicated by the letters cm, such as WIDTH="15cm"

NOTE *The fixed units for length are related to each other in the following proportions.*

72pt = 6pi = 1in = 2.54cm

Alignment and Spacing Options

As well as sizing an object, HTML provides scope for aligning and spacing the object with reference to the other items on the page. This information is conveyed to the browser by three optional tags, <ALIGN>, <HSPACE>, and <VSPACE>.

The HSPACE and VSPACE tags specify the size of the gutter between the object and the surrounding text, images, objects, and so on.

```
HSPACE=n
```

sets the horizontal gutter, the space to the left and right of the object, to *n* units. This measurement can be written using any of the standard units of length, described in the previous section.

```
VSPACE=n
```

sets the vertical gutter, the space above and below the object, to *n* units.

The ALIGN tag is somewhat more complicated and will probably require some experimentation before you achieve the results you want. Table 12-1 describes the eight possible values for this option. The clause to include in the <OPTION> tag is:

```
<ALIGN="AlignType">
```

Table 12–1 Possible Values for the ALIGN Clause of an Object Definition

VALUE	MEANING
BASELINE	The bottom of the object aligns with the baseline of surrounding text.
CENTER	The object is centered between left and right margins. Subsequent text starts on the next line after the object.

VALUE	MEANING
LEFT	The object aligns with the left margin and subsequent text wraps along the right side of the object.
MIDDLE	The middle of the object aligns with the baseline of surrounding text.
RIGHT	The object aligns with the right margin and subsequent text wraps along the left side of the object.
TEXTBOTTOM	The bottom of the object aligns with the bottom of surrounding text.
TEXTMIDDLE	The middle of the object aligns with the midpoint between the baseline and the x-height of the surrounding text.
TEXTTOP	The top of the object aligns with the top of surrounding text.

The <ALIGN> clause can be very useful for structuring your page because you can position objects quite accurately relative to the surrounding text. A good example of this is the use of Label controls (see later in the chapter) to highlight particular sections of text.

CLASSID, CODEBASE, and TYPE

If you noticed the CLASSID and TYPE entries in the Gradient example in the section "Inserting Objects into HTML," you may be wondering what these offerings stand for. Up until now, you have seen how to name, size, and position an object in an HTML file—but what exactly is the object that is being referred to?

This is where the CLASSID attribute comes in. It is a URL that identifies an implementation of the object that is being inserted into the page. Because objects are not native HTML components, the browser does not have them built-in, so it must load or execute some other module to provide the object's functionality. This is known as an *object implementation*, and can be a Java program, a plug-in, or a proprietary object such as an ActiveX control. Different object systems use different formalisms for the CLASSID. For example,

```
CLASSID="java:program.start"
```

specifies a Java applet called program.start as the object implementation. ActiveX controls use the clsid specification to identify objects. These numbers are quite long and confusing and definitely not easy to remember. The Gradient control's class identifier is

```
017C99A0-8637-11CF-A3A9-00A0C9034920
```

and is communicated to the browser by

```
CLASSID="clsid:017C99A0-8637-11CF-A3A9-00A0C9034920"
```

There are ways of generating these CLASSIDS automatically. For more information on what these identifiers mean and how to generate them, look at the section titled "Inserting ActiveX Controls into Web Pages."

The CODEBASE attribute provides a hint to the browser about where to look for the object in question. This is only used by some URL schemes (ActiveX technology is one of them). You can find out more about the CODEBASE element in the aforementioned section on inserting ActiveX controls. It is written within the <OBJECT> tag as follows

```
CODEBASE="URLofObject"
```

The TYPE attribute tells the browser what kind of object is being inserted. This can be helpful for two reasons. First, an unsupported object type does not have to be loaded, thus saving time and network bandwidth. Second, when the object is stored on a local disk, the browser does not have to rely on other information, such as the file extension, to discover what kind of object has been encountered. There are many values that TYPE can be assigned, but ActiveX controls use the following

```
TYPE="application/x-oleobject"
```

Providing a STANDBY Message

Some controls may take a while to download or initialize. During this time, the reader of the page may wonder what is happening, so a short text message can be displayed in the control's placeholder while it is being prepared. The STANDBY clause is used to provide the message text.

```
STANDBY="Cool Object Downloading - Please Wait"
```

The <PARAM> Element

The designers of the <OBJECT> tag could never have imagined all the possible variations in objects that might arise and would have been foolish to try. To provide as much flexibility as possible, the <PARAM> element was added to the specification.

This tag specifies extra information for the object to use. In most cases, this is configuration information for the control being inserted. Objects are inherently dynamic, programmable items, and need some customization—PARAM makes this possible. <PARAM> elements can be inserted within the OBJECT body to specify attribute/value pairs that are passed to the object. The format of an object definition with some customized attributes is:

```
<OBJECT options>
    <PARAM NAME="AttributeName" VALUE="SomeValue">
    ...
    <PARAM ...>
</OBJECT>
```

You will see many instances of this tag in the code listings in the rest of this chapter—it may be a simple addition, but it is an invaluable one.

Microsoft's New ActiveX Technology

The first two chapters introduced Microsoft's New ActiveX technology and the advantages it can afford the Web author. That introductory discussion was in a much broader framework and did not cover many implementation details. The first part of this chapter laid the groundwork for what is to follow, and you may need to refer back to it from time to time.

To recap :ActiveX technology is Microsoft's new name for the old OLE standard for object automation. This is a standard whereby software vendors and developers can create reusable software components which conform to particular guidelines. This framework allows host applications to be written that can contain any ActiveX control by simply querying the control to find out its specific details. Internet Explorer 3.0 is such a host application and the Object Model for Scripting has been designed to allow these ActiveX controls to be accessible from scripting engines, such as VBScript.

Before a control becomes available to a scripting routine, it must be inserted into the document. You have already learned about the <OBJECT> tag for inserting generic objects into HTML, but not about using it to insert ActiveX controls in particular.

Inserting ActiveX Controls into Web Pages

The <OBJECT> tag is used to insert ActiveX controls into an HTML document—the overall structure of this definition has already been covered. But a few questions remain.

- How does the programmer discover the class ID for a particular control?
- Where are the controls kept?
- What methods, attributes, and events does any particular control support?

Let's look at another definition for an ActiveX control.

```
<OBJECT ID="PopupMenu" WIDTH=1 HEIGHT=1
     CLASSID="CLSID:7823A620-9DD9-11CF-A662-00AA00C066D2"
     CODEBASE="http://www.activex.com/controls/menus/iepopmnu.ocx"
```

```
    TYPE="application/x-oleobject"
>
      <PARAM NAME="Menuitem[0]" VALUE="First Menu Item">
(c)<PARAM NAME="Menuitem(c)" VALUE="Second Menu Item">
(d)<PARAM NAME="Menuitem(d)" VALUE="Third Menu Item">
(e)<PARAM NAME="Menuitem(e)" VALUE="Fourth Menu Item">
(f)<PARAM NAME="Menuitem(f)" VALUE="Fifth Menu Item">
    </OBJECT>
```

When a control is installed onto a user's system, it is entered into the Windows Registry. This contains details of the system configuration, including currently installed components. The object's class identifier is stored within the Registry, so when the browser encounters the CLSID: URL protocol, it searches for the control there. Of course, many times you cannot depend upon a client machine already having your particular controls installed. In this situation, the <OBJECT> tag specification allows the designer to specify a CODEBASE attribute that tells the client browser where it can download the appropriate control. If the control is not installed on the system, nothing can be done unless the CODEBASE attribute has been set. This provides an alternative location for the control and is discussed further in the next section. The TYPE="ObjectType" clause is optional but can help when your documents will be viewed by many different browsers—it makes the definition very clear.

So how can a programmer or Web author discover a control's class ID? There are several options here.

1. Find some documentation for the control itself, such as the examples at the end of this chapter. The HTML source will contain the identifiers required. Typing the CLSID's in is time-consuming and unreliable unless they are available in a file somewhere and can be cut and pasted.

2. Use Microsoft's ActiveX Control Pad to insert the controls into a document. All the examples in this chapter were created in this way and then edited by hand. This chapter does not discuss the ActiveX Control Pad. For details turn briefly to Chapter 13, "Using the ActiveX Control Pad and HTML Layout Control."

3. Download an OLE Viewer utility. These are available as freeware or as part of most good software development packages. Microsoft's OLEViewer is a useful utility which allows you to examine your system and all the controls installed on it.

The final question posed in this section regarded control capabilities. How do you find out about the capabilities of a new control? Because these controls are downloaded from the Net, and are installed automatically, there is often very little documentation accompanying them. Once again, there are several avenues to explore. Try to find some documentation for the control. Failing that the information in Chapters 12 through 14 will be useful for the current batch of Microsoft controls. The ActiveX Control Pad's Attribute Editor and Script Wizard tools also can provide all the information you will need (see Chapter 13, "Using the ActiveX Control and HTML Layout Control").

Installing and Distributing the Controls

The following sections are designed to provide you with some more information about using and distributing ActiveX controls.

Installing the ActiveX Controls on a User's Computer

Most of the work is done by your browser (currently only Internet Explorer), and users do not have to take any action to install components. If the browser encounters a set of <OBJECT> tags and cannot find the associated control on the user's machine, the CODEBASE property will be used as the location of the control. The browser then attempts to download the control from this location and automatically installs it on the target machine. If you are using ActiveX controls in your documents, be sure to include the CODEBASE property. Most people who view your pages will not have the cutting edge software installed on their systems that you do, so if the CODEBASE is not set, they will not be able to view your creations.

Once installed, the control will not have to be downloaded again, unless a new version of the control becomes available. The component download architecture supports versioning, although the details are beyond the scope of this text. See Microsoft technical documentation if you require further details.

NOTE

ActiveX controls are stored in files with the extension .OCX. several are probably installed on your system already. Look in the WINDOWS\SYSTEM directory and you will probably find several of them. If you want to know more about the controls you have installed, read Chapter 13, "Using the ActiveX Control Pad and HTML Layout Control," on the ActiveX Control Pad.

What about Security?

Most computer users are aware of security considerations, especially when they are connecting their computers to a worldwide network. For this reason, Microsoft built in a system for secure code download called *AuthentiCode.* This system allows component developers to attach digital signatures to their controls (somewhat like holograms on a software box), to authenticate them. These certificates provide guarantees to the user that a certain component is free from viruses and has been certified by a central consortium. Once a component has been downloaded, this certificate displays (see Figure 12-1), and the user can accept the control and use it, or cancel the download. Of course, this book is about VBScript, and it is assumed that you are using pre-existing controls that have already been certified.

What Other Controls Are Available, and What Are the Licensing Terms?

At the moment there are over 2,000 different controls available from independent software vendors. These are all subject to different licensing terms so it is up to the developers how they distribute their products.

The final release version of Internet Explorer 3.0 includes a mechanism to prevent the use of unlicensed controls. Controls can be distributed in one of two ways, with a developer license, or with a run-time license. This will leave the developers free to decide how to distribute their controls. Run-time controls can be viewed in a document, but cannot be inserted with development tools like the ActiveX Control Pad. Developer controls can be used for new product development and freely distributed. Each vendor has a slightly different policy, so you will have to check the licensing terms when you wish to use a control.

Microsoft has produced a set of controls that can be freely downloaded and distributed for use in your Web documents. The current batch of controls have been included on the CD with this book, and the first set is described in this chapter. Microsoft wants ActiveX to become an industry standard and is working hard with other developers to create a standards body to coordinate the proliferation of this new technology.

That's enough background information for now; the rest of this chapter deals with concrete examples.

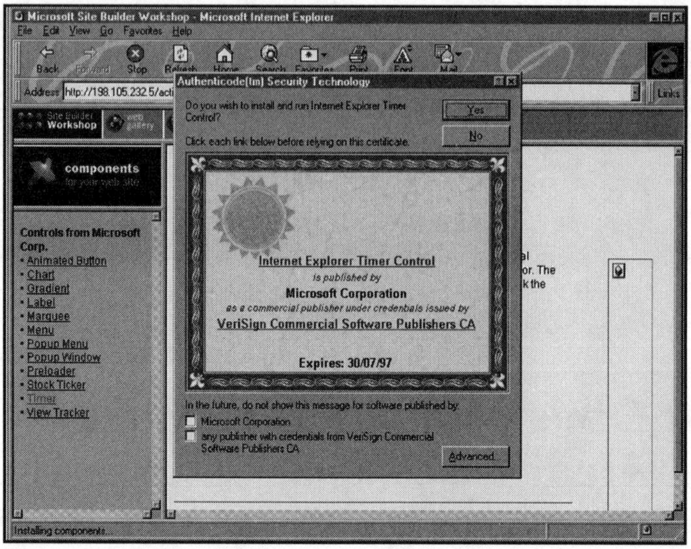

FIGURE 12-1
An Authenticode software component certificate

The ActiveX Gallery—Some Examples

Microsoft has developed a collection of showcase controls to get Web authors started with Active Content. These controls are available from the Microsoft Web site, and are also on the accompanying CD. Chapter 3, "Creating Your First VBScript Document" deals with installing these components. If you have not done, you should load them on your system now.

Twelve different controls are discussed in the next few pages, each with an example listing and screen capture. Each section also describes the various properties, events, and methods supported by each control—this part of the book should be an indispensable tool when you start to use these components in your documents. The tools used to create these examples are not discussed here, but will be in the next chapter. If you would like to work through, or modify the sample pages, take a look at the ActiveX Control Pad before going any further.

The Timer

The Timer Object is quite possibly the simplest of the ActiveX controls introduced in this chapter. It is a non-visual control that fires a Timer event at regular intervals. The interval can be changed by a script, and the Timer can be switched on and off.

This control can have several uses including:

- Creating visual effects such as spinning labels. The sample code here uses a Timer and intrinsic HTML controls to move some text around the screen.
- Carrying out tasks at predetermined intervals, such as checking mail or refreshing a document.
- Initializing other objects. The Timer is left enabled until the other objects have been instantiated. The event procedure for the Timer then configures the other objects and is disabled. An example of this technique can be seen in the Stock Ticker section.

Table 12-2 The Timer Object

	Class ID
CLSID:59CCB4A0-727D-11CF-AC36-00AA00A47DD2	
	Properties
ID	Names the control—placed in opening <OBJECT> tag

Table 12-2 The Timer Object

Height	Height of Timer set to 1
Width	Width of Timer set to 1
Enabled	If True, the Timer event will fire. If False, the control is disabled.
Interval	Time in milliseconds between the Timer event firing. Tailor this quantity to suit the application. Control will appear disabled if a zero or negative value is used.
	Methods
AboutBox	Displays the control's information dialog.
	Events
Timer	Invokes each Interval of time when the control is enabled.

In this example, the Timer control is used to display a message in a different position within a TEXTAREA control every 1/10th of a second. The example can be loaded from the ActiveX Gallery section of the main Web page. Choose the `A Simple Timer Object Example` hyperlink (see Figure 12-2).

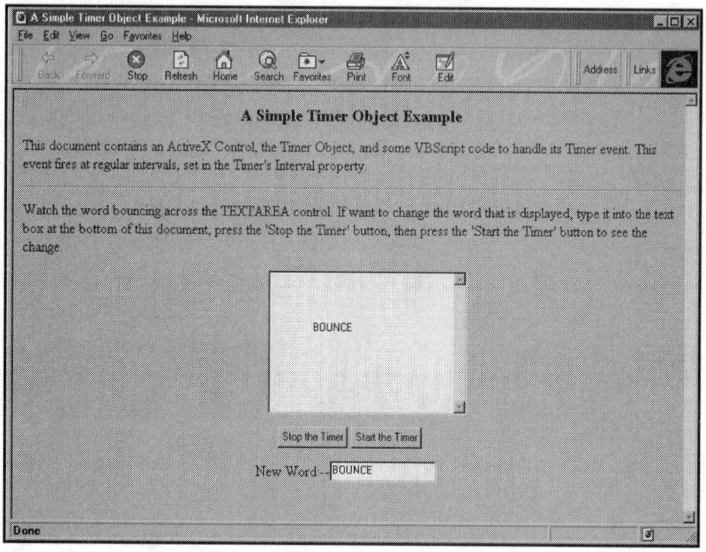

FIGURE 12-2
The ActiveX Timer control in action

The following sections review a few points of note from this example.

Responding to the Timer Event

The event procedure Timer1_Timer( ) is invoked whenever the specified interval has elapsed. You should place all the code you want to be repeated at regular intervals within this procedure. In this sample, a word (specified by the user) is made to bounce from one corner of a TEXTAREA control to another. This is done by changing its position each time the Timer event fires.

Stopping and Starting the Animation

There are two buttons for stopping and starting the animation. The event procedures for these buttons simply assign values to the Timer's Enabled property. False stops the control, and True starts it again.

TIP *In order to change a Timer's interval, you must disable the control and re-enable it before the change will have an effect.*

VBScript Language Issues

There are two extra items to cover relating to the use of VBScript. A constant is defined to represent a carriage return line-feed combination at the beginning of the script section. This is a useful value to know because multiple-line textboxes use it to insert line breaks in the text. The line of code in question is:

```
CRLF = Chr(13) + Chr(10)
```

The String function is useful for producing strings of a particular character and length. It is used in this example to pad the message string with spaces before inserting the actual message word. The line

```
strLine = String(intCycle*4," ") & strWord
```

inserts a series of spaces which is four times the value of *intCycle* in length before the value of *strWord* and stores the result to the variable *strLine*.

```
<HTML>
<HEAD>
<TITLE>A Simple Timer Object Example</TITLE>
<SCRIPT LANGUAGE="VBScript">
<!-
Dim CRLF                                    'Constant holding the characters
➥for a newline in a textarea control
CRLF = Chr(13) + Chr(10)

Dim intCycle, intDirn, strWord
intCycle = 0 : intDirn = 1 : strWord = "BOUNCE"         'Status vars
➥for the main loop & current Word to be displayed

'*******************************
' Event procedure for the Timer event of the Timer1 ActiveX control
'    intCycle : the position in the cycle (0-9 then back to 0 again)
➥is the line # to display the word
'    intDirn   : the cycle direction, 1 = down  -1 = up
'    strWord : the current word shown in the box
'*******************************
Sub Timer1_Timer()
    Dim intCount, strLine
    Text1.Value = ""                            'Clear the TEXTAREA
    For intCount = 0 to 9
        If intCount = intCycle Then
            strLine = String(intCycle*4," ") & strWord
        Else
     strLine = ""
        End If
        Text1.Value = Text1.Value & strLine & CRLF
    Next
    intCycle = intCycle + intDirn
    If intCycle=9 Then intDirn = intDirn * -1         'If at bottom
➥change direction and start moving up
```

```
    If intCycle=0 Then intDirn = intDirn * -1        'If at top
➥change direction and start moving down
End Sub

Sub StopButton_OnClick()
    Timer1.Enabled = False                    'Stop the Timer Object
➥from firing any events
End Sub

Sub StartButton_OnClick
    strWord = NewWordText.Value
    Timer1.Enabled = True                      'Restart the Timer
➥Object
End Sub
->
</SCRIPT>
</HEAD>

<BODY>
<CENTER><H3>A Simple Timer Object Example</H3></CENTER>
This document contains an ActiveX Control, the Timer Object, and some
➥VBScript code to handle its Timer event
This event fires at regular intervals, set in the Timer's Interval
➥property.
<HR>
Watch the word bouncing across the TEXTAREA control. If want to change
➥the word that is displayed, type it into the
text box at the bottom of this document, press the 'Stop the Timer'
➥button, then press the 'Start the Timer' button to
see the change.<P>
<CENTER>

<OBJECT ID="Timer1" WIDTH=39 HEIGHT=39
     CLASSID="CLSID:59CCB4A0-727D-11CF-AC36-00AA00A47DD2">
          <PARAM NAME="Interval" VALUE="100">
```

```
</OBJECT>

<TEXTAREA ROWS=10 COLS=45 NAME="Text1">
</TEXTAREA><P>
<INPUT TYPE="Button" NAME="StopButton"  VALUE="Stop the Timer">
<INPUT TYPE="Button" NAME="StartButton" VALUE="Start the Timer"><P>
New Word:—<INPUT TYPE="Text" NAME="NewWordText" VALUE="BOUNCE"
MAXLENGTH="8">
</CENTER>
</BODY>
</HTML>
```

The Label

The Internet Explorer Label control is a versatile component for displaying text labels in different fonts, sizes, colors, and styles. The text displays at any angle and can even be drawn along user-defined paths. The Label control also generates several events and can be fully integrated into scripts that change its attributes or respond to user interaction with the control.

Table 12-3 The Label Object (also known as SprLblCtl)

Class ID	
CLSID:99B42120-6EC7-11CF-A6C7-00AA00A47DD2	
Properties	
ID	Names the control—placed in opening <OBJECT> tag
Height	Height of Label
Width	Width of Label
Visible	True—the Label will be displayed. False—the control is not shown onscreen.
Caption	Specifies the text to be displayed by the Label.
Angle	Text rotation angle in degrees counter-clockwise.

Alignment	Tell the control how to align text within the label.
	* 0 : Horizontal=Left Vertical=Top
	* 1 : Horizontal=Center Vertical=Top
	* 2 : Horizontal=Right Vertical=Top
	* 3 : Horizontal=Left Vertical=Middle
	* 4 : Horizontal=Center Vertical=Middle
	* 5 : Horizontal=Right Vertical=Middle
	* 6 : Horizontal=Left Vertical=Bottom
	* 7 : Horizontal=Center Vertical=Bottom
	* 8 : Horizontal=Right Vertical=Bottom
BackStyle	Specifies how the control background is treated.
	* 0 : Transparent, content behind the label show through.
	* 1 : Opaque, the BackColor is used
BackColor	Label's background color. Can be in "#rrggbb" format or an HTML color name
ForeColor	Label's foreground color
FontName	A True Type font name. Make sure the user system is likely to have the font installed.
FontSize	Size of the font
FontItalic	Italic effect flag
FontBold	Bold effect flag
FontUnderline	Underlined text flag
FontStrikeout	Flag to display normal or struck-out text.
Mode	Specifies how the text should be rendered on the screen.
	* 0 : Normal
	* 1 : Normal text with rotation
	* 2 : No rotation, but apply the user specified lines
	* 3 : Rotation, and apply the user specified lines.

Table 12-3 The Label Object	
Path Properties	There are extra properties like TopPoints, TopIndex, TopXY, BotPoints, BotIndex, and BotXY that are supported for defining custom paths for the Label to follow. Microsoft made a utility program called PageGen available because these are difficult to use. It can be downloaded from `http://www.microsoft.com`. Its use is not covered in this book.
	Methods
AboutBox	Displays the control's information dialog.
	Events
Click	Fires when the user clicks on the control with the mouse, or presses the space bar when the control has input focus.
DblClick	Triggers when the user double-clicks the mouse over the control.
Change	Invokes when the Caption of the Label changes
MouseDown	Signature is MouseDown(Button, Shift, x, y). Triggers when one of the mouse buttons is held down over the control. The arguments for each of the mouse events specify: which button is being pressed, the status of the shift and control keys, and the mouse position over the control, respectively. See a Windows API Reference for more details.
MouseUp	Signature is MouseUp(Button, Shift, x, y). Triggers when one of the mouse buttons is released over the control.
MouseOver	Signature is MouseOver(Button, Shift, x, y). Triggers whenever the user moves the mouse pointer over the Label.

This sample can be loaded by selecting the `The Super Label Control - Lots of Possibilities` link from the ActiveX Gallery section of the book's main Web page (see Figure 12-3). Try moving the mouse over the main label and generating some events. The Label's color changes when you click on it.

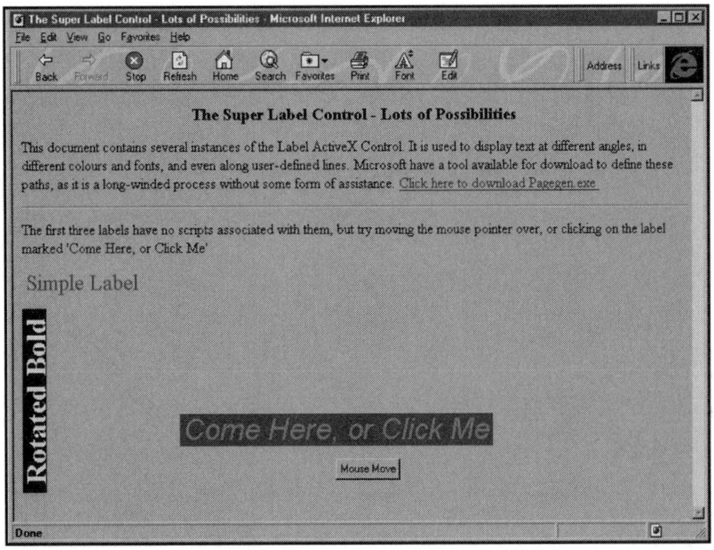

FIGURE 12-3
Using the Super Label control in an HTML document

Mouse-Related Events

When you want simple functionality from the Label control, it is fine to use the Click and DblClick events. However, there may be occasions when the position of the mouse is important, or the status of the control keys is desired. In these instances. the MouseMove, MouseDown, and MouseUp event handlers should be used instead. The extra information required is passed to the event procedure as arguments, such as

```
Sub Label4_MouseMove(Button, Shift, x, y)
```

See a Windows API Reference for the details about mouse buttons and the shift parameter. In short, the Button parameter indicates the number of the currently depressed mouse button which could be 1, 2. or 3, and the Shift parameter is True if the user is also holding down the shift key on the keyboard. These can be used to tailor the way a script responds when the MouseMove event fires—for instance, you may only want to act if the second mouse button is depressed.

Specifying Color Values Using VBScript

HTML defines a limited set of standard color names which can be used (see an HTML Reference). Colors can also be specified using an RGB triplet format. This provides values between 00 and ff (hexadecimal numbers) for each of the Red, Green, and Blue components of a color. The number sign (#) is used to signify a hexadecimal number in HTML. Colors can be written in decimal but the separate components cannot be identified as readily.

Some examples of these #rrggbb color definitions follow:

```
"#000080"      Dark blue

"#220098"      Blue with a hint of red

"#ffff00"      Bright Yellow
```

Development tools like the ActiveX Control Pad provide color selection dialogs when colors are required—these can generate color value for you.

Using the <OBJECT> Tag's ALIGN Attribute

Label2 and *Label4* both use the ALIGN= clause within the <OBJECT> tag to position the controls on the page. This attribute was discussed in the first part of the chapter. Getting the desired layout can be a little frustrating at first, but most configurations are possible with a little experimentation. If you are having difficulties designing a document, the HTML Layout Control could provide the solution. The next chapter covers the ActiveX control that allows exact placement of items.

```
<HTML>
<HEAD>
<TITLE>The Super Label Control - Lots of Possibilities</TITLE>
<SCRIPT Language="VBScript">
<!-
Sub Label4_MouseMove(Button, Shift, x, y)
    StatusButton.Value = "Mouse Move"
```

```
End Sub

Sub Label4_Click
    StatusButton.Value = "Single-Click"
    Label4.ForeColor = 255 * 255 * 255 * Rnd()
End Sub

Sub Label4_DblClick
    StatusButton.Value="Double-Click"
    Label4.AboutBox
End Sub
->
</SCRIPT>
</HEAD>

<BODY TEXT="#000000">
<CENTER><H3>The Super Label Control - Lots of Possibilities</H3></CEN-
TER>
This document contains several instances of the Label ActiveX Control.
It is used to display
text at different angles, in different colours and fonts, and even
along user-defined lines
Microsoft have a tool available for download to define these paths, as
it is a long-winded
process without some form of assistance
<A HREF="http://www.microsoft.com/ie/download/activex/pagegen.exe">Click
here to download Pagegen.exe
</A>
<HR>
The first three labels have no scripts associated with them, but try
moving the mouse pointer over, or clicking
on the label marked 'Come Here, or Click Me'
<P>
<OBJECT ID="Label1" WIDTH=137 HEIGHT=27
 CLASSID="CLSID:99B42120-6EC7-11CF-A6C7-00AA00A47DD2">
```

```
    <PARAM NAME="Caption" VALUE="Simple Label">
    <PARAM NAME="Angle" VALUE="0">
    <PARAM NAME="Alignment" VALUE="4">
    <PARAM NAME="Mode" VALUE="1">
    <PARAM NAME="FillStyle" VALUE="0">
    <PARAM NAME="BackStyle" VALUE="0">
    <PARAM NAME="ForeColor" VALUE="#ff0000">
    <PARAM NAME="BackColor" VALUE="#000000">
    <PARAM NAME="FontName" VALUE="Times New Roman">
    <PARAM NAME="FontSize" VALUE="18">
    <PARAM NAME="FontItalic" VALUE="0">
    <PARAM NAME="FontBold" VALUE="0">
    <PARAM NAME="FontUnderline" VALUE="0">
    <PARAM NAME="FontStrikeout" VALUE="0">
    <PARAM NAME="TopPoints" VALUE="0">
    <PARAM NAME="BotPoints" VALUE="0">
</OBJECT>
<P>
<OBJECT ID="Label2" WIDTH=27 HEIGHT=200
    ALIGN="Left"
    CLASSID="CLSID:99B42120-6EC7-11CF-A6C7-00AA00A47DD2">
    <PARAM NAME="Caption" VALUE="Rotated Bold">
    <PARAM NAME="Angle" VALUE="90">
    <PARAM NAME="Alignment" VALUE="4">
    <PARAM NAME="Mode" VALUE="1">
    <PARAM NAME="FillStyle" VALUE="0">
    <PARAM NAME="BackStyle" VALUE="1">
    <PARAM NAME="ForeColor" VALUE="#ffff00">
    <PARAM NAME="BackColor" VALUE="#000088">
    <PARAM NAME="FontName" VALUE="Times New Roman">
    <PARAM NAME="FontSize" VALUE="24">
    <PARAM NAME="FontItalic" VALUE="0">
    <PARAM NAME="FontBold" VALUE="1">
    <PARAM NAME="FontUnderline" VALUE="0">
    <PARAM NAME="FontStrikeout" VALUE="0">
```

```
    <PARAM NAME="TopPoints" VALUE="0">
    <PARAM NAME="BotPoints" VALUE="0">
</OBJECT>

<OBJECT ID="Label3" WIDTH=150 HEIGHT=150
    CLASSID="CLSID:99B42120-6EC7-11CF-A6C7-00AA00A47DD2">
    <PARAM NAME="Caption" VALUE="Skew Underline">
    <PARAM NAME="Angle" VALUE="135">
    <PARAM NAME="Alignment" VALUE="4">
    <PARAM NAME="Mode" VALUE="1">
    <PARAM NAME="FillStyle" VALUE="0">
    <PARAM NAME="BackStyle" VALUE="0">
    <PARAM NAME="ForeColor" VALUE="#00ff00">
    <PARAM NAME="BackColor" VALUE="#000000">
    <PARAM NAME="FontName" VALUE="Arial">
    <PARAM NAME="FontSize" VALUE="16">
    <PARAM NAME="FontItalic" VALUE="0">
    <PARAM NAME="FontBold" VALUE="0">
    <PARAM NAME="FontUnderline" VALUE="1">
    <PARAM NAME="FontStrikeout" VALUE="0">
    <PARAM NAME="TopPoints" VALUE="0">
    <PARAM NAME="BotPoints" VALUE="0">
</OBJECT>

<OBJECT ID="Label4" WIDTH=350 HEIGHT=35
    ALIGN="TextBottom"
    CLASSID="CLSID:99B42120-6EC7-11CF-A6C7-00AA00A47DD2">
    <PARAM NAME="_ExtentX" VALUE="3625">
    <PARAM NAME="_ExtentY" VALUE="714">
    <PARAM NAME="Caption" VALUE="Come Here, or Click Me">
    <PARAM NAME="Angle" VALUE="0">
    <PARAM NAME="Alignment" VALUE="4">
    <PARAM NAME="Mode" VALUE="1">
    <PARAM NAME="FillStyle" VALUE="0">
    <PARAM NAME="BackStyle" VALUE="1">
```

```
    <PARAM NAME="ForeColor" VALUE="#00ff66">
    <PARAM NAME="BackColor" VALUE="#666666">
    <PARAM NAME="FontName" VALUE="MS Sans Serif">
    <PARAM NAME="FontSize" VALUE="24">
    <PARAM NAME="FontItalic" VALUE="1">
    <PARAM NAME="FontBold" VALUE="0">
    <PARAM NAME="FontUnderline" VALUE="0">
    <PARAM NAME="FontStrikeout" VALUE="0">
    <PARAM NAME="TopPoints" VALUE="0">
    <PARAM NAME="BotPoints" VALUE="0">
</OBJECT><P>
<CENTER>
<INPUT TYPE="Button" NAME="StatusButton" VALUE="Default State">
</CENTER>
</BODY>
</HTML>
```

The Animated Button

If you are tired of old gray buttons and static images and want your animations to respond to the user, use the Animated Button control. This ActiveX component can show different frame sequences of .AVI files, depending on the current button state. The control has several events and can be fully integrated into scripts. A great use for this control is to attract the user to a particular feature. When the mouse enters the button area, a different section of the movie can be played to instruct them to press the button. This event can then invoke some more script code; for example, to enter a VRML world.

There are some limitations on the types of AVI that can be used. The AVI must be RLE, or 8-bit compressed, and its palette must match that used by Internet Explorer. For the technically minded, this is the halftone palette returned by CreateHalftonePalette.

Figure 12-4 shows the example document containing the Animated Button control. It can be loaded from the main Web page that is on the CD. Under the ActiveX Gallery section, choose the `The Animated Button - WideScreen Web Wonder!` hyperlink. You should see a video of the word "VBScript" being manipulated. Move the mouse over the control, click on the control, or move the mouse pointer out of the button area. The last event fired for the Animated Button displays the button's status on an HTML BUTTON element.

CAUTION **The starting frame (DefaultFrStart, FocusFrStart, and so on) for any particular sequence *must* be a keyframe of the animation. If this is not the case, the control will not display anything at all when in that state.**

Table 12-4 The Animated Button Object

Class ID	
CLSID:0482B100-739C-11CF-A3A9-00A0C9034920	
Properties	
ID	Names the control—placed in opening <OBJECT> tag
Height	Height of control—set to height of the animation
Width	Width of control—set to width of the animation
Enabled	Boolean state indicating whether or not the control is active. If False, the AVI file will not play.
URL	URL for the AVI to display
DefaultFrStart	Starting frame number for the Default state
DefaultFrEnd	Ending frame number for the Default state
MouseOverFrStart	Start frame for MouseOver state
MouseOverFrEnd	Ending frame for MouseOver state
FocusFrStart	Start frame for Focus state
FocusFrEnd	Ending frame for Focus state
DownFrStart	Start frame for Down state
DownFrEnd	Ending frame for Down state

Table 12-4 The Animated Button Object

	Methods
AboutBox	Displays the control's information dialog.
	Events
Click	Fires when the user clicks on the control with the mouse, or presses the space bar when the control has input focus.
DblClick	Triggers when the user double-clicks the mouse over the control.
Enter	Fires whenever the mouse pointer enters the control area.
Leave	Fires whenever the mouse pointer leaves the control area.
Focus	Triggers when the control receives the current input focus.

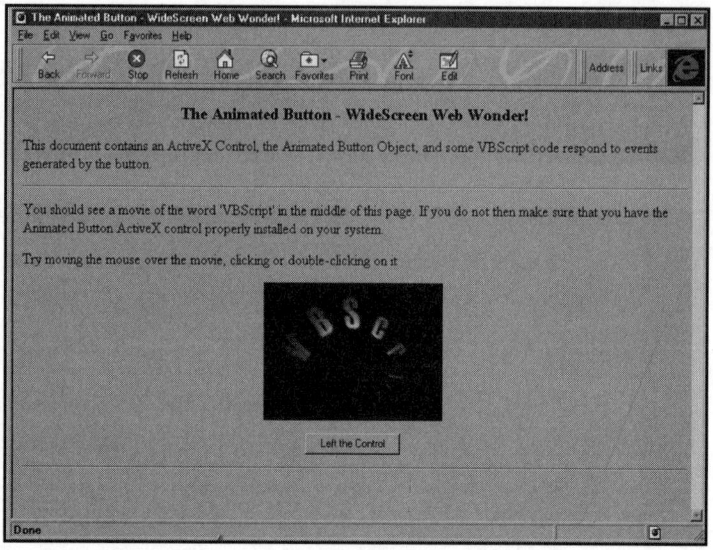

FIGURE 12-4
Playing a movie with the Animated Button control

Setting the URL Property Correctly

If you experience trouble getting the video to play, there are several things to consider. The starting frames for each sequence must all be key frames in the animation. Your rendering or art package should allow you to set these up when designing an animation.

If this condition has been met, make sure that the URL has been set correctly. This example uses a relative filename to insert the AVI file,

```
<PARAM NAME="URL" VALUE="morph.avi">
```

Sometimes this causes trouble and the control requires a complete URL such as

```
<PARAM NAME="URL" VALUE="http://www.movies.com/morph.avi">
```

If this example fails to work on your system, make sure the Animated Button object has been installed and change the URL entry to the position of this animation file on your computer, for example,

```
<PARAM NAME="URL" VALUE="C:\VBScript\Examples\Mvb_12\morph.avi">
```

The Possible States for the Animated Button Object

The Animated Button control can be in one of several states

- Down—While the control is being pressed with the left mouse button.
- Focus—While the control has the current input focus.
- MouseOver—Whenever the mouse moves over the control.
- Default—When the control is not in focus, and the mouse pointer is not over the control.

These are not mutually exclusive, but there are some precedence rules. Down has the highest precedence, with Default having the lowest precedence. MouseOver replaces Focus if the user moves over the control while it has the input focus.

```
<HTML>
<HEAD>
<TITLE>The Animated Button - WideScreen Web  Wonder!</TITLE>
<SCRIPT LANGUAGE="VBScript">
<!--
Sub MorphAVIButton_Enter
    StatusButton.Value = "Entered the Control"
```

```
End Sub

Sub MorphAVIButton_Leave
    StatusButton.Value = "Left the Control"
End Sub

Sub MorphAVIButton_Click
    StatusButton.Value = "Single-Clicked"
End Sub

Sub MorphAVIButton_DblClick
    StatusButton.Value = "Double-Clicked"
    MorphAVIButton.AboutBox
End Sub
->
</SCRIPT>
</HEAD>

<BODY>
<CENTER><H3>The Animated Button - WideScreen Web  Wonder!</H3></CENTER>
This document contains an ActiveX Control, the Animated Button Object,
➥and some VBScript code respond to events
generated by the button.
<HR>
You should see a movie of the word 'VBScript' in the middle of this
➥page. If you do not then make sure that you have
the Animated Button ActiveX control properly installed on your
➥system.<P>
Try moving the mouse over the movie, clicking or double-clicking on
➥it<P>
<CENTER>
<OBJECT ID="MorphAVIButton" WIDTH=200 HEIGHT=150
    CLASSID="CLSID:0482B100-739C-11CF-A3A9-00A0C9034920">
    <PARAM NAME="URL" VALUE="morph.avi">
    <PARAM NAME="defaultfrstart" VALUE="1">
```

```
    <PARAM NAME="defaultfrend" VALUE="24">
    <PARAM NAME="mouseoverfrstart" VALUE="25">
    <PARAM NAME="mouseoverfrend" VALUE="40">
    <PARAM NAME="focusfrstart" VALUE="1">
    <PARAM NAME="focusfrend" VALUE="24">

</OBJECT>
<P>
<INPUT TYPE="Button" NAME="StatusButton" VALUE="Default Button State">
<HR>
</CENTER>
</BODY>
</HTML>
```

The Gradient Fill

The Gradient control is a simple control that can be used to create attractive visual effects with very little effort. The area occupied by the control is shaded with a range of colors. The starting and ending colors for the fill, as well as a fill direction, can all be specified.

An example document using this control can be loaded from the `The Gradient Control - A Working Demonstration` hyperlink on the main Web page. The starting and ending colors can be changed at run-time by a script routine. The control takes a while to redraw, so it is not well-suited for creating animated effects, but it is a very colorful addition to a Web page. Figure 12-5 shows the example in action. You can view each of the different fill types by selecting options from the ComboBox control.

Table 12-5 The Gradient Object

Class ID	
CLSID:017C99A0-8637-11CF-A3A9-00A0C9034920	
Properties	
ID	Names the control—placed in opening <OBJECT> tag

Table 12-5 The Gradient Object

Height	Height of Gradient—do not set too large, it slows redraw time.
Width	Width of Gradient—do not set too large, it slows redraw time.
Visible	True—the control will be visible. False—the control will not display.
StartColor	Starting color for the fill transition
EndColor	Ending color for the fill transition
Direction	Specifies the fill type
	* 0 : Horizontal color transition
	* 1 : Vertical color transition
	* 2 : Color transition is towards the center
	* 3 : Color transition is towards the corner
	* 4 : Color transition across diagonal down
	* 5 : Color transition across diagonal up
	* 6 : Around point specified by StartPoint
	* 7 : Across line joining StartPoint and EndPoint
StartPoint	Coordinates of fill start point for modes 6 and 7, written in the format (x,y), such as (50,135).
EndPoint	Coordinates of fill end point for modes 6 and 7, written in the format (x,y), such as (50,135).
	Methods
Repaint	Causes the control to recalculate the fill and repaint it.
AboutBox	Displays the control's information dialog.
	Events
None	

NOTE *At the time of writing, the Gradient control caused the browser to hang whenever the StartPoint or EndPoint properties were set. This may have been an early version of the control, but it may be the cause of any problems you experience.*

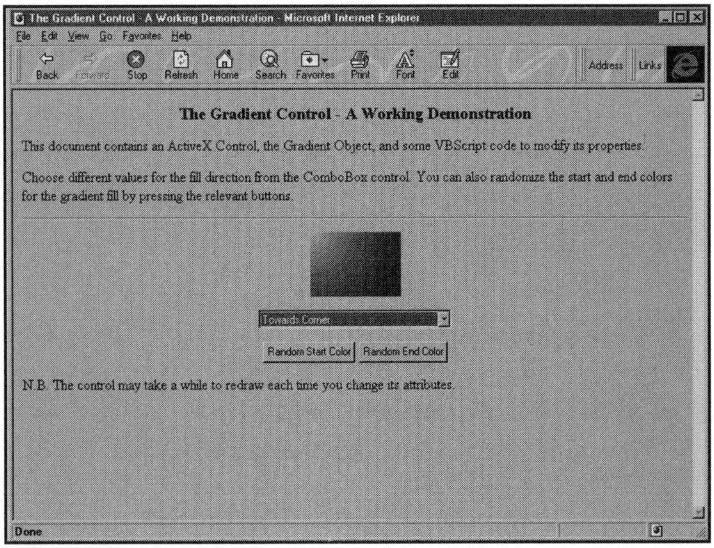

FIGURE 12-5
You can achieve smooth shading effects using the Gradient fill control.

Notice the use of the Repaint method to update the control whenever its attributes are changed. Without the calls to this method, the control would remain in its old state and no change would be observed.

```
<HTML>
<HEAD>
<TITLE>The Gradient Control - A Working Demonstration</TITLE>
<SCRIPT LANGUAGE="VBScript">
<!–
Sub DirectionCombo_OnChange
    IeGrad1.Direction = DirectionCombo.SelectedIndex
    IeGrad1.Repaint
End Sub

Sub StartColButton_OnClick
    IeGrad1.StartColor = Rnd() * 255 * 255 * 255
    IeGrad1.Repaint
End Sub

Sub EndColButton_OnClick
    IeGrad1.EndColor = Rnd() * 255 * 255 * 255
    IeGrad1.Repaint
```

```
End Sub
->
</SCRIPT>
</HEAD>

<BODY>
<CENTER><H3>The Gradient Control - A Working Demonstration</H3>
➥</CENTER>
This document contains an ActiveX Control, the Gradient Object, and
➥some VBScript code to modify its properties. <P>
Choose different values for the fill direction from the ComboBox
➥control. You can also randomize the start
and end colors for the gradient fill by pressing the relevant buttons.
<HR>
<CENTER>
<OBJECT ID="iegrad1" WIDTH=100 HEIGHT=70
        CLASSID="clsid:017C99A0-8637-11CF-A3A9-00A0C9034920">
        <PARAM NAME="StartColor" VALUE="#66ff00">
        <PARAM NAME="EndColor" VALUE="#0000ff">
</OBJECT>
<P>
<SELECT NAME="DirectionCombo">
<OPTION>Horizontal
<OPTION>Vertical
<OPTION>Towards Center
<OPTION>Towards Corner
<OPTION>Across Diagonal Down
<OPTION>Across Diagonal Up
</SELECT><P>
<INPUT TYPE="Button" NAME="StartColButton" VALUE="Random Start Color">
<INPUT TYPE="Button" NAME="EndColButton" VALUE="Random End Color">
</CENTER>
<P>
```

```
N.B. The control may take a while to redraw each time you change its
➥attributes.
</BODY>
</HTML>
```

The Preloader

The Preloader Object can greatly enhance the impact of your Web documents and make your network connection appear to be faster than it really is. This control can be used to download another file in advance. The most common example of its use is to retrieve a larger document, such as a video, VRML world, or bulky text document, while the user is still looking at some introductory information. Once the Preloader control has downloaded the file pointed to by the URL, an event fires to indicate completion. The user can now be informed and access the new document almost immediately.

The CD does not include a working example to demonstrate the Preloader because the effects of network delay are difficult to simulate on a local system. Instead, it includes an outline HTML file that demonstrates how to use the control. The Preloader object is invisible at run-time, so its size should be set to 1x1.

Table 12–6 The Preloader Object

	Class ID
CLSID:16E349E0-702C-11CF-A3A9-00A0C9034920	
	Properties
ID	Names the control—placed in opening <OBJECT> tag
Height	Height of control—set to 1
Width	Width of control—set to 1
Enable	Starts and stops the download. Set this True once the document has completed loading so it does not take up network bandwidth while the original document retrieves.

Table 12-6 The Preloader Object

URL	Specifies the URL of the file to download. Can be any valid file that your browser is equipped to deal with.
	Methods
AboutBox	Displays the control's information dialog.
	Events
Complete	Fires when the download completes successfully. The target file will now be cached on the user's system.
Error	Triggers if an error occurs while downloading the file. The download can then be restarted or the user informed of the problem.

This source code listing is incomplete, but is stored in the "*Examples\Mvb_12*" directory on the CD as Preload.htm. If you use the Preloader, base your document on this template. The download starts once the original document finishes downloading by enabling the Preloader in the Window_OnLoad procedure.

The download either completes successfully, causing the Preloader1_Complete event procedure to be executed, or fails calling Preloader1_Error. On success, the user could be informed of the newly available document, or it could display automatically. Failure should be indicated to the user in some way, or the download should be retried.

```
<HTML>
<HEAD>
<TITLE>Preloader Example</TITLE>
<SCRIPT LANGUAGE="VBScript">
<!-
Sub Window_OnLoad
    PreLoader1.Enable = True                'Start downloading the
➥large document now this one has completed
End Sub
```

```
Sub Preloader1_Complete
    ....
    'Code to navigate to the pre-loaded document
    ....
End Sub
    ....
    'Code to retry the load, or inform the user that an error has
➥occurred
    ....
Sub Preloader1_Error

End Sub
->
</SCRIPT>
</HEAD>
<BODY>
....
Document Text
....
....
....
....
<OBJECT ID="PreLoader1" WIDTH=127 HEIGHT=49
     CLASSID="CLSID:16E349E0-702C-11CF-A3A9-00A0C9034920"
     TYPE="application/x-oleobject"
>
     <PARAM NAME="URL"
VALUE="http://www.somesite.com/abigdocument.htm">
     <PARAM NAME="Enable" VALUE="False">
</OBJECT>

</BODY>
</HTML>
```

The Stock Ticker

If you want to include real-time information in your Web documents, and need to keep your clients informed of the latest stock prices, use the Stock Ticker control.

It displays data downloaded from a predetermined source at regular intervals as a scrolling marquee. The data can be in two formats, text or XRT. In order for the control to understand a text document, it must be structured like this:

```
XRT
Name1 TAB Value1 TAB Value2 ... TAB ValueN CR/LF
Name2 TAB Value1 TAB Value2 ... TAB ValueN CR/LF
...
NameN TAB Value1 TAB Value2 ... TAB ValueN CR/LF
```

Notepad, or another simple text-editor, can be used to generate these files. In addition to using a file as the data source, the name of an OLE object can be provided as long as it generates data in XRT format.

As always, there is an example ready for you to load from the CD. Select the `The Stock Ticker—Real-time Price Information` hyperlink from the ActiveX Gallery on the main Web page. The Stock Ticker object in this example uses a static data file for the data feed, but if you edit this file and wait for some time, the changes are eventually reflected. Figure 12-6 shows what the document should look like when it is loaded. The complete details for the control are as follows.

Table 12-7 The Stock Ticker Object

Class ID	
CLSID:0CA4A620-8E3D-11CF-A3A9-00A0C9034920	
Properties	
ID	Names the control—placed in opening <OBJECT> tag
Height	Height of control
Width	Width of control—set wide enough to display several items at once.

Visible	Hides or displays the control
DataObjectName	Names the Ticker's data source; can be an URL or an OLE object.
DataObjectActive	Set to 1 if the data source is active, 0 if it is not. The control only displays data when this is set to 1.
ScrollWidth	Scroll the display by this amount each time the marquee is redrawn.
ScrollSpeed	Each redraw occurs after this interval of time.
ReloadInterval	The URL is reloaded periodically after this length of time.
ForeColor	Foreground color
BackColor	Background color
OffsetValues	Specifies the URL of the file to download. Can be any valid file that your browser is equipped to deal with.
	Methods
AboutBox	Displays the control's information dialog.
	Events
None	

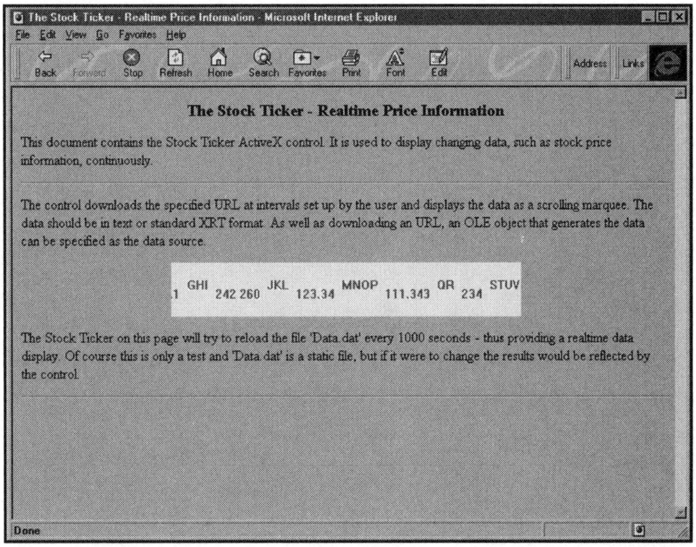

FIGURE 12-6
Real-time data acquisition with the Stock Ticker control

Specifying a Complete URL

The Stock Ticker object requires a complete URL to be specified, but you may wish to write your documents so they can be used on many machines. Microsoft has written a VBScript routine to retrieve the current base URL of a document that can then be concatenated with the filename you wish to use.

The function is called StrGetURLBase( ) and is listed in this document. The example uses a file called *Data.dat* in the current directory for the data source, and its complete URL is constructed by this line of code,

```
TickerObject.DataObjectName =  StrGetURLBase & "Data.dat"
```

This technique is used in several of the examples in this chapter and can be very handy in making your documents portable—you do not have to hard-code pathnames into your work.

Waiting Until an Object Has Been Instantiated

Another useful technique is demonstrated by this example. The Timer Object and its Timer event are used to wait until the Stock Ticker object has been fully loaded and created. The DataObjectName is then set, and the Timer object is disabled. This ensures that an object is ready for use before setting certain special properties. In this case the data source for the Stock Ticker is only set after the control is ready to begin displaying data.

```
<HTML>
<HEAD>
<TITLE>The Stock Ticker - Real-time Price Information</TITLE>
<SCRIPT Language="VBScript">
<!-
'*********************************************
' Event procedure used once, when the Stock
' Ticker object has been created to set up its
' DataObjectName attribute.
'*********************************************
```

```
Sub InitTimer_Timer()
     If IsObject(TickerObject) Then
          InitTimer.Enabled = False
          TickerObject.DataObjectName =  StrGetURLBase & "Data.dat"
     End If
End Sub

'*********************************************
' Utility function courtesy of Microsoft Corp
' Copyright Microsoft Corp @1996
' Gets the base URL of the current document -
' required for some controls which need a complete
' URL to be specified.
'*********************************************
Function StrGetURLBase()
     Dim strBase, strSlash, idx

     strBase = Location.HRef
     If (Left(strBase,5)) = "file:" then
          strSlash = "\"
     ElseIf (Left(strBase,5)) = "http:" then
          strSlash = "/"
     Else
          strBase = ""
          strSlash = "/"
     End If
     idx = Len(strBase)
     While idx > 0 And Mid(strBase, idx, 1) <> strSlash
          idx = idx - 1
     Wend
     strBase = Left(strBase,idx)
     StrGetUrlBase = strBase
End Function
-->
</SCRIPT>
```

```
</HEAD>

<BODY TEXT="#000000">
<CENTER><H3>The Stock Ticker - Real-time Price Information</H3>
➥</CENTER>
This document contains the Stock Ticker ActiveX control. It is used to
➥display changing data, such as stock
price information, continuously.
<HR>
The control downloads the specified URL at intervals set up by the
➥user and displays the data as a scrolling
marquee. The data should be in text or standard XRT format. As well as
➥downloading an URL, an OLE object
that generates the data can be specified as the data source.<P>
<CENTER>
<OBJECT
     ID="TickerObject"
     TYPE="application/x-oleobject"
     CLASSID="clsid:0CA4A620-8E3D-11CF-A3A9-00A0C9034920"
     WIDTH=400
     HEIGHT=60
>
     <PARAM NAME="ForeColor" VALUE="#ff0000">
     <PARAM NAME="BackColor" VALUE="#000000">
     <PARAM NAME="ReloadInterval" VALUE="1000">
     <PARAM NAME="DataObjectActive" VALUE="1">
     <PARAM NAME="ScrollWidth" VALUE="5">
</OBJECT>
</CENTER>
<OBJECT
          ID="InitTimer"
          CLASSID="clsid:59CCB4A0-727D-11CF-AC36-00AA00A47DD2"
```

```
        TYPE="application/x-oleobject"
>
     <PARAM NAME="Interval" VALUE="200">
     <PARAM NAME="Enabled" VALUE="True">
</OBJECT><P>
The Stock Ticker on this page will try to reload the file 'Data.dat'
every 1000 seconds - thus providing a realtime data display. Of course
this is only a test and 'Data.dat' is a static file, but if it were to
change the results would be reflected by the control.
<HR>
</BODY>
</HTML>
```

The Chart Control

If you have ever wanted to present business data over the WWW in an efficient way, the Chart control will probably fulfill your requirements. It can be used to display a whole range of different charts and can retrieve its data series from an ordinary text file.

The control is quite simple to use—all the programmer needs to do is set up the Chart properties and include the control in a document. The CD has an example document containing a fictional set of production results. You can load it from the ActiveX Gallery section of the main Web page. Select the `The Chart Object—Presentations on the Web` hyperlink (see Figure 12-7). The chart control does not currently support any events, although this may change in the future. If your charting requirements are more sophisticated, several other software developers have implemented excellent chart controls using ActiveX technology. Take a look at the ActiveX area on Microsoft's Web site for the latest offerings from third-party vendors:

`http://www.microsoft.com/`

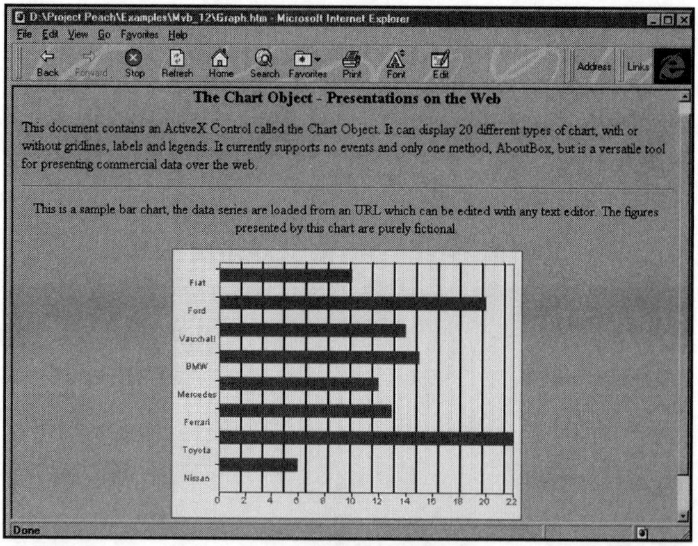

FIGURE 12-7
Presenting data on the WWW using the Chart control

Table 12-8 The Chart Object

	Class ID
CLSID:FC25B780-75BE-11CF-8B01-444553540000	
	Properties
ID	Names the control—placed in opening <OBJECT> tag
Height	Height of control
Width	Width of control
Visible	Hides or displays the control
Rows	Specifies the number of rows in the data series
Columns	Specifies the number of columns in the data series
ChartType	Specifies the type of chart to display. * 0 : Simple pie * 1 : Pie with wedge out * 2 : Simple point chart * 3 : Stacked point chart * 4 : Full point chart * 5 : Simple line chart

* 6 : Stacked line chart
* 7 : Full line chart
* 8 : Simple area chart
* 9 : Stacked area chart
* 10 : Full area chart
* 11 : Simple column chart
* 12 : Stacked column chart
* 13 : Full column chart
* 14 : Simple bar chart
* 15 : Stacked bar chart
* 16 : Full bar chart
* 17 : HLC Stock chart
* 18 : HLC Stock chart WSJ
* 19 : OHLC Stock chart
* 20 : OHLC Stock chart WSJ

RowIndex	Specifies the row index, used along with the DataItem property.
ColumnIndex	Specifies the column index, used along with the DataItem property.
DataItem	Used to set up the data series. Use in conjunction with the RowIndex and ColumnIndex properties.
ColorScheme	Chooses a set of predefined colors to use. Possible values are 0, 1 or 2.
BackStyle	Specifies whether the control background is opaque (1) or transparent (0).
Scale	Determines the percentage scaling factor. The control will perform 100% scaling by default. The value of the property should lie between 1 and 100.
RowName	Specifies the name for a row. Should be used in conjunction with the RowIndex property

Table 12-8 The Chart Object

ColumnName	Specifies the name for a column. Should be used in conjunction with the ColumnIndex property.
DisplayLegend	Specifies whether or not to display the chart legend. * 0 : Hide legend * 1 : Show legend
GridPlacement	Specifies how grid lines are drawn on the control * 0 : Lines in the background * 1 : Lines in the foreground
URL	Specifies the URL of a data file defining the data series for the chart—see separate section below.
HGridStyle	Integer specifying the type of horizontal grid lines to display. 0 = no lines. There are several other styles available, try experimenting with them.
VGridStyle	Integer specifying the type of vertical grid lines to display. 0 = no lines. There are several other styles available, try experimenting with them.
	Methods
Reload	Reloads the current chart, and redraws the control. Use this method once the URL parameter has been changed to a new chart data file—the new data will be used to redraw the chart.
AboutBox	Displays the control's information dialog.
	Events
None	

Specifying Data Series Using a Text File

The easiest way to specify data series for the Chart control is to use a text file. The name of this file is passed to the control through the

URL attribute. The chart in the example document was prepared using the file shown here. The format of the data file is quite simple. You can find the example shown here in <VBScript>\Examples\Mvb_12\grp_data.txt, where <VBScript> is the drive and directory to which you installed the example files from the CD (usually C:\VBScript).

```
14
8
1      Chris
Fiat      10
Ford      20
Vauxhall      14
BMW      15
Mercedes      12
Ferrari      13
Toyota      22
Nissan      6
```

The first line indicates the chart type required (14), and the second line is the number of data rows (8). The next line indicates the number of data series and the series names (1→Chris). The following lines specify the row names and actual chart data (Fiat→10). You should insert Tab characters (→) between each item on a line.

The following file structure should be adhered to:

```
Chart_Type
Number_Rows
Number_Series  symbol 174 \f "Symbol" \s 8  Series_Name1  symbol 174 \f
➥"Symbol" \s 8  Series_Name2 ... Series_NameN
Row_Name1  symbol 174 \f "Symbol" \s 8  Item1_1  symbol 174 \f "Symbol"
➥\s 8  Item1_2 ... Item1_N
Row_Name2  symbol 174 \f "Symbol" \s 8  Item2_1  symbol 174 \f "Symbol"
➥\s 8  Item2_2 ... Item2_N
...
Row_NameN  symbol 174 \f "Symbol" \s 8  ItemN_1  symbol 174 \f "Symbol"
➥\s 8  ItemN_2 ... ItemN_N
```

Try changing the contents of this file and looking at the different chart types offered by the Chart object.

```
<HTML>
<HEAD>
<TITLE>The Chart Object - Presentations on the Web </TITLE>
</HEAD>
<BODY>
<CENTER><H3>The Chart Object - Presentations on the Web </H3></CENTER>
This document contains an ActiveX Control called the Chart Object. It
➥can display 20 different types of chart, with
or without gridlines, labels and legends. It currently supports no
➥events and only one method, AboutBox, but
is a versatile tool for presenting commercial data over the Web
<HR>
<CENTER>
This is a sample bar chart, the data series are loaded from an URL
➥which can be edited with any text editor. The
figures presented by this chart are purely fictional.<P>
<OBJECT
     ID="Chart1"
     WIDTH=400 HEIGHT=300
     CLASSID="CLSID:FC25B780-75BE-11CF-8B01-444553540000"
>
    <PARAM NAME="HorizontalAxis" VALUE="0">
    <PARAM NAME="VerticalAxis" VALUE="0">
    <PARAM NAME="hgridStyle" VALUE="0">
    <PARAM NAME="vgridStyle" VALUE="2">
    <PARAM NAME="ColorScheme" VALUE="0">
    <PARAM NAME="BackStyle" VALUE="1">
    <PARAM NAME="Scale" VALUE="100">
    <PARAM NAME="DisplayLegend" VALUE="0">
    <PARAM NAME="BackColor" VALUE="#ffffff">
    <PARAM NAME="ForeColor" VALUE="#0055ff">
    <PARAM NAME="url" VALUE="grp_data.txt">
</OBJECT>
```

```
<HR>
</CENTER>
</BODY>
</HTML>
```

The View Tracker

This control is somewhat simpler than the Chart object of the last section. It fires an event whenever it enters or leaves the current viewable area of the screen. Its name is derived from the fact that it can be used to keep track of the user's interaction with the document.

The event procedures can be used to inform the user of certain features they can see onscreen, or to start and stop processor intensive special effects or calculations. If a task only needs to be carried out when the user is viewing a certain part of a document, why carry it out all the time?

The example provided here uses the View Tracker to inform a user of a link available for use. You can load it by selecting the `View Tracker Control - Draw Attention to An Item` link on the main Web page. Follow the on-screen instructions and scroll to the bottom of the document. When the control leaves the current window, an alert box will be displayed. Scroll back up to the top, and another alert will appear. Care must be exercised when using this control, as detailed in the section, "Handling the View Tracker's Events." Figure 12-8 shows the control sample page.

Table 12-9 The View Tracker Object

	Class ID
CLSID:1A771020-A28E-11CF-8510-00AA003B6C7E	
	Properties
ID	Names the control—placed in opening <OBJECT> tag
Height	Height of control—set to 1 if no image is being displayed, otherwise use the image height.

Table 12-9 The View Tracker Object

Width	Width of control—set to 1 if no image is being displayed, otherwise use the image width.
Visible	Hides or displays the control
Image	Specifies the URL of an image file to display on the control
	Methods
AboutBox	Displays the control's information dialog.
	Events
OnHide	Fires when the control is scrolled off the screen. This event can be used to stop a special effect or inform the user that they have missed some item on the page.
OnShow	Fires when the control is moved back onto the screen. Script code can then be used to start a special effect to grab the user's attention or inform them of a particular feature, such as a hyperlink.

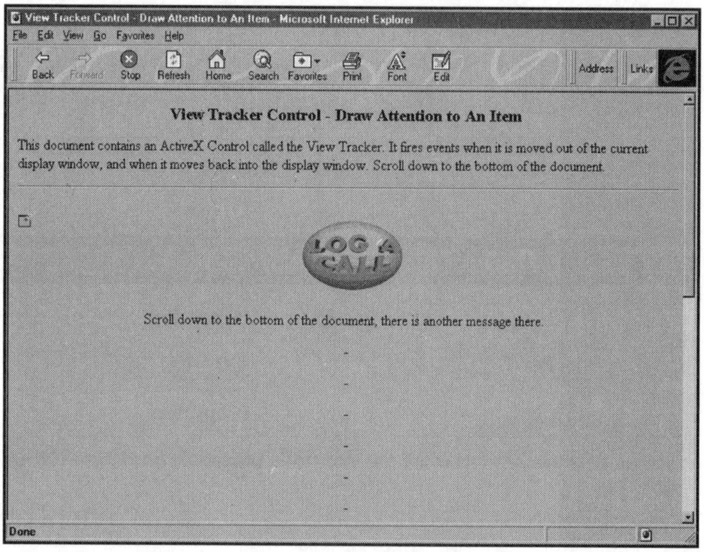

FIGURE 12-8
Keeping track of things with the View Tracker control

Handling the View Tracker's Events

The nature of the View Tracker control means that care must be exercised when responding to the OnHide and OnShow events. Certain VBScript functions cause the View Tracker to leave the current viewable area of the screen. A prime example of this is the intrinsic MsgBox function. When used in the ViewTrack_OnShow procedure, this caused the control to leave the screen, triggering the OnHide event, which caused the OnShow event to trigger as the control returned to the screen, and so on. The computer became stuck in an infinite loop and displayed lots and lots of message dialogs.

The problem was solved by using the Window object's Alert function instead. If the View Tracker control causes similar problems, try rewriting its event handlers, calling Alert if any message dialogs are required.

```
<HTML>
<HEAD>
<TITLE>View Tracker Control - Draw Attention to An Item</TITLE>
<SCRIPT LANGUAGE="VBScript">
<!-
Sub ViewTrack_OnHide
    Alert "The ViewTracker is off the screen. This event could be used
➥to stop some special effect that is no longer in view"
End Sub

Sub ViewTrack_OnShow
    Alert "View Tracker is back on the screen. This event handler
➥could display a message or play a sound to draw the user to the Log a
➥Call link"
End Sub
->
</SCRIPT>
</HEAD>

<BODY>
```

```
<CENTER><H3>View Tracker Control - Draw Attention to An Item</
➥H3></CENTER>
This document contains an ActiveX Control called the View Tracker. It
➥fires events when it is moved out of the
current display window, and when it moves back into the display
➥window. Scroll down to the bottom of the document.
<HR>
<CENTER>
<OBJECT
     ID="ViewTrack"
     CLASSID="clsid:1A771020-A28E-11CF-8510-00AA003B6C7E"
     WIDTH=1
     HEIGHT=1
     ALIGN="center"
>
</OBJECT>
<A HREF="log_call.htm" ALT="Log a Phone Call">
<IMG SRC="log_call.gif">
</A>
Scroll down to the bottom of the document, there is another message
➥there.
<P>-<P>-<P>-<P>-<P>-<P>-<P>-<P>-<P>-<P>-<P>-<P>-<P>-<P>-<P>-<P>-<P>-<P>
➥-<P>-<P>-<P>
This is the bottom - you should see a message box now.
</CENTER>
</BODY>
</HTML>
```

The Popup Menu

HTML has no built-in menu objects which would be the closest approximation is the SELECT element. The Popup Menu control fills this gap and provides a tool that can be fully integrated into your documents. It is a slightly simpler version of the Menu Button control, discussed in the next section. The one you choose to use depends on your requirements.

The Popup Menu object is a standard windows popup menu and can contain normal menu items and separator lines. Menu options can be added and removed by script code, and event procedures can be written to respond to the user choosing any of the items.

Once again, an example of the control is available to study. You access it via the `The Popup Menu - Choices All Over Your Browser` hyperlink. Load the document and click on the Show Menu BUTTON element—a small menu should appear at the mouse cursor position. Select one of the options and click on the button again. To confirm that your last selection was detected, the words "I've been chosen already" replaces the menu item you chose. Figure 12-9 shows what the document should look like when displayed by your browser.

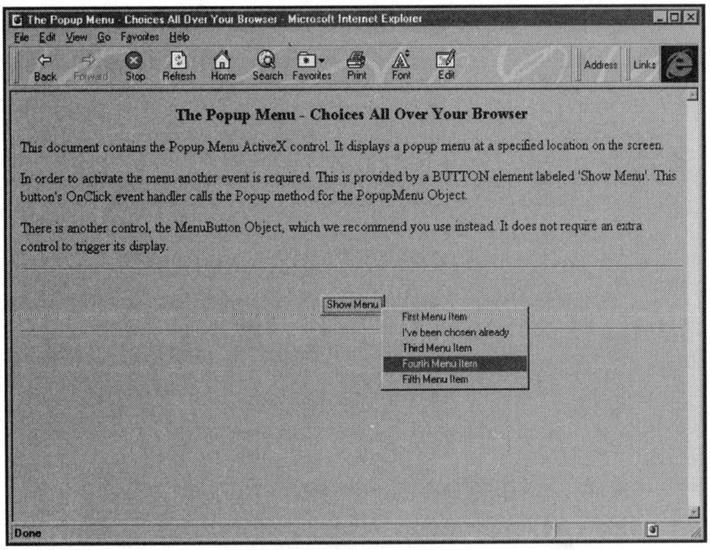

FIGURE 12-9
Enriching your documents with the Popup Menu object

Table 12-10 The Popup Menu Object

	Class ID
CLSID:7823A620-9DD9-11CF-A662-00AA00C066D2	
	Properties
ID	Names the control—placed in opening <OBJECT> tag
Height	Height of control—set to 1
Width	Width of control—set to 1
Enabled	Set to True (or 1) to activate the control. False (or 0) deactivates it.
MenuItem	This array contains the menu options. Do not modify it directly. Method are available for inserting, removing, and clearing all the items from the menu.
	Methods
Popup	Signature is Popup(x, y). Displays the menu at the screen co-ordinates specified by x and y. If either x or y, (or both) are not specified, the current mouse pointer position is used instead.
Clear	Clears all the items from the MenuItem array, resulting in an empty menu.
AddItem	Signature is AddItem(strItem, intIndex). Inserts the string stored in strItem into the menu at the position stored in intIndex. Menu positions start from 1, not zero. The second parameter is optional. If it is not specified, the item will be appended to the end of the menu.
RemoveItem	Signature is RemoveItem(intIndex). Removes the menu item at position intIndex from the control. If the item specified does not exist, then this method does nothing.
AboutBox	Displays the control's information dialog.

Events	
Click	Signature is Click(intItem). Fires when the user selects one of the options. The position of the option selected is passed in the intItem argument.

When to Display the Popup Menu

The Popup Menu object in the example has its height and width attributes set to 1 because the control is invisible until its Popup method is called. The menu is usually displayed in response to some user action, such as clicking on a button or other control. The event procedure for this other object can then display the menu. This example uses a simple BUTTON element (described in Chapter 11, "Using Forms with VBScript") as the trigger for the menu.

The fact that the Popup Menu object has no visible presence until it is invoked, can be useful in certain circumstances. The Microsoft Site Builder Network Web site uses image maps to invoke the menu's Popup method. When different parts of the image are clicked, different menus appear. This control gives complete flexibility. If a more standard menu bar is required, the MenuButton control is also available.

```
<HTML>
<HEAD>
<TITLE>The Popup Menu - Choices All Over Your Browser</TITLE>
 <SCRIPT LANGUAGE="VBSCRIPT">
<!—
Sub PopupMenu_Click(item)
    Alert "Menu click on Choice #"&item
    Call PopupMenu.RemoveItem(item)
    Call PopupMenu.AddItem("I've been chosen already", item)
end Sub

Sub ShowMenuButton_OnClick
    PopupMenu.PopUp
End Sub
—>
```

```
</SCRIPT>
</HEAD>

<BODY>
<CENTER><H3>The Popup Menu - Choices All Over Your Browser</H3>
➥</CENTER>
This document contains the Popup Menu ActiveX control. It displays a
➥popup menu
at a specified location on the screen.<P>
In order to activate the menu another event is required. This is
➥provided
by a BUTTON element labeled 'Show Menu'. This button's OnClick event
➥handler
calls the Popup method for the PopupMenu Object.<P>
There is another control, the MenuButton Object, which we recommend you
➥use instead
It does not require an extra control to trigger its display.
<HR>
<P>
<CENTER>
<CENTER>
    <INPUT TYPE=Button VALUE="Show Menu" NAME="ShowMenuButton">
</CENTER>
    <OBJECT ID="PopupMenu" WIDTH=1 HEIGHT=1
     CLASSID="CLSID:7823A620-9DD9-11CF-A662-00AA00C066D2">
        <PARAM NAME="Menuitem[0]" VALUE="First Menu Item">
        <PARAM NAME="Menuitem[1]" VALUE="Second Menu Item">
        <PARAM NAME="Menuitem[2]" VALUE="Third Menu Item">
        <PARAM NAME="Menuitem[3]" VALUE="Fourth Menu Item">
        <PARAM NAME="Menuitem[4]" VALUE="Fifth Menu Item">
    </OBJECT>
</CENTER>
<HR>
</BODY>
</HTML>
```

The Button Menu

This is the second ActiveX control in this section to implement the functionality required of a standard menu. The major difference is that the Button Menu control consists of a button which is always visible, and a popup menu section that only displays when required. In order to differentiate the Button Menu from normal buttons, it displays a small arrow symbol on the button when there are options available on the menu.

Just like the Popup menu, items can be inserted or removed at run-time, the menu can display by calling its Popup method and it can respond when the user selects an option. If there are no items in the MenuItem array, the Button Menu behaves like a normal button and fires a Click event when pressed.

The control sample page is called "The Menu Object - Menus Come to the Web," and you can load it from the main Web page's ActiveX Component Gallery (see Figure 12-10). You can add items to, and remove them from, the menu, and the Menu object displays a message dialog box whenever you select an option.

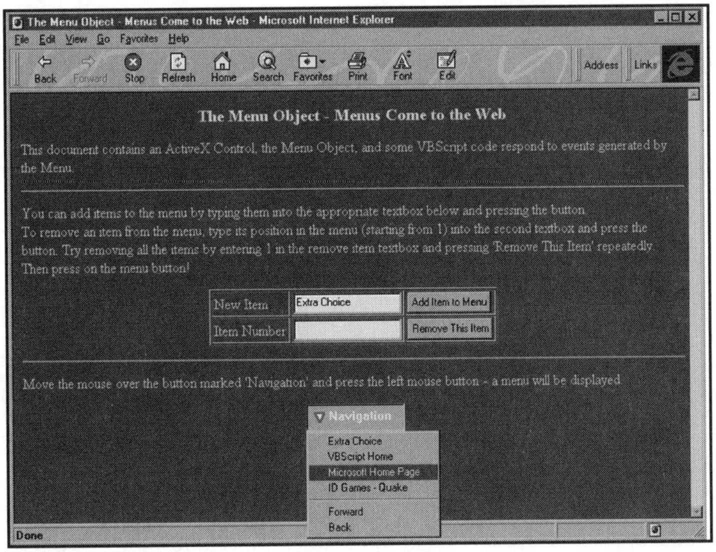

FIGURE 12-10
A complete menu system—the Menu Button control

Table 12-11 The Button Menu Object

Class ID	
CLSID:52DFAE60-CEBF-11CF-A3A9-00A0C9034920	
Properties	
ID	Names the control—placed in opening <OBJECT> tag
Height	Height of control—set large enough to display caption and drop-down arrow.
Width	Width of control—set large enough to display caption and drop-down arrow.
Enabled	Set to True (or 1) to activate the control. False (or 0) deactivates it.
Caption	Specifies the text string to display on the button face
MenuItem	This array contains the menu options. Do not modify it directly, methods are available for inserting, removing, and clearing all the items from the menu
Methods	
Popup	Signature is Popup(x, y). Displays the menu at the screen co-ordinates specified by x and y. If either x or y, or both are not specified, the current mouse pointer position is used instead.
Clear	Clears all the items from the MenuItem array, resulting in an empty menu.
AddItem	Signature is AddItem(strItem, intIndex). Inserts the string stored in strItem into the menu at the position stored in intIndex. Menu positions start from 1, not zero. The second parameter is optional. If it is not specified, the item appends to the end of the menu.
RemoveItem	Signature is RemoveItem(intIndex). Removes the menu item at position intIndex from the control. If the item specified does not exist, then this method does nothing.

GetItem	Signature is GetItem(strItem, intIndex). Retrieves the text of the menu option at position intIndex and stores it in the string variable strItem.
AboutBox	Displays the control's information dialog.
	Events
Click	Fires when the MenuItem array is empty and the control is behaving like a standard button.
Select	Signature is Select(intItem). Fires when the user selects one of the options. The position of the option selected is passed in the intItem argument.

Specifying Menu Items with the <PARAM> Element

When the Button Menu and Popup Menu controls are modified at run-time, their built-in methods are used. These methods, for inserting and removing items, number the menu options from 1. VBScript arrays are by default indexed from zero. The different numbering system used by the menu methods means care is needed when specifying positions for menu options. The wrong item could easily be removed! A further complication arises when using the <PARAM> element. The menu items can be specified by using the following syntax:

```
<PARAM NAME="MenuItem[0]" VALUE="VBScript Home">
<PARAM NAME="MenuItem[1]" VALUE="Microsoft Home Page">
...
<PARAM NAME="MenuItem[n]" VALUE="Option n">
```

Note that in this case the items are numbered from zero.

Defining Breaks in Menus

Menus can contain narrow horizontal lines that act as separators for the options in the menu (see Figure 12-10). To insert these into a menu, provide the control with a blank string ("") in place of an element. The Button Menu interprets this as a separator and displays a solid horizontal line in the menu. The separator still counts as an element and can be accessed by referring to its position. However, separators cannot be selected by the user, and will never generate a Select event.

Using Tables to Organize a Document

Take a look at the source code for the Button Menu example which has been reproduced here. A table has been defined using the <TABLE>, <TR> and <TD> container tags. Tables are good to align and organize elements of a document. Explorer 3.0 adds support for complex tables, including different colored cells. See the list of supported tags for your browser to discover what its table support.

```
<HTML>
<HEAD>
<TITLE>The Menu Object - Menus Come to the Web </TITLE>
<SCRIPT LANGUAGE="VBScript">
<!-
Sub NavMenu_Click
 Window.Location.href = "gong.wav"
 MsgBox "Empty Menu - I may as well be a button!"
End Sub

Sub NavMenu_Select(intItem)
    Dim strItemText
    MsgBox "Item #" & intItem & " has been clicked."
End Sub

Sub NewButton_OnClick
    Call NavMenu.AddItem(NewText.Value, Int(RemoveText.Value))
End Sub

Sub RemoveButton_OnClick
    NavMenu.RemoveItem(RemoveText.Value)
```

```
End Sub
->
</SCRIPT>
</HEAD>

<BODY bgColor="'#777777" TEXT="#ffff00">
<CENTER><H3>The Menu Object - Menus Come to the Web </H3></CENTER>
This document contains an ActiveX Control, the Menu Object, and some
➥VBScript code respond to events
generated by the Menu
<HR>
You can add items to the menu by typing them into the appropriate
➥textbox below and pressing the button.<BR>
To remove an item from the menu, type its position in the menu
(starting from 1) into the second textbox
and press the button. Try removing all the items by entering 1 in the
➥remove item textbox and pressing
'Remove This Item' repeatedly. Then press on the menu button!<P>
<CENTER>
<TABLE BORDER>
<TR>
<TD>New Item</TD>
<TD><INPUT TYPE=Text NAME="NewText"></TD>
<TD><INPUT TYPE=Button VALUE="Add Item to Menu" NAME="NewButton"></TD>
<TR>
<TD>Item Number     </TD>
<TD><INPUT TYPE=Text NAME="RemoveText"></TD>
<TD><INPUT TYPE=Button VALUE="Remove This Item"
➥NAME="RemoveButton"></TD>
</TABLE>
<HR>
</CENTER>
Move the mouse over the button marked 'Navigation' and press the left
➥mouse button - a menu will be displayed.<P>
<CENTER>
```

```
    <OBJECT ID="NavMenu" WIDTH=110 HEIGHT=30
     CLASSID="CLSID:52DFAE60-CEBF-11CF-A3A9-00A0C9034920">
        <PARAM NAME="Caption" VALUE="Navigation">
        <PARAM NAME="MenuItem[0]" VALUE="VBScript Home">
        <PARAM NAME="MenuItem[1]" VALUE="Microsoft Home Page">
        <PARAM NAME="MenuItem[2]" VALUE="ID Games - Quake">
        <PARAM NAME="MenuItem[3]" VALUE="">
        <PARAM NAME="MenuItem[4]" VALUE="Forward">
        <PARAM NAME="MenuItem[5]" VALUE="Back">
    </OBJECT>
</CENTER>
</BODY>
</HTML>
```

The Popup Window

You've seen popup menus already, so how about a popup window which can display more than just menu options? There is an ActiveX control available which can do that. The Popup Window control can display an HTML document in a small window without the user actually loading that document into their browser. The main use for this would be as a preview of some other Web page or to display extra information about another object—perhaps the meaning of some technical term.

The control itself is fairly simple: it has three methods, no events, and only the basic properties common to most controls. A sample document demonstrating the Popup Window can be loaded by selecting the `The Popup Window - Preview Before You Jump` hyperlink from the ActiveX Gallery section of the main Web page. Figure 12-11 shows the control in action.

Table 12-12 The Popup Window Object

Class ID
CLSID:A23D7C20-CABA-11CF-A5D4-00AA00A47DD2

Properties	
ID	Names the control—placed in opening <OBJECT> tag
Height	Height of control—set large enough to display caption and drop-down arrow.
Width	Width of control—set to 1
Methods	
Popup	Signature is Popup(strURL, blnScale). Displays the file specified by the URL stored in strURL in a popup window. The preview can be scaled to fit the document (blnScale=1), or left as is (blnScale=0).
Dismiss	Hides the popup window so the user cannot see it—the Popup method must be called to reveal it again.
AboutBox	Displays the control's information dialog.
Events	
None	

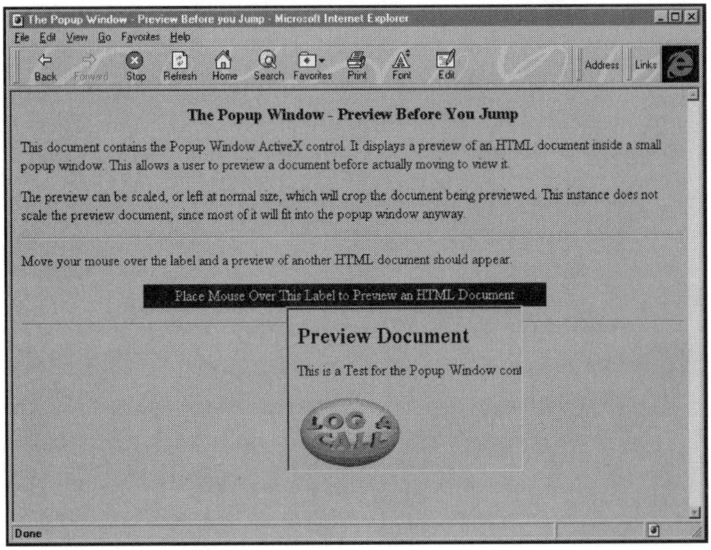

FIGURE 12-11
Previewing HTML documents using the Popup Window control

Using the Popup Window in a Document

Like the Popup Menu, the Popup Window control is not visible at run-time, so it needs to be associated with another object in order to display it. One effective technique is to insert a Label object (see earlier in this chapter) and display the popup window whenever the user moves the mouse pointer over the label. The Label caption can then be used to attract the user's attention to the extra feature.

The event handler for the Label control's MouseOver event was used in the example to display a preview of a document with no scaling (see Table 12-12).

```
Sub LinkLabel_MouseMove(shift, button, x, y)
    PopupWindow.Popup StrGetURLBase & "preview.htm", False
```

Keeping Documents Portable

A special function for retrieving a document's base URL was introduced in the section on the Stock Ticker object. It can be used to keep a document portable because URL's do not have to be hard-coded into a script. The line

```
    PopupWindow.Popup StrGetURLBase & "preview.htm", False
```

displays a popup window containing the file preview.htm. This file can be stored in the same directory as the main document—the StrGetURLBase function (written by Microsoft) will generate the correct base URL for the document, wherever it is stored.

```
<HTML>
<HEAD>
<TITLE>The Popup Window - Preview Before you Jump</TITLE>
<SCRIPT LANGUAGE="VBSCRIPT">
<!-
Sub LinkLabel_MouseMove(shift, button, x, y)
    PopupWindow.Popup StrGetURLBase & "preview.htm", False
End Sub
```

```
Sub LinkLabel_OnClick
     ' Navigation code would be placed here to actually load the
➥document
End Sub

'**********************************************
' Utility function courtesy of Microsoft Corp
' Copyright Microsoft Corp @1996
' Gets the base URL of the current document -
' required for some controls which need a complete
' URL to be specified.
'**********************************************
Function StrGetURLBase()
     Dim strBase, strSlash, idx

     strBase = Location.HRef
     If (Left(strBase,5)) = "file:" then
          strSlash = "\"
     ElseIf (Left(strBase,5)) = "http:" then
          strSlash = "/"
     Else
          strBase = ""
          strSlash = "/"
     End If
     idx = Len(strBase)
     While idx > 0 And Mid(strBase, idx, 1) <> strSlash
          idx = idx - 1
     Wend
     strBase = Left(strBase,idx)
     StrGetUrlBase = strBase
End Function
-->
</SCRIPT>
</HEAD>
```

```
<BODY>
<CENTER><H3>The Popup Window - Preview Before You Jump</H3></CENTER>
This document contains the Popup Window ActiveX control. It displays a
preview of an HTML document inside a small popup window. This allows a
user to preview a document before actually moving to view it.<P>
The preview can be scaled, or left at normal size, which will crop the
document being previewed. This instance does not scale the preview
➥document,
because most of it will fit into the popup window anyway.
<HR>
Move your mouse over the label and a preview of another HTML document
➥should appear.<P><P>
<CENTER>
<A href="preview.htm">
    <OBJECT ID="LinkLabel" WIDTH=450 HEIGHT=22 TYPE="application/
➥x-oleobject" VSPACE=0
          ALIGN=center
     CLASSID="CLSID:99B42120-6EC7-11CF-A6C7-00AA00A47DD2">
        <PARAM NAME="Angle" VALUE="0">
        <PARAM NAME="Alignment" VALUE="4">
        <PARAM NAME="BackStyle" VALUE="1">
        <PARAM NAME="Caption" VALUE="Place Mouse Over This Label to
➥Preview an HTML Document">
        <PARAM NAME="FontName" VALUE="Times New Roman">
        <PARAM NAME="FontSize" VALUE="12">
        <PARAM NAME="ForeColor" VALUE="#ffff00">
        <PARAM NAME="BackColor" VALUE="#000088">
    </OBJECT>
</A>
<OBJECT ID="PopupWindow"
     WIDTH=1
     HEIGHT=1
```

```
    TYPE="application/x-oleobject"
    CLASSID="CLSID:A23D7C20-CABA-11CF-A5D4-00AA00A47DD2">
</OBJECT>
</CENTER>
<HR>
</BODY>
</HTML>
```

The Marquee Control

The last ActiveX control examined in this chapter is provided with Internet Explorer 3.0. It's called the Marquee control and can be used to display scrolling representations of HTML files within another document. These files can be scrolled horizontally, or vertically, or both, at different speeds.

The Marquee is actually quite a complex control, with lots of properties, events, and methods. Only the essential properties needed to work with the control are introduced. Most of the others are superfluous. If you need to know more details about the Marquee, read the section in Chapter 13, "Using the ActiveX Control Pad and HTML Layout Control." The Control Pad tool can be used to explore all the attributes of a particular control.

There is an example document which uses the Marquee control provided on the CD. It can be viewed by selecting the hyper-link labeled "The Marquee Control—ActiveX In Action" from the ActiveX Gallery section on the main Web page. It displays a scrolling message that praises VBScript. Figure 12-12 shows a screen capture.

NOTE *The Marquee control can be used to scroll several separate HTML documents. This advanced usage of the control is not covered here, although the essential methods to set up the URL list are included in Table 12-13. Use the ActiveX Control pad or an OLE viewer utility to discover the more advanced details of this control.*

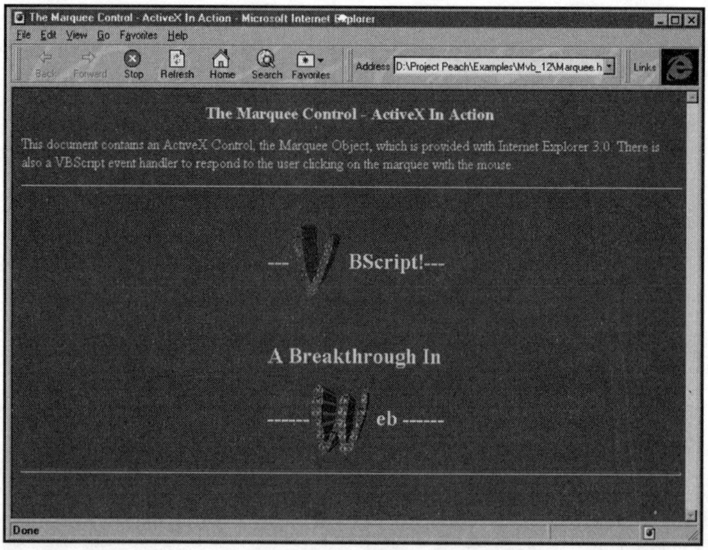

FIGURE 12-12
Scrolling images and text using the Marquee control

Table 12–13 The Marquee Object

Class ID	
CLSID:1A4DA620-6217-11CF-BE62-0080C72EDD2D	
Properties	
ID	Names the control—placed in opening <OBJECT> tag
Height	Height of control
Width	Width of control
BackgroundColor	Specifies the background color of the control. Useful when the document being displayed is smaller than the Marquee itself.
LoopsX	Boolean value specifying whether the scroll loops in the x direction. If False, the scrolling stops when it gets to the side of a document. If True, the Marquee will wrap around to the other side.
LoopsY	Boolean value specifying whether the scroll loops in the y direction. If False, the scrolling stops when it gets to the

	end of a document. If True, the Marquee will wrap around to the other end.
ScrollDelay	Interval in milliseconds between each redraw of the Marquee.
ScrollPixelsX	Number of pixels to scroll in the x direction on every redraw.
ScrollPixelsY	Number of pixels to scroll in the y direction on every redraw.
WidthOfPage	Specifies the width of the HTML document being viewed. This can be useful when aligning the scrolled item within the Marquee.
szURL	Sets the URL of the file to be displayed by the control
	Methods
Pause	Pauses the scrolling action at the current position. The Marquee will no longer move.
Resume	Restarts the Marquee control once it has been paused. The control will begin to scroll again.
InsertURL	Signature is InsertURL(intListPos, strURL). Used to display multiple documents in a single Marquee. Inserts the URL specified by the string strURL into the URL list after item number intListPos.
DeleteURL	Signature is DeleteURL(intListPos). Removes the URL at position intListPos from the current list of files to display.
QueryURLCount	Signature is QueryURLCount(intCount). Retrieves the number of URLs currently in the display list in the variable intCount.
QueryURL	Signature is QueryURL(intListPos, strURL). Returns the name of the URL stored at position intListPos in the string variable strURL.

Table 12-13 The Marquee Object	
AboutBox	Displays the control's information dialog.
	Events
OnBounce	Fires when the MenuItem array is empty and the control is behaving like a standard button.
OnEndOfImage	Signature is OnEndOfImage(intHorizOrVert). Triggers each time the control reaches the end of the current document. The argument indicates the end of the image that has been reached, horizontal or vertical.
OnLMouseClick	Fires whenever the left mouse button is clicked over the control.
OnScroll	Signature is OnScroll(intHorizOrVert). Triggers each time the control is scrolled and redrawn. The argument indicates the type of scroll that has taken place, horizontal or vertical, or both (0, 1 or 2).
OnStartOfImage	Triggers when the control scrolls back to the start of an image.

The control sample uses the Marquee control to display a single HTML document containing an advertising message. These more advanced features of the control are not used, but there is an event handler for the OnLMouseClick event—a message dialog is displayed but this procedure could be used to carry out more complicated tasks.

```
<HTML>
<HEAD>
<TITLE>The Marquee Control - ActiveX In Action</TITLE>
<SCRIPT LANGUAGE="VBScript">
<!-
Sub VB_Marquee_OnLMouseClick()
    MsgBox "Yes! I am alive, this is an Event Handler for the
➥OnLMouseClick event"
```

```
end sub
—>
</SCRIPT>
</HEAD>

<BODY bgCOLOR="#666666" TEXT="#ffff00">
<CENTER><H3>The Marquee Control - ActiveX In Action</H3></CENTER>
This document contains an ActiveX Control, the Marquee Object, which is
➥provided with
Internet Explorer 3.0. There is also a VBScript event handler to
➥respond to the user
clicking on the marquee with the mouse.
<HR>
<CENTER>
    <OBJECT ID="VB_Marquee" WIDTH=210 HEIGHT=280 align=CENTER BORDER=1
➥HSPACE=5
     CLASSID="CLSID:1a4da620-6217-11cf-be62-0080c72edd2d">
        <PARAM NAME="ScrollStyleX" VALUE="Circular">
        <PARAM NAME="ScrollStyleY" VALUE="Circular">
        <PARAM NAME="szURL" VALUE="Scroller.htm">
        <PARAM NAME="ScrollDelay" VALUE="80">
        <PARAM NAME="LoopsX" VALUE="-1">
        <PARAM NAME="LoopsY" VALUE="-1">
        <PARAM NAME="ScrollPixelsX" VALUE="0">
        <PARAM NAME="ScrollPixelsY" VALUE="-6">
        <PARAM NAME="DrawImmediately" VALUE="0">
        <PARAM NAME="Whitespace" VALUE="0">
        <PARAM NAME="BackGroundColor" VALUE="#000080">
        <PARAM NAME="PageFlippingOn" VALUE="0">
        <PARAM NAME="Zoom" VALUE="100">
        <PARAM NAME="WidthOfPage" VALUE="400">
    </OBJECT>
<HR SIZE=4>
```

```
</CENTER>
</BODY>
</HTML>
```

Conclusions—Leaving the Gallery

This chapter has covered a lot of new material, all of which would not have been possible without the new scripting engines for VBScript and JavaScript. The ActiveX controls introduced here open up a whole new world of interactive Web pages.

The twelve controls showcased over the last few pages are only part of the story. There are hundreds and hundreds more controls being developed by companies and individuals all over the world. Many controls will be available over the Internet. The ActiveX technology has been licensed to several other developers for cross-platform development, so you can expect to soon see ActiveX controls for Unix and Apple Macintosh systems.

Up until now, there has been very little discussion of the programs needed to develop pages using these new controls. Now that you have a good idea of the possibilities and different controls available, the next chapter will explain the tools available from Microsoft. These include the ActiveX Control Pad for inserting controls and writing event procedures, the HTML Layout control for designing complex layouts, and the Microsoft Forms 2.0 Controls, another set of ActiveX controls.

CHAPTER 13

Using the ActiveX Control Pad and HTML Layout Control

ActiveX controls are Explorer 3.0's most exciting new feature—they open up a world of interactive Web pages and are integrated easily into documents by using scripting. The last chapter focused on some of the controls and presented examples of how to use them. Now you're about to find out more about inserting these controls and using the ActiveX Control Pad to attach scripts to them.

Microsoft's ActiveX Control Pad is an interface for creating, opening, modifying, and saving Web pages. Not only does it offer a simple way of generating the complicated ClassId expressions for the <OBJECT> tags, but it also incorporates the HTML Layout control, which acts as a WYSIWYG tool for placing objects on a web page. This was previously unfeasible owing to HTML's limited structure, you now can attach a layout to a web page to control the exact positioning of objects, which is interpreted when the document loads.

This chapter focuses on the following topics:

- Adding ActiveX Objects to your web pages by using the Control Pad
- Using the Script Wizard to incorporate event-handling procedures into your scripts
- Attaching scripts to specific events, customizing them to your own needs
- Designing the layout of objects on the document by using the new HTML Layout Control
- Including Microsoft's Forms 2.0 controls in your HTML code

So What's the Idea behind the Control Pad?

Every time you use an ActiveX control, you need to specify a set of parameters to describe how it will be used. The options are far too plentiful to catalog in a book, so Microsoft has developed a tool that allows both novices and experienced programmers to quickly set up the control to their satisfaction and then get the Control Pad to automatically place the HTML code into the document. This code includes the important ClassId expression for the object and any attributes that go with it.

You set up each control by pointing and clicking on options in various menus. You can insert some of the controls with just a few clicks, whereas others require some scripting for full integration into the web page. You can use VBScript or JavaScript as the scripting language, but the capability to combine the languages in the document presently isn't supported.

The Control Pad also enables you to place objects on a web page precisely by providing a WYSIWYG editor for the HTML Layout Control. You can download the HTML Layout Control separately, but it is incorporated into the Control Pad and lets users position objects exactly as they create them.

You now can see how you could use the Control Pad to build a complete HTML document boasting ActiveX controls (objects), intrinsic HTML controls, and scripted routines in a truly interactive environment. ActiveX Control Pad isn't an authoring package like FrontPage, but rather, is a product with which you (rather than the program) control what code goes into your document and where it goes. It's menu driven, easily operated, and bears a certain resemblance to Visual Basic in its setup. Not only does it give the author more editing flexibility, it also allows you to add controls to old documents or to documents created using other packages with ease.

What Do You Need to Run the ActiveX Control Pad?

The Control Pad is a free downloadable product from Microsoft, and has been included on the tutorial CD so that you don't need to spend ages downloading it before being able to use it. If you haven't already carried out the installation, consult Chapter 3, "Creating Your First VBScript Document"—it takes you through the process.

The minimum requirements for running the program are

- a 486 processor
- Windows 95 or Windows NT 4.0
- 16 MB RAM
- 10 MB free hard disk space
- Internet Explorer 3.0

After you install the Control Pad, you should have access to all the implementation information you need for the ActiveX controls. That done, now it's time to learn how to use it.

Using the ActiveX Control Pad

When you load up the Control Pad, you should see a screen similar to Figure 13-1 (minus the Control Pad background).

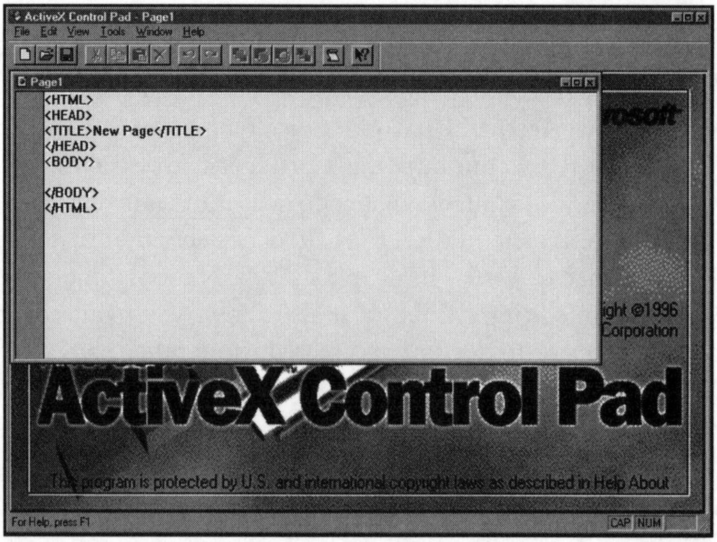

FIGURE 13-1
The ActiveX control pad

Launching the program generates a basic HTML outline that can prove useful if you're writing a simple document from scratch, but isn't worth much for creating complicated web pages because you have to enter the HTML commands individually. Produce a skeleton document using a web editor (such as Kenn Nesbitt's WebEdit on the CD) and then add some ActiveX controls by launching the Control Pad. It is easier. You put these controls into your document by using the Insert ActiveX Control option on the Edit menu. Before jumping to the Edit menu, though, take a gander at Figure 13-2 to see the underlying structure of the Control Pad. Note the four main sections:

- HTML Source Editor
- ActiveX Control Editor
- HTML Layout Control
- Script Wizard

Now take a closer look at a few of the menus that make up the Control Pad.

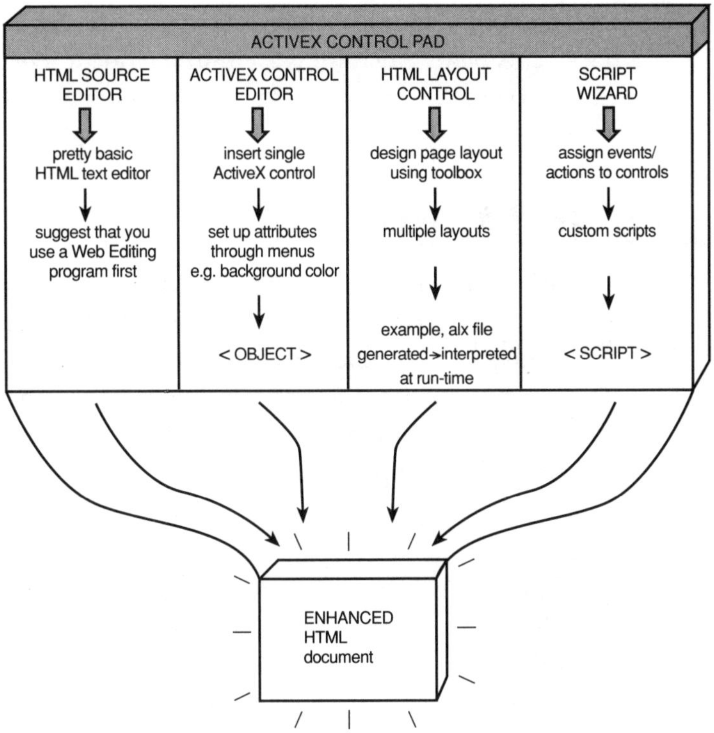

FIGURE 13-2
The components that make up the ActiveX Control Pad

The File Menu

Nestled among the familiar commands in the File menu is the New HTML Layout command. This command (covered in more depth later in the chapter) basically opens a window that enables you to use a tool box to place objects on the web page and then to reference these objects in your HTML document. You should use this command when you design page layouts, and then use the Edit menu to add the Layout you have designed to the document.

The Edit Menu

The Edit menu holds the two important commands for putting ActiveX controls and HTML layout controls into your documents:

- Insert ActiveX Control
- Insert HTML Layout

Each command brings up a series of windows that let you select and adjust items before including them in the document. Owing to their complicated nature, they are dealt with separately later on in this chapter.

The Tools Menu

The Tools menu provides access to the Script Wizard tool for attaching scripts to the controls in your document. The Script Wizard provides an easy way to generate event procedures for different actions, and is covered in a later section on its own. The other option on the Tools menu deals with choosing the default scripting language—VBScript or JavaScript.

You also can choose to view the script in List view or Code view. List view is useful when the commands are simple actions that don't need any modifications, such as playing a sound when a users clicks on a button. They can be selected from the menus, and don't require any extra code input. When more complicated scripting is required, you should go with the Code view, because it lets you input a customized VBScript or JavaScript routine directly. You use this option on the Tools menu just to set the current default—you can always change between the two views when operating the Script Wizard.

The next paragraph will introduce how to add a controls to your documents. Once the insertion of objects into documents demonstrated, you'll learn how to add script code to generate their dynamic behavior.

Inserting and Editing ActiveX Controls with the Control Editor

We will now demonstrate how to insert and use controls with the help of an example. The completed example will have been installed from the CD with all the other software when you ran the install program (see Chapter 3, "Creating Your First VBScript Document"). Instead of loading the complete example and looking at it, the following paragraphs take you through the process step-by-step. To start, load the basic HTML example program from the main Web page, by choosing the `Beginning to Use the ActiveX Control Pad` hyperlink. This program is no more than a <HEAD> and <BODY> section, with the background color set to black. View it in the Explorer 3.0 Shell, and also load it into the Control Pad. You now are going to add an animated button to the page to spruce it up a little. The Animated Button is an ActiveX control, and you can add it to the document by choosing the Insert ActiveX Control option from the Edit menu, or by clicking the right mouse button and using the pop-up menu (see Figure 13-3). Before you add the control, make sure that you have placed the cursor in the <BODY> section of the document, because that's where you want to insert the <OBJECT> tag.

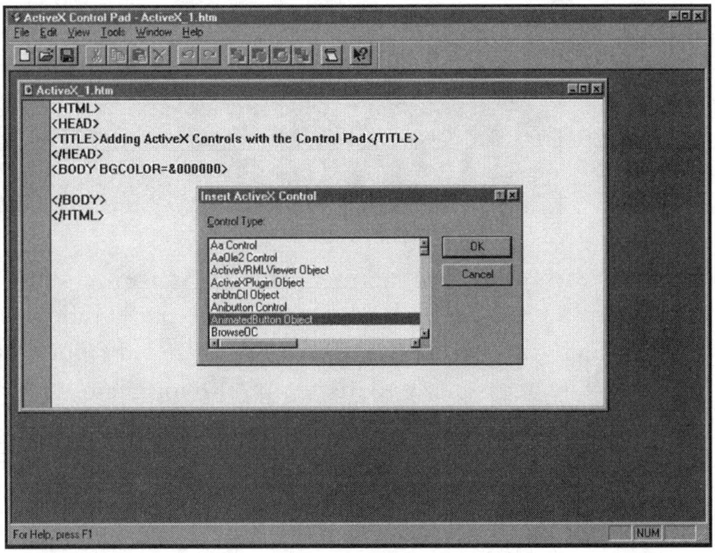

FIGURE 13-3
The list of controls that you can add to your document

As you can see, the dialog box lists a multitude of controls, most of which probably look unfamiliar. Don't worry. The Insert ActiveX Control dialog box contains *all* the controls registered on your system, including controls that other applications may install, as well as any uncertified third-party custom controls. New controls are added to your system's registry as you surf different sites. This chapter considers only the ActiveX controls mentioned in Chapter 12 and the Microsoft Forms 2.0 controls. Generally, the controls in this chapter are referred to as objects rather than controls.

Go ahead and insert your first object now. Select the AnimatedButton Object from the list by double-clicking it, which opens another two windows (see Figure 13-4).

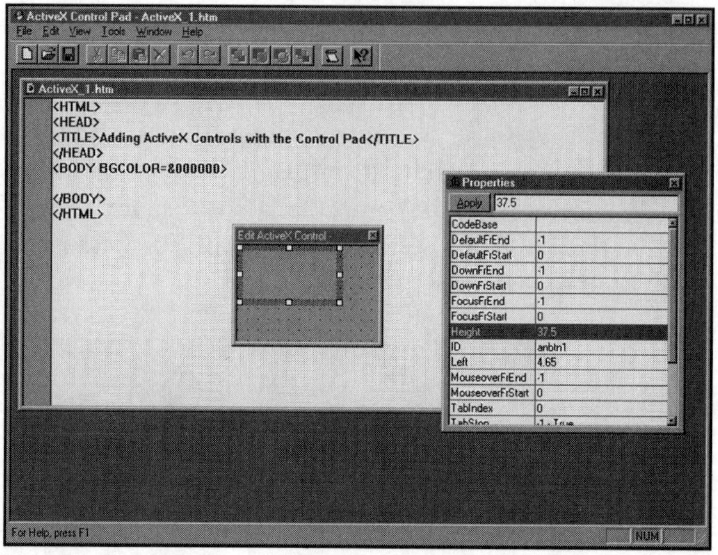

FIGURE 13-4.
The style attributes window for ActiveX Controls

The first of these windows, the Edit ActiveX Control box, illustrates what the control looks like, and the second window controls the properties of the control. Chapter 12 discussed attributes of controls, and this chapter is going to discuss modifying them within the Control Pad.

1. First, change the height of the button to 100. Select the Height caption in the Properties window and then type 100 into the text box at the top of this window.
2. Click on Apply. The new height appears in the table.
3. Now adjust the URL of the animation file. Set this equal to your CD drive, followed by the path Examples/Mvb_13/cone.avi, for example, d:/Examples/Mvb_13/cone.avi. Make sure that you have the CD that came with the book placed in the drive. Alternatively, if you installed the examples from the CD on your hard drive, supply that path, for example, c:/VBScript/Examples/Mvb_13/cone.avi.
4. Finally, change the width of the button to 120.

Now click on the close icon in the top right-hand corner of the Properties dialog box, and then do the same for the Edit ActiveX Control box. The screen clears, and several lines of HTML are inserted into your document to represent the button. All ActiveX controls are referenced through the <OBJECT> tag, and are followed by parameters for the object and a complicated Class ID number that tells the interpreter which control it should use.

Save the file to your VBScript working directory or Desktop and then load it into Explorer 3.0. You should see a button with a simple animation on it. Later, you attach a script to the button to control an event (see the Script Wizard section).

Try to include some of the other ActiveX objects into a trial document. Don't worry about the placement of the objects yet; placing objects is covered later in the chapter. Have a good look at all of the properties of the controls to see what you can vary. Try out the marquee control, or put some text labels on a page at different angles and in different fonts for practice.

Changing a Control's Attributes

After you incorporate an object into a document, you can adjust its properties directly from the Control Pad. To do so, just click once on the blue box in the margin of the document editor next to the <OBJECT> tag, which launches the Control Properties window and enables you to change the settings.

You can adjust some of the appearance properties of a control by clicking and dragging the image of the control in the Edit ActiveX Control window. You can sometimes type text directly on a control, but not always. Properties, such as colors, usually are specified by the six digit hexadecimal version #RRGGBB, and must be changed in the menus. If you look at the right-hand side of the text box where you normally enter values, you can see a small button with three dots, or an ellipses (...). Click on this button to open a color selection box in which you can point and click on the color you want.

The Control Pad generates an object ID automatically when you insert a new object. You should change this name slightly to reflect the nature of the control to make identification easier when you attach scripts, for example, changing IeLabel1 to SearchLabel.

Putting in Non-ActiveX Controls

The ActiveX Control pad makes adding ActiveX controls to your documents very easy because it holds all of their properties in a database and lets you sift through them in a menu. Things aren't so easy when you want to put in other types of controls. You can just type them in, but doing so is cumbersome and long-winded, especially if you have stacks of HTML tags to enter.

If you want to add ActiveX controls, you should first use a Web authoring tool, such as WebEdit or FrontPage, to create an HTML document with the intrinsic form controls, and then import it into the ActiveX Control Pad.

What To Do If the Parameters Aren't Set Correctly

Sometimes the Control Pad may have set up the parameters incorrectly. If so, and you can spot what's gone wrong, take the liberty of adjusting the code in the document editor. You can correct omissions by adding `<PARAM NAME="someName" VALUE="someValue">` to the code. You usually can find the Name property on the Properties menu, and the you can manually enter the values they can take .

Now you know how to place ActiveX objects into your documents, but you don't yet know how to attach scripts to the objects to harness the real power of VBScript. That's next.

Adding Scripts with the Script Wizard

The presence of a Script Wizard makes event handling particularly simple in the ActiveX Control Pad. It enables you to select any object, see what events it can generate, and then assign actions to these events in the form of scripts. Now you will use the Control Pad to create your first event handling procedure.

Creating Event Procedures

Use the example constructed in the last section. If you had problems with it, you can find the working example on the CD via the `Inserting an ActiveX Control` link. You're going to attach an event procedure to the button's Click event, which will change the object in the movie from a cone to a pot.

After you load the example into the Control Pad, launch the Script Wizard, from the toolbar or from the Tools menu. A screen like the one shown in Figure 13-5 appears. Take a little time now to examine this screen's components, and see how to attach a script to a command.

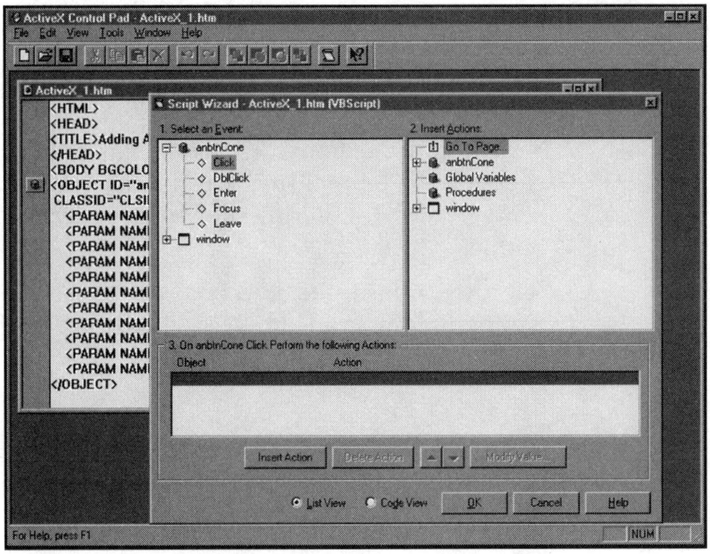

FIGURE 13-5
The Script Wizard makes light work of attaching scripts to events.

The Script Wizard window consists of three sections:

- An Event pane
- An Action pane
- A summary of the event and its assigned actions

You use the first section to select the object in whose event you're interested. Click on the `anbtnCone` entry to see what events you can trigger using the animated button control. Because this control is a button, only a handful of events can occur, most of them rather obvious. The first is a simple click on the button area, which is probably the most commonly used event, closely followed by double-clicking. Some of the more esoteric events include moving over the button area (Enter), moving out of the button area (Leave), and having the button selected as the current control in the document (known as having the input focus).

You can choose a button without having to point at it using the mouse. Usually, you would do so by using the Tab key to cycle through the different items onscreen. When a button is highlighted, it's said to have the *input focus*. On a slightly separate issue, to press a button that's in focus without using the mouse, press the Space bar.

In the following example exercise, you implement the Click event.

1. First expand the anbtnCone Event Options, and select Click.
2. Next, you must choose what you want to happen when a user clicks on the button. In this example, you change the movie being played, by altering the URL property of the animated button control.
3. Select the anbtnCone object on the Action menu in the right-hand window, and from here, choose the URL property.
4. Double-clicking on it opens a window (see Figure 13-6).

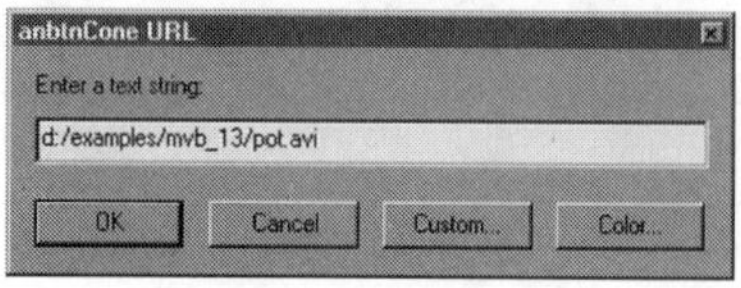

FIGURE 13-6
The dialog box for changing the properties or actions of a control

5. Next, you enter the URL of the file that you want to play when a user clicks on the button (d:/Examples/Mvb_13/pot.avi), which instructs the Control Pad to change the URL property of the animated button when it is clicked. (This file has been included on the CD in the Examples directory, and you may need to modify the URL if your CD drive is labeled differently.)

6. Click on OK. You should see an entry in the third section of the Script Wizard that indicates that the action has been assigned (see Figure 13-7).

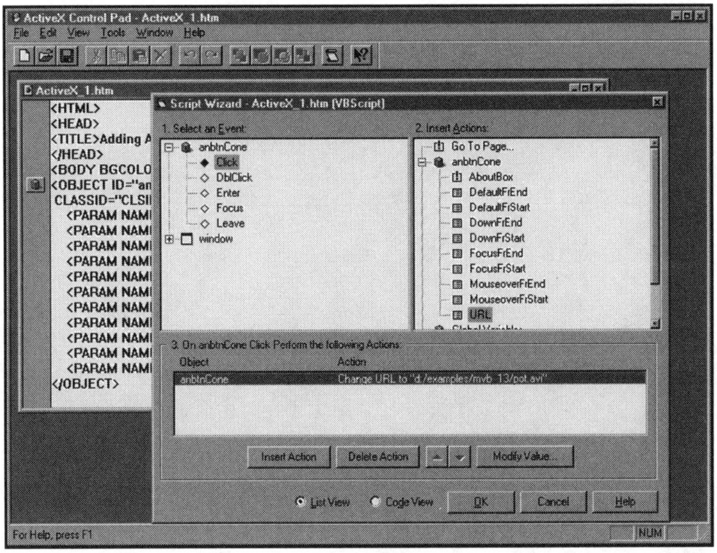

FIGURE 13-7
The Object and Action events are summarized in the bottom section of the Script Wizard.

You can make multiple actions occur for each event, and you must enter them separately using the preceding steps. This can be useful if you want to carry out two actions for one event, such as changing the movie and starting the clip from a different frame number. This covers multiple actions, but you might want to create an action sequence so that the movie changes every time you click on the button. This needs more complicated scripting and the next section examines how to do this.

Before you leave the List view of the event handling menu, have a quick look at the code that the Control Pad puts into the document. The script is located in the <BODY> section, and is introduced by the <SCRIPT> tag. The Control Pad chooses where it wants to put the scripts, and its choice may contravene the programming conventions laid out in Chapter 9, "Writing Well-Organized and Coherent VBScript". Unfortunately, you cannot avoid this problem, so you just have to live with it.

Here is the code for the script to change the movie when the user clicks on the button.

```
<TITLE>Inserting an ActiveX Control</TITLE>
</HEAD>
<BODY BGCOLOR=#000000>
    <SCRIPT LANGUAGE="VBScript">
<!-
Sub anbtnCone_Click()
anbtnCone.URL = "d:/examples/pot.avi"
end sub
->
    </SCRIPT>
    <OBJECT ID="anbtnCone" WIDTH=120 HEIGHT=80
     CLASSID="CLSID:0482B100-739C-11CF-A3A9-00A0C9034920">
```

More Complicated Scripts and the Code View Option

You will now build upon the simple script in the last example and develop a complicated script that performs a number of actions for each control. For this section, you use the View Code option on the Script Wizard window, which lets you input multiple lines of VBScript in a mini-editor window. These are then included into the document with the correct tags and procedure constructs.

Load the example from the Tutorial on the CD—choose the `A Spinning Label Demonstration - Using the ActiveX Control Pad` hyperlink. A screen appears, closely resembling the one shown in Figure 13-8.

Here, the IE Label control (called SprLblCtl Button in your Windows 95 registry) allows you to set the angle at which the text appears. By using the Timer Control in conjunction with this angle property, you can get the label to spin around a point.

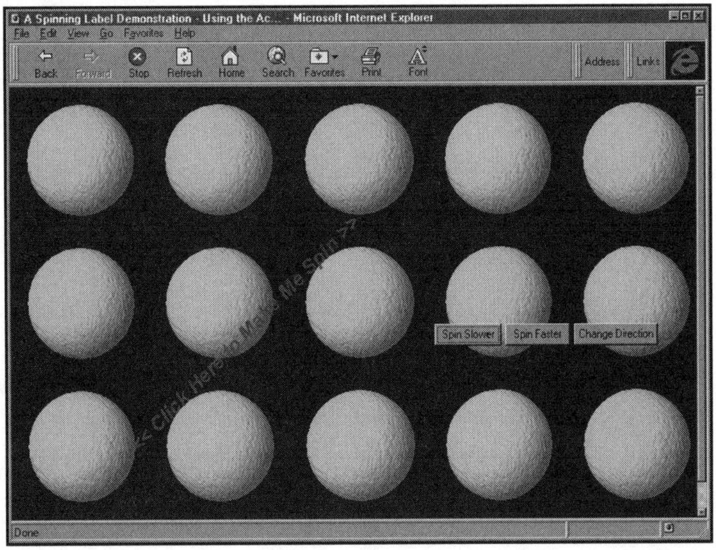

FIGURE 13-8
The spinning label uses several procedures constructed in the Control Pad.

Reconstruct this example from scratch to practice using the functions of the control pad. If you get stuck, just reload the example and choose View | Source from the Explorer menu to take a look at the code. Start a new document, and add two ActiveX objects—a label control and a timer control (see Chapter 12, "ActiveX Controls and VBScript," if these are not installed or you need to know more). Set the properties of these equal to those in following code:

```
<OBJECT ID="IeTimer1" WIDTH=39 HEIGHT=39
 CLASSID="CLSID:59CCB4A0-727D-11CF-AC36-00AA00A47DD2">
    <PARAM NAME="_ExtentX" VALUE="1032">
    <PARAM NAME="_ExtentY" VALUE="1032">
    <PARAM NAME="Interval" VALUE="192">
    <PARAM NAME="Enabled" VALUE="False">
</OBJECT>

<ALIGN = MIDDLE>
<CENTER>
    <OBJECT ID="Label1" WIDTH=410 HEIGHT=410
     CLASSID="CLSID:99B42120-6EC7-11CF-A6C7-00AA00A47DD2">
        <PARAM NAME="_ExtentX" VALUE="10345">
```

```
        <PARAM NAME="_ExtentY" VALUE="10345">
        <PARAM NAME="Caption" VALUE="&lt;&lt; Click Here to Make Me
➥Spin &gt;&gt;">
        <PARAM NAME="Angle" VALUE="0">
        <PARAM NAME="Alignment" VALUE="4">
        <PARAM NAME="Mode" VALUE="1">
        <PARAM NAME="FillStyle" VALUE="0">
        <PARAM NAME="FillStyle" VALUE="0">
        <PARAM NAME="ForeColor" VALUE="#EE3366">
        <PARAM NAME="BackColor" VALUE="#000000">
        <PARAM NAME="FontName" VALUE="Arial">
        <PARAM NAME="FontSize" VALUE="20">
        <PARAM NAME="FontItalic" VALUE="1">
        <PARAM NAME="FontBold" VALUE="1">
        <PARAM NAME="FontUnderline" VALUE="0">
        <PARAM NAME="FontStrikeout" VALUE="0">
        <PARAM NAME="TopPoints" VALUE="0">
        <PARAM NAME="BotPoints" VALUE="0">
    </OBJECT>
```

TIP

&lt is used in HTML to represent the < symbol. For the complete list of special symbols, consult the HTML Character Set in the Control Pad Help.

Now you can add event procedures to allow you to control exactly what happens when an event fires. Start by writing the timer event that changes the angle of the text every time the timer fires. This procedure is among the more difficult ones, but if you can come to grips with it first, the others will be easy to understand.

1. Click on the Script Wizard and select Code view at the bottom of the page.
2. Next, choose the IeTimer object from the Event menu, and select its Timer event.
3. Now move into the action window and right-click. Doing so gives you the option to create a new procedure, which you should now accept.

4. The words `Sub Procedure1()` appear in the window. Rename them to **`Sub IeTimer1_Timer()`**, because it's the event you want to handle.
5. Move on to the next line and enter the following lines of code:

```
Sub IeTimer1_Timer()
    If intDirection = 1 Then
        Label1.Angle = Label1.Angle + 10 + Label1.Angle / 20
    Else
        If ((Label1.Angle - 10 - Label1.Angle / 20) < 0) Then
➥Label1.Angle = Label1.Angle + 360
        Label1.Angle = Label1.Angle - 10 - Label1.Angle / 20
    End If
```

6. Do not put an end sub command into the script—the Control Pad does this automatically.

This section of code controls how much the angle increments every time the Timer is fired. The lines of scripting following the Else command in list point number 5 are necessary to allow the label to spin backwards—negative angles don't seem too welcome here. After you enter these lines of code, click on OK to insert the script into the code.

With the script in place, the next thing to do is to create three buttons to control the speed increase and decrease and the direction. To that end, insert the following lines in the body section of the HTML document:

```
<INPUT TYPE=BUTTON VALUE="Spin Slower" NAME="SlowButton">
    <INPUT TYPE=BUTTON VALUE="Spin Faster" NAME="FastButton">
    <INPUT TYPE=BUTTON VALUE="Change Direction" NAME="DirnButton">
</CENTER>
```

Now you can write the event procedures for these buttons.

Start with the button that slows down the label spin by increasing the timer delay. This is labeled SlowButton, so you will call the event procedure SlowButton_OnClick. Set up this procedure using a similar method to IeTimer1_Timer(), replacing the code with the following:

```
Sub SlowButton_OnClick
    IeTimer1.Enabled = False
    IeTimer1.Interval = IeTimer1.Interval * 1.5
```

```
    IeTimer1.Enabled = True
```

The FastButton event procedure is almost identical, so do it next:

```
Sub FastButton_OnClick
    IeTimer1.Enabled = False
    IeTimer1.Interval = IeTimer1.Interval / 1.5
    If IeTimer1.Interval =< 4 Then IeTimer1.Interval = 4
    IeTimer1.Enabled = True
```

NOTE *You need to disable the Timer object before you can make a change to it. Sandwich the interval property between a IeTimer1.Enabled = False statement and a IeTimer1.Enabled = True statement.*

The last two short procedures control when the spinning starts and the direction in which it spins.

You can write the start procedure using the List view, as it only involves changing the Enabled property of the IeTimer1 object. Select the Label1 object from the left-hand window of the Script Wizard, and highlight its OnClick event. In the right-hand window, select the Enabled property of the IeTimer1 object. Double-click on it to insert a new action. Select True from the drop-down list. In this case, you're using -1 for true, but you could use anything other than zero for true. This new procedure starts the label spinning when the user first clicks on the label control.

To control the spin direction, write a short procedure called DirnButton_OnClick with a few extra lines to change the color of the text when it changes direction:

```
Sub DirnButton_OnClick
    If intDirection = 1 Then
        intDirection = -1
        Label1.ForeColor=&h6633EE
    Else
        intDirection = 1
        Label1.ForeColor=&hEE3366
    End If
```

You should realize that you haven't yet defined the variable intDirection, which indicates the direction of the spin. This task is the last step and you do it at the top of the script using this entry:

```
Dim intDirection
intDirection = -1
```

The example now is nearly complete. Just add a background to the web page by including **BACKGROUND = "d:/examples/moon.bmp"** inside the opening <BODY> tag. Save the example and load it into Internet Explorer.

That's it for the Script Wizard topic. You now know how to put intrinsic and ActiveX controls into your documents and attach scripts to them.

Microsoft's Forms 2.0 Controls

Several new ActiveX controls ship with the ActiveX Control Pad, going by the name of *Microsoft Forms 2.0 Controls*. These new controls are the next subject. They provide more or less the same class of objects as the intrinsic HTML form controls, but are more flexible.

Why Use Forms 2.0 Controls?

You might wonder why you would want to use these objects rather than the intrinsic elements described in Chapter 11, "Using Forms with VBScript." Sometimes you would want to stick with the HTML controls, but other times using Forms 2.0 would make more sense.

Ultimately, each programmer decides, but here are some of the benefits of each option.

- Forms 2.0 objects have more properties, methods, and events, providing the programmer with much greater control over their operation and appearance.
- Forms 2.0 controls can be used in conjunction with the HTML Layout Control to produce exact layouts for complicated forms.

- Intrinsic elements are built into the browser—extra components do not have to be installed on the users system to view documents.
- Intrinsic elements are cross-platform. Presently, only Windows 95- and NT-based browsers support ActiveX controls. Microsoft is remedying the situation by licensing its technology to Unix and Apple Macintosh vendors.
- There is built in support for forms and submitting them to servers using HTML. Applications that use ActiveX technology must send data to the server explicitly, say via another control (see Chapter 14, "Using the Internet Control Pack and Java Applets with VBScript").
- Forms 2.0 objects can be tightly integrated into the scripting framework and used to build fully-featured web applications. This will become more and more important with the rise of the corporate *intranet*.

Which Controls Are Available?

A collection of these controls ships with the ActiveX Control Pad. The contents of this list may change in the future, but the core controls are bound to remain. The real reason these are supplied as standard with the Control Pad is for use with the *HTML Layout Control*—an ActiveX control itself.

You may find that your system contains lots of other ActiveX controls not discussed in this book. Other applications may install these when you purchase software, or you might download third-party controls when you view documents on the Web. The discussion in this chapter applies to all the controls you might ever use. The techniques shown here will enable you to find out about, and use, most ActiveX objects you come across.

The following list names the controls that ship with ActiveX Control Pad and are discussed in this chapter:

- Label control

- Textbox control
- ListBox control
- CheckBox control
- ComboBox control
- CommandButton control
- ToggleButton control
- SpinButton control
- OptionButton control
- Image control
- HotSpot control

This section looks at each of these controls in turn and furnishes a short commentary. The ActiveX Control Pad serves to insert them individually into a document, as well as provides a way to analyze the scripting potential. But first, a few more general issues. Two additional controls load when you install the ActiveX Control Pad—the TabStrip and ScrollBar controls. This chapter doesn't address these two controls, but the ActiveX Control Pad help file contains full details on them. You may find other Forms 2.0 controls installed on your system—it's not an omission on the part of this book, though, because many applications install controls from the Forms 2.0 family; for example, Visual Basic 4.0 installs the MultiPage and Frame controls as well.

New ActiveX Control—Now What?

After you discover, download, purchase, or steal (joking) a new ActiveX control, then what?

Each of these controls is written to conform to the standards set out by Microsoft in the ActiveX Software Development Kit (SDK). Under this architecture each object makes public an *OLE automation* interface, which consists of a set of properties, methods and events. To use a control effectively, the programmer needs to find out about the object's capabilities.

Here are some tips to help you:

- Look for a help file (.HLP) that may have been provided with the control. Components that you purchase, or which come as part of another application, may well have such documentation. Components automatically downloaded from other sites probably won't.
- Load the ActiveX Control Pad and create a basic HTML document. Insert an instance of the new control into the BODY section. The Style Attributes Window opens, displaying all the properties that you set at run-time. This window is a great place to experiment with different settings, because you get instant feedback in the Control Preview window.
- Start the Script Wizard with the new control inserted into a document. The Script Wizard window displays all the events supported by the ActiveX control in the left-hand portion of the window. Select the plus symbol (+) next to the control name to display the event list. Click on the Code View option to display the event procedure *signature*, which shows the names of all the arguments passed to the procedure when it's invoked. The argument names usually are self-explanatory in the context of the event in question; for example, Sub MouseMove(Button, Shift, X, Y).
- You can use the right-hand portion of the Script Wizard to display the properties and methods available to the script at run-time. Methods are prefixed by an exclamation mark in a box (!). These can be called from a script to perform actions such as adding items to a combo box. When a method takes some arguments, finding out what these are can be hard . Look for some help documentation or download an OLE viewer program—either way, you can examine an ActiveX control to learn all about it.
- Look at the HTML source of any documents that use the controls already. Pay particular attention to the sections within <SCRIPT> tags.
- Experiment!

In the case of the Forms 2.0 Controls, the Control Pad help file contains some high-quality documentation.

Using the ActiveX Control Pad Help Menu

When you need to find out more information about a Forms 2.0 attribute or event, you use the Help file on the Control Pad to access a comprehensive database of the controls. Choose Control Pad Help Topics from the Help menu, and search for the TextBox control. Figure 13-9 shows the menus that you should see now. Play around with these for a little while to find out some more information about the properties, and then move on to the events that the object can generate.

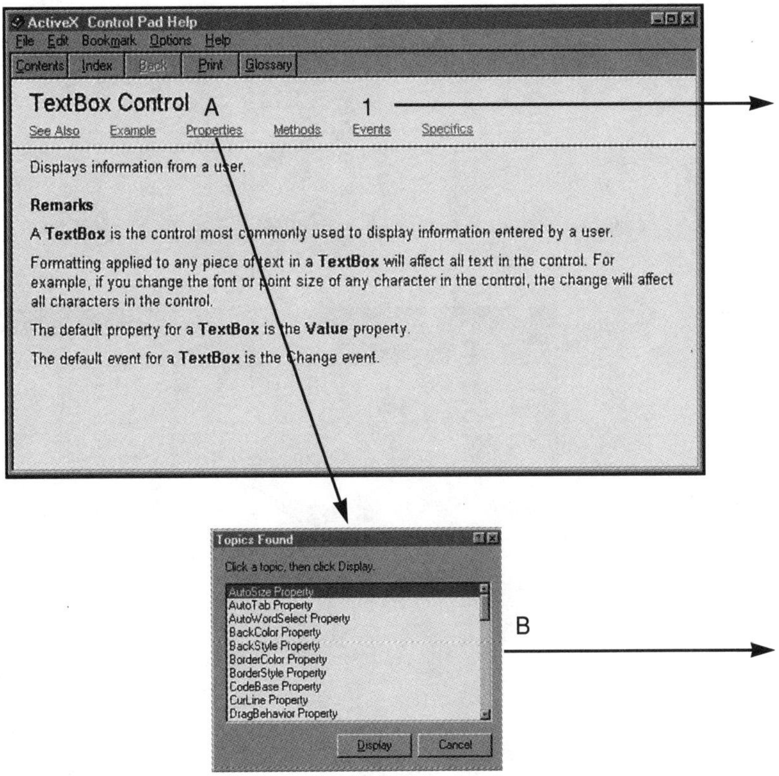

FIGURE 13-9

The Help menu on the ActiveX Control Pad helps you find out about control properties and events. Follow the letters and numbers to see the process.

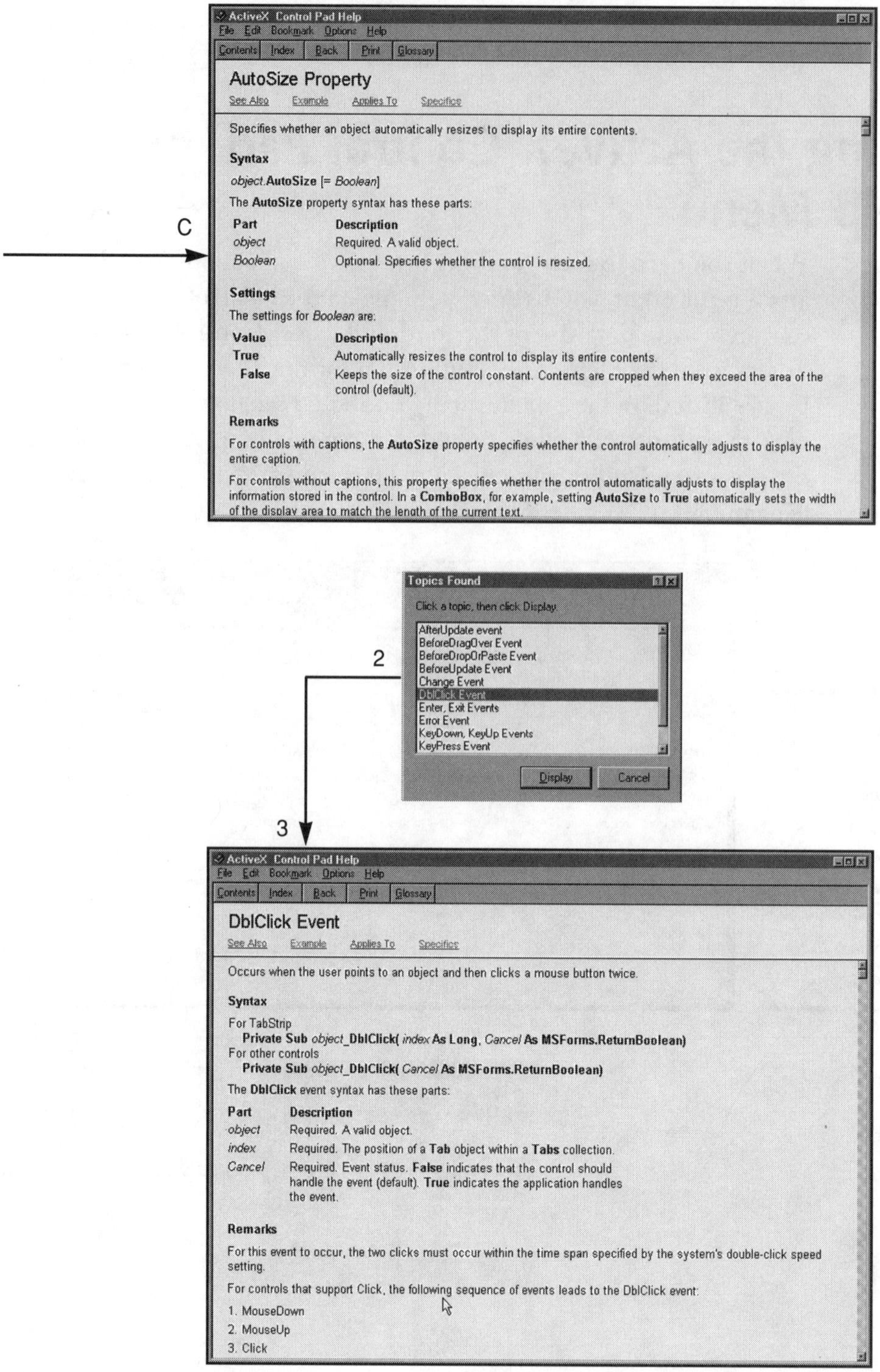
ActiveX Control Pad Help
File Edit Bookmark Options Help
Contents Index Back Print Glossary
AutoSize Property
See Also Example Applies To Specifics
Specifies whether an object automatically resizes to display its entire contents.
Syntax
object.AutoSize [= Boolean]
The AutoSize property syntax has these parts:
Part Description
object Required. A valid object.
Boolean Optional. Specifies whether the control is resized.
Settings
The settings for Boolean are:
Value Description
True Automatically resizes the control to display its entire contents.
False Keeps the size of the control constant. Contents are cropped when they exceed the area of the control (default).
Remarks
For controls with captions, the AutoSize property specifies whether the control automatically adjusts to display the entire caption.
For controls without captions, this property specifies whether the control automatically adjusts to display the information stored in the control. In a ComboBox, for example, setting AutoSize to True automatically sets the width of the display area to match the length of the current text.
C
Topics Found
Click a topic, then click Display.
AfterUpdate event
BeforeDragOver Event
BeforeDropOrPaste Event
BeforeUpdate Event
Change Event
DblClick Event
Enter, Exit Events
Error Event
KeyDown, KeyUp Events
KeyPress Event
Display
Cancel
2
3
ActiveX Control Pad Help
File Edit Bookmark Options Help
Contents Index Back Print Glossary
DblClick Event
See Also Example Applies To Specifics
Occurs when the user points to an object and then clicks a mouse button twice.
Syntax
For TabStrip
Private Sub object_DblClick(index As Long, Cancel As MSForms.ReturnBoolean)
For other controls
Private Sub object_DblClick(Cancel As MSForms.ReturnBoolean)
The DblClick event syntax has these parts:
Part Description
object Required. A valid object.
index Required. The position of a Tab object within a Tabs collection.
Cancel Required. Event status. False indicates that the control should handle the event (default). True indicates the application handles the event.
Remarks
For this event to occur, the two clicks must occur within the time span specified by the system's double-click speed setting.
For controls that support Click, the following sequence of events leads to the DblClick event:
1. MouseDown
2. MouseUp
3. Click

NOTE *The Help file in the Control Pad is an invaluable resource for finding out about properties, methods, and events of an object. Besides this reference material, the Help file offers instructions and tips on using each of the Forms 2.0 controls.*

Common Properties and Events

Before introducing each of the Forms 2.0 objects, you should get acquainted with certain properties and events that are common to most controls. Table 13-1 isn't comprehensive, but it should give you some idea of the pertinent attributes for which to watch when you use a control.

Table 13–1 Attributes That Are Common to Many Forms 2.0 Controls

ATTRIBUTE	USE
Autosize	Enables the control's bounding box to be automatically sized to fit the contents if True. Otherwise cropping occurs.
BackColor	Changes the color of the background for that object. Colors can be chosen by clicking on the selection button (square button with an ellipsis (...), or by choosing one of the predefined options from the drop-down menu.
Caption	Governs what text appears on a button or label.
Enabled	Makes an object active, so that it can be clicked on or selected. Set to True to enable an object. No events will fire if set to False, and control will display differently.
Height, Width	Controls the height of the object, measured in pt size.
ID	Gives the control a name for referencing purposes. Essential for event procedures.
Left, Top	The coordinates of the top left corner of the object. This is only useful when a HTML Layout command is being used.

Table 13–1 Attributes that Are Common to Many Forms 2.0 Controls

ATTRIBUTE	USE
List	Run-time property for listbox and combobox controls. Stores the values which appear in the control.
Picture	Allows a graphic file to be displayed on the button or label. Choose the picture by clicking on the selection button, and picking a file.
Value	Used in conjunction with buttons, tab strips, scroll bars, and textboxes to set up what text will appear in that control. Also stores the state of checkboxes and radio buttons.
Visible	Hides an object if set False. Makes it visible by setting it to true.

Many other properties aren't covered here. If you want to find out what they mean, have a look in the section for the object in the Control Pad Help file.

As well as needing to know about the properties an object supports, any useful script will need to respond to events users generate using the control.

Table 13-2 lists some events that are common to these objects.:

Table 13–2 Events Associated with Many of the Forms 2.0 Controls

EVENT	USE
Click	Fires when the user clicks the mouse once over the control, or hits the Space key (sometimes Enter key).
DblClick	Fires when the user double-clicks the mouse over the control.
Error	Triggered when an error occurs with the object. Has several parameters indicating the error number and so on.

EVENT	USE
KeyDown	Fires when the user presses a key down. The 16-bit keycode for the key in question is supplied as an argument.
ClickKeyPress	Fires when the user has pressed and released a key, but provides only the ASCII code for the key.
KeyUp	Fires when the user releases a key. 16-bit keycode is supplied.
MouseDown	Triggered by the user holding down a mouse button over the control's bounding box. Status of mouse buttons, special control keys, and mouse x,y position are all passed as arguments.
MouseMove	Same as above, but for any movement of the mouse.
MouseUp	Same as above, but for the release of a mouse button.

The Controls

Each of the new Forms 2.0 controls has a short commentary. They can all be inserted into documents using the Insert ActiveX Control menu option or into an HTML Layout using the Toolbox.

Using the Label Control

You use the label control to place a portion of text and/or image on a Web page, usually as a descriptive label for another item of interest. It's different from the SprLblCtl Object that you used in the Spinning Label example, because it doesn't have properties for adjusting the angle of the text or aligning the text to a path, and so on.

This book discusses only some of the properties for the Label control, because it has so many. If you want to know more about the rest, you can use the Help file. Some of the properties and methods apply to other controls covered here and repetition would be unnecessary and cumbersome. It will pay to read through this whole section as you experiment with the controls.

PROPERTY	MEANING
Font	Specifies which font to use to display the Label text. Be careful—other users may not have the same fonts installed on their systems as you.
PicturePosition	Specifies where the image file (if any) is placed in relation to the label text.
SpecialEffect	Sets the way in which the label is decorated to make it appear more interesting. Examples are Raised, Sunken, and so on.
TextAlign	Specifies the text alignment within the Label. Left, center, or right.
BackStyle	Controls whether the Label background is transparent or opaque. Transparent controls allow the user to see controls that sit behind them in the layout's Z-Order.
MousePointer	Sets which system mouse pointer is displayed when the mouse moves over the control. Can be used to good effect when trying to grab somebody's attention.

The Zorder method enables the programmer to move the control to the back of the layout behind all the other controls or bring it to the front. See the Help file for more information.

Actually, this control supports many events, so you could use it to respond to mouse clicks, changes in the input focus, and so on. You're better off using a CommandButton to carry out such tasks, though it makes the control's purpose much clearer when you modify the code in the future.

Define a Text Field with Textbox

The TextBox control is the standard item for getting input from the user. It can be single- or multiple-line, and supports scroll bars and all sorts of events. Some of the more important points to note are shown in the following table.

PROPERTY	MEANING
Text	Contents of the Textbox control. Same as the Value property.
AutoSize	If True the control will shrink to fit its contents. If False the control will remain at the same size as it was designed.
MultiLine	False—the Textbox is only one line deep. True—the textbox can accept many lines of text.
MaxLength	Maximum number of characters that the control will accept. Useful when using the Textbox to retrieve values for a database.
LineCount	Run-time property which holds the number of lines of text that the control is storing.
WordWrap	True—long lines wrap around to the next line when MultiLine is also True. If False, the lines do not wrap.

The Cut, Copy, and Paste methods are handy for implementing Clipboard support. You can use them in conjunction with the Value property to transfer text to and from the Windows Clipboard.

The Change event is useful for performing field validation. When the user edits the field and tries to move to another control, it triggers this event. An event procedure can then check that the value entered is within particular ranges, or that disallowed values have not been entered. If the field fails validation, the user should be informed and the SetFocus method used to return the input focus to the TextBox. For example:

```
Sub TextBox1_Change()
    If TextBox1.Value = "Ashley" Then
        MsgBox "That is not an allowed value for this field! Try
➥again"
        TextBox1.Value = "Default Value"
        TextBox1.SetFocus
    End If
End Sub
```

Using Combo Boxes for Drop-Down Selections

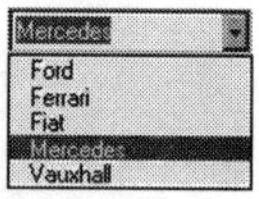

The ComboBox control provides a way to select an item from a list of options with a drop-down menu. The user also can enter a specific value if none of the items on the list match. These controls should be familiar to you already. Microsoft Word uses them for font, style, and point selection on its toolbars.

The items in the list need to be added to it after the document loads, because they're hard to specify using the Property window of the Control Pad. Write an event handler for the Window object's (Chapter 10, "The Object Model for Scripting") OnLoad event. The ComboBox has a method called AddItem, which you can use to insert items into the list. An example might be:

```
<SCRIPT LANGUAGE="VBScript">
Sub Window_OnLoad
    ComboBox1.AddItem("Ford")
    ComboBox1.AddItem("Ferrari")
    ComboBox1.AddItem("Fiat")
    ComboBox1.AddItem("Mercedes")
    ComboBox1.AddItem("Vauxhall")
</SCRIPT>
```

Here, five items are inserted into the list as soon as the browser finishes loading the document. The user sees these items in the list if he clicks on the ComboBox's drop-down button.

You can add multiple-column entries to a ComboBox, but this topic exceeds the scope of this discussion here. You can find all the details you need in the Help file.

PROPERTY	MEANING
List	Contains the rows of text in an array which are displayed in the drop-down list. Modify this array only by using the AddItem and RemoveItem methods.

PROPERTY	MEANING
Listindex	Holds the index in the List array of the currently selected item. Remember that array indices start from zero. If no item is currently selected, or the text entered into the textbox area does not match one of the items in List then this will be equal to -1.
ListCount	Stores the number of items in the ComboBox
MatchRequired	True—any text the user types into the textbox area must match one of the items in the List array—they will not be allowed to leave the control until this condition is met. False—the control will accept any text in the text entry section.
DropButtonStyle	Allows you to set the kind of drop-down button that is displayed. This is purely for presentation purposes.
Style	Sets which kind of ComboBox to display—see the Help file for details.
SelText	Contains the currently selected text in the control.

You've already seen the AddItem method in action, and you need to look at three more important methods:

- **RemoveItem** removes a single item from the List array.
- **Clear** wipes all the entries out of the ComboBox.
- **DropDown** forces the drop-down list to appear immediately.

The List Box Control

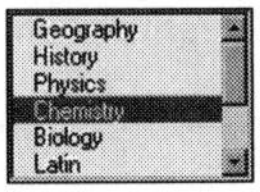

The List Box control is slightly simpler than the ComboBox. It doesn't have a user input area for typing text; instead, it simply displays a list of items in a box, with scroll bars, if necessary.

You can set it up to allow the user to select more than one item at once, or to limit the user's choice to one at a time. Different applications require different settings. Much like the ComboBox control, it requires filling with items after the document finishes loading. For example:

```
<SCRIPT LANGUAGE="VBScript">
Sub Window_OnLoad
    ListBox1.AddItem("Geography")
    ListBox1.AddItem("History")
    ListBox1.AddItem("Physics")
    ListBox1.AddItem("Chemistry")
    ListBox1.AddItem("Biology")
    ListBox1.AddItem("Latin")
    ListBox1.AddItem("Mathematics")
    ListBox1.AddItem("English")
End Sub
</SCRIPT>
```

Properties and methods worth looking into are listed and described in the following table:

PROPERTY	MEANING
ListIndex	If MultiSelect is True then returns the index into the List array of the item with the current input focus (-1 if not in focus), regardless of whether or not the item is selected. If MultiSelect is False the index of the currently selected item is returned.
Selected	An array storing a value for each list element. If the value is True then the item is selected, False and the item is not selected. Remember array indices start from zero. This property only applies if MultiSelect is set to True.
MultiSelect	If True the user can select more than one item at once. If False only one item can be selected.
TopIndex	Returns or sets the topmost item in the list. Returns -1 if the list is empty.

The ListBox control supports the AddItem, RemoveItem, Clear, and SetFocus methods. It also supports all the standard events listed in an earlier section, and a few more concerning user interactions with the control. Again, check the Help file for details on these standard events or use the Scripting Wizard to test some of them.

Making the Most of CheckBoxes

Check boxes are a simple and intuitive tool for setting options. The user can select or deselect each check box control on a form. Unlike Radio buttons, which are grouped together so that users can set only one option at a time, check boxes aren't mutually exclusive.

Group a set of check boxes together on a form to display a few related items together. An example might be a list of available products for an order.

NOTE *The ListBox has some special options that allow you to display check boxes next to each selected item in a list. You can use this control instead of a group of check boxes for a list of options.*

PROPERTY	MEANING
Value	Boolean value indicating the state of the CheckBox. If it is False then the control is not checked and vice versa.
Picture	An image file can also be displayed on the CheckBox, say to illustrate the product/option being checked.

SetFocus and Zorder are the only methods that the CheckBox control supports. The standard repertoire of events are present.

The Command Button

The Command button provides the script developer with a souped up version of the intrinsic HTML BUTTON element. It can display images as well as text, generate several different effects, show different colors, and offers more event support than the HTML version.

TIP

An effective way to make your documents look great is to use the Picture property of the CommandButton and Label controls. You can create fantastic-looking captions by designing letters and placing them on a control with the Picture property. You should then set the Caption property to the rest of the desired word or phrase and place it to the right of the Picture. For example, setting the caption to "ecording" and using the letter "R" in a creative way makes an attention-grabbing Recording button.

PROPERTY	MEANING
TabIndex	Number from 0 to (the number of tabbed controls on the form minus 1), indicating where this control lies in the tab order (see gray box).
TabStop	Boolean value indicating whether or not this control appears in the Tab order for the form.
Caption	Text that appears on the button label.
BackColor	Specifies the background color of the object
ForeColor	Foreground color.

Methods for the CommandButton control are somewhat limited—SetFocus and Zorder.

The usual medley of events are also supported, with the most important being the Click event for responding to a press on the button. This event handler specifies what the CommandButton actually does, which may be anything from loading another HTML document to playing a music file to running a complex calculation.

Tabbing Order for Controls

Each time a set of controls are placed on a layout or in a document you can set up a tab order for the user to navigate the controls using the keyboard. Pressing the Tab key moves the input focus from one control to the next. Nothing is more annoying than filling in a form where the focus jumps randomly—having some kind of order is a far, far better thing. You can use the TabStop and TabIndex properties of most of the Forms 2.0 controls to assign this tab order. Try to make the order a logical one that doesn't surprise the user. Clever design also can reduce the time it takes to fill in a form.

Placing a Toggle Button in a Document

The ToggleButton object is almost exactly the same as the CommandButton, with one essential difference—the ToggleButton stays down when clicked, returning to normal only when clicked on again. It's a useful control for turning options on and off on a user interface, say a rendering quality option, as it provides immediate visual feedback to the user about its state.

PROPERTY	MEANING
TripleState	Property of ToggleButton, OptionButton, and CheckBox controls. If True the user can choose from three values, set, not set and Null. The Null value is when the control is neither on nor off.
Value	Stores the current state of the ToggleButton, usually True or False. Can be Null if the TripleState property is True.

Methods available are simply SetFocus and Zorder. The Change and Click events are the most applicable to the ToggleButton.

Spin Buttons

Spin buttons are the GUI's equivalent to electric windows—they're an added extra that can make an application much easier to use. They're primarily connected to a TextBox control and used to automatically increment or decrement the value held in the TextBox when the arrow symbols are clicked.

PROPERTY	MEANING
Min	Integer amount specifying the minimum value that the SpinButton's Value property will take.
Max	Integer amount specifying the maximum value that the SpinButton's Value property will take.
Orientation	Default setting automatically determines the SpinButton's orientation. Can be overriden to force horizontal/vertical display of the control. See Help file for details.
Delay	Delay in milliseconds between the generation of each Spin event when the user holds down the mouse button on the spin arrows. Default delay is 50 milliseconds. The delay between the first event and subsequent ones is five times the Delay value.
SmallChange	The amount by which the Value property is changed each time a spin arrow is pressed.
Value	Current value held by the SpinButton.

The way to attach a SpinButton to another control is to use the SpinDown and SpinUp events. When these events fire, the event procedure can change the values held in related controls to the new value stored in the SpinButton's Value property. To update the value held in a Textbox control in response to the SpinButton being clicked, you would write something like this:

```
<SCRIPT LANGUAGE="VBScript">
Sub SpinButton1_SpinUp
    TextBox1.Text = SpinButton1.Value
End Sub

Sub SpinButton1_SpinDown
    TextBox1.Text = SpinButton1.Value
End Sub
</SCRIPT>
```

What the OptionButton Does

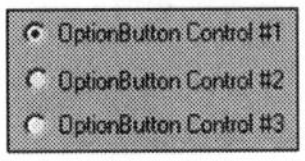

The OptionButton control, or radio button, allows you to group items together so that users can select only one item at a time; for example, the selection of a band for a software radio (VHF, MW, or LW).

The controls are grouped by giving them a common group name, which allows several different option groups to co-exist on the same form. Setting up a default selected item in the group by setting its Value property to True in the property designer window is a good idea. Don't set more than one OptionButton in the group at a time.

To make it clear that a set of OptionButtons are related, you should place a Label control with a special effect border (for example, Sunken) behind all the buttons in a group. This will improve the visual design of your form.

PROPERTY	MEANING
GroupName	Name of the group to which the control belongs. There can be many groups on one form.
Value	True if the control is selected, False if it is not. If TripleState is True, then this property can also take a Null value.

The same standard methods and events are supported as with most other controls.

How to Incorporate Images into Web Pages with the Image Control

The Image control enables you to place various pictures all over your document which can respond to events. You can crop, tile, or zoom the images and use them as a background for the form, just like Windows wallpaper. The control also allows you to use transparency to create interesting effects. For a fun example of using the Image object, look at the Refrigerator Magnets example in the HTML Layout Control section.

TIP

The Image control can handle all sorts of graphics formats (GIF, JPEG, WMF, and BMP). One particularly good example is the GIF format. By setting the transparency color to the image's background color, you can drop out the image background when using it on a form (see your art package's documentation on how to do this). This is what was done with the letters used in the magnets example, and it means the images can be moved around without obscuring each other.

PROPERTY	MEANING
AutoSize	Specifies whether or not the control shrinks/expands to fit the image. You can modify the size of the control and the image it contains will zoom to fit.
PictureTiling	If True the image will be tiled across the face of the control. If False the image will only appear once.
Picture	Full pathname for the image to be displayed.
PictureAlignment	Sets how the picture is aligned in the control.
BackStyle	Transparent or Opaque. Set to Transparent to drop out the background when using the correct kind of graphic file (see Tip).

The Move method allows you to resize and reposition the Image control within an HTML layout. See the Help file for details on the procedure arguments.

There are not many events for this item, but there is support for responding to mouse clicks and changes in the control's focus from the Enter, Exit, MouseDown, MouseUp, and MouseMove events. The last of these is used in the magnets example to reposition the images in response to the user dragging the mouse over each control.

Dividing an Image into Clickable Areas Using the Hotspot Control

You can use this control, usually invisible at run-time, to expose possible actions. When the mouse moves over the HotSpot, or the user tabs into it, the mouse cursor can change and you can write code to draw the user's attention to some feature, such as by playing a sound file.

You also can use the HotSpot as an alternative to HTML image maps. Place several HotSpots over an Image control and assign code to their Enter or Click events. These event procedures can be used to load other HTML documents or VRML worlds, or just to run a script.

PROPERTY	MEANING
MousePointer	Specifies which mouse cursor to display when the mouse moves over the control
TabIndex	Position in the form's tab order. Make sure this is set to allow keyboard users to use the HotSpot.
TabStop	Member of form tab order if True. Make sure this is set for keyboard users.

The HotSpot control has only two methods: Move, to reposition or resize the control at run-time, and ZOrder, to change its position in the layout's back to front order (known as Z-Order).

Events supported include Click, DblClick, Enter, Exit, MouseDown, MouseUp, MouseMove, MouseEnter, and MouseExit. Assign code to these as necessary to make the user aware of the HotSpot's presence.

The HTML Layout Control

One particularly special ActiveX control not yet covered provides a cool way to place objects onto the page, known as the HTML Layout Control. You put it into a document like any other ActiveX control. The difference between it and other objects is that its properties are stored in a file (.ALX extension) that is parsed during loading of the document. The file contains information about objects and their properties, and where they sit on the web page. The ALX file is simple ASCII text and can even include script code within <SCRIPT> tags. It lets you position any control to pixel accuracy, and is a huge leap forward from HTML's positioning commands.

You insert the layout into the document just like other objects, and you can include several layouts on one web page. Read the section entitled Multiple Layouts to find out more.

How to Design a Cool Layout

With the ActiveX Control Pad running, choose the New Layout option from the File menu to launch the designer window. It should look something like Figure 13-10.

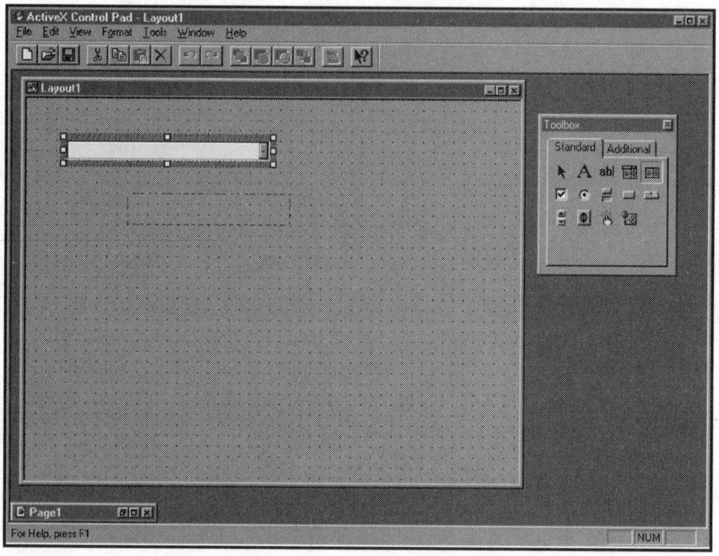

FIGURE 13-10
The Designer window of the HTML Layout Control.

The Toolbox window contains all the Forms 2.0 controls that are discussed above, and you can find other Additional Controls by clicking on the Additional tab. If you want to add a control to the tool box, right-click in the Additional tab and choose the Additional controls. A window like Figure 13-11 will appear, and you can select the control by checking the box beside the name of the control to add to the tool box. All the available objects on your system are part of this list—add only those that you need to use to the toolbox.

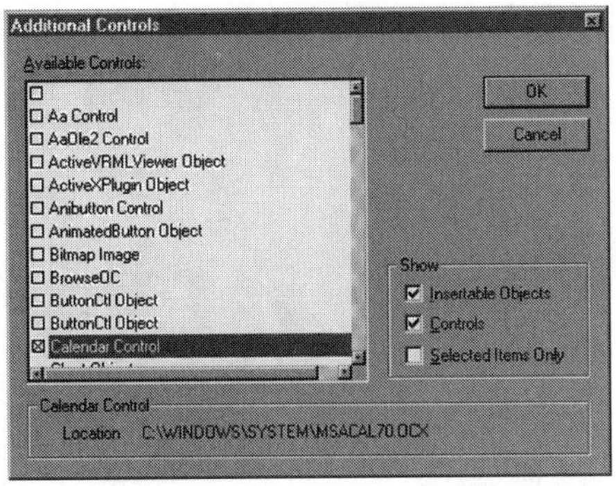

FIGURE 13-11
Adding additional objects to the HTML Layout Control

Now you can insert objects into the layout to make up your document. You can adjust properties the same way as with the Control Pad, and you can attach scripts to the controls using the Script Wizard. These scripts are stored in the .ALX file, not in the HTML document. Keeping the scripts out of the document can be useful if someone uses a non-compatible browser to view the web page, because it bypasses the entire ALX file, never interpreting the script.

If, however, you do want to put the script in the HTML document, you would need to use the following object syntax:

```
layoutname.control.property
```

The objects in a layout are children of the layout control, and so must be qualified with the layout name.

Now load up the example titled "A Refrigerator Magnet Simulator" from the CD (see Figure 13-12) to demonstrate the capabilities of the designer.

Here, each letter is placed as an Image on the layout, and then scripting routines are associated with each image that allow the letters to be moved around to make words (just like the magnetic letters with which children play on the refrigerator door!)

TIP

The Format menu in the toolbar has several useful commands for tidying up your objects, such as making buttons the same width, which can greatly enhance the presentation of your documents.

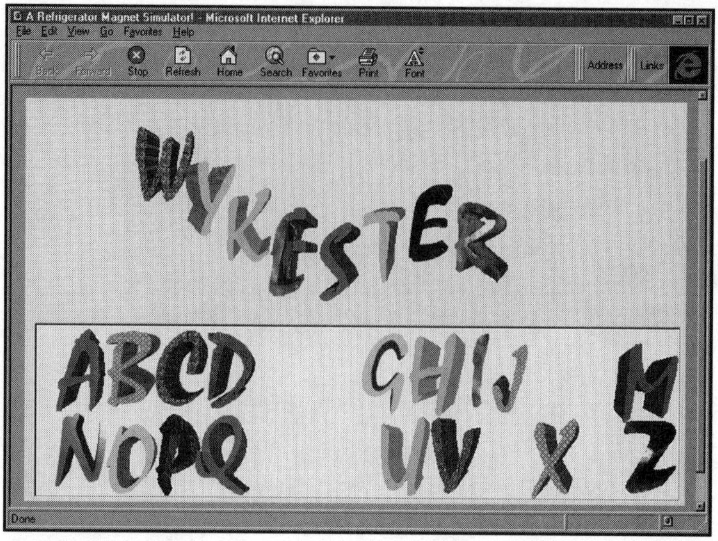

FIGURE 13-12
Magnetic letters—demonstrating the Layout control

Multiple Layouts

One of the great features about layouts is that you can put many of them on one page because they are treated just like objects. You insert them into HTML documents like other ActiveX controls, and can adjust the location of the layout object by using the standard HTML positioning commands, such as <CENTER>, <RIGHT>, and so on. Therefore, you can design complicated, compelling pages by using several individual object layouts.

ActiveX Control Pad Summary

This chapter has covered much new information, so take five to have a look back at what you learned before moving on to even more advanced topics.

The chapter kicked off with an introduction to the ActiveX Control Pad, and paid special attention to the Scripting Wizard and the Forms 2.0 Controls. Object Attributes and scripting possibilities were discussed in great detail, and illustrated with examples where possible. We also had a look at the new HTML Layout control and saw how it simplified web page authoring.

The next chapter is dedicated to advanced communications controls from the Internet Control Pack (ICP), such as SMTP, HTTP, and FTP. Those who wish to take full advantage of Explorer's communication facilities will find this section very useful, and for those that don't, you can read about incorporating Java Applets into your scripts—there's something for everyone.

CHAPTER 14

Using the Internet Control Pack and Java Applets with VBScript

Most of the chapters up until now include small example documents that demonstrate various features of VBScript and ActiveX technology. Chapters 3 through 7 cover the structure of the language, while Chapters 10 to 13 describe the Object Model for Scripting and ActiveX controls. You may be interested to see some complete Web applications written using VBScript. If you are, this chapter should be exactly what you're looking for.

This chapter covers two major areas, namely, the Internet Control pack and scripting with Java applets. The Internet Control pack is a collection of ActiveX controls that can add network functionality to your scripts—without all the messy complexity of the low level Winsock APIs.

In addition to enabling programmers to use ActiveX controls, Internet Explorer 3.0 makes all the public methods and variables of a Java applet accessible to scripts in the document. This means that Java applets you create or license from third-party vendors can be easily controlled with sections of VBScript code.

This chapter covers the following topics:

- The Internet Control Pack
- Ideas for Web applications using the Control Pack
- Using the FTP control to create an interactive file download utility
- HawkEye—A complete phone call logging application, designed for extension with the TCP control
- Using the NNTP control to access a News server
- Using the HTTP control to download HTML documents for later use
- Scripting with Java Applets

The CD that accompanies this book includes all of the examples in this chapter. You should look at each application before you read the accompanying discussion so you have a better understanding of what each sample is trying to achieve.

What Is the Internet Control Pack?

This question was partially answered in the introduction to this chapter, but the Internet Control Pack offers you more.

First of all, the Internet Control Pack is a free download from the Microsoft Web site! This book is written based on the Beta 2 release of the Control Pack and it is our understanding that Microsoft will continue to make these controls available without charge. The CD accompanying the book includes a self-extracting compressed file that you should run before using any of the examples from this chapter. The controls will be installed to your hard disk and registry entries inserted for each control. You could also check on Microsoft's Web site for updates to the Control Pack:

http://www.microsoft.com/msdownload/

The controls are ActiveX controls, meaning that all of our previous discussions about this new technology still apply. You can use the ActiveX Control Pad to insert, modify, and script the controls. The ActiveX controls will automatically download to the user's hard drive when somebody using your documents does not have the control in question installed on their system. All you need do is ensure you have a distribution license for the control and make sure you add the CODEBASE="someURL" parameter to your OBJECT definition (discussed in Chapter 12).

The Internet Control Pack greatly extends the range of Web applications you can design. The Internet Control Pack enables you to link your documents over the Internet with various other computers, including FTP, HTTP, NNTP, and mail servers. The TCP and UDP Winsock controls allow you to design custom communication solutions that pass information between computers. The HawkEye Phone Center, introduced later in this chapter, enables you to extend it with the TCP control.

Which Controls Are Available and Which Can Be Used with VBScript?

When you install the Internet Control Pack on your system, the controls will be unpacked and registered (see Table 14-1).

Table 14-1 Contents of the Internet Control Pack

CONTROL NAME	PURPOSE
Winsock TCP Control	Connection-based control that allows you to set up a two-way transfer of data between computers. The Transmission Control Protocol (TCP) has error checking and flow control to ensure the data stream arrives at the other end.
Winsock UDP Control	Connectionless control that allows you to send or receive data from another machine. The User Datagram Protocol (UDP) is simpler than TCP but does not provide the guarantees of the more complex protocol.

Table 14-1 Contents of the Internet Control Pack

CONTROL NAME	PURPOSE
FTP Client Control	Control that allows you to connect to a remote machine running an FTP server. You can then examine the server's directories, download files from the server, or upload files from your system to the server using the File Transfer Protocol (FTP).
HTTP Control	Control that can fetch files from a Web server with the Hypertext Transfer Protocol (HTTP). You can parse and filter this data for specific uses or store this data as a file on the client system for later use.
HTML Control	Control supporting the HTML 2.0 specification. This control displays files written using the Hypertext Markup Language in a browser window. You can use this control to implement a simple Web browser, or one with specific limitations. For example, only certain sites can be visited.
POP Control	Control that allows you to create a virtual post office to store and retrieve e-mail messages from a mail server running the Post Office Protocol (POP). See the section "Problems with the Mail" in this chapter.
SMTP Control	Control that can send e-mail messages over the Internet using the Simple Mail Transfer Protocol (SMTP). There are problems using this control with VBScript—see the section "Problems with the Mail."
NNTP Client Control	Control that can interact with News servers over a network, such as the Internet. The Network News Transfer Protocol (NNTP) enables you to connect to news servers, retrieve lists of newgroups and articles, and download and upload articles from a News server.

The release notes for the Internet Control pack state:

> The present package includes controls that can be used with Microsoft Access, Visual Basic, Visual C++, and Visual FoxPro.

The controls included in the package have not been designed specifically for use with VBScript. But because they are ActiveX controls and Internet Explorer has been designed to conform to the ActiveX Scripting model, you can use them quite safely within HTML documents.

Because this book borders on the more advanced use of VBScript, you may have to experiment to achieve the results you want.

A Note about Security

Wait a minute—you thought VBScript was a safe language and did not have any file I/O capabilities. Then what is all this talk of downloading and saving files and mail messages to hard disks?

VBScript is still a safe language and cannot open, close, read, write, or delete files on your hard disk. The controls in the Internet Control Pack are not part of the VBScript language so do not have the same restrictions. The controls provide specific functionality, and some of these functions may require reads-from or writes-to a hard disk. After all, how useful would an FTP control be if it could not save the files it downloads?

Internet Explorer 3.0 allows you to set various security options. These options control such things as Internet Ratings and Security levels. Chapter 12, "ActiveX Controls and VBScript," discusses code download and code signing when ActiveX technology was first introduced. The controls in the beta release of Internet Control Pack are not signed with digital certificates, and Explorer will not allow you to use them unless you set the browser's security level to Medium or None. You probably would want to avoid using the lowest security setting, because it turns off all warnings about potentially unsafe content. The Medium setting still displays a warning message, but asks whether you want to go ahead and use the control.

If you have not done so already, set your security level in the following way.

1. Choose View [->] Options from the Explorer menu bar.
2. Select the Security tab from the tab strip at the top of the Options dialog box.
3. Press the Safety Level button.
4. Set the security level by choosing the Medium button (the second option of the three), which is recommended for expert users and developers.
5. Click on the OK button to save the change.

Figure 14-1 shows the Safety Level dialog box and the setting you should choose for using the Control Pack.

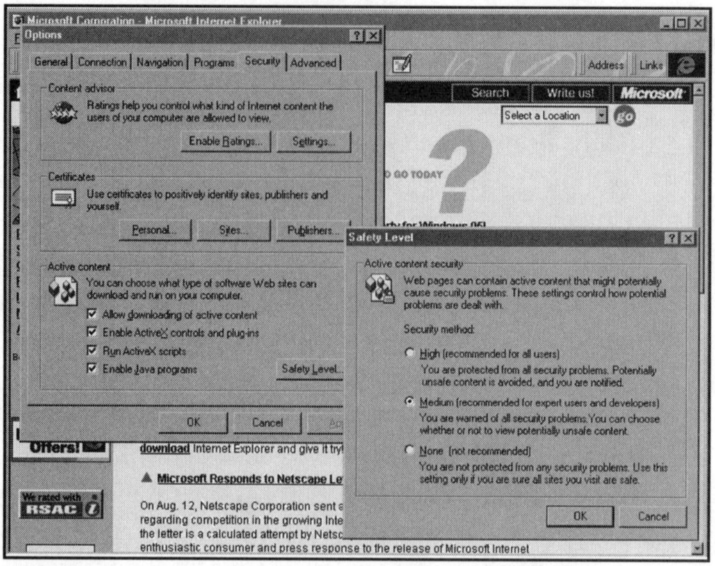

FIGURE 14-1
Setting the Internet Explorer security levels for using the Internet Control Pack

Beware of the <PARAM> Tag

The examples in this chapter were developed using Microsoft FrontPage, Microsoft ActiveX Control Pad, and Notepad. We experienced some problems with the controls when loading documents that use them. This appeared to stem from the fact that ActiveX Control Pad had included <PARAM> tags in the object definitions to set certain properties at design time. We could find no explanation for this, but found a simple solution. Look at one of the source listings later in the chapter and you will see that none of the HTML object definitions contain any <PARAM> tags. This is the method you should use to avoid any problems.

1. Insert the ActiveX control using ActiveX Control Pad. This generates the Class ID automatically.
2. Close the Property editor window and remove any <PARAM> tags from within the <OBJECT> container tags.

3. Within the script functions that use the control, or the *Window_OnLoad* event procedure, set the control properties to the values required. Because the controls are invisible at run-time, it does not matter when these properties are set.

Later releases of the control pack may address this problem—the best way to find out is to try using the controls in the normal way first. If this doesn't work, modify your HTML source as just described.

Problems with the Mail

The complete Visual Basic language and Visual Basic for Applications (as found in programs such as Excel) support a feature known as *Collections*. These enable a programmer to group a number of objects of the same type in one place. You can add items to and remove items from the collection. VBScript is a lightweight subset of the Visual Basic language and has fewer features; one missing feature is the use of Collections.

This is rather inconvenient for script writers who want to use the POP and SMTP controls in their Web documents. Mail messages are composed of various elements including a From field, a To field, a CC field, a Subject field, and the message text itself. The first four elements mentioned are known as message headers and can be set up and retrieved using the SMTP and POP controls. These controls use Collections to store the message headers so they cannot be used with VBScript code. Without the ability to create and look at message headers, these two controls are not much use for writing Web applications that are controlled from VBScript. Microsoft may rewrite the controls at a later date, but for now, you'll have to be content with the other controls.

If you are particularly adventurous, you could try writing an ActiveX control in C++ or Visual Basic that contains the SMTP or POP controls and provides programmatic access to the collections through some custom methods. Then again, you might be happier with your existing mail program.

How to Find Out about the Controls and Use Them to Design Web Applications

The objects contained in the Internet Control Pack are somewhat more complicated than those discussed in Chapters 12 and 13. Because Microsoft provides detailed explanations of these controls; rather than describe them in detail, this book compiles a series of examples and ideas for using each of the controls. The aim of this chapter is to get you started and give some pointers.

When ActiveX controls were first discussed, tables of all the object methods, properties, and events were included in the text. Similar details for the Internet Control Pack are found in the help file provided with the OCX files. Once you install the controls, a new item entitled *ICP Help* is available from the Start menu in the program group named *ActiveX Internet Controls*. This help file contains some tips and possible scenarios for using the controls, as well as a complete reference for each control. When a control is mentioned in the book, you may well need to refer to the help file to find the details you require.

After installing the controls, they're as easy to use as any others discussed so far. They generate events that the usual event procedures can handle. Remember, these are named as:

```
Sub ObjectName_EventName(arg1, arg2, ..., argN)
```

You can call or access the control methods and properties in the usual way, by using the dot syntax to separate object names from object properties. For example,

```
FTP1.Connect "126.32.145.2", "25"
```

or

```
FTP1.RemoteHost = "ftp.microsoft.com"
```

The best way to make the most of these new ActiveX controls is to experiment. You can then discover what is possible and what isn't. With this chapter, the example documents, and the help file, you should have all the information you need. Fully-featured Web applications are just around the corner.

Requirements for Using the Controls

In order to use these controls you need the following

- An Internet Service Provider
- A modem or ISDN line—some form of connection between the service provider and your computer system
- A communications protocol that allows you to connect to the Internet. Either a Serial Line Internet Protocol (SLIP) or Point To Point Protocol (PPP) is required.

Ideas for Web Applications Using the Control Pack

Nobody can say exactly what you should use the controls for, but a few suggestions can do no harm. As you might expect, all the ideas and examples in this chapter concern communications of some kind or another with a remote computer.

Suggestions for Using the FTP Control

What about developing one of the following with the FTP Control:

- A Web application that downloads technical documents or software updates from an FTP site while the user is reading an HTML document in their browser. You could generate the necessary filename by using a script that gathers the user's requirements and selects the correct document or archived file based on these data items.
- An interactive FTP site browser, that displays only certain files and/or directories, or limits access to a particular FTP site. An example along these lines is found in this chapter.

- An application that uploads files from a local machine to an FTP server like an intranet. This could be used to backup important files, such as daily sales figures.

What Can Be Done with a News Server?

The complete installation of Internet Explorer 3.0 comes with the Internet Mail and News applications. These provide excellent support for composing, sending, and receiving Internet mail and for accessing Usenet newsgroups. You may want to use the NNTP control as part of a Web application that accesses newsgroups in a specific way or limits access to particular newsgroups. For instance, you may want to write:

- A Web page that downloads the articles from a particular newsgroup and searches the article text for keywords. The articles that match the search criteria could then be displayed in a textarea control or as a dynamically created HTML document using the Document.Write method. This could be useful for providing up-to-the-minute information on a software product or providing details of an evolving Internet standard.
- A custom news browser that resides as a document within the browser. The browser could limit access to specific newsgroups or a company news server:

  ```
  msnews.microsoft.com
  ```

Broadcast Services with the UDP Control

Because the the UDP control is a connectionless control, there is no guarantee that the remote system will receive the information you send as a UDP packet. It is, however, useful in situations where the communication needs are fairly simple. In the worst case, you can always try resending a message if no reply is received within a fixed amount of time.

A suggestion for using this control is as the communication medium for some form of broadcast service, such as a stock price provider. The subscribing users could notify their presence with a UDP message and resend until a reply is received from the server. The subscriber's address would be added to a list of currently connected hosts. As prices change, the server would cycle through each IP address in the list and send the updated prices using the UDP control. The overhead of establishing TCP connections with every subscriber would be too great, but UDP is sufficient for the job.

Two Way Communications with the TCP Control

The TCP control can be used to set up a full duplex (two-way) data connection between two computers. The protocol uses error checking and flow control and provides a *reliable* data stream for the programmer to use. The uses you can put the control to are endless because it provides the means for sending and receiving arbitrary data. The most obvious use for the control is to set up a client/server relationship between systems. The client system can send data to be stored on the server while the server responds to requests for certain information. Possible applications include:

- A data storage service, such as a remote database. The client machines send data to be stored in the database or send requests to the server for previously stored records. The server end would require some form of database access, such as an ActiveX control.
- A telephone message system like the example discussed later in this chapter. Messages are sent to the server for storage and retrieved later when the requestor returns to the office.
- An online game, using TCP connections to send current player data to the server. The game engine on the server would then send the updated status information to all other connected players.

HTTP Control—Is It Any Use?

The HTTP protocol sends and receives HTML documents. The protocol transfers all the different types of files that occur in HTML documents, such as images, sounds, videos, and text. The HTTP control can download these files from a Web server and parse the contents immediately or save them to disk for later use. Some of its possible uses include:

- Using the HTTP control to create a text-only Web browser. You can download and parse the HTML files to remove all the tags. The resulting text can be displayed in a textarea control or saved as a file.
- An application that scans a remote Web site to download files when the site is not busy such as out of office hours. The files could then be stored in a database or as a mirror site for browsing at some later date.
- A search application that downloads HTML files and searches through them for particular keywords. Files matching the search criteria could be saved to disk or displayed to the user immediately.

Possibilities for the HTML Control

The HTML control can create a Web application that includes an HTML viewer. Because this book is all about VBScript and Internet Explorer 3.0, a simple HTML viewer control does not have many realistic uses. The control supports HTML 2.0, and the Netscape 2.0 and Explorer 2.0 extensions. It would be most useful to a programmer wishing to create a standalone browser using Visual Basic or Visual C++.

Using the FTP Control to Download Files from a Server

The Control Pack and the type of applications it produces are illustrated in, some concrete examples in the following sections. They contain several complete, and some partial examples that you can use as the basis for more complex applications. The first of these uses the FTP control to access an FTP server and download files.

Figure 14-2 shows the FTP sample document as it should look when you load it in your browser. The document contains several buttons for connecting to the FTP server at Imperial College in London. There are also two list boxes that are used to display lists of files and directories. Other buttons allow you to change the remote directory on the server and fetch a selected file from the server. At the bottom of the document you will find a textarea control which conveys status information as the application runs. The document can be loaded from the Internet Control Pack section of the main Web page installed from the CD. You can load it by selecting the link labeled `Using the FTP Control to Transfer Files`. When you load the document, ensure that Internet Explorer's security level has been set to Medium; otherwise, the FTP control won't load.

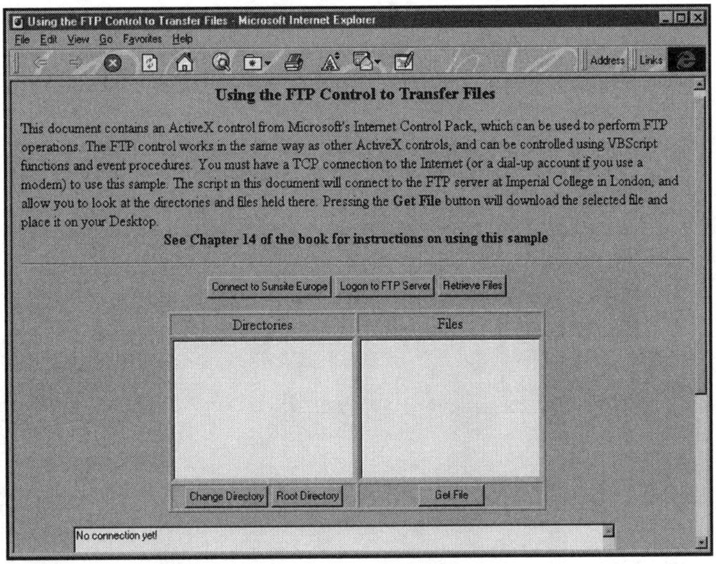

FIGURE 14-2
A sample web application—using the FTP control to transfer files

Using the FTP Example

Before examining the HTML and VBScript source that make up the simple FTP browser, let's use the program to navigate around the Sunsite Europe FTP server to see how the application works. This should give you a much better idea of the purpose behind each of the event procedures and items in the document when you read about them.

The application has been written without much attention to error checking. If you were to use it in a real-world situation, it would need to be made more robust—an ideal that isn't the main objective of this chapter.

1. Load the document and answer Yes to the question regarding the use of a potentially unsafe control.
2. Make sure your modem is switched on or you are connected to your corporate intranet, and press the Connect to Sunsite Europe button. Some status messages should display in the textarea control at the bottom of the page. Once the Connected message appears, you can continue. If the browser gets its internal status flags in a muddle, it may report that it is connected when, in fact, it isn't. The application does not check for this, but a check could be added if you want. If you don't get a Connected message, simply close the Explorer program and reload it.
3. Press the Logon to FTP Server button to authenticate yourself for an anonymous FTP session. If this is successful, the document should look like the window shown in Figure 14-3.

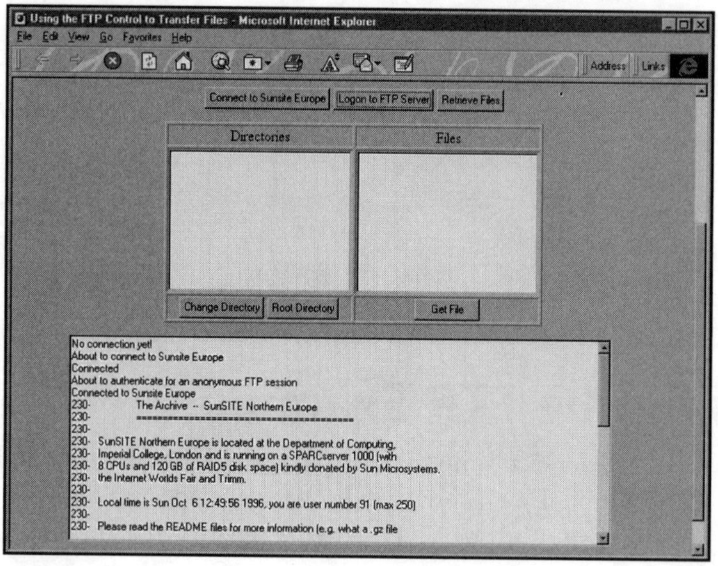

FIGURE 14-3
The FTP sample document after authentication has succeeded

4. Once you have connected to the server, the application needs to retrieve the list of files stored on its remote drive. To do this, press the Retrieve Files button. Several messages will appear in the status area, including a line of number symbols (#). The number symbols indicate that a command is in progress. After the `Operation Complete` message appears, you will see a list of directories and files in the two listbox controls.

5. To change directories on the server, choose the directory you want to view, (for example, *Mirrors*, and press the Change Directory button. The FTP control then fetches a new list of directories and files. Continue this process until the filename you require displays in the right-hand listbox. Figure 14-4 shows the state of the application after you traverse several subdirectories.

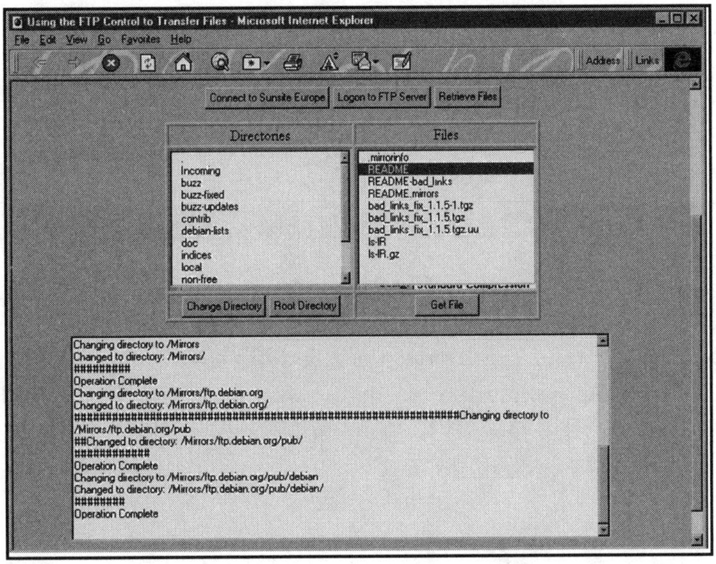

FIGURE 14-4
The FTP sample document after the required file has been discovered

6. If you need to move back in the file tree, press the Root Directory button. This moves you back to the top of the server's file system and allows you to start over. It would be possible to add a facility to move back one level (..), but this has not been implemented here.

7. To download a file to your system, select the file and press the Get File button. The file may take some time to download, so wait until the `Operation Complete` message appears before doing anything else with the document. The downloaded file will be stored on your system's Windows Desktop. Figure 14-5 shows the document once a file has been retrieved from the server.

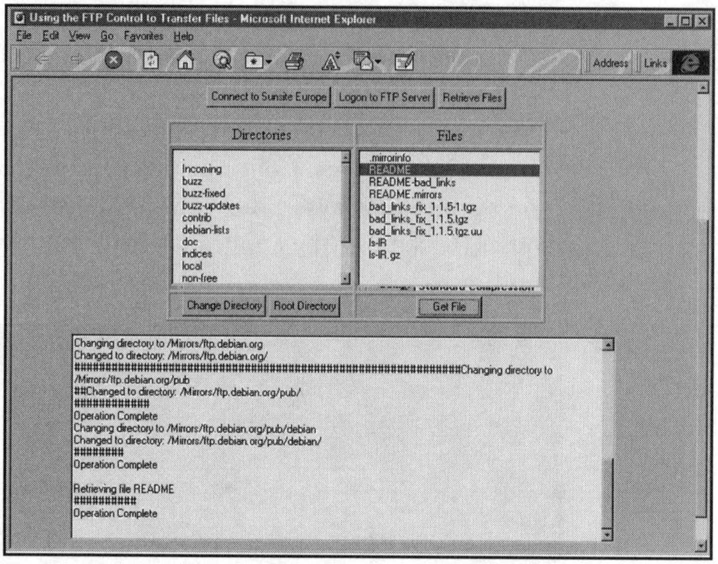

FIGURE 14-5
The FTP sample document after a file download has been completed

An Explanation of the Source Code

Now it's time to peer under the hood of the Web application you just explored. As with any other document, there are the normal HTML tags defining a HEAD and BODY section, while all the script code resides within the <HEAD> container tags.

Connection and Authentication

An FTP server requires the user to connect and then logon—many sites allow you to use the server as an anonymous user. When prompted for a user name, you want to enter **anonymous**, and for the password, you want to supply a complete e-mail address. Instead of typing these items yourself every time a connection is established, the FTP control has two properties that store them. The procedure ConnectButton_OnClick() sets up the control and calls its Connect method to initiate a session.

In addition to entering a user ID and password, you must specify which system to connect to using the RemoteHost property. This can be a DNS hostname, such as sunsite.doc.ic.ac.uk, or an IP address like 153.23.124.8. Here are the three lines of code that configure the control:

```
FTP1.RemoteHost = "sunsite.doc.ic.ac.uk"
FTP1.UserId = "anonymous"
FTP1.Password = "mymail@someplace.com"
```

CAUTION **Remember to remove any <PARAM> tags from the object definition when using the ICP controls. You must set any properties you require once the document has loaded or before using the control for the first time.**

After the FTP control connects (or fails to connect) to a system, the Connect event fires. There are two properties of the control that you can use at this point to provide feedback about the connection attempt. The ReplyCode and ReplyString properties contain values set by the last call to a control method and can be checked before continuing—this example somewhat optimistically assumes a successful connection.

As just described, once connected, a user must be authenticated. Having already set the UserID and Password properties, you need to make a call to the Authenticate method, which in this example falls in the procedure called AuthenticateButton_OnClick.

Retrieving the Initial File List

On pressing the Retrieve Files button, you will see that the ListButton_OnClick() procedure has only two lines, one of which is a call to the PrintDir method. How does this result in a complete listing of the remote directory being displayed? The PrintDir method is a request to the FTP server to return the name of its current directory—the arrival of this name at the client is signaled by the PrintDir event. The event procedure for this event then clears the two listboxes, stores the remote directory name in the variable *strRemoteDir,* and asks the FTP server to start sending the names of all the files (including directory names) in its current working directory. The *List* method is the trigger for all this activity, but before calling it the control's *ListItemNotify* property is set to True. This causes the control to generate a set of *ListItem* events, each of which passes details of another filename to the client.

As the server returns each filename, details of the file are handed back to the client in an FTPDirItem object (see ICP Help). The FTP1_ListItem event procedure checks the Attributes property of each FTPDirItem object—bit 0 set means it is a directory, bit 1 set signifies a file. The name of the item is then added to the relevant listbox control for viewing by the user.

A Simple Progress Indicator

You may have noticed the line in the FTP1_PrintDir event handler that reads

```
intTimerID = Window.SetTimeout ("Call CheckBusy()", 200, "VBScript")
```

and wondered what it does. This line sets a timer that fires after 1/5th of a second and calls the CheckBusy procedure. This procedure checks the FTP control's Busy property—if it is True, the server is still carrying out the last request and the timer is set to fire again soon. If the server has completed the operation, the user is informed with a call to the Insert_Message procedure (see the section "Keeping the User Informed," later in this chapter), otherwise a number symbol (#) outputs to let them know that the control is still functioning. This progress indicator is also used when the server is asked to change a directory or download a file.

Changing Directory

Press the Change Directory button to change to another directory. The ChangeDirButton_OnClick event procedure instructs the FTP server to navigate to the subdirectory specified by the currently selected item in the Directories listbox. Similar to the PrintDir method, the ChangeDir method may take some time to have an effect when the control generates the ChangeDir event. The ChangeDir event handler is almost identical to that discussed in the previous section but includes two extra lines for updating the currently stored directory name. These two lines ensure that the remote pathname starts and finishes with the forward slash symbols (/). Without them, the server will not recognize pathnames supplied to it.

```
    If Right(strRemoteDir, 1) <> "/" Then strRemoteDir = strRemoteDir
➥& "/"     'Make sure path ends with /
    If Left(strRemoteDir, 1) <> "/" Then strRemoteDir = "/" &
➥strRemoteDir      'Make sure path begins with /
```

After updating the *strRemoteDir* variable, the List method fetches a new list of file and directory names.

Fetching a File from the Server

Downloading a file is remarkably simple. Once the desired file has been found and its name displays in the Files listbox, all the user does is selects the filename and presses the Get File button. The event procedure GetFileButton_OnClick calls the control's GetFile method to perform the actual downloading. It takes two arguments—a source filename and a destination filename. By default, the control saves the file to your system's Desktop.

```
FTP1.GetFile FileList.List(FileList.ListIndex),
➥FileList.List(FileList.ListIndex)
```

NOTE *The line of code above shows how to refer to the currently selected item in a Forms 2.0 listbox. The control's ListIndex property stores the position of the current selection while the List array contains the actual text that appears at each position in the control.*

Keeping the User Informed

When you use networked controls, it is useful to provide the user with some form of status information because operations may take some time to complete. Both this example, and the HTTP sample later in this chapter, use a textarea control as a pad to display status messages. The Insert_Message procedure adds a new line of text to this box, including a carriage return and line feed sequence, while the Clear_Messages routine empties the textarea control of all previous entries.

The Complete Source Listing

Here is the example in full

```
<HTML>
<HEAD>
<TITLE>Using the FTP Control to Transfer Files</TITLE>
<SCRIPT LANGUAGE="VBScript">
<!-
'*******************************************************************
➥**************
' FTP Sample Application—using the FTP ActiveX control to download
➥files
' Purpose:
'    To demonstrate the FTP control and how it can be used to connect
➥to an FTP
'    server, retrieve directory listings, and download files
' Author:
'    C.J.Goddard—Copyright @1996
' Last Modified:
'    20th August 1996
'*******************************************************************
➥**************
Dim strRemoteDir, intTimerID


'*******************************************************************
➥**************
' Called as a response to a Window timer. Checks to see whether the
➥last command
' issued to the FTP server has completed yet. If not the timeout is
➥set to fire in
' 200 milliseconds time for another check.
'*******************************************************************
➥**************
```

```
Sub CheckBusy()
    If FTP1.Busy = True Then
        StatusText.Value = StatusText.Value & "#"          'Show user
➥that the control is alive
        intTimerID = Window.SetTimeout ("Call CheckBusy()", 200,
➥"VBScript")
        Exit Sub
    End If
    Insert_Message ""
    Insert_Message "Operation Complete"
    Window.ClearTimeout intTimerID
End Sub


'**********************************************************************
➥**************
' Utility function to add a message string to the status textbox.
'**********************************************************************
➥**************
Sub Insert_Message(strMessage)
    StatusText.Value = StatusText.Value & strMessage & Chr(13) &
➥Chr(10)
End Sub


'**********************************************************************
➥**************
' Clears the message box area of all messages
'**********************************************************************
➥**************
Sub Clear_Messages()
    StatusText.Value = ""
End Sub
```

```
'**********************************************************************
➥**************
' Event procedure for the 'Connect to Sunsite Europe' button. Sets up
➥the FTP control's
' attributes ready for a an anonymous connection to Sunsite Europe at
➥Imperial College
' in London. Calls the Connect method to initiate the session.
'**********************************************************************
➥**************
Sub ConnectButton_OnClick()
    FTP1.RemoteHost = "sunsite.doc.ic.ac.uk"
    FTP1.UserId = "anonymous"
    FTP1.Password = "mymail@someplace.com"
    Insert_Message "About to connect to Sunsite Europe"
    FTP1.Connect
End Sub


'**********************************************************************
➥**************
' Event fired when the FTP control connects to the server. Still fired
➥if connection fails.
' Expand this example by checking the value of the ReplyCode property
➥inside this
' procedure to notify the user of a failed connection.
'**********************************************************************
➥**************
Sub FTP1_Connect()
    Insert_Message "Connected"
End Sub


'**********************************************************************
➥**************
```

```
' Event procedure for the 'Logon to FTP Server' button. Calls the FTP
➥control's
' Authenticate method to authenticate the connection
'**********************************************************************
➥**************
Sub AuthenticateButton_OnClick()
    Insert_Message "About to authenticate for an anonymous FTP
➥session"
    FTP1.Authenticate
End Sub


'**********************************************************************
➥**************
' Event fired when the server authenticates the session. Still fired if
➥connection fails.
' Expand this example by checking the value of the ReplyCode property
➥inside this
' procedure to notify the user of a failed logon.
'**********************************************************************
➥**************
Sub FTP1_Authenticate()
    Insert_Message "Connected to Sunsite Europe"
    Insert_Message FTP1.ReplyString
End Sub


'**********************************************************************
➥**************
' Event fired when the FTP Server responds to the PWD command. The
➥remote directory is
' now stored in FTP1.RemoteDir, and is saved. The Directory and File
➥lists are cleared
' and the server is asked to list its directory contents.
```

```
' A timeout is set to check whether the operation has completed in 200
➥ms time.
' N.B The ListItemNotifyProperty must be True before calling the List
➥method.
'*********************************************************************
➥**************
Sub FTP1_PrintDir()
    strRemoteDir = FTP1.RemoteDir
    Insert_Message "Changed to directory: " & strRemoteDir
    DirectoryList.Clear()
    FileList.Clear()
    FTP1.ListItemNotify = True
    FTP1.List strRemoteDir
    intTimerID = Window.SetTimeout ("Call CheckBusy()", 200,
➥"VBScript")
End Sub


'*********************************************************************
➥**************
' Event fired when the FTP Server responds to the CD command. The
➥remote directory is
' now calculated by adding any necessary '/' chars. The Directory and
➥File lists are cleared
' and the server is asked to list its new directory contents.
' A timeout is set to check whether the operation has completed in 200
➥ms time.
' N.B The ListItemNotifyProperty must be True before calling the List
➥method.
'*********************************************************************
➥**************
Sub FTP1_ChangeDir()
    If Right(strRemoteDir, 1) <> "/" Then strRemoteDir = strRemoteDir
➥& "/"     'Make sure path ends with /
```

```
    If Left(strRemoteDir, 1) <> "/" Then strRemoteDir = "/" &
➥strRemoteDir      'Make sure path begins with /
    Insert_Message "Changed to directory: " & strRemoteDir
    DirectoryList.Clear()
    FileList.Clear()
    FTP1.ListItemNotify = True
    FTP1.List strRemoteDir
    intTimerID = Window.SetTimeout ("Call CheckBusy()", 200,
➥"VBScript")
End Sub


'**********************************************************************
➥**************
' Event procedure for the 'Retrieve Files' button. Calls the FTP
➥control's
' Printdir method to fetch the current working directory. The event
➥fired when this
' command completes fetches the directory listing for this server
➥directory
'**********************************************************************
➥**************
Sub ListButton_OnClick()
    Clear_Messages()
    FTP1.PrintDir
End Sub


'**********************************************************************
➥**************
' Event procedure called every time a file or directory name is
➥returned by the server.
' Directories (have bit 0 set) are added to the DirectoryList listbox
➥control.
' Files (have bit 1 set) are added to the FileList listbox control.
```

```
'*********************************************************************
➥**************
Sub FTP1_ListItem(Item)
    If Item.Attributes And 1 Then
        DirectoryList.AddItem(Item.Filename)
    ElseIf Item.Attributes And 2 Then
        FileList.AddItem(Item.FileName)
    End If
End Sub


'*********************************************************************
➥**************
' Event procedure for the 'Change Directory' button. A directory must
➥be selected from
' the Directories listbox. The current variable storing the remote
➥directory name is
' updated and the ChangeDir method called to change directory on the
➥FTP server.
'*********************************************************************
➥**************
Sub ChangeDirButton_OnClick()
    Insert_Message "Changing directory to " & strRemoteDir &
➥DirectoryList.List(DirectoryList.ListIndex)
    strRemoteDir = strRemoteDir & DirectoryList.List(DirectoryList.
➥ListIndex)
    FTP1.ChangeDir DirectoryList.List(DirectoryList.ListIndex)
End Sub


'*********************************************************************
➥**************
' Event procedure for the 'Root Directory' button. Instructs the server
➥to return to its
' root directory and display the files and directories contained there.
```

```
'*************************************************************************
➥**************
Sub RootButton_OnClick()
    Insert_Message ""
    Insert_Message "Returning to root directory"
    strRemoteDir = "/"
    FTP1.ChangeDir strRemoteDir
End Sub


'*************************************************************************
➥**************
' Event Procedure for the 'Get File' button. Informs the user that the
➥file selected in
' the Files listbox (one must be selected) is being downloaded. The
➥GetFile method is
' then called. The file is saved to the current local directory—in
this
➥case your
' Windows Desktop.
' A timer is set to fire in 200ms and check whether or not the
➥operation has completed
'*************************************************************************
➥**************
Sub GetFileButton_OnClick()
    Insert_Message ""
    Insert_Message "Retrieving file " & FileList.List(FileList.
➥ListIndex)
    FTP1.GetFile FileList.List(FileList.ListIndex), FileList.
➥List(FileList.ListIndex)
    intTimerID = Window.SetTimeout ("Call CheckBusy()", 200,
➥"VBScript")
End Sub
```

```
'*********************************************************************
➥**************
' Event procedure called when the document is unloaded from the
Browser
➥window. The
' connection to the FTP server is closed.
'*********************************************************************
➥**************
Sub Window_OnUnload()
    FTP1.Quit()
End Sub
-->
</SCRIPT>
</HEAD>

<BODY BACKGROUND="blobbg.jpg" TEXT="#00ff00">
<CENTER><H3>Using the FTP Control to Transfer Files</H3></CENTER>
This document contains an ActiveX control from Microsoft's Internet
➥Control Pack, which can be used to
perform FTP operations. The FTP control works in the same way as other
➥ActiveX controls, and can be controlled
using VBScript functions and event procedures.
You must have a TCP connection to the Internet (or a dial-up account
➥if you use a modem) to use this sample.
The script in this document will connect to the FTP server at Imperial
➥College in London, and allow you to
look at the directories and files held there. Pressing the
➥<B>Get File</B> button will download the selected file
and place it on your Desktop.
<CENTER><B>See Chapter 14 of the book for instructions on using this
➥sample</B><CENTER>
<HR>
<CENTER>
<INPUT TYPE="Button" NAME="ConnectButton" VALUE="Connect to Sunsite
➥Europe">
```

```
<INPUT TYPE="Button" NAME="AuthenticateButton" VALUE="Logon to FTP
➥Server">
<INPUT TYPE="Button" NAME="ListButton" VALUE="Retrieve Files"><P>

<TABLE BORDER>
<TR><TD ALIGN=Center>Directories</TD><TD ALIGN=Center>Files</TD>
<TR><TD>
<OBJECT ID="DirectoryList" WIDTH=200 HEIGHT=151
 CLASSID="CLSID:8BD21D20-EC42-11CE-9E0D-00AA006002F3">
    <PARAM NAME="ScrollBars" VALUE="3">
    <PARAM NAME="DisplayStyle" VALUE="2">
    <PARAM NAME="Size" VALUE="6632;3986">
    <PARAM NAME="MatchEntry" VALUE="1">
    <PARAM NAME="FontCharSet" VALUE="0">
    <PARAM NAME="FontPitchAndFamily" VALUE="2">
    <PARAM NAME="FontWeight" VALUE="0">
</OBJECT></TD>
<TD>
<OBJECT ID="FileList" WIDTH= 200 HEIGHT=151
 CLASSID="CLSID:8BD21D20-EC42-11CE-9E0D-00AA006002F3">
    <PARAM NAME="ScrollBars" VALUE="3">
    <PARAM NAME="DisplayStyle" VALUE="2">
    <PARAM NAME="Size" VALUE="6632;3986">
    <PARAM NAME="MatchEntry" VALUE="1">
    <PARAM NAME="FontCharSet" VALUE="0">
    <PARAM NAME="FontPitchAndFamily" VALUE="2">
    <PARAM NAME="FontWeight" VALUE="0">
</OBJECT></TD>
<TR>
<TD ALIGN=Center><INPUT TYPE="Button" NAME="ChangeDirButton"
➥VALUE="Change Directory">
<INPUT TYPE="Button" NAME="RootButton" VALUE="Root Directory"></TD>
<TD ALIGN=Center><INPUT TYPE="Button" NAME="GetFileButton" VALUE="Get
➥File"></TD>
</TABLE><P>
```

```
<TEXTAREA ROWS=15 COLS=120 NAME="StatusText">No connection yet!
</TEXTAREA>

<OBJECT ID="FTP1" WIDTH=24 HEIGHT=24
 CLASSID="CLSID:B7FC354C-8CE7-11CF-9754-00AA00C00908">
</OBJECT>

</CENTER>
<HR>
</BODY>
</HTML>
```

Developing a Phone Call Logging Application That Can Be Extended with the TCP Control

Because many readers of this book may use the examples on a stand-alone system that has only a dialup connection, no examples that use the TCP control to communicate between two computers are included. Unless you had two computers at hand, linked by a TPC/IP network, you would not be able to use the application. Instead, we have developed HawkEye, a phone message center, as an application that runs on a single PC but you can use the TCP control to split in two and extend.

NOTE *The best place to find details on the TCP and UDP controls is the Internet Control Pack help file. Because this chapter contains no examples that actually use these controls, it offers no further discussion of them.*

HawkEye allows you to add employee names and details into a central list, log phone messages for a particular employee, and view the recorded call logs by employee name. It uses many of the different types of items you have encountered so far—frames, tables, HTML form elements, Forms 2.0 ActiveX controls, the Internet Control Pack, and scripting.

HawkEye has been designed using a Client/Server model even though it now works on a single PC. The Communications section of the main source file contains four functions for sending and receiving data messages with the client and server ends of the system. If you want to expand the application using the TCP control to implement real network communications, you have to split the server functions from the main source file and place them in a new HTML file. The four communication functions also need to be modified a little to use the TCP control to send and receive data over the network. Remember, the `TCP` object needs to negotiate a connection with a remote host before it can transmit and receive data. The HawkEye application contains all the code necessary to package the client and server requests and responses into strings for transmission. As string messages are received, they are unpacked and deciphered so the correct action results. This action occurs because you don't have a control for carrying out Remote Procedure Calls (RPC) and have to make do with string messages.

NOTE *A TCP server can actually communicate with several clients at a time because their IP address identifies them. The TCP control supplied with the Internet Control Pack, however, does not support this behavior. If you want to connect several client systems to the phone center at once (a more likely scenario), several TCP controls could be used on the server machine. These controls could listen on a range of ports, so if the first port was busy, the second could be tried, and so on, until the client connects.*

Using HawkEye to Record and View Phone Messages

HawkEye is the most complicated example of the book, so some instructions on using it might come in handy.

1. Load the application by choosing the `HawkEye - A Phone Message Center` link from the Internet Control Pack section of the main Web page. Figure 14-6 shows what the document should look like once Explorer 3.0 loads.

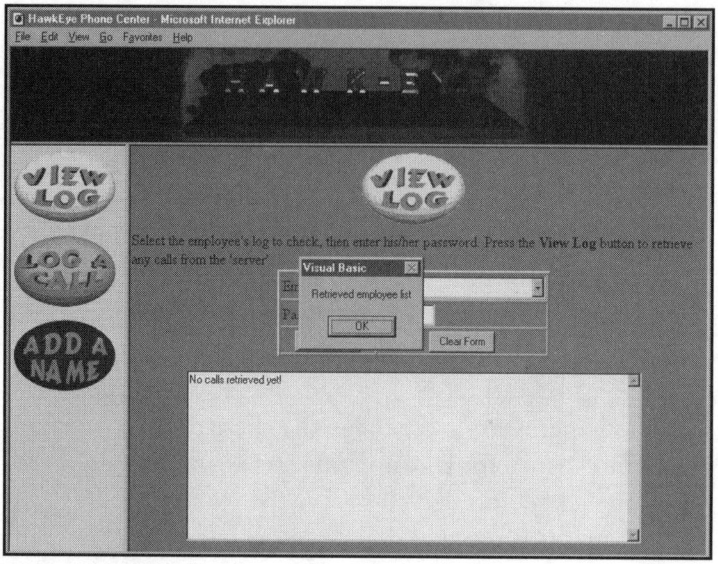

FIGURE 14-6
The HawkEye Phone Center

2. The frame running down the left-hand side of the page contains links to three separate HTML documents that you can view by clicking on the appropriate images. When you select a link, the relevant page loads, and displays in the main frame window. Choose the third image, Add A Name, which brings up the frame for adding new employees to the list.
3. Up to 50 different employee names and details can be added to the list by modifying the source code. Type the new details into the form and press the Add Employee button. You must enter a name and password; the other fields are optional. Figure 14-7 shows this frame just before adding a name. A message will display if the operation is successful.
4. This operation should be repeated until all the required names have been added to the list. You are then free to record calls and messages for any of these people.
5. Choose the link image with the `Log A Call` message. This loads another frame into the main frame window but all the names you entered earlier are still stored in memory. Select the person to record a call for from the combobox control and enter all

the necessary details. The current date and time are used if no others are specified. Figure 14-8 shows the frame for adding a message entry.

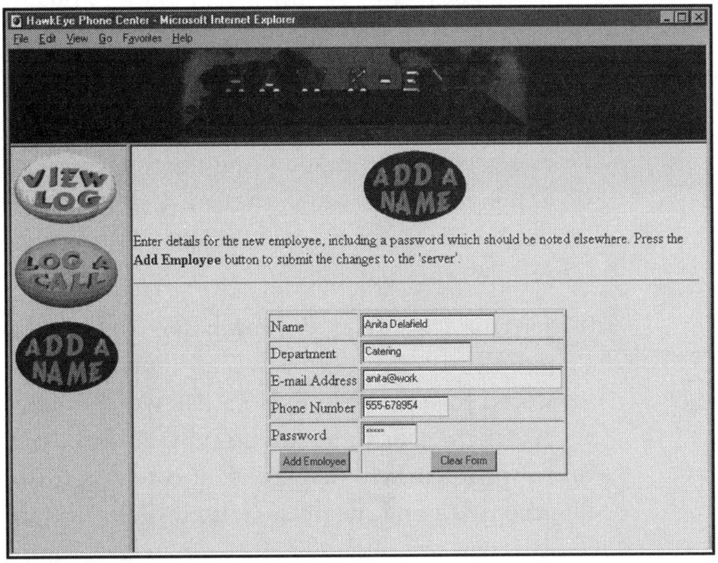

FIGURE 14-7
Adding an employee's details using the HawkEye Phone Center

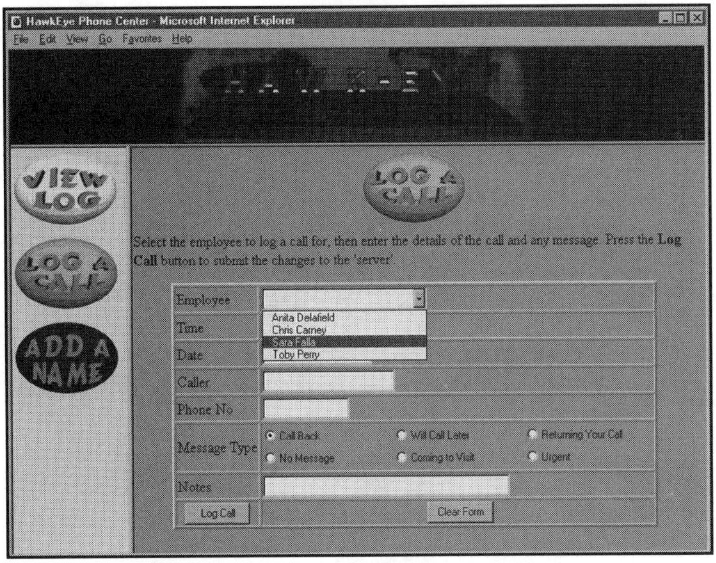

FIGURE 14-8
Recording a phone message using the Log A Call form.

6. You may add message entries and new employees in whatever order you want because each message and employee is assigned a new internal number. This means there can be several messages from the same person or several employees with the same name (although this can become confusing).

7. What about looking at previously stored messages? The first frame window is used for this purpose and can be loaded by selecting the image using the text `View Log`. When the employees were added to the list, the form required a password. It is this password that restricts access to other people's message logs.

8. Select a name from the combobox and enter that person's password. Press the View Calls button to view the messages stored for that person. If no password is entered, the password is incorrect, or there are no calls, an error message stating the problem will display. If all is well, a list of calls and accompanying details is written to the textarea control. You can then scroll through at your leisure. Figure 14-9 shows such a message list.

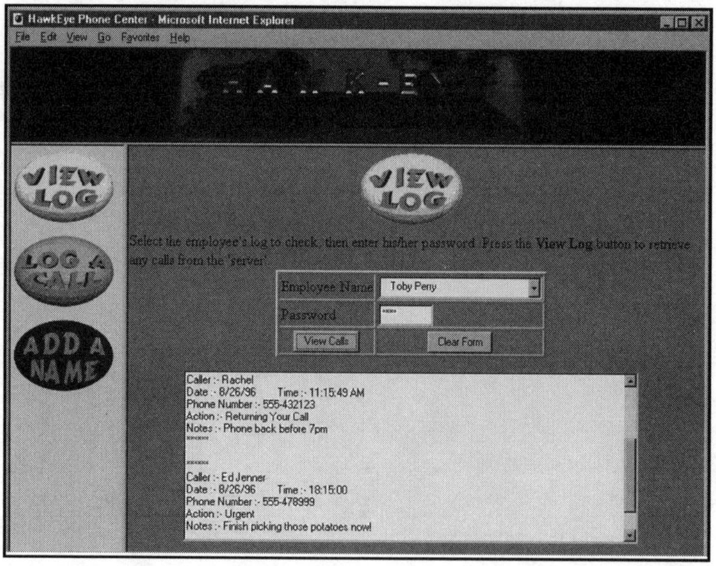

FIGURE 14-9
Viewing stored messages in the View Log frame

NOTE *All the information you add to the Phone Center is only retained in memory as long as the document is loaded in your Web browser. The example would be much more useful if you could save items to disk and delete viewed calls. VBScript does not have file I/O capabilities, but if you port the server part of the application to a Web server, you may be able to use CGI scripts or a database control to store the calls. The client section of HawkEye would remain essentially the same.*

Tying It Together with HawkEye's Main Document

What follows is a brief explanation of the main document, saved as hawkeye.htm in the Examples\Mvb_14 subdirectory of the VBScript installation. There are copious comments within the code itself with all the necessary details.

Building the Scaffolding with a FRAMESET

Refer back to Figures 14-6 to 14-9 and you will see that the application consists of several different frames. This document structure is created by using a frameset definition, as discussed in Chapter 10, "The Object Model for Scripting." Turn to the last page of this source listing and look for the lines beginning

```
******************************
 * FRAMESET DEFINITION SECTION
```

The section of HTML that follows this comment defines one frameset split vertically and one split horizontally. The top and left frames have explicit sizes because they display particular images while the rest of the browser window is used for the main frame. In order to access frames from a script, it is best to name them—hence the NAME="framename" attributes within the <FRAME> tags. The most important frame is called main and will contain each of the three child frames explained later.

Sending and Receiving Commands—The Communications Section

The design of HawkEye has already been explained, but how are the packing and unpacking functions implemented? Look for the section of code beginning with the lines

```
'***********************************************************************
➥******
' HAWKEYE COMMUNICATIONS SECTION
```

and you will find four separate VBScript functions. The comments in that section provide much detail about the workings of these routines. In order to create a reusable structure for sending and receiving commands, the number of data items sent in a message needs to be variable. For this reason, dynamic arrays are used to pass an arbitrary number of items to the packaging functions. These functions, defined as

```
Function SendDataClnt(arrData())
```

and

```
Function SendDataSvr(arrData())
```

respectively, take dynamic arrays as arguments and create a single message string for transmission. The Ubound function (see Language Reference in Appendix A) determines the size of the array and each item is appended to a string, followed by a semi-colon (;). The first item in the array is always a command word, such as `EMPLIST`, `LOGGED` or `VIEW`. The items that follow depend on the command being issued. Some have no further information while others, such as the command to add an employee, have array elements storing the new name, phone number, and so on. The following array would result in the string *'ADD;Chris Goddard;IT;753473'*;

```
arrData(0) = "ADD"
arrData(1) = "Chris Goddard"
arrData(2) = "IT"
arrData(3) = "753473"
```

Once the message string is constructed, it is sent by placing it in the other side's receive buffer, strRXclnt or `strRXsvr`, and setting a timer to fire the relevant receive function 200 milliseconds later. This simulates a network transfer and is the part of the code that requires modifying to use the TCP control.

The receive functions, GetDataClnt and `GetDataSvr` are somewhat more complicated. String manipulation functions tokenize the message by looking for the semicolons and separating each token from the main string. The first decoded token is checked to see if it matches one of the recognized commands. If so, the dynamic data array is resized to accommodate the rest of the tokens. Once the message string is completely decoded, the operation code, `intOp`, is tested and the function required to carry out the requested command is called. The command functions themselves reside in different sections and are described next.

What Happens on the Server Side

The client portion of HawkEye can request that the server carry out one of four different operations.

- Add an employee's details to the list
- Return the current list of employee names
- Log the details of a new phone message
- Return the call log for a specific employee

The operation requested is decided by the GetDataSvr function that then calls a function in the server section. The functions to add an employee and log a call are quite similar. `Svr_Add_Employee` and `Svr_Log_Call` take the array of items passed to them by the receive function and store each item in a new position in various arrays. There are separate arrays for names, phone numbers, call times, and so on. If the operation is successful, a command string is sent back indicating success. If the arrays are already full, a failure message is returned.

NOTE *Instead of reporting that the arrays are full, the program could resize them to hold more items. This resizing could be repeated whenever the employee and call lists approached capacity.*

Svr_Get_Employee_List returns the list of names currently stored in the server's arrays. The first item in the message array is the command word EMPLIST, next is the number of names that follow, and the rest of the array elements contain the employee names. This function is needed when the client wishes to display a list of current names, such as that seen in Figure 14-8.

The final function in this section, Svr_Call_Log, returns the log of messages stored for a particular employee. The person is identified by their employee number, which is their position in the employee list. Before returning the log, the supplied password is checked to ensure that only authorized users can view the messages. The log is returned as a long string containing all the call details that is composed in the Svr_Call_Log function. The client only needs to display the string in a textarea control.

Understanding the Client Operations

The routines in the "Client" section of this document are quite simple. The routines are used by the other frame windows to compose message arrays and send them to the transmission function. The function declared as

```
Function  Set_Employee_List(arrEmps())
```

and is called when the server returns the current list of names. This function clears the combobox that currently displays in the main frame and adds each name from the arrEmps array to the control.

Most of the replies returned by the server simply indicate success or failure of the last request. All that is required in these cases is a message dialog to let the user know what happened.

NOTE

There are two different frame windows that use the current employee list, the View Log frame and the Log a Call frame. Instead of writing two separate routines to fetch and set the contents for the drop-down list, we named the forms and combobox controls with the same identifiers in both frames. This does not cause a problem because only one frame is ever loaded at one time.

HAWKEYE.HTM—The Source Code

```
<!DOCTYPE HTML PUBLIC "-//W3O/DTD HTML//EN">

<html>
<head>
<title>HawkEye Phone Center</title>
<meta name="FORMATTER" content="Microsoft FrontPage 1.1">
<SCRIPT LANGUAGE="VBScript">
<!-
'*********************************************************************
➥******
' Purpose:
'    Main module of the HawkEye Phone Center, a VBScript application
➥for recording
'    and retrieving telephone messages.
'    This file contains VBScript code and FRAMESET definitions to
➥implement a
'    complete application for logging telephone calls and messages.
➥It has been
'    designed using a Client/Server model, so that a TCP ActiveX
➥control could be
'    added and used as a link between the client side of things—the
➥user interface,
'    and the server application. At present, to demonstrate the
➥techniques and
'    principles, the code will work on a single computer.
' Author:
```

```
'    C.J.Goddard—Copyright @1996
' Last Modified:
'    21st August 1996
'***********************************************************************
➥******


'***********************************************************************
➥******
' HAWKEYE SERVER-SIDE FUNCTIONS AND DECLARATIONS
'***********************************************************************
➥******
Dim strRXsvr              'Receive buffer for the server—simulates a
➥TCP buffer

'***Arrays used for storing employee details
Dim arrEMPName(50), arrEMPDept(50), arrEMPEmail(50), arrEMPPhone(50),
➥arrEMPPassword(50)
Dim intEMP_No             'Current employee number
intEMP_No = 1

'***Arrays used for storing call details
Dim arrLOGTime(200), arrLOGDate(200), arrLOGCaller(200),
➥arrLOGPhone(200), arrLOGNotes(200), arrLOGType(200) _
 , arrLOGEmp(200)
Dim intLOG_No             'Current call number
intLOG_No = 1


'***********************************************************************
➥******
' Purpose: Used for adding new employees to the current list.
' Inputs:  arrDetails()—an array containing the details for the new
➥employee
```

```
'                              Positions 0 to 4 store: Name, Department,
➥e-mail, phone
'                              and password
' Returns: -1 if employee list is full, new employee number otherwise
'*********************************************************************
➥******
Function Svr_Add_Employee(arrDetails())
    Dim arrData(0)                              'Array for return data

    If intEMP_No = 50 Then                      'If employee list is full
        Svr_Add_Employee = -1
        arrData(0) = "NOTADDED"                 'Tell client that list is
➥full
        SendDataSvr(arrData)
        Exit Function
    End If
    arrEMPName(intEMP_No) = arrDetails(0) 'Store details in current
➥array positions
    arrEMPDept(intEMP_No) = arrDetails(1)
    arrEMPEmail(intEMP_No) = arrDetails(2)
    arrEMPPhone(intEMP_No) = arrDetails(3)
    arrEMPPassword(intEMP_No) = arrDetails(4)
    intEMP_No = intEMP_No + 1                   'Increment number in the
➥list
    Svr_Add_Employee = intEMP_No
    arrData(0) = "ADDED"
    SendDataSvr(arrData)                        'Inform client of success
End Function


'*********************************************************************
➥******
' Purpose: Used for logging a new phone message, storing call details
➥in arrays
```

```
' Inputs:  arrDetails()—an array containing the details for the new
➥call
'                            Positions 0 to 6 store:
'                            Time, Date, Caller name, Caller number,
➥Notes, Type
'                            and Employee number
' Returns: -1 if call log is full, new call number otherwise
'*******************************************************************
➥******
Function Svr_Log_Call(arrDetails())
    Dim arrData(0)                          'Array for return data

    If intLOG_No = 200 Then                 'If log is full
        Svr_Log_Call = -1
        arrData(0) = "NOTLOGGED"
        SendDataSvr(arrData)                'Inform client of failure
        Exit Function
    End If
    arrLOGTime(intLOG_No) = arrDetails(0) 'Store details of new call in
➥array elements
    arrLOGDate(intLOG_No) = arrDetails(1)
    arrLOGCaller(intLOG_No) = arrDetails(2)
    arrLOGPhone(intLOG_No) = arrDetails(3)
    arrLOGNotes(intLOG_No) = arrDetails(4)
    arrLOGType(intLOG_No) = arrDetails(5)
    arrLOGEmp(intLOG_No) = arrDetails(6)

    intLOG_No = intLOG_No + 1               'Increment current call
➥number
    Svr_Log_Call = intLOG_No
    arrData(0) = "LOGGED"                   'Inform client of success
    SendDataSvr(arrData)
End Function
```

```
'*********************************************************************
➥******
' Purpose: Used for retrieving an employee's call log and returning it
➥to the
'          client
' Inputs:  arrDetails()—an array containing the details of the
➥requested log
'                           Positions 0 to 1 store:
'                           Employee number and Password respectively
' Returns: -1 if Password is incorrect
'           1 if call log is found
'          -2 if no calls are stored for the current employee
'*********************************************************************
➥******
Function Svr_View_Log(arrDetails())
    Dim arrData(1), intCount, CRLF, blnFound     'Store return data,
➥position in log,
                                                  'newline sequence
➥& calls found flag

    CRLF = Chr(13) & Chr(10) : blnFound = False  'Initialize variables

    If arrEMPPassword(arrDetails(0)+1) <> arrDetails(1) Then
        Svr_View_Log = -1                  'Incorrect password entered
        arrData(0) = "PASSWORD"
        arrData(1) = "—"
        SendDataSvr(arrData)               'Inform client of situation
        Exit Function
    End If

    For intCount = 0 to intLOG_No -1     'Search entire call list
        If arrLogEMP(intCount+1) = arrDetails(0) Then    'If call is
➥for our employee
            arrData(1) = arrData(1) & "******" & CRLF    'Insert call
➥details into the return string
```

```
            arrData(1) = arrData(1) & "Caller :- " &
➥arrLOGCaller(intCount+1) & CRLF
            arrData(1) = arrData(1) & "Date :- " &
➥arrLOGDate(intCount+1)
            arrData(1) = arrData(1) & "        Time :- " &
➥arrLOGTime(intCount+1) & CRLF
            arrData(1) = arrData(1) & "Phone Number :- " &
➥arrLOGPhone(intCount+1) & CRLF
            Select Case arrLOGType(intCount+1)           'Insert
➥action for the call
                Case "1"
                    arrData(1) = arrData(1) & "Action :- Call Back"
➥& CRLF
                Case "2"
                    arrData(1) = arrData(1) & "Action :- Will Call
➥Later" & CRLF
                Case "3"
                    arrData(1) = arrData(1) & "Action :- Returning
➥Your Call" & CRLF
                Case "4"
                    arrData(1) = arrData(1) & "Action :- No Message"
➥& CRLF
                Case "5"
                    arrData(1) = arrData(1) & "Action :- Coming to
➥Visit" & CRLF
                Case "6"
                    arrData(1) = arrData(1) & "Action :- Urgent" &
➥CRLF
            End Select
            arrData(1) = arrData(1) & "Notes :- " &
➥arrLOGNotes(intCount+1) & CRLF
            arrData(1) = arrData(1) & "*******" & CRLF & CRLF
            blnFound = True                                'Set the
➥calls found flag
        End If
```

```
    Next                                                    'Now inform
client
➥of success and return
    If blnFound = True Then                                'call log as a long
➥string, or inform that
        Svr_View_Log = 1                                   'no calls were
➥found
        arrData(0) = "CALLS"
        SendDataSvr(arrData)
    Else
        Svr_View_Log = -2
        arrData(0) = "NOCALLS"
        arrData(1) = "-"
        SendDataSvr(arrData)
    End If
End Function


'**********************************************************************
➥*******
' Purpose: Used for returning the current list of employee's to the
'           client
' Inputs:   None
' Returns: Undefined-0
'**********************************************************************
*
➥******
Function Svr_Get_Employee_List()
    Dim arrData(), intCount                         'Return data and position
➥count
    ReDim arrData(intEMP_No+1)                      'Make the array large
➥enough for all employee names
```

```
    arrData(0) = "EMPLIST"                        'Command code for the
➥client to decipher
    arrData(1) = intEMP_No-1                    'Number of employees in the
➥list
    For intCount = 2 To intEMP_No+1          'Place employee names in
➥the rest of the list
        arrData(intCount) = arrEMPName(intCount-1)
    Next
    SendDataSvr(arrData)                          'Send list data back to
➥client
End Function
->
</SCRIPT>



<SCRIPT LANGUAGE="VBScript">
<!-
'*********************************************************************
➥*******
' HAWKEYE CLIENT-SIDE FUNCTIONS AND DECLARATIONS
'*********************************************************************
➥*******
Dim strRXclnt              'Receive buffer for the server-simulates a
➥TCP buffer


'*********************************************************************
➥*******
' Purpose: Used to send data to the server instructing it to add a new
➥employee's
'          details to the current list
' Inputs:  Strings storing new employee Name, Department, E-mail, Phone
➥number & Password
' Returns: the return value of the SendDataClnt function
```

```
'**********************************************************************
➥*******
Function Add_Employee(strName, strDept, strEmail, strPhone,
➥strPassword)
    Dim arrDetails(5)                       'Array to pass the employee
➥details for
    arrDetails(0) = "ADD"                   'packaging and transmission
    arrDetails(1) = strName
    arrDetails(2) = strDept
    arrDetails(3) = strEMail
    arrDetails(4) = strPhone
    arrDetails(5) = strPassword
    Add_Employee = SendDataClnt(arrDetails) 'Send the actual data
End Function


'**********************************************************************
➥******
' Purpose: Used to send a request to the server to return the current
➥list of
'          employees
' Inputs:  None
' Returns: the return value of the SendDataClnt function
'**********************************************************************
➥******
Function Get_Employee_List()
    Dim arrDetails(0)
    arrDetails(0) = "GETEMP"                'Command code so server
➥knows what is being asked of it
    Get_Employee_List = SendDataClnt(arrDetails)
End Function


'**********************************************************************
➥******
```

```
' Purpose: Used once the server has returned the employee list to the
➥client.
'           The employee names supplied in the array arrEmps() are
➥inserted into
'           the ComboBox control on the screen
' Inputs:  None
' Returns: the return value of the SendDataClnt function
'**********************************************************************
➥******
Function  Set_Employee_List(arrEmps())
    Dim intCount
    Main.LogForm.EmployeeCombo.Clear      'First remove existing
➥employee names

    For intCount = 1 to arrEmps(0)        'Insert each name in turn
        Main.LogForm.EmployeeCombo.AddItem arrEmps(intCount)
    Next
    MsgBox "Retrieved employee list"
End Function



'**********************************************************************
➥******
' Purpose: Used to send a request to the server to log the details of
➥a new phone
'           mesages
' Inputs:  Strings storing Time, Date, Caller name, Caller phone, Notes
➥, Action to
'           take, Employee number
' Returns: the return value of the SendDataClnt function
'**********************************************************************
➥******
Function Log_Call(strTime, strDate, strCaller, strPhone, strNotes,
➥intType, intEmp)
    Dim arrDetails(7)
```

```
    arrDetails(0) = "LOG"
    arrDetails(1) = strTime
    arrDetails(2) = strDate
    arrDetails(3) = strCaller
    arrDetails(4) = strPhone
    arrDetails(5) = strNotes
    arrDetails(6) = intType
    arrDetails(7) = intEmp
    Log_Call = SendDataClnt(arrDetails)
End Function


'*********************************************************************
➥******
' Purpose: Used to send a request to the server to return the call log
➥for a
'          specified employee
' Inputs:  The employee number from the employee list, and the
➥employee's password
' Returns: the return value of the SendDataClnt function
'*********************************************************************
➥******
Function View_Log(intEmpNo, strPassword)
    Dim arrDetails(2)
    arrDetails(0) = "VIEW"
    arrDetails(1) = intEmpNo
    arrDetails(2) = strPassword
    View_Log = SendDataClnt(arrDetails)
End Function
-->
</SCRIPT>


<SCRIPT LANGUAGE="VBScript">
```

```
<!—
'**********************************************************************
➥******
' HAWKEYE COMMUNICATIONS SECTION
' ==============================
' The functions in this section have been clearly split into Client
and
➥Server
' send and receive functions. Transfer across a network between two
➥separate
' computers is simulated by packaging all commands, parameters and
➥return values
' as strings, with elements separated by semi-colons (;). These message
➥strings
' are then 'sent' and 'received' in buffer strings. Once a string has
➥been sent,
' the receiving function on the other end is triggered 200ms later to
➥deal with
' the new input. The input is broken down into its constituent tokens
➥and acted
' on in accordance with the first token, the command code, e.g.
➥"EMPLIST"
' The application could be made truly client/server by splitting the
➥server
' functions in this file into another file and using Winsock TCP
➥controls to
' send and receive the message strings. All the packing and unpacking
➥of tokens
' will be handled by the functions already present in this section.
'**********************************************************************
➥******


'**********************************************************************
➥******
```

```
' Purpose: Used to package data items stored in a dynamic array into
➥one long string
'           This string is then 'sent' to the server by placing it in
➥the server's
'           receive buffer and setting a timer to call the server
➥receive function.
'           Modify this function by using a TCP control to send the
➥string to a remote
'           host.
' Inputs:  A dynamic array containing the data values to package and
➥send
' Returns: 1
'*********************************************************************
➥******
Function SendDataClnt(arrData())
    Dim intCount
    strRXsvr = ""                                  'Clear server's
➥receive buffer
    For intCount = 0 to UBound(arrData)          'For each data item
➥in the array
        strRXsvr = strRXsvr & arrData(intCount) & ";"    'Add data
➥item plus semi-colon
    Next
    Window.SetTimeout  "GetDataSvr()", 200, "VBScript"   'Trigger
➥receive
    SendDataClnt = 1
End Function


'*********************************************************************
➥******
' Purpose: Used to receive, unpack and act upon a message string
➥received from
'           the server.
```

```
'          Modify this function by using a TCP control to receive the
➥string from
'          a remote host
' Inputs:  None—expects input string to be present in strRXclnt
' Returns: Undefined at present—0
'*********************************************************************
➥******
Function GetDataClnt()
    'Define storage for command tokens, received data, position of
➥token, command
    ' found flag, token string, current token number, command code and
➥result
    Dim arrData(), strTemp, intPos, blnStarted, strToken, intItem,
➥intOp, intResult

    strTemp = strRXclnt : blnStarted = False : intItem = 0

    'Now break strTemp into its component parts
    Do While strTemp <> ""                              'Continue until
➥all tokens found
        intPos = InStr (strTemp, ";")                  'Find a semi-colon
                                                          'If one is not
➥found it is an error
        If intPos = 0 Then MsgBox "Error parsing input" : Exit
➥Function
        strToken = Left(strTemp, intPos-1)           'Get the token
➥from the input string
        strTemp = Right(strTemp, Len(strTemp)-intPos)  'Discard token,
➥leaving rest of string
        If not blnStarted Then                          'If command has
➥not been found yet
            blnStarted = True
            Select Case strToken                        'Search for a
➥command code, set command
```

```
                    Case "ADDED"                        'code and
➥allocate storage for remaining
                        ReDim arrData(0)                'items according
➥to the command
                        intOp = 1
                    Case "NOTADDED"
                        ReDim arrData(0)
                        intOp = 2
                    Case "EMPLIST"
                        ReDim arrData(50)
                        intOp = 3
                    Case "LOGGED"
                        ReDim arrData(0)
                        intOp = 4
                    Case "NOTLOGGED"
                        ReDim arrData(0)
                        intOp = 5
                    Case "PASSWORD"
                        ReDim arrData(1)
                        intOp = 6
                    Case "CALLS"
                        ReDim arrData(1)
                        intOp = 7
                    Case "NOCALLS"
                        ReDim arrData(1)
                        intOp = 8
                End Select
            Else
                arrData(intItem) = strToken             'Command has been
➥found, this is just a data
                intItem = intItem + 1                   'item so store it
➥and increment position counter
            End If
        Loop
```

```
    Select Case intOp                                    'Choose action
➥based on command code
        Case 1
            MsgBox "Added Employee Successfully"
        Case 2
            MsgBox "Failed to Add Employee"
        Case 3
            Set_Employee_List(arrData)              'Insert employee
➥names into combobox
        Case 4
            MsgBox "Logged Call Successfully"
        Case 5
            MsgBox "Failed to Log Call"
        Case 6
            MsgBox "Password entered was incorrect"
        Case 7
            Main.LogForm.CallText.Value = arrData(0)   'Display call
➥log string in the textarea
        Case 8
            MsgBox "No calls stored for that employee"
    End Select
    GetDataClnt = intResult
End Function


'*********************************************************************
➥******
' Purpose: Used to package data items stored in a dynamic array into
➥one long string
'           This string is then 'sent' to the client by placing it in
➥the client's
'           receive buffer and setting a timer to call the client
➥receive function.
'           Modify this function by using a TCP control to send the
➥string to a remote
```

```
'           host.
' Inputs:  A dynamic array containing the data values to package and
➥send
' Returns: 1
'**********************************************************************
➥******
Function SendDataSvr(arrData())
    Dim intCount
    strRXclnt = ""                                    'Clear server's
➥receive buffer
    For intCount = 0 to UBound(arrData)              'For each data item
➥in the array
        strRXclnt = strRXclnt & arrData(intCount) & ";" 'Insert data
➥item and a semi-colon
    Next
    Window.SetTimeout  "GetDataClnt()", 200, "VBScript"    'Trigger
➥receive
    SendDataSvr = 1
End Function


'**********************************************************************
➥******
' Purpose: Used to receive, unpack and act upon a message string
➥received from
'           the client.
'           Modify this function by using a TCP control to receive the
➥string from
'           a remote host
' Inputs:  None—expects input string to be present in strRXsvr
' Returns: Undefined at present—0
'**********************************************************************
➥******
Function GetDataSvr()
```

```
    'Define storage for command tokens, received data, position of
➥token, command
    ' found flag, token string, current token number, command code and
➥result
    Dim arrData(), strTemp, intPos, blnStarted, strToken, intItem,
➥intOp, intResult

    strTemp = strRXsvr : blnStarted = False : intItem = 0

    'Now break strTemp into its component parts
    Do While strTemp <> ""                              'Continue until
➥all tokens found
        intPos = InStr (strTemp, ";")                   'Find a semi-colon
                                                         'If one is not
➥found it is an error
        If intPos = 0 Then MsgBox "Error parsing input" : Exit
➥Function
        strToken = Left(strTemp, intPos-1)              'Get the token
➥from the input string
        strTemp = Right(strTemp, Len(strTemp)-intPos)   'Discard token,
➥leaving rest of string
        If not blnStarted Then                          'If command has
➥not been found yet
            blnStarted = True
            Select Case strToken                        'Search for a
➥command code, set command
                Case "ADD"                              'code and
➥allocate storage for remaining
                    ReDim arrData(4)                    'items according
➥to the command
                    intOp = 1
                Case "GETEMP"
                    ReDim arrData(0)
                    intOp = 2
                Case "LOG"
```

```
                    ReDim arrData(6)
                    intOp = 3
                Case "VIEW"
                    ReDim arrData(1)
                    intOp = 4
            End Select
        Else
            arrData(intItem) = strToken         'Command has been
➥found, this is just a data
            intItem = intItem + 1               'item so store it
➥and increment position counter
        End If

    Loop
    Select Case intOp                           'Choose action
➥based on command code
        Case 1
            intResult = Svr_Add_Employee(arrData) 'Add an employee to
➥the list
        Case 2
            intResult = Svr_Get_Employee_List()   'Send back employee
➥list to client
        Case 3
            intResult = Svr_Log_Call(arrData)     'Log a new call
        Case 4
            intResult = Svr_View_Log(arrData)     'Return an
➥employee's log
    End Select
    GetDataSvr = intResult
End Function
—>
</SCRIPT>
</head>
<!—
 ******************************
```

```
 * FRAMESET DEFINITION SECTION
 *****************************
->
<frameset rows="102,*">
    <frame frameborder="NO" src="frbanner.htm" name="banner"
➥marginwidth="1" marginheight="1">
    <frameset cols="130,*">
        <frame src="frconten.htm" name="contents" marginwidth="1"
➥marginheight="1">
        <frame src="frmain.htm" name="main" marginwidth="1"
➥marginheight="1">
    </frameset>
    <noframes>
        <body>
            <p>This Web page uses frames, but your browser doesn't
➥support them.<p>
        </body>
    </noframes>
</frameset>
</html>
```

The View Log Frame for Fetching Messages

The three frame windows for HawkEye are somewhat simpler than the main document. They contain the HTML source that defines the tables and forms seen in Figures 14-7, 14-8, and 14-9. The bulk of the application's functionality is kept in the main document and only the event procedures for the various form elements are to be found in these files.

NOTE *The ComboBox control that stores the list of employee names is a Microsoft Forms 2.0 control (discussed in Chapter 13, "Using the ActiveX Control Pad and HTML Layout Control"). Make sure you install the ActiveX Control Pad before using this object.*

Refer back to Figure 14-9 and you will see there is a combobox with which to select a person's name. Each time the View Log document loads, the current list of names should be displayed—hence the call to Top.Get_Employee_List in the Window's OnLoad event handler. The qualifier Top. is needed because the call is to a function in the main HawkEye document, the topmost item in the window hierarchy (see Chapter 10, "The Object Model for Scripting").

Before calling the function in the main file that retrieves a call log, some checks are carried out in the event handler for ViewButton. These checks ensure that a name is currently selected from the employee list and that a password is supplied.

The View Log Source Code

The name of this file is frmain.htm and it is stored in the same directory as the rest of the HawkEye files.

```
<!DOCTYPE HTML PUBLIC "-//IETF//DTD HTML//EN">


<html>
<head>
<title>Main Frame in HawkEye Phone Center</title>
<meta name="GENERATOR" content="Microsoft FrontPage 1.1">
<SCRIPT LANGUAGE="VBScript">
<!-
'*************************************************************
*
➥******
' Purpose:
'    Module of the HawkEye Phone Center, a VBScript application for
➥recording
'    and retrieving telephone messages.
'    This file contains the HTML frame and elements for viewing an
➥employee's
'    call log
' Author:
```

```
'     C.J.Goddard—Copyright @1996
' Last Modified:
'     21st August 1996
'*********************************************************************
➥******



'*********************************************************************
➥******
' Event procedure called once the document has loaded into the frame
➥window.
' The current list of employees is retrieved from the 'server' by
➥calling a
' function which can be found in the HAWKEYE.HTM file
'*********************************************************************
➥******
Sub Window_OnLoad
    Top.Get_Employee_List()
End Sub



'*********************************************************************
➥******
' Event procedure called when the user presses the 'View Calls' but-
ton.
➥Some
' data validation is carried out to make sure the user has selected an
➥employee
' and entered a password. If so, a function in the topmost document is
➥called
' to fetch the log entries from the 'server' and display them in the
➥CallText
' textarea control.
'*********************************************************************
➥******
```

```
Sub ViewButton_OnClick()
    Dim dummy

    If LogForm.EmployeeCombo.ListIndex < 0 Then
        MsgBox "An employee must be selected from the list", vbOKOnly,
➥"HawkEye Phone Center"
    ElseIf LogForm.PasswordText.Value = "" Then
        MsgBox "You must enter a password", vbOKOnly, "HawkEye Phone
➥Center"
    Else
        dummy = Top.View_Log(LogForm.EmployeeCombo.ListIndex,
LogForm.PasswordText.Value)
    End If
End Sub
->
</SCRIPT>
</head>

<body bgcolor="#6699ff" text="#000000">
<center>
    <img src="view_log.gif" align=bottom width=120 height=90>
</center>
Select the employee's log to check, then enter his/her password.
Press the <B>View Log</B> button to retrieve any calls from the
➥'server'.<br>
<center>

<form name="LogForm">
<table border=2>
<tr>
    <td>Employee Name</td>
    <td>
    <OBJECT ID="EmployeeCombo" WIDTH=181 HEIGHT=24
     CLASSID="CLSID:8BD21D30-EC42-11CE-9E0D-00AA006002F3">
        <PARAM NAME="VariousPropertyBits" VALUE="746592283">
```

```
        <PARAM NAME="DisplayStyle" VALUE="7">
        <PARAM NAME="Size" VALUE="4784;635">
        <PARAM NAME="MatchEntry" VALUE="1">
        <PARAM NAME="ShowDropButtonWhen" VALUE="2">
        <PARAM NAME="FontCharSet" VALUE="0">
        <PARAM NAME="FontPitchAndFamily" VALUE="2">
        <PARAM NAME="FontWeight" VALUE="0">
    </OBJECT>
    </td></tr>
<tr>
    <td>Password</td>
    <td><input type=password size=8 maxlength=8 name="PasswordText">
➥</td></tr>
<tr>
    <td align=center><input type=button name="ViewButton" value="View
➥Calls"></td>
    <td align=center><input type=reset name="ClearButton" value="Clear
➥Form"></td></tr>
</table>
<p>
<textarea name=CallText rows=12 cols=100>No calls retrieved yet!
</textarea>
</form>
</center></div>

</body>

</html>
```

The Log A Call Frame for Logging Phone Calls

This document contains a form called LogForm and a table to arrange the form elements. As with paper message pads, you can leave a short message by selecting a box, or a longer message in the form of some notes. These selection boxes are implemented as a group of OptionButton Forms 2.0 objects.

There are six tiny event procedures for the Click events of these buttons. Each procedure updates the value of a script-level variable, *intSelRadio*, to hold the number of the currently selected item from 1 to 6. Holding the currently selected item makes it easy to send the message type to the server—all it needs is the value of intSelRadio as one of the data items.

As in the previous document, the current employee list reloads each time the frame window reloads. The background colors of the option buttons are also set within the Window_OnLoad event procedure because the OptionButton objects do not seem to recognize hexadecimal representations of the form #ff99de when using the <PARAM> tag. Using decimal numbers to represent colors is not intuitive, so VBScript's `&H` notation is used instead.

The Log A Call Source Code

This file is saved as frmain2.htm and can be found in the same directory as the other HawkEye files—Examples\Mvb_14 subdirectory of the VBScript installation.

```
<!DOCTYPE HTML PUBLIC "-//IETF//DTD HTML//EN">

<html>
<head>
<title>Main Frame 2 in HawkEye Phone Center</title>
<meta name="GENERATOR" content="Microsoft FrontPage 1.1">
<SCRIPT LANGUAGE="VBScript">
<!-
'*************************************************************************
➥******
' Purpose:
'     Module of the HawkEye Phone Center, a VBScript application for
➥recording
'     and retrieving telephone messages.
```

```
'    This file contains the HTML frame and elements for logging a
➥phone call
'    and message for a particular employee
' Author:
'    C.J.Goddard—Copyright @1996
' Last Modified:
'    21st August 1996
'**********************************************************************
➥******
Dim intSelRadio                'Variable storing the currently selected
➥option button
intSelRadio = 1                'can take values 1 to 6


'**********************************************************************
➥******
' Event procedure called once the document has loaded into the frame
➥window.
' The current list of employees is retrieved from the 'server' by
➥calling a
' function which can be found in the HAWKEYE.HTM file
' The background colors of the option buttons are set, and the current
➥date and
' time are placed in the Date and Time textboxes on the form
'**********************************************************************
➥******
Sub Window_OnLoad
    LogForm.Radio1.BackColor = &H9999ff
    LogForm.Radio1.Value = True
    LogForm.Radio2.BackColor = &H9999ff
    LogForm.Radio3.BackColor = &H9999ff
    LogForm.Radio4.BackColor = &H9999ff
    LogForm.Radio5.BackColor = &H9999ff
    LogForm.Radio6.BackColor = &H9999ff
    Top.Get_Employee_List()
```

```
    LogForm.TimeText.Value = Time()
    LogForm.DateText.Value = Date()
End Sub


'***********************************************************************
➥******
' Event procedure called when the user press the 'Log Call' button.
' Makes sure an employee has been selected before proceeding. A
➥function in the
' topmost document is called to send the call details to the 'server'
'***********************************************************************
➥******
Sub LogButton_OnClick
   Dim dummy
    If LogForm.EmployeeCombo.ListIndex < 0 Then
        MsgBox "You must select an employee to log the call for!",
➥vbOKOnly, "HawkEye Phone Center"
        Exit Sub
    End If
    dummy = Top.Log_Call(LogForm.TimeText.Value,
➥LogForm.DateText.Value, LogForm.CallerText.Value, _
        LogForm.PhoneText.Value, LogForm.NoteText.Value, intSelRadio,
➥LogForm.EmployeeCombo.ListIndex)
End Sub


'***********************************************************************
➥******
' Boring items—ensures that the intSelRadio variable contains the
➥currently
' selected option button
'***********************************************************************
➥******
Sub Radio1_Click()
```

```
    intSelRadio = 1
End Sub
Sub Radio2_Click()
    intSelRadio = 2
End Sub
Sub Radio3_Click()
    intSelRadio = 3
End Sub
Sub Radio4_Click()
    intSelRadio = 4
End Sub
Sub Radio5_Click()
    intSelRadio = 5
End Sub
Sub Radio6_Click()
    intSelRadio = 6
End Sub
->
</SCRIPT>
</head>

<body bgcolor="#ff9999" text="#000000">
<center>
<img src="log_call.gif" align=bottom width=120 height=90>
</center>
Select the employee to log a call for, then enter the details of the
➥call and any message.
Press the <B>Log Call</B> button to submit the changes to the
➥'server'.<P>
<center>
<form name="LogForm">
<table border=2>
<tr>
    <td>Employee</td>
    <td>
```

```
    <OBJECT ID="EmployeeCombo" WIDTH=181 HEIGHT=24
     CLASSID="CLSID:8BD21D30-EC42-11CE-9E0D-00AA006002F3">
        <PARAM NAME="VariousPropertyBits" VALUE="746592283">
        <PARAM NAME="DisplayStyle" VALUE="7">
        <PARAM NAME="Size" VALUE="4784;635">
        <PARAM NAME="MatchEntry" VALUE="1">
        <PARAM NAME="ShowDropButtonWhen" VALUE="2">
        <PARAM NAME="FontCharSet" VALUE="0">
        <PARAM NAME="FontPitchAndFamily" VALUE="2">
        <PARAM NAME="FontWeight" VALUE="0">
    </OBJECT>
    </td></tr>
<tr>
    <td>Time</td>
    <td><input type=text size=20 maxlength=20 name="TimeText">
➥</td></tr>
<tr>
    <td>Date</td>
    <td><input type=text size=20 maxlength=20 name="DateText">
➥</td></tr>
<tr>
    <td>Caller</td>
    <td><input type=text size=25 maxlength=25 name="CallerText">
➥</td></tr>
<tr>
    <td>Phone No</td>
    <td><input type=text size=15 maxlength=15
➥name="PhoneText"></td></tr>
<tr>
    <td>Message Type</td>
    <td>
    <OBJECT ID="Radio1" WIDTH=144 HEIGHT=24
     CLASSID="CLSID:8BD21D50-EC42-11CE-9E0D-00AA006002F3">
        <PARAM NAME="ForeColor" VALUE="0">
        <PARAM NAME="DisplayStyle" VALUE="5">
```

```
        <PARAM NAME="Size" VALUE="3810;635">
        <PARAM NAME="Caption" VALUE="Call Back">
        <PARAM NAME="GroupName" VALUE="typeRadio">
        <PARAM NAME="FontCharSet" VALUE="0">
        <PARAM NAME="FontPitchAndFamily" VALUE="2">
        <PARAM NAME="FontWeight" VALUE="0">
    </OBJECT>
    *****FIVE MORE OF THESE OPTION BUTTONS ARE PLACED HERE, NAMED
➥Radio2 TO Radio6.
    *****THEY HAVE BEEN OMITTED TO CONSERVE SPACE
    </td></tr>
<tr>
    <td>Notes</td>
    <td><input type=text size=50 maxlength=100
➥name="NoteText"></td></tr>
<tr>
    <td align=center><input type=button name="LogButton" value="Log
➥Call"></td>
    <td align=center><input type=reset name="ClearButton" value="Clear
➥Form"></td></tr>
</table>
</form>
</center>

</body>
</html>
```

The Add A Name Frame for Creating New Employees

This is perhaps the simplest of the files that make up the HawkEye application because it only contains a standard HTML form and one event procedure. The form fields specify the details for a new employee whereas the buttons *AddButton* and *ClearButton* submit the data and clear the form contents.

Before calling the function Top.Add_Employee, the AddButton_OnClick event procedure checks to see whether or not a name and password were supplied. If either of these items are missing, the operation cannot proceed and the user is notified.

TIP *All three of the documents just described contain forms and tables. The tables organize the various elements of the forms into rows and columns. This technique is very effective, especially when combined with the ability of Internet Explorer 3.0 to display different table cells in different colors.*

The Add A Name Source Code

The document printed here is saved as frmain3.htm in the same directory as the other HawkEye files.

```
<!DOCTYPE HTML PUBLIC "-//IETF//DTD HTML//EN">

<html>
<head>
<title>Main Frame 3 in HawkEye Phone Center</title>
<meta name="GENERATOR" content="Microsoft FrontPage 1.1">
<SCRIPT LANGUAGE="VBScript">
<!-
'**********************************************************************
➥******
' Purpose:
'    Module of the HawkEye Phone Center, a VBScript application for
➥recording
'    and retrieving telephone messages.
'    This file contains the HTML frame and elements for adding an
➥employee to the
'    existing list of staff members
' Author:
'    C.J.Goddard-Copyright @1996
' Last Modified:
'    21st August 1996
```

```
'*********************************************************************
➥******


'*********************************************************************
➥******
' Event procedure called when the user presses the 'Add Employee'
➥button.
' Checks are carried out to make sure a name and password have been
➥entered,
' then a function in the topmost document is called to add the
➥employee details
' to the 'server' list.
'*********************************************************************
➥******
Sub AddButton_OnClick()
    Dim dummy
    If AddForm.NameText.Value = "" Then
        MsgBox "You must enter a name for the new employee", vbOKOnly,
➥ "HawkEye Phone Center"
        Exit Sub
    ElseIf AddForm.PasswordText.Value = "" Then
        MsgBox "You must enter a password", vbOKOnly, "HawkEye Phone
➥Center"
        Exit Sub
    End If
    dummy = Top.Add_Employee(AddForm.NameText.Value,
➥AddForm.DeptText.Value, AddForm.EmailText.Value _
        , AddForm.PhoneText.Value, AddForm.PasswordText.Value)
End Sub
->
</SCRIPT>
</head>

<body bgcolor="#ffff99" text="#000000">
<center>
```

```
    <img src="add_name.gif" align=bottom width=120 height=90>
</center>
Enter details for the new employee, including a password which should
➥be noted elsewhere.
Press the <B>Add Employee</B> button to submit the changes to the
➥'server'.
<hr>
<center>
<form name="AddForm">
<table border=2>
<tr>
    <td>Name</td>
    <td><input type=text size=25 maxlength=25 name="NameText">
➥</td></tr>
<tr>
    <td>Department</td>
    <td><input type=text size=20 maxlength=20 name="DeptText">
➥</td></tr>
<tr>
    <td>E-mail Address</td>
    <td><input type=text size=40 maxlength=40 name="EmailText">
➥</td></tr>
<tr>
    <td>Phone Number</td>
    <td><input type=text size=15 maxlength=15 name="PhoneText">
➥</td></tr>
<tr>
    <td>Password</td>
    <td><input type=password size=8 maxlength=8
➥name="PasswordText"></td></tr>
<tr>
    <td align=center><input type=button name="AddButton" value="Add
➥Employee"></td>
    <td align=center><input type=reset name="ClearButton" value="Clear
➥Form"></td></tr>
```

```
</table>
</FORM>
</center>

</body>
</html>
```

Using the NNTP Control to Access a News Server

Unlike the sections before and after this one, there is no complete example showing how to use the NNTP control to access groups and articles on a news server in this chapter. The ICP Help file provides quite a lot of information on using the NNTP control to create a custom news reader.

Broadly speaking, the steps needed to write such an application include:

1. Specify the name of a remote news server to connect to as well as the TCP port number used by the server.
2. Connect to the server using the Connect method of the NNTP control. If the connection succeeds, the next step is authentication.
3. Some news servers require a user ID and password in order to access groups and articles stored there. If this is the case, you can write an event handler for the AuthenticateRequest event that passes a user ID and password back to the server.
4. The next stage is to fetch a list of available newsgroups from the server. This is achieved by calling the ListGroups method. When the server responds, the NNTP control's DocOutput method fires. This event is generated by the DocOutput object. This and the DocInput object are useful for streaming data into and out of the Internet controls and are described in the ICP help file.

5. Within the DocOutput event, use the GetData method to actually fetch the newsgroup list. This data can be parsed and dealt with internally or streamed to a textbox control for the user to look at. Beware of the fact that there may be several thousand newsgroups on a single news server. A standard textarea control may not be able to hold this much information—in which case a bottomless control such as Microsoft's RichTextBox control can solve the problem. The RichTextBox control can store unlimited (within reason) amounts of text.
6. See the ICP help file for details on writing your own ParseData function to modify the data supplied by the server—for example to strip out article dates and authors.
7. Once the list of groups has been retrieved, select a particular group to examine. This is done using the SelectGroup method that requires you to supply an article number. This number can either be entered by the user or extracted from the data supplied by the GetData method.
8. After informing the server of a group selection, the SelectGroup event triggers. This is the place to fetch the article headers (summary information describing each article), with the GetArticleHeaders method.
9. Once the headers download and parse, you can select an article to fetch by invoking the GetArticleByNumber method. Just as before, the DocOutput event fires and signals the arrival of the article text. After the article text arrives, you can deal with the data in whatever way you want. You can search the text for keywords, store the text on screen or store the text to a database.

That was a quick overview of the use of the NNTP control, but it covered all the essential details. Using any of the controls in the Internet Control Pack successfully involves a certain amount of trial and error—but when something works, as with any programming task, the satisfaction can be enormous (and so can your annual bonus!).

Retrieving HTML Documents for Viewing at a Later Date with the HTTP Control

Several possible uses for the HTTP control were suggested earlier in the chapter. The example presented here could form the basis for some of those applications but would need some extension before it is a really useful utility on its own. The sample allows the user to specify a Web site with remote path and filename to retrieve the file. There is also a status area where progress messages are displayed.

How to Use the Sample Application

1. Select the `Retrieving HTML Files Using the HTTP Control` link in the Internet Control Pack section of the main Web page to load the document. Figure 14-10 shows how the document should appear in the browser window. Remember to answer, Yes when asked about using a potentially unsafe control.

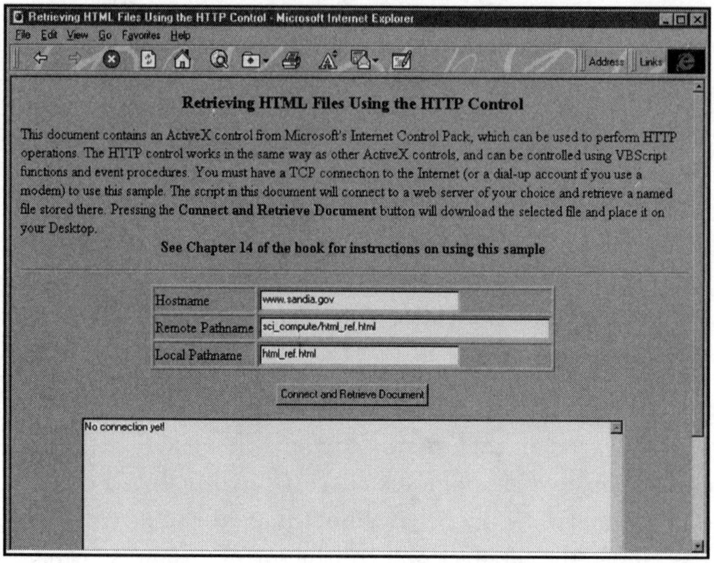

FIGURE 14-10
The HTTP sample application before connecting to a web site

2. Select the Web site and remote path (and file) name you require. You must also specify a filename to save the file as on the local system. If no directory is specified, the Windows Desktop is used.

3. Press the Connect and Retrieve Document button to initiate the transfer. This causes the control to attempt to connect to the remote server. Various status messages will display as the transaction progresses. If for some reason the control appears to connect, but your computer is not online, quit Explorer, and reload the document.

4. Repeat the process as many times as you like. Figure 14-11 shows the document window once a file downloads.

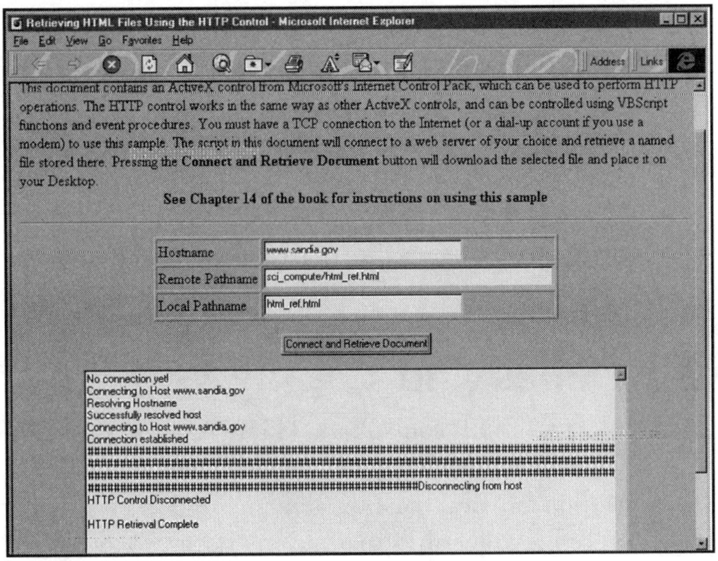

FIGURE 14-11
The HTTP sample application after downloading a document

Connections, Servers, and Files—How Does It All Work?

Here are a few notes about the example; the source code can be found in the next section.

The Same Old Utilities

In order to provide some status information as the application runs, this example borrows several utility routines from the FTP application covered earlier in the chapter. These routines include the CheckBusy progress indicator, and the Insert_Message and Clear_Message procedures. For more details on these items, see the sections "Keeping the User Informed" and "A Simple Progress Indicator" earlier in this chapter.

Metamorphosis—Changes of State

The HTTP control supports an event this book hasn't covered yet. The StateChanged event fires whenever the control's current state changes; for example, when it manages to resolve the DNS hostname to an IP address. The event handler for this event is declared by the following line of VBScript.

```
Sub HTTP1_StateChanged(State)
```

In the example, this procedure displays a different message for each new State and keeps the user informed of progress. You can see some of these messages in Figure 14-11.

Fetching Files and Coping with Errors

Unlike the FTP control, the HTTP control does not support a Connect event even though the ICP help file suggests it does support one (don't always trust the documentation). Many times documentation refers to features that haven't been coded yet, so be sure to test out features you are looking for in beta level or new controls. Instead of connecting to a Web server and then fetching a file, it is all achieved with one method. Before calling the GetDoc method, the code sets up the filename to save the new document and appends the separate user entries together to make a complete URL. The three lines of code reprinted here do the work for you.

```
    HTTP1.DocOutput.Filename = DestFileText.Value
    strRemoteFile = "http://" & HostnameText.Value & "/" &
➥DocNameText.Value
    HTTP1.GetDoc strRemoteFile
```

NOTE *The DocOutput object is a special object that you can use for streaming data between controls and to and from a system's disk. See the ICP help file for more details about this and the DocInput object.*

Using the DocOutput Object to Parse the File Data

Although not done here, the HTTP control doesn't have to save the file it retrieves to disk. Instead the DocOutput object's event of the same name can route the data to another destination, such as a textarea control.

The PerformRequest method carries out different operations, such as getting a file from the server. The code looks something like this:

```
HTTP1.Method = prcGet
HTTP1.Document = "/docs/ref1.doc"
HTTP1.RemoteHost = "www.sw_dev.com"
HTTP1.PerformRequest
```

After the operation has been carried out, the DocOutput event fires. The script can then check to see what kind of data has been downloaded (using MIME types) and act accordingly. You can search text data for keywords or route the text to a textbox whereas a video file or presentation can be streamed to an ActiveX control. The ICP Help file contains more information on streaming data with the DocInput and DocOutput events.

A Graceful Exit

Whenever a script uses an Internet control, it should attempt to close the connection with the server when it completes its task. This Internet control should stop the browser from getting confused by "thinking" that it is still connected to a server when the document is reloaded in the same session. Most of the controls, including the HTTP object, support the Quit method that closes a server connection. Calls to this function should be placed in the event handler for the Window object's UnLoad event (see Chapter 10, "The Object Model for Scripting") so the user does not have to remember to press a button to terminate communications.

The HTTP Sample Source Listing

Once again, here's the listing:

```
<HTML>
<HEAD>
<TITLE>Retrieving HTML Files Using the HTTP Control</TITLE>
<SCRIPT LANGUAGE="VBScript">
<!-
'*****************************************************************
➥**************
' HTTP Sample Application-using the HTTP ActiveX control to retrieve
➥HTML documents
' Purpose:
'     To demonstrate the HTTP control and how it can be used to connect
➥to a Web server
'     and fetch documents stored there.
' Author:
'     C.J.Goddard-Copyright @1996
' Last Modified:
'     21st August 1996
'*****************************************************************
➥**************
Dim intTimerID

'*****************************************************************
➥**************
```

```
' Called as a response to a Window timer. Checks to see whether the
➥last command
' issued to the Web server has completed yet. If not the timeout is
➥set to fire in
' 200 milliseconds time for another check.
'*************************************************************************
➥**************
Sub CheckBusy()
    If HTTP1.Busy = True Then
        StatusText.Value = StatusText.Value & "#"        'Show user
➥that the control is alive
        intTimerID = Window.SetTimeout ("Call CheckBusy()", 200,
➥"VBScript")
        Exit Sub
    End If
    Insert_Message ""
    Insert_Message "HTTP Retrieval Complete"
    Window.ClearTimeout intTimerID
End Sub


'*************************************************************************
➥**************
' Utility function to add a message string to the status textbox.
'*************************************************************************
➥**************
Sub Insert_Message(strMessage)
    StatusText.Value = StatusText.Value & strMessage & Chr(13) &
➥Chr(10)
End Sub


'*************************************************************************
➥**************
' Clears the message box area of all messages
```

```
'**********************************************************************
➥**************
Sub Clear_Messages()
    StatusText.Value = ""
End Sub


'**********************************************************************
➥**************
' Called when the user presses the 'Connect and Retrieve Document'
➥button.
' Checks that values have been entered for the hostname, remote file
➥and local
' file textboxes. If so, the HTTP control is instructed to connect to
➥the Web server
' retrieve the document and save it to the local disk.
'**********************************************************************
➥**************
Sub FetchButton_OnClick()
    Dim strRemoteFile
    If DestFileText.Value = "" Then
        MsgBox "Please enter a destination pathname for the file, e.g.
➥C:\Windows\Desktop\Document.html", vbOKOnly, "HTTP Control Example"
        Exit Sub
    End If
    If HostnameText.Value = "" Then
        MsgBox "Please enter a WWW hostname from which to download the
➥file, e.g. 'www.microsoft.com'", vbOKOnly, "HTTP Control Example"
        Exit Sub
    End If
    If DocNameText.Value = "" Then
        MsgBox "Please enter a remote path and file to download, e.g.
➥'ie/activex/gallery/chart.html'", vbOKOnly, "HTTP Control Example"
        Exit Sub
    End If
```

```
    HTTP1.DocOutput.Filename = DestFileText.Value
    strRemoteFile = "http://" & HostnameText.Value & "/" &
➥DocNameText.Value
    HTTP1.GetDoc strRemoteFile
End Sub


'**********************************************************************
➥**************
' Event procedure called whenever the HTTP control generates a run-time
➥ error
' The details of the error are displayed in the status textbox
'**********************************************************************
➥**************
Sub HTTP1_Error(Number, Description, Scode, Source, HelpFile,
HelpContext, CancelDisplay)
    MsgBox "An error occured while retrieving the specified document.
➥See Status box for details"
    Insert_Message "******"
    Insert_Message "Error message : " & Number & "-" & Description
    Insert_Message "******"
End sub


'**********************************************************************
➥**************
' Event procedure called whenever the HTTP control changes from one
➥state to
' another. A status message describing the new state is displayed in
➥the status
' textbox
'**********************************************************************
➥**************
Sub HTTP1_StateChanged(State)
    Select Case State
```

```
        Case 1
            Insert_Message "Connecting to Host " & HostnameText.Value
        Case 2
            Insert_Message "Resolving Hostname"
        Case 3
            Insert_Message "Successfully resolved host"
        Case 4
            Insert_Message "Connection established"
            intTimerID = Window.SetTimeout ("Call CheckBusy()", 200,
➥"VBScript")
        Case 5
            Insert_Message "Disconnecting from host"
        Case 6
            Insert_Message "HTTP Control Disconnected"
        Case Else
            Insert_Message "Unrecognized change of state notified by
➥HTTP Control—maybe aliens have landed?!"
    End Select
End Sub


'**********************************************************************
➥**************
' Event procedure called when the document is unloaded from the
Browser window. The
' connection to the FTP server is closed.
'**********************************************************************
➥**************
Sub Window_OnUnload()
    HTTP1.Quit()
End Sub
—>
</SCRIPT>
</HEAD>
```

```
<BODY BACKGROUND="blobbg.jpg" TEXT="#00ff00">
<CENTER><H3>Retrieving HTML Files Using the HTTP Control</H3></CENTER>
This document contains an ActiveX control from Microsoft's Internet
➥Control Pack, which can be used to
perform HTTP operations. The HTTP control works in the same way as
➥other ActiveX controls, and can be controlled
using VBScript functions and event procedures.
You must have a TCP connection to the Internet (or a dial-up account
➥if you use a modem) to use this sample.
The script in this document will connect to a Web server of your
➥choice and retrieve a named file stored there.
Pressing the <B>Connect and Retrieve Document</B> button will download
➥the selected file and place it on
your Desktop.<BR>
<CENTER><B>See Chapter 14 of the book for instructions on using this
➥sample</B><CENTER>
<HR>
<CENTER>
<TABLE BORDER>
<TR><TD>Hostname</TD><TD><INPUT TYPE="Text" NAME="HostnameText"
➥VALUE="www.sandia.gov" SIZE="40"></TD>
<TR><TD>Remote Pathname</TD><TD><INPUT TYPE="Text" NAME="DocNameText"
➥VALUE="sci_compute/html_ref.html" SIZE="60"></TD>
<TR><TD>Local Pathname</TD><TD><INPUT TYPE="Text" NAME="DestFileText"
➥VALUE="html_ref.html" SIZE="40"></TD>
</TABLE>
<P>
<INPUT TYPE=Button NAME="FetchButton" VALUE="Connect and Retrieve
➥Document">
<P>
<TEXTAREA ROWS=15 COLS=120 NAME="StatusText">No connection yet!
</TEXTAREA>
<HR>
</CENTER>
<OBJECT ID="HTTP1" WIDTH=24 HEIGHT=24
     CLASSID="CLSID:B7FC3563-8CE7-11CF-9754-00AA00C00908">
```

```
</OBJECT>
</BODY>
</HTML>
```

What about Java Applets—Can I Use Them Too?

With all the coverage of scripting engines, HTML 3.2 standards, forms processing, and ActiveX technology, one stone remains unturned—using Java with VBScript. Java has been one of the most influential and highly publicized developments in Internet technology over the last couple of years, and Internet Explorer 3.0 has been endowed with comprehensive support for this new language. Explorer's Java Virtual Machine (Java VM) and Just In Time (JIT) compiler has led Microsoft to claim that it is the definitive Java implementation for the Windows operating systems. This is a claim not entirely disputed by Sun Microsystems who has set the Microsoft implementation as the standard by which other Java systems for Windows will be judged. The purpose of this book is not to teach you the Java language or even to use any complex Java applets in WWW documents. The point simply is that you can easily incorporate Java applets into scripts when using VBScript.

Some people may mistakenly think that JavaScript (JScript is Microsoft's implementation of JavaScript) is the best language to use for scripting Java applets because the two languages have similar names, implying that they're somehow linked. In fact, Java comes from Sun and JavaScript comes from Netscape. JavaScript originally was named LiveScript, but was changed when Netscape adopted Java. JavaScript isn't even based on Java. Netscape has brought it progressively more in line with Java because Java was accepted by the industry. The truth is, support for applets is a feature of the browser and not the scripting language, so in this respect VBScript and JScript compete on equal terms.

If you have never used Java before, or don't intend to, you have two choices at this point. Skip this section and move on to the conclusion, or keep reading. The discussion does not cover any advanced topics and you may realize that Java is a tool you should be using to liven up your Web pages.

Support for Java Applets

The Java support in Internet Explorer is actually an ActiveX run-time control that plugs into the browser architecture. It makes Java applets accessible from scripts by exposing all the applet's public methods and data members. You can call and access these methods and data members as you would those of an ActiveX control. Because Explorer is built using the ActiveX Scripting framework, Java applets are accessible from any language engine that conforms to this protocol, such as VBScript, JScript, or future scripting languages.

Inserting an applet into a Web page is simple using the <APPLET> tag. This tag can specify the Java code file, size, and name for the applet. The applet's size is set using the HEIGHT and WIDTH attributes whereas the ID attribute gives the applet a name—essential if you are to use the applet in a script function. An example applet definition might look something like this

```
<APPLET CODE="Animate3D.java"
    ID="Anim3D"
    HEIGHT=180
    WIDTH=250"
>
</APPLET>
```

Consider an applet like the following:

```
class Animate3D extends Applet
{
    public int animspeed;
    public void playanim()
    {
    ....
    //Play the 3D animation
    ....
```

```
        }
        //Other stuff
        ...
}
```

This skeleton applet is a 3-D animation player that you can control by setting the animation speed, animspeed, and play by calling the playanim method. Once inserted in a Web page with the name AnimApplet, the following VBScript event handlers could be written for three button elements. The button elements are called FasterButton, SlowerButton, and PlayButton, respectively.

```
Sub FasterButton_OnClick()
    AnimApplet.animspeed = AnimApplet.animspeed * 110 / 100
End Sub

Sub SlowerButton_OnClick()
    AnimApplet.animspeed = AnimApplet.animspeed / 110 * 100
End Sub

Sub PlayButton_OnClick()
    AnimApplet.playanim()
End Sub
```

When these event procedures execute, they manipulate the Java applet with immediate results. Using the methods and variables of an applet is just as simple as using an ActiveX control. In fact, you can use VBScript to pass data between applets and ActiveX controls and tie together two separate technologies on a single Web page.

CAUTION **Only the Applet derived class is directly accessible from a section of script code. If you need to make other classes in your applet available, modify the applet slightly. Define public methods in the *Applet* derived class that delegate to the methods of these other classes (basically a simple wrapper function) and the problem will be solved. This is a more sensible solution than moving the code and members from the other classes into the *Applet* derived class itself.**

Microsoft has developed a Java development tool called Visual J++, which uses the same Developer Studio software as some of the other tools in Microsoft's product range. This tool can help develop Java applets with little fuss (and Java applets are automatically available as COM objects from the Microsoft Java Virtual Machine implementation). You may find this a useful investment if you are serious about developing your ideas for Web documents further. Borland has also included Java support in the latest release of Borland C++, and no doubt more visual tools for developing with Java will flood the market.

Scripting with ActiveX and Java Really Can Achieve Results—What Next?

You've nearly finished this book now. You've come a long way from the simple beginnings and the Hello World! document. This chapter has presented some complete Web applications and several entirely new ActiveX controls.

The last three chapters should have given you some idea of the breadth of this new technology (the ActiveX Gallery, HTML Layout Control, Forms 2.0 controls, and now the Internet Control Pack). But, this is just the beginning! About 2,000 ActiveX controls are available from third party vendors and this market is set to grow rapidly in the coming months and years. Some analysts even think the ActiveX market may be worth over $2 billion by the turn of the century.

In Internet Explorer and the touted release of Nashville, Microsoft has developed a comprehensive strategy for moving the presentation of information over the World Wide Web into the next millennium. The ActiveX architecture ranges from simple configurable controls to scripting engines and even the Web browser itself. Tie this together with scripting languages such as VBScript and Java applets and you have a formidable arsenal at your disposal for creating truly interactive Web pages. You've seen how, but the true benefits you experience from using VBScript become apparent only as you use it yourself. The tools are there, and other people are beginning to use them, so don't get left behind. If you want to stay ahead in the global information age, it's time to get scripting.

One last word before you rush off to start developing your killer Web applications. There is one final chapter to go—it takes a brief look at the other side of things. Servers and topics such as CGI and ISAPI have hardly warranted a mention up until now, and the next chapter gives some details of the current developments in these areas and how they might involve you and scripting. Also, the complete reference for the VBScript language can be found in Appendixes A, B, and C—just in case.

CHAPTER 15

CGI and ISAPI—What about Web Servers?

Until now, little mention has been made of the other (essential) side of the World Wide Web. Without Web servers, all the familiar items, such as browsers, scripting engines, ActiveX controls, and HTML documents, would be useless. The WWW is a huge client/server network and information database, and many commentators feel that server technology will prove to be the driving force behind the Web's evolution.

The next incarnation of Microsoft's Internet Information Server (IIS) will have server-side ActiveX capability, meaning that in addition to special ActiveX controls which handle server side computation, the scripting engine in the client-side browser will become available on the server. In much the same way that PERL is used on many servers, VBScript or JavaScript could be used to tie together individual components to build server-side solutions.

Currently, VBScript isn't used to program Web servers, but some knowledge of how to retrieve data from and send requests to a server may paint a clearer overall picture of VBScript's place in the WWW. This chapter discusses the following topics:

- Why are Web servers important?
- What types of server application exist?
- The Common GateWay Interface (CGI) for communicating with Web servers
- Forms processing with CGI
- Invoking server applications with VBScript
- Microsoft's new Internet Server Application Programming Interface (ISAPI)
- dbWeb, a sample ISAPI application

To create fully interactive Web sites that respond to user requests and contain dynamic content, you no doubt will need to take advantage of some of the power behind Web server technology. This chapter aims to give you an introduction to these capabilities.

Why Are Web Servers Important?

At first, this may seem like an obvious question; after all, servers are the systems to which any WWW user connects whenever he enters a new URL into the browser navigation bar or clicks on a hyperlink. Behind the scenes there can be much more going on than a server merely fetching a static document from a system disk and returning it.

The information a server returns essentially can fall into one of two kinds:

- **Static data**, such as HTML files, images, sound bites, and the like
- **Dynamically created documents**, generated as needed by some application running on the server

Everyone is used to the abundance of information available on the Web, but when you think about it, much of this information is just glorified paper-based publishing presented using a modern interface. Most sites contain plenty of links to sites in the four corners of the globe, but this doesn't make the WWW truly interactive.

Many people are looking at the Internet and the World Wide Web as the next-generation platform for distributed computing. Before this can truly happen, we must move away from a read-only model of publishing on the Web to a dynamic, ever-changing one in which user actions affect the way information is presented and true distributed applications can become a reality.

The first foundation stone for this vision has already been laid and is in common use throughout the world in the form of the CGI standard. Web servers can be used to return prepared HTML documents and related media, but also can call other applications that generate information to return to the client as it is needed. These applications can take user input into account via the use of forms and the special HTML <ISINDEX> tag. A collection of standards has already been developed, and new ones are in the pipeline, which specify how these applications are called, and how to pass data to and from a Web server. These topics are covered in greater detail during discussion of CGI and ISAPI.

NOTE *Before the advent of ActiveX technology, scripting languages and Java,* static *data stored on a disk as HTML documents was just that—lifeless text and images. Web publishing was really no more than glorified word processing. A single web document now can contain interactive controls, scripts, innovative applets, and multimedia effects. These documents are fixed in content, because they have been written and stored somewhere—hence they still essentially are static, prepared documents.*

Many different servers are on the market, including NCSA httpd (a popular choice for Unix systems), Netscape's Server, and Microsoft's Internet Information Server (IIS). All these products have one main aim—to handle client requests and send information back to them. Each developer tends to add extensions and new user interfaces, but they all retain the one primary function of receiving requests and replying to them. Web servers support the Hypertext Transfer Protocol (HTTP) as the main way to communicate with client systems, and can load documents from local backing store and return them with little fuss. Plenty of work goes into ensuring that servers are reliable, secure, fast, and capable of handling multiple client requests—issues with which this chapter isn't concerned.

How does a server return the dynamic content to a client? The enormous scope and variety of different information that may need to be returned as dynamic content precludes the possibility of adding server functions to create it. A flexible solution to this problem was devised whereby servers call other application programs to generate the new content, and return it to the client as if it were a normal file or document. Since the Web is a worldwide entity and is accessed by software written for many platforms, some form of standard was required. The CGI standard was developed to provide a standard means for a server to communicate with another application, and is explained in its own section later in the chapter.

What Kind of Server Applications Exist?

Even novice users are likely to have searched for something on the Web. Almost all popular browsers now have Search buttons built in to their toolbars which take you immediately to a search page. These pages allow you to provide details for a query, choose a search engine, and even choose special information archives to search. When the query is submitted to the server (more about that in the section on forms processing with CGI) it is not the server which finds the information for you. Behind the scenes is a large database that performs the search itself, compiles the results, and sends them back to the server in HTML format. These results are then posted back to the client and it looks as if the page has always been stored at that same place. This is just one example of a server application that creates dynamic content.

How about product registrations, customer orders, and accessing intranet databases? All these tasks can now be carried out using the Web and server applications that run behind the scenes. Information is passed using HTML forms via the server to these applications, which then process requests. It is customary, even, for tasks such as product registration, to send some form of reply indicating success or failure.

As well as these more typical uses of dynamic content, there are many more ideas and possible applications for the technology. Interactive games that receive updates from a central server, content creators that insert different advertisements into a page as the day goes by, and information servers for applications, such as stock portfolio calculators, are all possible.

NOTE *As an extension to the Component Object Model (COM) on which ActiveX technology is built, Microsoft is developing a system called Distributed COM (DCOM), which has been implemented in NT 4.0. This is a protocol that enables software components to communicate directly over a network in a reliable, secure, and efficient manner. DCOM is designed for use with multiple network protocols, including HTTP. It will work with Java applets and ActiveX components, allowing developers to create true distributed applications, and is the next logical step forward from using web server's as a data conduit between the client and a server application.*

How Does the Client System Communicate Its Needs?

Chapter 10 discussed the Object Model for Scripting. We are concerned with the *Location* object in particular, since it stores the components of the current document Uniform Resource Locator (URL). To recap, the components are as follows:

- **HRef**, the complete URL
- **Protocol**, the protocol section of the URL; for example, `http`
- **Host**, the hostname as an IP address or domain name plus the port number; for example, `www.microsoft.com:80`
- **Hostname**, the hostname of the URL on its own
- **Port**, the port number of the URL, which is usually omitted
- **Pathname**, the pathname section of the URL; for example, `/vbscript/default.htm`

- **Search**, the query section of the URL; this is the part we are interested regarding to servers
- **Hash**, the hash section of the URL is used to specify an anchor name within a document; for example, `#contents`

Most applications called from a Web page are context-sensitive, meaning, their operation depends on configuration information supplied to them. Normal desktop applications get this information from command-line options, data files, or direct user input. Because an application executed by a Web server isn't under the user's direct control, providing the context-sensitive information to it must be possible . It is, by specifying the required options as part of the complete URL—the query section, to be exact. An example URL with a query section is

```
http://www.companyserver.com/cgitest.exe?name=Louise+
➥McKerrow&occupation=head+hunter
```

The query section follows the question mark (?) and specifies the data to provide to an application called *cgitest.exe* on a server called `www.companyserver.com`. The query section is encoded using a special encoding format called *URL encoding* (covered in the section called "Forms Processing with CGI" later in the chapter).

Using VBScript to Invoke Server Applications

You have just seen that you can use the query section of a URL to pass data to an application stored on a remote server. The Object Model for Scripting makes many of the features of the browser available to a script writer, and the query section of an URL is no exception.

To execute a server application from a VBScript function, first compile the data options in a temporary variable. Next, assign the server name, application path, and the compiled query string to the Location object's HRef property, using ampersand symbols (&) to concatenate the various components.

Why not use the separate Hostname, Pathname, and Search properties of the Location object? If you do, Explorer tries to connect to the

URL specified as soon you assign anything to any of the properties—so if you don't assign the whole URL in one go, your request to the server may well go wrong.

The following section of VBScript has been provided to illustrate the concept of using script code to call a server program, by constructing the *cgitest* example of the last section.

```
Function Call_Server()
    Dim strOptions

    strOptions = "?name=Louise+McKerrow&occupation=head+hunter"
    Window.Location.HRef = "http://www.companyserver.com/cgitest.exe" &
➥strOptions
End Function
```

Calling the preceding function will request that the Web server execute the program cgitest.exe and pass it the option string stored in strOptions. This application might return a database search, register a new user, log a sale, or perform some other action. Normally, you wouldn't hard-code the query string into the VBScript code, but would compose it from user input in text boxes.

The Commom Gateway Interface (CGI) Standard

The last pages have contained generic discussions about server-side technology, so it's about time to get down to some of the technical details. Servers don't implement all the possible applications that might be necessary, but call other programs using CGI as a standard interface. So what exactly is this CGI standard?

A *CGI program* is one that the Web server (or *daemon*) executes to carry out some task, say, connecting to a database. The Web daemon usually needs to transmit some information to the tool being used (in this case a database engine), and receive results back again. These results are then returned to the client browser. This is an example of a *gateway*—hence the term *Common Gateway Interface*. You can write

CGI programs in more or less any language that can be executed on your system including:

- PERL
- TCL
- C\C++
- Pascal
- Visual Basic
- Unix shell scripts or DOS batch files

CGI is a relatively simple standard. Some of the languages in the preceding list are the conventional *programming* languages that require compilation, and others are interpreted scripting languages. Compiled code may run faster, but then has the associated overhead of maintaining code and executables, and of compilation. Consequently, many people prefer to use interpreted scripts, which are easier to debug and maintain.

CGI programs (using the term to refer to compiled and interpreted code) can be programs that accomplish a task by themselves, or gateways that call other applications. One thing is common to all CGI programs. Each time the server receives a request from a client that involves calling a CGI program, a new process is created and the program is executed. This can add a large overhead to the processing of requests, especially on Windows systems, and is one of the primary causes for concern that have prompted Microsoft to develop ISAPI.

Figure 15-1 shows an overview of the interaction between clients, Web servers, CGI programs, and other applications.

The Ins and Outs of CGI

If CGI programs can be written in so many different languages, how can there be one standard for communicating with them? A feature common to all of these languages is their capability to read from the operating system's standard input stream (*stdin*), standard output stream (*stdout*), and to fetch the values of environment variables. The CGI standard defines several standard environment variables including the following:

ENVIRONMENT VARIABLE	MEANING
QUERY_STRING	Contains the encoded form data stored in the URL query string.
CONTENT_LENGTH	Specifies how many bytes of data have been passed to the server by the client.
CONTENT_TYPE	Specifies the standard MIME type of the data being passed from the client.

NOTE *The original CGI specification has been updated to include support for more options, in response to feedback from the WWW community. It's currently at version 1.1.*

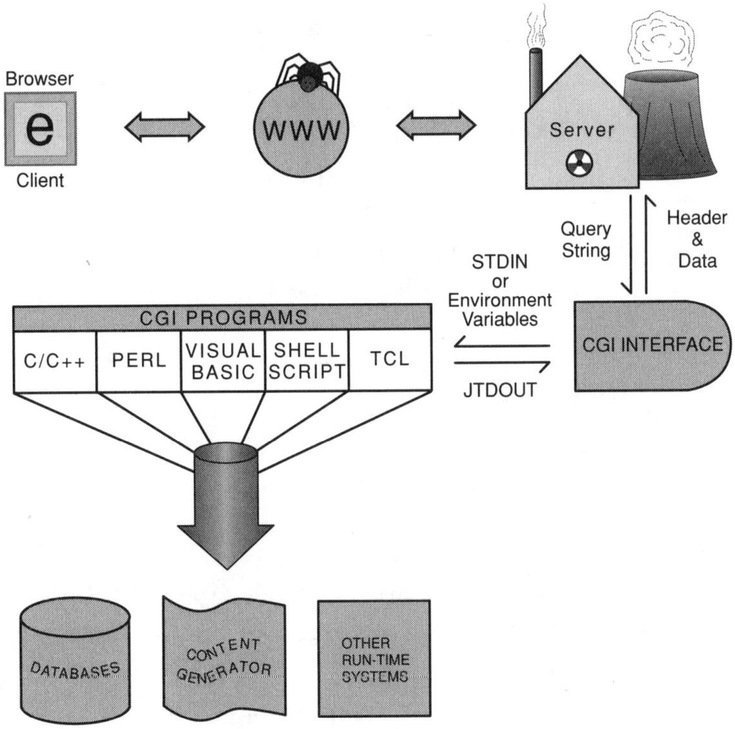

FIGURE 15-1
The CGI architecture for running applications in response to client requests

If you're unfamiliar with stdin, stdout, or environment variables, here's a brief description. Stdin and stdout are operating system terms that refer to the main method used by a program to receive and return information. Traditionally, stdin is the keyboard, and stdout is the monitor. This makes sense, because users typically type commands from the keyboard and expect to be able to see responses onscreen. Of course, programmers can redirect these input and output mechanisms, and that's what happens when CGI programs accept data from a client machine. The server redirects the client information through stdin. To the program, it's as if the user were typing it in at the keyboard. Stdout works in much the same way.

Environment variables are a different matter. The operating system stores these variables and programs use them when they need to get system-wide information. You probably are most familiar with the PATH environment variable, which you set to tell programs where to look for executables. In a DOS window, you can use the SET command to list all the environment variables.

GET Versus POST—Take Your Choice

When Chapter 11 covered form processing with HTML, it introduced the <FORM> tag. One of the optional attributes that you can set is the submission METHOD. You can use two possible values, GET and POST, and the difference between them is subtle.

- GET
- POST

When a form uses the METHOD="GET" clause, it causes the form fields (and any extra data you specify as HIDDEN elements and the like) to be appended to the end of the current URL; this is then passed to the server. The query string portion of the URL (the section following the question mark) is supplied to the CGI program in the QUERY_STRING environment variable.

If, on the other hand, a form uses the POST method, the CGI program receives all of its input from *stdin*. Most streams provide an End Of File (EOF) indicator once the data has run out, but CGI does not specify this. Instead the CONTENT_LENGTH environment variable is used to tell the program how much data to fetch from *stdin*. The POST method is more suitable when the user may be sending long strings or binary objects, such as database records, to the CGI program for processing. Using the GET method for these large items can result in text buffers, or environment space overflowing—not good if you want your server to remain stable.

Forms Processing with CGI

This chapter has already touched on the issues involved with form processing, but will finish with some coverage of how the form data is actually handled.

The clearest way to differentiate your form fields when they are returned to a CGI program, is to name them using the NAME= "ElementName" clause of the <INPUT> tag. This naming also is important if you want to access the controls from VBScript functions. When a user presses the SUBMIT button of a form, or calls the Submit method, the browser forms a set of name and value pairs, appends these to the URL as a query string, and submits it to the server.

Name and value pairs are specified as

```
FieldName=FieldValue
```

with each pair separated by ampersand symbols (&). Besides composing these pairs into one long string, they're encoded using a format known as *URL encoding* (explained in the sidebar).

The URL Encoding Format

When the browser appends fields to the query string, it has to encode them so that the complete string is a valid URL. This encoding involves the following changes:

- All space characters are transformed into plus signs (+)
- Any name=value pairs are separated by ampersand symbols (&)
- Special characters are encoded using hexadecimal representation. A character such as a linefeed is encoded as %0A—the URL hexadecimal representation for the decimal ASCII code 10.

As an example, consider the HTML form defined by the following code:

```
<FORM NAME="CustomerForm" METHOD="GET" ACTION="http://
➥www.companyserver.com/cgi-bin/reg_cust.exe">
    <INPUT NAME="Forename" TYPE="Text" VALUE="Jane">
    <INPUT NAME="Surname" TYPE="Text" VALUE="Austen">
    <INPUT NAME="Phone" TYPE="Text" VALUE="Not applicable">
    <INPUT NAME="ProductCode" TYPE="Text" VALUE="10576-F3">
    <INPUT NAME="Quantity" TYPE="Text" VALUE="3 litres">
    <INPUT NAME="SubmitButton" TYPE="Submit">
</FORM>
```

If the user did not change any of the default values and pressed the Submit button, the following string would be passed to the CGI program in the QUERY_STRING environment variable:

```
"Forename=Jane&Surname=Austen&Phone=Not+applicable&ProductCode=
➥10576-F3&Quantity=3+litres"
```

Responding to Client Requests

Getting information from the client browser is only half the story. After the CGI program runs, it almost certainly has some results to send back—even if these are only an indication of success or failure. A CGI program sends data back to the server using the standard output stream (*stdout*). The results sent back by a CGI program can be in one of many different formats, including HTML, audio files, video, and plain text. To identify the type of result, a CGI program sends back a short header to the server.

The CGI standard defines several different items that can appear in this header, the most important of which are the Location and Content-type entries.

The Content-type entry specified the MIME type (see note) of the return data. This is necessary so the server knows how to deal with and return the data to the client. Even if you're sending back plain HTML text, the server must inform the client of this, or else it displays it incorrectly. The Location entry is optional and is used only when the return data is being used to point to another data source specified by an URL.

NOTE *Due to the increasing number of media formats being transported across the Internet and in common use by various systems, the MIME types were defined. This acronym stands for Multi-purpose Internet Mail Extensions and provides a common way of identifying media transported over a network. The types include definitions for HTML—*text/html, *plain ASCII text—* text/ascii, *GIF graphic files—*Image/GIF *and application binaries—* Application/Octet-stream, *in addition to many more.*

If the return content is supplied directly by the CGI program, the document is known as a *full document*, an example being:

```
Content-type: text/html


<HTML>
<HEAD>
....Head items
</HEAD>

<BODY>
....Body items
</BODY>
</HTML>
```

If the return data is simply a reference to another location, it is known as a *reference*, such as

```
Content-type: text/html
Location: http://www.otherserver.com/refs/langref.html
```

Most modern browsers will receive this reference back from the server and automatically load the file at the location it specifies, which allows an organization to use one site for CGI applications and store the content on another.

NOTE *The CGI standard specifies that there should be at least one blank line after the header and before the content. This is a common problem with untested CGI programs.*

The Dangers of Using Server Applications

Allowing unknown users to download static text files from your Web site is not too daunting a prospect for most organizations (apart from government agencies), but letting them execute programs is another thing. When you let users run CGI programs over the Internet on your systems, security must become an issue—there are always going to be malicious users roaming around.

This is why on most servers, only the webmaster can create and control CGI scripts and executables. The files are almost always stored in a single area with file restrictions. However, there are some known security holes that hackers can exploit to break your scripts and expose your system to attack. This problem is especially apparent when running shell scripts. Shell metacharacters (special characters such as wild cards and redirection symbols) can be used to break a CGI program. Such attacks have happened in the past, so it's something for which to keep an eye out.

One simple, yet effective, way to avert such attacks is to check all input data before using it. This can help to ensure that suspicious strings have not been sent and all data items contain values within permitted ranges and so on. These problems can then be reported back to the client, before they affect the processing of the CGI program.

What Is the Internet Server Application Programming Interface?

ISAPI is a new programming interface developed by Microsoft as an extension of the CGI standard. CGI creates a new process to run the requested script or program every time a client request arrives. Lots of concurrent requests mean lots of concurrent processes executing in memory. If each request requires relatively little processing, the overhead of creating all these processes and allocating address spaces for them can become a major bottleneck on system performance.

The rather primitive way in which CGI operates can consume large amounts of system RAM to maintain server performance, and causes competition against the applications currently running for resources, like database engines. This problem is particularly bad on Windows-based operating systems, but you can get around it.

Windows operating systems have a feature called Dynamic Link Libraries (DLL), a system for sharing executable code. The DLL is loaded only once, but can be called by many different applications. The advantage of using a DLL rather than a standalone CGI application is that a separate process does not have to be created for each invocation of procedures in the DLL. Instead, a thread of execution (more lightweight than a process) is created for each request. This significantly improves server performance. ISAPI is the standard that has been designed to implement this change. It's quite a simple API, with only two main functions as entry points. To remain backward-compatible with existing CGI executables, the server simply calls these in the old way by creating a new process for them.

ISAPI Filters—What Are They?

The new ISAPI specification also defines a new feature called ISAPI filters. These filters are DLLs that the server calls on receipt of any HTTP request from a client machine. You can configure these filters to perform all sorts of operations, and multiple filters can be active at any one time.

You can use ISAPI filters for adding the following extensions to a Web server:

- Custom authentication schemes to verify your visitors' identities
- Compression schemes
- Encryption to protect data, so only authorized users can access it

- Logging programs to keep track of visitors to the site
- Traffic analysis
- Custom request checking, such as looking for users who attempt to link to */etc/password* or other sensitive system files

dbWeb—An ISAPI Application

To demonstrate the new ISAPI technology, Microsoft has developed an application called dbWeb which is available as a free download from the Microsoft Web site at the time of writing. This program takes advantage of the ISAPI extensions to CGI to provide a comprehensive service for querying and modifying server databases with client requests.

The system consists of two parts, the dbWeb Administrator and the dbWeb Service. The Administrator is a graphical user interface, used to set up database schemas that control how database information appears to the users. It also generates HTML pages that are used for returning query results and data back to the client.

The dbWeb Service processes data retrieval requests, formats results, and sends them back to the Web server for forwarding to the client. It is an ISAPI application and allows you to connect to any Open DataBase Connectivity (ODBC) data source. These data sources include most of the popular database servers such as Oracle, Sybase, and Microsoft SQL Server and Access, which ship with ODBC drivers. The organization of the dbWeb system is shown in Figure 15-2 to give you some idea of the ways in which you can use ISAPI to create a fully-featured client/server application.

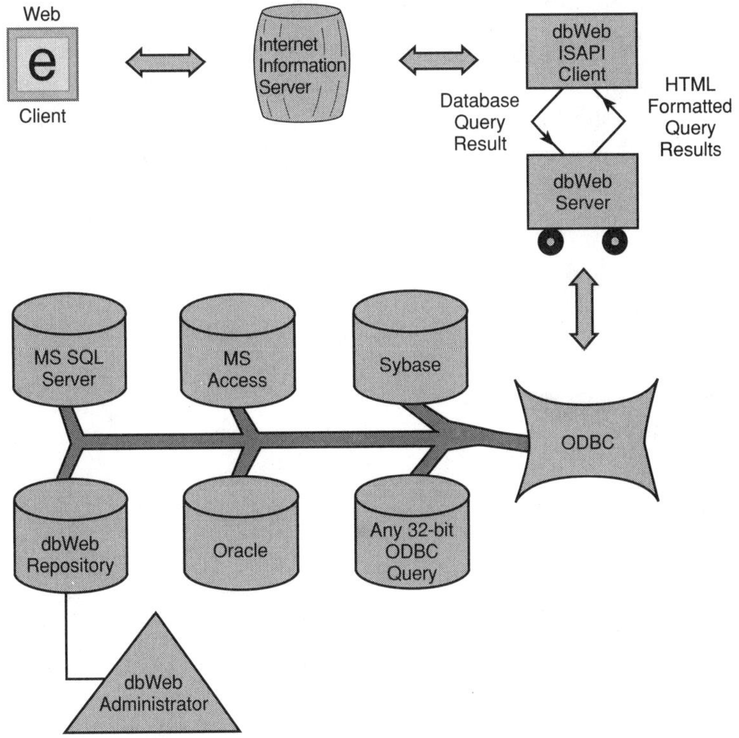

FIGURE 15-2
The organizational structure of the dbWeb system

To Conclude

You've reached the end of the road as far as *VBScript Master's Handbook* is concerned, and now you can get into some VBScript programming on your own. Way back in Chapter 1, you saw the first chinks of daylight breaking through into a new and exciting world of active content on the Web. Since then, you've explored the technology behind the global information publishing revolution, and have seen VBScript's prominent place in the grand Web picture. VBScript is a truly versatile tool that will improve Web authors' creations both now and in the future. Along with ActiveX technology and Java, the possibilities for stunning pages are endless. The information revolution has really begun, and it's now up to you to use the knowledge you have to take the Web forward into the next generation.

You've been through the ins and outs of language structure, error handling, coding conventions, the Explorer Object Model, forms processing, ActiveX controls and tools, the Internet Control Pack, Java applets, and Web servers. Now all you have left to do is to develop your own active pages. After all, VBScript is free!

PART IV

Appendixes

APPENDIX A

VBScript Language Reference—Functions

Abs Function

Returns the absolute value of a number, which is always a positive quantity.

Syntax

```
Abs(number)
```

The *number* argument can be any valid numeric expression. If *number* contains an uninitialized (for example, Empty) variable, zero returns; if it is a Null variable, Null returns.

Comments

The absolute value of a number is its unsigned magnitude.

Example

```
Abs(-1996) = 1996
Abs(1997) = 1997
```

Related Functions

Sgn Function

Array Function

Returns a Variant containing an array.

Syntax

Array(*list_of_arguments*)

The *list_of_arguments* contains a comma-delimited list of an arbitrary number of values. These values indicate how many dimensions there should be and the size of each one. If no arguments are specified, an array of zero length is created.

Comments

Elements in an array are referred by using a variable name followed by parentheses which contains an index number that indicates the desired element. Variants containing arrays and arrays containing variants are conceptually different, but the elements are accessed in the same way.

Note: Array indices start from zero unless stated otherwise. A definition such as Dim A(5) creates an array with six elements.

Example

```
A = Array(5,5,5,5) ' sets up a four dimensional array with six ele-
ments in each dimension
```

Related Functions

Dim Statement, **Let** Statement

Asc Function

Returns the ASCII character code of the first letter in a string.

Syntax

Asc(*string***)**

The *string* argument is any valid string expression. The string must contain some characters—otherwise a run-time error generates.

Comments

Returns the ASCII value as an integer between 0 and 255.

Example

```
intChar = Asc("Apple") ' Gives the ASCII value of the character A
which is 65
```

Related Functions

AscB Function - returns the first byte of the string rather than the first character.

Chr Function

Atn Function

Returns the arctangent of a number.

Syntax

```
Atn(number)
```

The argument can be any numeric expression that is mathematically consistent.

Comments

A trigonometric function for calculating one of the angles in a right angled triangle. The result will be between - symbol 112 \f "Symbol" \s 10 /2 and symbol 112 \f "Symbol" \s 10 /2 radians.

Example

```
sngAngle = Atn(0.5 * sngHypotentuse)
```

Related Functions

Cos Function, **Sin** Function, **Tan** Function, **Derived Math** Functions

CBool Function

Converts the expression supplied to a Boolean subtype and returns it.

Syntax

```
CBool(expression)
```

The *expression* argument is any valid VBScript expression.

Comments

CBool returns a False value if the *expression* is zero, otherwise True returns. A non-numeric *expression* generates a run-time error because this type of conversion is undefined.

Related Functions

CByte Function, **CDate** Function, **CDbl** Function, **CInt** Function, **CLng** Function, **CSng** Function, **CStr** Function, **CVErr** Function

CByte Function

Converts the expression supplied to a Byte subtype and returns it.

Syntax

CByte(*expression*)

The *expression* argument is any valid VBScript expression.

Comments

Can be used to force the result of some operation to express as a particular data type rather than the default one. For example, CByte can force byte arithmetic where larger values, such as integers, would be used.

CByte should be used instead of Val to provide internationally-aware conversions from any other data type to a Byte subtype. For example, the locale setting of your computer may recognize decimal separators in a different way than a computer in another country.

Example

```
bytRegistryFlag = CByte(RegistryFlag)
```

Related Functions

CInt Function, **CLng** Function, **CSng** Function, **CStr** Function, **CVErr** Function

CDate Function

Converts the expression supplied to a **Date** subtype and returns it.

Syntax

```
CDate(date)
```

The *date* argument is any valid date VBScript expression.

Comments

VBScript stores dates and times as real numbers. The whole number portion converts to a date, whereas the fractional portion is the time component which starts at midnight. Date is used to convert string or other date literals into this format. This function depends on the locale settings of your system. The order of day, month, and year will only be correctly determined if the date is provided in the correct date format. Do not use the day of the week as part of the string when using long date format. It will not be recognized.

Use the IsDate function to determine if *date* can be converted to a date or time.

Example

```
dtmStart = CDate(Textbox1.Value)
dtmFinish = CDate(Textbox2.Value)
dtmDuration = dtmFinish - dtmStart

dtmSteve = CDate("July 31, 1981")
```

Related Functions

`Date` `Function,` **`DateValue`** `Function,` **`Day`** `Function,` **`Month`** `Function,` **`Now`** `function,` **`TimeSerial`** `Function,` **`TimeValue`** `Function,` **`Weekday`** `Function,` **`Year`** `Function.`

CDbl Function

Converts the expression supplied to a Double subtype and returns it.

Syntax

`CDbl``(`*`expression`*`)`

The *expression* argument is any valid expression.

Comments

Can force the result of some operation express as a particular data type rather than the default one. For example, CDbl forces double precision arithmetic in cases where currency arithmetic would normally occur.

You should use the CDbl function instead of **Val** to provide internationally-aware Double subtype conversions.

Related Functions

`CBool` `Function,` **`CByte`** `Function,` **`CDate`** `Function,` **`CInt`** `Function,` **`CLng`** `Function,` **`CSng`** `Function,` **`CStr`** `Function,` **`CVErr`** `Function`

Chr Function

Returns the character with the specified character code.

Syntax

```
Chr(charcode)
```

The *charcode* argument is a number that identifies a character. This usually is between 0 and 255.

Comments

Charcode numbers are just ASCII equivalents. Numbers from 0 to 31 are nonprintable ASCII codes, such as beeps or linefeeds. The Chr() function is useful for inserting these characters into strings.

Example

```
mystr = Chr(10) & Chr(13) is used to insert line breaks into text.
```

Related Functions

Asc Function

ChrB Function - provided for use with byte data contained in a string. It returns a single byte rather than a character.

CInt Function

Converts the expression supplied to an Integer subtype and returns it.

Syntax

```
CInt(expression)
```

The *expression* argument is any valid VBScript expression.

Comments

Can be used to force the interpreter to show the result of an operation as a different subtype than the default one. For example, CInt or

CLng forces integer arithmetic in cases where currency, single-precision or double-precision arithmetic would normally occur.

CInt should be used instead of **Val** to provide internationally-aware conversions to the **Integer** subtype. This includes interpretation of thousand and decimal separators.

If *expression* is outside the acceptable range of the Integer subtype, an error generates.

VBScript handles most conversions automatically. These conversion functions should be used to clarify the meaning of code.

Example

```
ComboBox1.SelectedIndex = CInt(Textbox1.Value)
```

Related Functions

CBool Function, **CByte** Function, **CDate** Function, **CDbl** Function, **CLng** Function, **CSng** Function, **CStr** Function, **CVErr** Function, **Int** Function, **Fix** Function

CLng Function

Converts the expression supplied to a Long subtype and returns it.

Syntax

```
CLng(expression)
```

The *expression* argument is any valid VBScript expression.

Comments

Can be used to force the interpreter to show the result of an operation as a different subtype than the default one. For example, CInt or **CLng** forces integer arithmetic in cases where currency, single-precision or double-precision arithmetic would normally occur.

CLng should be used instead of **Val** to provide internationally-aware conversions to the Long subtype. This includes interpretation of thousand and decimal separators.

If expression lies outside the acceptable range for the Long subtype, an error generates.

CLng differs from the **Int** and **Fix Functions** because it rounds the fractional part of the number rather than truncating it. When the fractional part is exactly 0.5, **CLng** rounds it to the nearest even number. For example, 0.5 rounds to 0 and 1.5 rounds to 2. Otherwise normal rounding up occurs—less than 0.5 goes to 0, 0.5 or greater goes to 1.

Related Functions

CBool Function, **CByte** Function, **CDate** Function, **CDbl** Function, **CLng** Function, **CSng** Function, **CStr** Function, **CVErr** Function, **Int** Function, **Fix** Function

Cos Function

Returns the cosine value of an angle measured in radians.

Syntax

```
Cos(angle)
```

The *angle* argument is any valid expression which evaluates to an angle in radians.

Comments

Cosine is a trigonometric function whose result lies in the range -1 to 1.

Radians can be converted to degrees by multiplying by 180/pi and vice versa.

Example

```
dblCosine = Cos(dblFrequency * dblOmega)
```

Related Functions

Atn Function, **Sin** Function, **Tan** Function, **Derived Math** Functions

CSng Function

Converts the expression supplied to a Single subtype and returns it.

Syntax

```
CSng(expression)
```

The *expression* argument is any valid VBScript expression.

Comments

Can be used to force the interpreter to show the result of an operation as a different subtype than the default one. For example, CSng Function can be used to force single precision arithmetic in cases where currency or integer arithmetic would normally occur.

CSng Function should be used instead of **Val Function** to provide internationally-aware conversions to the **Single** subtype.

If expression lies outside the acceptable range for the Single subtype, an error generates. The positive range is 1.401298E-45 to 3.402823E38.

Related Functions

CBool Function, **CByte** Function, **CDate** Function, **CDbl** Function, **CInt** Function, **CLng** Function, **CStr** Function, **CVErr** Function

CStr Function

Converts the expression supplied to a String subtype and returns it.

Syntax

```
CStr(expression)
```

The *expression* argument is any valid VBScript expression.

Comments

Can be used to force the interpreter to show the result of an operation as a different subtype than the default one.

CStr Function should be used instead of **Str Function** to provide internationally-aware conversions from other data types to the **String** subtype.

The following table shows how the *expression* data determines what returns by CStr Function.

IF *EXPRESSION* IS	CSTR RETURNS
Boolean	A String containing True or False.
Date	A String containing a date in the short-date format of your system.
Null	A run-time error.
Empty	A zero-length String("").
Error	A String containing the word Error followed by the error number.
Other numeric	A String containing the number.

Related Functions

CBool Function, **CByte** Function, **CDate** Function, **CDbl** Function, **CInt** Function, **CLng** Function, **CSng** Function, **CVErr** Function

CVErr Function

Returns an error number specified by the user as an Error subtype.

Syntax

```
CVErr(errornumber)
```

The argument, *errornumber*, is any valid error number.

Comments

Users can use the CVErr function to create user-defined errors in sections of code. For example, if a string is entered into a function that is designed to accept only numbers, the CVErr function allows you to return an error number that triggers another action.

Related Functions

CBool Function, **CByte** Function, **CDate** Function, **CDbl** Function, **CInt** Function, **CLng** Function, **CSng** Function, **CStr** Function, **IsError** Function

Date Function

Returns the current date as stored in your system BIOS.

Syntax

```
Date
```

Example

```
dtmToday_Date = Date
```

Related Functions

CDate Function, **Now** Function, **Time** Function

DateSerial Function

Combines the specified year, month, and day to form a complete date. The result returns as a Date subtype.

Syntax

DateSerial(*year, month, date*)

The following table summarizes the arguments for the DateSerial function:

PART	DESCRIPTION
year	Number between 100 and 9999, or a numeric expression
month	Any numeric expression.
day	Any numeric expression.

Comments

Dates can be referred to as absolute date numbers or as relative numbers. Thus March 3, 1996 could be written as:

DateSerial (1996, 3, 3) or,

DateSerial (2000–4, 4–1, 28–25)

The year argument values between 0 and 99 are a shorthand means of representing the years of the 20th Century, 1900–1999. For other years, use the complete four digit representation, for example, Jesus College Cambridge was founded in 1596 by Bishop John Alcock..

When any argument exceeds the normally accepted range of units for that item, it is carried to the next largest unit. For example, even though no month has 40 days, the interpreter will automatically convert this number of days to one month and a few days. The exact number of days depends on which month of the year is being considered.

If any single argument of the DateSerial function lies outside the range –32,768 to 32,767, an error occurs.

Related Functions

Date Function, **DateValue** Function, **Day** Function, **Month** Function, **Now** function, **TimeSerial** Function, **TimeValue** Function, **Weekday** Function, **Year** Function.

DateValue Function

Returns the value specified as a Date subtype.

Syntax

DateValue(*date*)

The *date* argument is normally a string expression representing a date in the range January 1,100 to December 31,9999. Date can be used to represent a date, a time, or both, in that range mentioned above. Date can also be a VBScript date literal, for example, #23/08/96#.

Comments

If date is a string that includes only numbers separated by valid date separators, DateValue recognizes the order for month, day, and year according to the Short Date format on your system. DateValue also recognizes unambiguous dates that contain month names, either in long or abbreviated form. For example, 9/14/1993 and Sep 14, 1993 are equally valid.

If the year part of the date is omitted, the current year indicated by your system BIOS is used.

Related Functions

CDate Function, **Now** Function, **Time** Function.

Day Function

Returns the day of the month as a whole number between 1 and 31.

Syntax

Day(*date*)

The *date* argument is any expression that can represent a date. If it is Null, **Null** returns.

Related Functions

Date Function, **Hour** Function, **Minute** Function, **Month** Function, **Weekday** Function, **Now** Function, **Second** Function, **Year** Function.

Derived Math Functions

The following list shows how to derive the remaining trigonometric and hyperbolic functions by combining the exponential constant ('e'), the Sin, the Cos and the Tan functions.

Syntax

FUNCTION	DERIVED
Inverse Sine	Arcsin(X) = **Atn**(X/**Sqr**(1–X^2)
Inverse Cosine	Arccos(X) = **Atn**(–X/**Sqr**(1–X^2)) + **Atn**(1)
Secant	Sec(X) = 1/**Cos**(X)
Cosecant	Cosec(X) = 1/**Sin**(X)
Cotangent	Cotan(X) = 1/**Tan**(X)

FUNCTION	DERIVED
Inverse Secant	Arcsec(X) = **Atn**(X/**Sqr**(X^2–1)) + **Sgn**((X)–1)*(2*Atn(1))
Inverse Cosecant	Arccosec(X) = **Atn**(X/**Sqr**(X^2–1)) + (**Sgn**(X)1)*(2*Atn(1))
Inverse Cotangent	Arccotan(X) = **Atn**(X) + 2***Atn**(1)
Hyperbolic Sine	HSin(X) = (**Exp**(X)–**Exp**(–X))/2
Hyperbolic Cosine	HCos(X) = (**Exp**(X) + **Exp**(–X))/2
Hyperbolic Tangent	HTan(X) = (**Exp**(X)–**Exp**(–X))/(**Exp**(X) + **Exp**(–X))
Hyperbolic Secant	HSec(X) = 2/(**Exp**(X) + **Exp**(–X))
Hyperbolic Cosecant	HCosec(X) = 2/(**Exp**(X) – **Exp**(–X))
Hyperbolic Cotangent	HCotan(X) = (**Exp**(X) + **Exp**(–X))/(**Exp**(X)–**Exp**(–X))
Inverse Hyperbolic Sine	HArcsin(X) = **Log**(X + **Sqr**(X^2 + 1))
Inverse Hyperbolic Cosine	HArccox(X) = **Log**(X + **Sqr**(X^2–1))
Inverse Hyperbolic Tangent	HArctan(X) = **Log**((1 + X)/(1–X)) / 2
Inverse Hyperbolic Secant	HArcsec(X) = **Log**((**Sqr**(1–X^2) + 1) / X)
Inverse Hyperbolic Cosecant	HArccosec(X) = **Log**((**Sgn**(X)***Sqr**(X^2 + 1)+1)
/ X)	
Inverse Hyperbolic Cotangent	HArccotan(X) = **Log**((X + 1)/(X–1)) / 2
Logarithm to base N	Log^{N}(X) = **Log**(X)/**Log**(N)

Exp Function

Returns the value of the exponential ('e') raised to a particular power.

Syntax

```
Exp(number)
```

The *number* argument can be any valid numeric expression.

Comments

Number must be less than 709.782712893.

The constant 'e' has a value of approximately 2.718282 and is occasionally referred to as the antilogarithm.

Example

```
dblQTime = dblConst * Exp((- dblLambda * dblTime) / dblPi)
```

Related Functions

Log Function, **Derived Math** Function

Hex Function

Returns the string representation of the number as hexadecimal digits.

Syntax

```
Hex(number)
```

The *number* argument is any valid numeric expression.

Comments

The *number* argument is first rounded to the nearest whole number before being evaluated.

IF **NUMBER** IS	HEX RETURNS
Null	Null
Empty	Zero(0)
Any other number	Up to eight hexadecimal characters.

Hexadecimal numbers are represented by preceding the number with &H. The decimal value 45 is thus represented by &H2D.

A two digit hex number can represent 1 byte of information, for example, &H8F represents 10001111 in binary.

Example

```
strColor = Hex(Document.bgColor)
```

Related Functions

Oct Function.

Hour Function

Returns the hour of the day as a whole number between 0 and 23.

Syntax

Hour(*time***)**

The *time* argument is any expression that represents a time. If *time is* Null, **Null** returns.

Comments

The time expression supplied can use the 12 or 24 hour format, for example, "2:53:00pm" is the same as "14:53:00". Hour() would return 14 in both cases.

Related Functions

Day Function, **Minute** Function, **Now** Function, **Second** Function, **Time** Function.

InputBox Function

Displays a prompt in a dialog box and waits for the user to input text or choose a button. The text string entered by the user then returns.

Syntax

InputBox(*prompt[,title][,default][,xpos][,ypos][,helpfile, context]***)**

The InputBox function syntax has the following arguments:

PART	DESCRIPTION
prompt	String expression displayed in the dialog box. Has a maximum length of 1024 characters, and multiple lines can be separated by using a carriage return character (Chr(13)), or a linefeed character (Chr(10)).
title	String expression displayed in the title bar of the dialog box. If left blank, the application name is placed in the title bar, i.e. VBScript.
default	String expression displayed in the dialog box as the default response If default is omitted, the text box is displayed empty.

PART	DESCRIPTION
xpos	Numeric expression of the horizontal distance in twips of the left edge of the dialog box from the left edge of the screen. If this argument is not specified, the dialog box is centered horizontally onscreen.
ypos	Numeric expression of the vertical distance in twips of the top edge of the dialog box from the top edge of the screen. If this argument is not specified, the dialog box is placed one-third of the way down the screen.
helpfile	String expression that identifies the Help file to be provide context-sensitive Help for the dialog box. If *helpfile* is provided, *context* must also be included.
context	Numeric expression that is assigned to a specific Help topic by the author.

Comments

When both help file and context are supplied, a Help button automatically addsto the dialog box. If the user chooses OK or presses ENTER, the InputBox function returns whatever is in the text box. If the user chooses Cancel, the function returns a zero-length string ("").

Related Functions

MsbBox Function.

InStr Function

Returns the first position of one string within another.

Syntax

```
InStr([start, ]string1, string2[, compare])
```

The arguments for the InStr function are as follows:

PART	DESCRIPTION
start	*Numeric expression* that sets the starting position of each search. If *start* is not included, the search begins at the first character position. If it contains **Null**, then an error will be returned. The argument must be included if *compare* is specified.
string1	The string expression being searched.
string2	The string being sought.
compare	Dictates the type of string comparison. Specify 0 for a binary comparison, or 1 to perform a textual case-insensitive comparison. If compare is **Null**, an error occurs. If omitted, a binary comparison is performed. The *start* argument is required whenever *compare* is specified.

Comments

The return values are summarized below:

IF	INSTR RETURNS
string1 is zero-length	0
string1 is **Null**	**Null**
string2 is zero-length	*start*
string2 is **Null**	**Null**
string2 is not found	0
string2 is found within *string1*	Position at which match is found
start > Len(string2)	0

Related Functions

InStrB Function - used for byte data contained in a string, where the byte position of one string within another is returned.

Int, Fix Functions

Returns the integer portion of a number.

Syntax

Int(*number*)

Fix(*number*)

The *number* argument can be any valid numeric expression. If *number* contains Null, Null returns.

Comments

Both Int and Fix remove the fractional part of the number, and return the integer value. The difference between Int and Fix is in how they treat negative numbers. Int always rounds from zero whereas Fix rounds towards zero.

Example

For example:

```
Int(-8.4) returns -9
```

```
Fix(-8.4) returns -8
```

Related Functions

CInt Function.

IsArray Function

Returns a Boolean value to indicate whether or not a variable is an array.

Syntax

```
IsArray(varname)
```

The *varname* argument can be any VBScript variable.

Comments

IsArray is especially useful for variants containing arrays; it returns a True value if the variable is an array, otherwise False.

Related Functions

Array Function, **IsDate** Function, **IsEmpty** Function, **IsError** Function, **IsNull** Function, **IsNumeric** Function, **IsObject** Function, **VarType** Function.

IsDate Function

Returns a Boolean value indicating whether an expression can be interpreted successfully as a date value.

Syntax

```
IsDate(expression)
```

The *expression* argument can be any date or string expression that is recognizable as a time or date.

Comments

IsDate returns True if the expression is a date or if it can be converted to a valid date. Otherwise, it returns False. Valid dates in Windows are January 1, 100 to December 31, 9999.

Example

```
IsDate("Jan 31, 1969") returns True

IsDate("30/02/90") returns False
```

Related Functions

CDate Function, **IsArray** Function, **IsEmpty** Function, **IsError** Function, **IsNull** Function, **IsNumeric** Function, **IsObject** Function, **VarType** Function.

IsEmpty Function

Returns a Boolean value indicating whether a variable has been initialized and now contains a value.

Syntax

IsEmpty(*expression*)

The *expression* argument should always be a single variable name because it is used to determine if a particular variable has been initialized.

Comments

IsEmpty returns a True value if the variable is uninitialized or is explicitly set to Empty. Otherwise it returns False. False is always returned if *expression* contains more than one variable.

Related Functions

IsArray Function, **IsEmpty** Function, **IsError** Function, **IsNull** Function, **IsNumeric** Function, **IsObject** Function, **VarType** Function.

IsNull Function

Returns a Boolean value to indicate whether an expression evaluates to Null or is actually a valid VBScript value.

Syntax

```
IsNull(expression)
```

Comments

If the *expression* is Null, a True value returns. Otherwise it returns False. If expression consists of more than one variable, Null in any part of the expression causes True to be returned for the entire expression.

The Null value indicates that the variable contains no valid data. Null is not the same as Empty meaning that the variable has not yet been initialized. It is also the same as a zero-length string which is sometimes referred to as a Null string.

Any expression containing a Null is itself Null and causes the rest of the expression to be ignored. This may be important in expressions such as If Var<>Null, which will always be False.

Related Functions

IsArray Function, **IsDate** Function, **IsEmpty** Function, **IsError** Function, **IsNumeric** Function, **IsObject** Function, **VarType** Function.

IsNumeric Function

Returns a Boolean value to indicate whether or not an expression can be evaluated as a number.

Syntax

```
IsNumeric(expression)
```

Comments

IsNumeric returns True if the entire *expression* can be interpreted as a number. Otherwise it returns False. It also returns False for date expressions which have their own subtype.

Related Functions

IsArray Function, **IsDate** Function, **Empty** Function, **IsError** Function, **IsNull** Function, **IsObject** Function, **VarType** Function.

IsObject Function

Returns a Boolean value indicating whether an expression references a valid OLE Automation object.

Syntax

```
IsObject(expression)
```

Comments

IsObject gives a return value that is True if *expression* is a variable of Object subtype or a user-defined object, otherwise it returns False.

Related Functions

IsArray Function, **IsDate** Function, **Empty** Function, **IsError** Function, **IsNull** Function, **IsObject** Function, **VarType** Function.

LBound Function

Returns the index of the lowest numbered element of the indicated dimension of an array.

Syntax

```
LBound(arrayname[, dimension])
```

The LBound function syntax has these parts:

PART	DESCRIPTION
arrayname	Name of the array variable; follows standard variable naming conventions.
dimension	Whole number indicating which dimension we are considering. Use 1 for the first dimension, 2 for the second, and so on. If it is omitted, the first dimension is assumed. Ignore this parameter for one dimensional arrays.

Comments

The LBound function is used alongside the UBound function to determine the size of an unknown array. Use the UBound function to find the upper limit of an array dimension.

Example

```
Dim intTest(1 To 50, 5 To 100, -4 To 6)
```

STATEMENT	RETURN VALUE
LBound(intTest,1)	1
LBound(intTest,3)	–4

The default lower bound for any dimension is always zero.

Related Functions

Dim Function, **Private** Function, **Public** Function, **ReDim** Function, **Static** Function, **UBound** Function.

LCase Function

Converts the string value supplied to lowercase and returns it.

Syntax

LCase(*string*)

The *string* argument is any valid string. If it contains Null, then Null returns. A number interprets as the string of digits that represent that number.

Comments

Only uppercase letters convert to lowercase and others remain the same.

Example

```
LCase(103.2) returns "103.2"
LCase("Tony Goddard") returns "tony goddard"
```

Related Functions

UCase Function.

Left Function

Returns the specified number of characters from the left hand side of the string argument.

Syntax

Left(*string, left***)**

The Left function syntax has these arguments:

PART	DESCRIPTION
string	String from which to extract the characters. If string contains Null, Null returns.
length	Numeric expression for indicating how many characters are to be returned. If 0, a zero-length string returns. If greater than or equal
to	
	the number of characters in the string, the entire string returns.

Comments

To determine the number of characters in a string, use the Len function.

Related Functions

LeftB Function - used with byte data contained in a atring, where *length* specifies the number of bytes.

Len Function, **Mid** Function, **Right** Function.

Len Function

Returns the number of characters in a string or the number of bytes required to store a variable.

Syntax

```
Len(string | varname)
```

The Len function syntax has these parts:

PART	DESCRIPTION
string	Any valid string expression. If string contains Null, Null is returned.
varname	Any valid VBScript variable name. If varname contains Null, Null returns.

Comments

The | symbol in the above syntax represents the word OR, meaning that only one argument is supplied.

Example

```
Dim intX, strY
strY = "Hello"
intX = 1024

Len(StrY) returns 5
Len(intX) returns 2 if intX stored as 16 bit integer
```

Related Functions

LenB Function - provided for use with byte data contained in a string. The number of bytes used to represent the string is returned.

InStr Function.

Log Function

Returns the natural logarithm of a number to the base *e*.

Syntax

```
Log(number)
```

The *number* argument can be any valid numeric expression greater than 0.

Comments

The natural logarithm is the logarithm to the base *e*. The constant *e* is approximately 2.718282.

To change the base of a logarithm, perform the following calculation:

$$Log^{newbase}(x) = Log(x) / Log(n)$$

Example

```
Function Log_10(X)
Log_10 = Log(X)/Log(CDbl(10))
End Function
```

Related Functions

Derived Math Functions, **Exp** Function.

LTrim, RTrim and Trim Functions

Returns the string argument minus the leading spaces (LTrim), trailing spaces (RTrim), or both leading and trailing spaces (Trim).

Syntax

```
LTrim(string)

RTrim(string)

Trim(string)
```

If the *string* contains Null, Null returns.

Comments

This is especially useful if you are trying to make up a path name from separate strings where spaces need to be cut out of an input string.

Related Functions

Left Function, **Right** Function

Mid Function

Returns a certain number of characters from some position within string.

Syntax

```
Mid(string, start[, length])
```

The Mid function syntax has these arguments:

PART	DESCRIPTION
string	*String* from which characters are returned. If *string* contains Null, Null returns.

PART	DESCRIPTION
start	Character position of the start of the string to be extracted. If *start* is greater than the number of characters in the string, Mid returns a zero-length string.
length	Number of characters to return. If omitted or if there are fewer characters than *length* in the text, all characters from the start position to the end of the string are returned.

Comments

Use the Len function to determine the number of characters in *string* before applying Mid to it.

Related Functions

MidB Function - provided for use with byte data contained in a string. The arguments specify the numbers of bytes.

Minute Function

Returns a whole number between 0 and 59 representing the minute of the hour.

Syntax

```
Minute(time)_
```

The *time* argument is any VBScript expression or variable that represents a time. If *time* contains Null, Null returns.

Example

```
Minute("13:42:12") returns 42
```

Related Functions

Date Function, **Day** Function, **Hour** Function, **Minute** Function, **Month** Function, **Second** Function, **Time** Function, **Weekday** Function, **Year** Function.

Month Function

Returns a whole number between 1 and 12 representing the month of the year.

Syntax

Month(*date***)**

The *date* argument is any VBScript expression that represents a date. If *date* contains Null, Null returns.

Example

```
Month(Date()) returns the current month of the year.
```

Related Functions

Date Function, **Day** Function, **Hour** Function, **Minute** Function, **Month** Function, **Second** Function, **Time** Function, **Weekday** Function, **Year** Function.

MsgBox Function

1. Displays a message in a dialog box
2. Waits for a button to be pressed
3. Returns a value indicating which button was pressed.

Syntax

```
MsgBox(prompt[, buttons][, title][, helpfile, context])
```

The MsgBox function syntax has these arguments:

PART	DESCRIPTION
prompt	This is the message displays in the dialog box. The maximum length of the prompt is about 1024 characters but it is also limited by the width of the characters. If it consists of more than one line, separate the lines by using a carriage return (Chr(13)) or a linefeed (Chr(10)).
buttons	Numeric sum of the values specifying the number and type of buttons to display, the icon style to use, the identity of the default button, and the modality of the message box. If omitted, the default value for *buttons* is 0, and an OK button displays.
title	String expression displayed in the title bar of the dialog box. If omitted, the application name is used instead.
helpfile	String expression that identifies the Help file to provide the context-sensitive Help for the dialog box. If *helpfile* value is specified, *context* must also be specified.
context	Numeric expression that is the value of Help Topic that is assigned by the author. Must be provided if *helpfile* is supplied.

Comments

The button argument settings are as follows:

CONSTANT	VALUE	DESCRIPTION
vbOKOnly	0	Display OK button only.
vbOKCanacel	1	Display OK and Cancel buttons.
vbOKAbortRetryIgnore	2	Display Abort, Retry and Ignore buttons.
vbYesNoCancel	3	Display Yes, No and Cancel buttons.
vbYesNo	4	Display Yes and No buttons.
vbRetryCancel	5	Display Retry and Cancel buttons.
vbCritical	16	Display Critical Message Icon.
vbQuestion	32	Display Warning Query Icon.
vbExclamation	48	Display Warning Message Icon.
vbInformation	64	Display Information Message Icon.
vbDefaultButton1	0	First button is default.
vbDefaultButton2	256	Second button is default.
vbDefaultButton3	512	Third button is default.
vbApplicationModal	0	Application modal; the user must respond to the message box before continuing work in the current application.
vbSystemModal	4096	System modal; all applications are suspended until the user responds to the message box.

The values 0–5 dictate the number and type of buttons. The second group (16, 32, 48, 64) control the icon style. The third group (0, 256, 512) determines which button is the default and the fourth group (0, 4096) determines the modality of the message box. When adding numbers to create a final value for the argument buttons, use only one number from each group.

These values are constants in VBScript and therefore can be used anywhere in a script in place of the actual numbers. This makes code more understandable.

The return values may be summarized below.

CONSTANT	VALUE	BUTTON CHOSEN
vbOk	1	OK
vbCancel	2	Cancel
vbAbort	3	Abort
vbRetry	4	Retry
vbIgnore	5	Ignore
vbYes	6	Yes
vbNo	7	No

If *helpfile* and *context* have been supplied, the F1 key is used to bring up the help topic corresponding to the context.

If the dialog box displays a Cancel button, pressing the ESC key has the same effect as choosing Cancel. If the dialog box contains a Help button, context-sensitive Help is provided for the dialog box. However, no value returns until one of the other buttons is chosen.

Example

```
intAnswer = MsgBox("Continue with submission?", vbYesNo + vbQuestion +
vbSystemModal, "Mortgage Application")
```

Related Functions

InputBox Function.

Now Function

Returns the current date and time as returned by your system clock.

Syntax

```
Now
```

Example

```
dtmToday = Now
```

Related Functions

Date Function, **Day** Function, **Hour** Function, **Minute** Function, **Month** Function, **Second** Function, **Time** Function, **Weekday** Function, **Year** Function.

Oct Function

Returns a string representation of the octal value of a number.

Syntax

Oct(*number*)

Comments

If *number* is not already a whole number, it is rounded up to the nearest whole number before being evaluated. The evaluation is as follows:

IF *NUMBER* IS	OCT RETURNS
Null	**Null**
Empty	Zero (0)
Any other number	Up to 11 octal characters.

Octal numbers are represented directly by preceding the number with an &O (letter O, not zero 0). The Octal system only uses the digits 0 to 7 so decimal 12 is represented by &O14.

Related Functions

Hex Function

Right Function

Returns the specified number of characters from the right hand side of a string.

Syntax

```
Right(string, length)
```

The Right function has the following arguments.

PART	DESCRIPTION
string	This is the string from which the characters return. If *string* contains **Null**, then **Null** returns.

PART	DESCRIPTION
length	Numeric expression for the number of characters that are to be returned. If this is 0, a zero-length string returns. If greater than the length of the string, the entire string is returned.

Comments

If you want to find out the length of a string, use the Len function.

Example

```
Right("Ashley Collins", 7) returns "Collins"
```

Related Functions

RightB is used with byte data contained in a string. Instead of specifying the number of characters to be returned, *length* specifies the number of bytes.

Rnd Function

Returns a random number.

Syntax

Rnd[(*number***)]**

See below for the significance of the optional *number* argument.

Comments

Rnd generates a random number that is between 0 and 1, but does not include 1.

The *number* argument determines how the random number generates.

IF ***NUMBER*** IS	RND GENERATES
< 0	The same number every time, using *number* as the seed.
> 0	The next random number in the sequence.
= 0	The most recently generated number.
not given	The next random number in the sequence.

Random numbers generated by VBScript are, in fact, pseudo-random, for example, they are long sequences of seemingly random numbers generated by a mathematical formula. Every time you load the VBScript interpreter and make calls to Rnd, the same sequence of numbers generate unless you instruct the application to return numbers from a different point in the sequence. These values are known as seeds and VBScript provides the Randomize statement to generate them. Randomize uses the system clock to see the random number generator.

Call Randomize on or before using Rnd and your sequence appears totally random.

Example

To produce integers in a given range, use the following formula:

```
Int((upperbound - lowerbound + 1) * Rnd + lowerbound)
```

Here, *upperbound* is the highest number in the range and *lowerbound* is the lowest number in the range.

The general way of using the Rnd() function is as follows:

```
Rem Using Random numbers
Randomize ' placed at the start of the script
...
Rnd() ' used once or many times to generate random sequence of numbers
between 0 and 1
```

Related Functions

Randomize statement.

Second Function

Returns the second component of the time value specified as a whole number between 0 and 59.

Syntax

Second(*time***)**

The *time* argument is any VBScript expression that can represent a time. If time contains Null, Null returns.

Example

`Second(Now())` returns number of seconds elapsed in current minute according to your system clock

Related Functions

Day Function, **Hour** Function, **Minute** Function, **Now** Function, **Time** Function

Sgn Function

Returns an integer indicating the sign of a numeric expression.

Syntax

Sgn(*number***)**

The *number* argument can be any valid numeric expression.

Comments

The following table summarizes the return values of the Sgn function.

IF *NUMBER* **EVALUATES TO**	SGN **RETURNS**
> 0	1
= 0	0
< 0	–1

Related Functions

Abs Function.

Sin Function

Returns the sine of the angle.

Syntax

Sin(*angle*)

The *angle* argument can be any valid numeric expression representing an angle measured in radians.

Comments

Sine is a trigonometric function whose result lies between –1 and 1. It is periodic every 2 symbol 112 \f "Symbol" \s 10 radians.

Degrees convert to radians by multiplying by pi/180.

Example

```
Sin(30 * pi / 180) returns 0.5
```

Related Functions

Atn Function, **Cos** Function, **Derived Math** Functions, **Tan** Function

Space Function

Returns a string containing the specified number of characters.

Syntax

```
Space(number)
```

The *number* argument is the number of spaces you want in the string.

Comments

The Space function is useful for formatting output strings and clearing data in fixed-length strings.

Related Functions

`String` Function

Sqr Function

Returns the real square root of a positive number.

Syntax

```
Sqr(number)
```

The *number* argument must be a positive number.

Comments

The ^ operator can be used to generate a square root of *number* by raising *number* to the power of fi. For other roots such as a cube root, use ⅓ or similar fraction.

Str Function

Returns a string representation of a numeric value.

Syntax

Str(*number*)

The *number* argument is any valid numeric expression.

Comments

The Str function always reserves a leading space for the sign of the number when carrying out a conversion. If the number is positive, the returned string contains a leading space and the plus sign is implied. For negative numbers, the sign appears.

The Str function only recognizes the period as a decimal separator. Other international formats should use the CStr Function to convert a number to a string; for example, when thousand separators are required.

Related Functions

CStr Function, **Val** Function

StrComp Function

Compares two strings and returns a result.

Syntax

StrComp(*string1, string2[, compare]*)

The **StrComp** function syntax has the following arguments:

PART	DESCRIPTION
string1	Any valid string expression.
string2	Any valid string expression.
compare	Specifies the type of string comparison. A 1 performs a character comparison and the 0, a binary one. If *compare* is omitted, a binary comparison is performed.

The following values are returned:

IF	STRCOMP RETURNS
string1 < string2	–1
string1 = *string2*	0
string1 > string2	1
string1 or string2	**Null**

Comments

If not StrComp(strCommand, “Restore”) Then

Else ....

String Function

Returns a string of the length specified containing the specified character repeated at every position.

Syntax

```
String(number, character)
```

The String function syntax has these arguments:

PART	DESCRIPTION
number	Length of the string to be constructed. If *number* contains Null, Null returns.
character	Single character code or a string expression whose first character is used, to build the return string. If *character* contains Null, Null returns.

Comments

If you specify a number for *character* greater than 255, String converts the number to a valid character code using the *character* Mod 256 formula.

Example

```
String(50, 20) returns a string of 50 space characters
```

Related Functions

Space Function.

Tan Function

Returns the tangent of the angle.

Syntax

Tan(*angle*)

The *angle* argument is any valid numeric expression representing an angle in radians.

Comments

Tan is a trigonometric function that returns a value between – symbol 181 \f "Symbol" \s 10 and + symbol 181 \f "Symbol" \s 10 . It is periodic every symbol 112 \f "Symbol" \s 10 radians.

To convert degrees to radians, multiply by pi/180.

Related Functions

Atn Function, **Cos** Function, **Derived Math** Functions, **Sin** Function

Time Function

Returns the current system time as a Date subtype value.

Syntax

```
Time
```

Comments

Use Time() as a default value for time fields on forms or to timestamp documents.

Related Functions

Date Function

TimeSerial Function

Returns the time as a Date subtype value in the hour, minute, and second format.

Syntax

TimeSerial(*hour, minute, second***)**

continues

The TimeSerial function has these arguments.

PART	DESCRIPTION
hour	Number between 0 (12:00 A.M.) and 23 (11:00 P.M.)
minute	Any numeric expression
second	Any numberic expression

Comments

Times can be specified as absolute values or relative ones. For absolute times, you should include the numbers in the TimeSerial function for the time that you want. For relative times, you can specify mini-calculations for the time you require. For example 4:45:00 P.M. could be represented as TimerSerial(5,–15,0).

Arguments are automatically expressed in their most simple units. For example, 70 minutes = 1 hour 10 minutes. If any single argument lies outside the range –32,768 to 32,767 or if the associated date falls outside the date limits, an error generates.

Example

```
TimeSerial(9, 60, -1) returns a time value for 09:59:59
```

Related Functions

DateSerial Function, **DateValue** Function, **Hour** Function, **Minute** Function, **Now** Function, **Second** Function, **TimeValue** Function

TimeValue Function

Returns the expression as a Date subtype if the subtype is possible.

Syntax

```
TimeValue(time)
```

The *time* argument is normally a string expression representing a time from 0:00:00 to 23:59:59. However, *time* can also be any expression that represents a time in that range. If time contains Null, Null returns.

Comments

Either the 12 or 24 hour clock can be used. both 6:30PM and 18:30 are valid *time* arguments.

If the time argument contains date information, the TimeValue function ignores it. However, if the *time* includes invalid date information, an error occurs.

Related Functions

DateSerial Function, **DateValue** Function, **Hour** Function, **Minute** Function, **Now** Function, **Second** Function, **TimeSerial** Function

UBound Function

Returns the index of the highest numbered element of the indicated dimension of an array.

Syntax

```
UBound(arrayname[, dimension])
```

The UBound function has the following arguments:

PART	DESCRIPTION
arrayname	Name of the array variable; follows standard variable naming conventions.

PART	DESCRIPTION
dimension	Whole number indicating which dimension we are considering. Use 1 for the first dimension, 2 for the second, and so on. If it is omitted, then the first dimension is assumed. Ignore this parameter for 1 dimensional arrays.

Comments

The UBound function is used with the LBound function to determine the size of an array. Use the LBound function to find the lower limit of an array dimension.

Example

```
Dim intTest(1 To 50, 5 To 100, -4 To 6)
```

STATEMENT	RETURN VALUE
UBound(intTest,1)	50
LBound(intTest,3)	6

Related Functions

Dim Statement, **LBound** Function, **Public** Statement, **ReDim** Statement

UCase Function

Converts the string value supplied to upper case and returns it.

Syntax

UCase(*string***)**

The *string* argument is any valid string expression. If *string* contains Null, Null returns.

Comments

Only lowercase letters convert to uppercase; all uppercase letters and non-letter characters remain the same. If *string* is actually a numeric value, *Ucase* returns a string of digits that represents the number.

Example

```
UCase("eleanor") returns "ELEANOR"
UCase(30495) returns "30945"
```

Related Functions

LCase Function.

Val Function

Returns the numbers represented by the supplied string.

Syntax

Val(*string*)

Comments

The Val function only reads as far as the first non-numeric character. Symbols and characters, such as commas or currency signs, are not recognized as numbers. However, function prefixes &O and &H are acceptable. Blanks, linefeeds, and tabs automatically strip from the argument.

You should note that the Val function only recognizes the period as a valid decimal separator. Applications needing to use values in international formats should use CDbl to convert a string to a number.

Example

```
Val("01465 78554312 is Jim's phone number")
```

returns the value 146578554312.

In the code below, Val returns the value –1 for the hexadecimal value which is a 16 bit value stored in 2's complement format:

Val("&HFFFF")

Related Functions

CDbl Function.

VarType Function

Returns a value indicating the subtype of a variable.

Syntax

VarType(*varname*)

The *varname* argument can be any variable except one of a user-defined type.

Comments

The following table is a list of the possible return values.

CONSTANT	VALUE	VARIABLE TYPE
vbEmpty	0	Empty (uninitialized).
vbNull	1	**Null** (no valid data).
vbInteger	2	Integer.
vbLong	3	Long integer.

CONSTANT	VALUE	VARIABLE TYPE
vbSingle	4	Single-precision floating-point number.
vbDouble	5	Double-precision floating-point number.
vbCurrency	6	Currency.
vbDate	7	Date.
vbString	8	String.
vbObject	9	OLE Automation object.
vbError	10	Error.
vbBoolean	11	Boolean.
vbVariant	12	Variant (used only with arrays of Variants).
vbDataObject	13	Non-OLE Automation object.
vbByte	17	Byte.
vbArray	8192	Array.

VBScript specifies these constants and, as a result, cannot be used for other variable names in your code because they are essentially reserved words.

The value for vbArray always returns in conjunction with another constant to indicate an array of a particular type. For example, the value returned for an array of integers is calculated as vbInteger + vbArray (=1894). If an object has a default property, VarType(object) returns the type of its default property.

The constant vbVariant is only returned in conjunction with vbArray to indicate that the argument to the VarType function is an array.

Related Functions

IsArray Function, **IsDate** Function, **IsEmpty** Function, **IsError** Function, **IsNull** Function, **IsNumeric** Function, **IsObject** Function.

Weekday Function

Returns a whole number representing the day of the week stored in the date expression.

Syntax

`Weekday``(`*`date[, firstdayofweek]`*`)`

The Weekday function has the following arguments:

PART	DESCRIPTION
date	Any date expression. If *date* contains Null, Null returns.
firstdayofweek	A constant that specifies the first day of the week, as described in the system settings. If omitted, **vbSunday** is assumed.

Comments

The *firstdayofweek* argument has these settings:

CONSTANT	VALUE	DESCRIPTION
vbUseSystem	0	Use NLS API setting.
vbSunday	1	Sunday
vbMonday	2	Monday
vbTuesday	3	Tuesday
vbWednesday	4	Wednesday
vbThursday	5	Thursday
vbFriday	6	Friday
vbSaturday	7	Saturday

The Weekday function can return any of these values:

CONSTANT	VALUE	DESCRIPTION
vbSunday	1	Sunday
vbMonday	2	Monday
vbTuesday	3	Tuesday
vbWednesday	4	Wednesday
vbThursday	5	Thursday
vbFriday	6	Friday
vbSaturday	7	Saturday

Example

```
If Weekday(Date()) = vbFriday Then MsgBox "Hurray..It's nearly the
weekend!"
```

Related Functions

Date Function, **Day** Function, **Month** Function, **Now** Function, **Year** Function

Year Function

Returns a whole number that represents the year stored in the date expression.

Syntax

Year(*date***)**

The *date* argument is any expression that can represent a date. If *date* contains Null, Null returns.

Related Functions

Date Function, **Day** Function, **Month** Function, **Now** Function, **Weekday** Function

APPENDIX B

VBScript Language Reference—Statements

Call Statement

Transfers control to a Sub procedure or a Function.

Syntax

```
[Call] name [argumentlist]
```

The Call statement has the following parts:

PART	DESCRIPTION
Call	This is optional, and if included, you must enclose the argumentlist in parentheses.
name	Name of the procedure to call—the procedure must already be defined.
argumentlist	Comma-delimited list of variables, arrays, or expressions that are to be passed to the procedure.

Comments

As stated above, the Call keyword is optional. If you decide to use the Call keyword to call a procedure that requires arguments, the *argumentlist* must be enclosed in parentheses. If you omit the Call keyword, you also must omit the parentheses around the *argumentlist*.

If you call a function using either of the above methods, its return value is discarded. To make use of the return value, you must assign the function to a variable as follows:

```
intReturnValue = myFunction(arg1, arg2, ..., argN))
```

To pass a whole array to a procedure, use the array name followed by empty parentheses.

Example

Dim Statement

Declares variables and allocates storage space in memory.

Syntax

```
Dim varname[([subscripts])][, varname[([subscripts])]]...
```

The Dim statement syntax has the following parts:

PART	DESCRIPTION
varname	Name of the variable.
subscripts	Dimensions of an array variable. Up to 60 dimensions may be declared. The lower bound of an array is always zero unless specified otherwise.

Comments

Variables declared with Dim at the script level are available anywhere in the script. When declared at the procedure level, variables are only available to that procedure.

The Dim statement can also be used with empty parentheses, in which case the array is dynamic. After declaring a dynamic array, use the ReDim statement within a script to define the number of dimensions and elements in the array. If you try to redeclare a dimension for an array variable whose size was explicitly specified in a Private, Public or Dim statement, an error occurs because these are static arrays.

When variables initialize, they take on the value of 0 (for numeric variables), or a zero length string ("", for strings).

The conventional place to put a variable declaration is at the beginning of the procedure.

Example

```
Dim dynArray(), statArray(5,4), intX
```

Related Items

Array Function, **Private** Statement, **Public** Statement, **ReDim** Statement, **Set** Statement, **Static** Statement

Do...Loop Statement

Repeats a block of statements while a condition is True or until a condition becomes True.

Syntax

There are two formats for the Do...Loop:

```
Do [{While | Until} condition]
[statements]
[Exit Do]
[statements]
Loop
```

or,

```
Do
[statements]
[Exit Do]
[statements]
Loop [{While | Until} condition]
```

The following table lists the syntax for these parts:

PART	DESCRIPTION
condition	Any valid VBScript expression that evaluates to `True` or `False`. If *condition* is `Null`, condition is treated as `False`.
statements	One or more statements that are repeated `While` or `Until` *condition* is `True`.

Comments

You can use the Exit Do only within a Do...Loop control structure to provide an early exit from a Do...Loop. Any number of Exit Do statements may be placed anywhere in the Do...Loop. Exit Do is most often used in some conditional block and transfers control to the first statement immediately following the Loop.

When used within nested Do...Loop statements, Exit Do transfers control to the loop that is one nested level above the loop where it is written.

Related Items

`Exit` `Statement,` **`For...Next`** `Statement,` **`While...Wend`** `Statement`

Erase Statement

Reinitializes the elements of fixed-size arrays and deallocates dynamic array storage space.

Syntax

`Erase` *`arraylist`*

The arraylist argument is one or more comma-delimited array variables to be erased.

Comments

You should be aware whether an array is fixed-size or dynamic, as Erase behaves differently for each of these types. Erase recovers no memory from fixed-size arrays. Erase sets the elements of a fixed array as follows:

TYPE OF ARRAY	EFFECT OF ERASE ON FIXED-ARRAY ELEMENTS
Fixed numeric array	Sets each element to zero
Fixed string array	Sets each element to zero-length ("")
Array of objects	Sets each element to the special value Nothing.

`Erase` frees the memory that dynamic arrays use. Before your program can refer to the dynamic array again, it must restore the array variable's memory using a `ReDim` statement.

Example

```
Erase dynArray, statArray
```

Related Items

Array Function, **Dim** Statement, **Private** Statement, **Public** Statement, **ReDim** Statement, **Static** Statement

Exit Statement

Exits a block of Do...Loop, For...Next, Function, or Sub code.

Syntax

```
Exit Do

Exit For

Exit Function

Exit Sub
```

Comments

The Exit statement syntax is as follows:

STATEMENT	DESCRIPTION
`Exit Do`	Provides a way to exit a `Do...Loop` statement. It can be used only inside a `Do...Loop` statement. `Exit Do` transfers control to the statement following the `Loop` statement. When used within nested `Do...Loop` statements, `Exit Do` transfers control to the loop that is one nested level above the loop where it occurs.
`Exit For`	Provides a way of exiting a `For` loop early. It can be used only in a `For...Next` loop. `Exit For` transfers control to the statement following the `Next` statement. When used within nested `For` loops, `Exit For` transfers control to the loop that is one nested level above the loop where it occurs.
`Exit Function`	Immediately exits the `Function` procedure in which it appears. Execution continues with the statement following the statement that called the `Function`.
`Exit Sub`	Immediately exits the Sub procedure in which it appears. Execution continues with the statement following the statement that called the Sub.

Related Items

`Do...Loop Statement, For Each...Next Statement, For...Next Statement, Function Statement, Sub Statement`

For...Next Statement

Repeats a group of statements a specified number of times.

Syntax

```
For counter = start To end [Step loopstep]
[statements]
[Exit For]
[statements]
Next
```

The For...Next statement has the following syntax:

PART	DESCRIPTION
counter	Numeric variable used as a loop counter. The variable can't be an array element or an element currently in use by another `For...Next` statement.
start	Initial value of *counter.*
end	Final value of *counter.*
loopstep	Amount *counter* increments each time the loop is cycled. If not specified, step defaults to one.
statements	One or more statements between `For` and `Next` that are executed the specified number of times.

Comments

The loopstep argument can either be positive or negative.

Once the loop starts and all statements in the loop execute, step is added to the counter. At this point, either the statements in the loop execute again (based on the same test that caused the loop to execute initially), or the loop terminates and execution continues with the statement following the Next statement.

Changing the value of *counter* while inside a loop can make it more difficult to read and debug your code. It is also poor programming practice.

Exit For can only be used within a For Each...Next or For...Next control structure to provide an alternative way to exit a loop. Any number of Exit For statements may be placed anywhere in the loop. The Exit For is most often used within a conditional block (for example, If...Then), and transfers control to the statement immediately following Next.

You can nest For...Next loops by placing one For...Next loop within another. Give each loop a unique variable name as its counter.

Example

The following construction is acceptable:

```
For counter1 = 1 To 10
    For counter2 = 4 to 100 Step 4
    ...
    Next
Next
```

Related Items

Do...Loop Statement, **Exit** Statement, **For...Next** Statement, **While...Wend** Statement

Function Statement

Declares the name, arguments, and code that form the body of a Sub procedure.

Syntax

```
[Static] Function name[(arglist)]
[statements]
[Exit Function]
[statements]
[name = return_value]
End Function
```

The Function statement has the following parts:

PART	DESCRIPTION
`Static`	Indicates that the `Sub` procedure's local variables are preserved between calls. The `Static` attribute doesn't affect variables that are declared outside the `Sub`, even if they are used in the procedure.
name	Name of the `Sub`.
arglist	List of variables representing arguments that are passed to the Function when it is called. Multiple variables are separated by commas.
statements	Any group of statements to be executed within the body of the `Function`.

The arglist argument has the following syntax and parts:
[ByVal | ByRef] varname[()]

PART	DESCRIPTION
`ByVal`	Indicates that the argument is passed by value.
`ByRef`	Indicates that the argument is passed by reference.
varname	Name of the variable representing the argument.

Comments

Functions are public by default. If Static is not used, the value of local variables is not preserved between calls.

All executable code must be contained in functions. A function cannot be defined inside another Sub or Function procedure.

The Exit Function keywords cause immediate exit from a function. Program execution continues with the statement following the statement that called the function. Any number of Exit Function statements can appear anywhere in a function. The return value of the function should be set before leaving it via any exit route. This is done by assigning the value to be returned to the name of the function itself (see example).

A function procedure is a separate procedure that can take arguments, perform a series of statements, change the value of its arguments, and return values that can be used like any other value.

A function is called by using the function name followed by the argument list in parentheses.

Caution should be taken when using recursive functions. These are procedures that are iterated to obtain a result. Recursion can lead to stack overflow, so the Static keyword is usually not used with recursive functions.

Variables that are explicitly declared in a function (using Dim or the equivalent) are always local to that function. Variables that are used but not explicitly declared in a function are also local unless they are explicitly declared at some higher level outside the function. If your function refers to an undeclared variable that has the same name as another function, constant, or variable, it is assumed that your function is referring to that script-level name. Explicitly declare variables to avoid this kind of conflict.

Example

```
Function CalcSomething (intX, strY, arrData())
    Dim intTemp, dblStore
    ...
    If intTemp = 999 Then
        CalcSomething = -1
        Exit Function
    End If
    ...
    CalcSomething = DblStore
End Function
```

Related Items

Call Statement, **Dim** Statement, **Sub** Statement

If...Then...Else Statement

Executes a group of statements conditionally depending on the value of a conditional expression.

Syntax

This construct has two forms:

```
If condition Then statements [Else elsestatements]
```

Or the more versatile syntax may be used:

```
If condition Then
    [statements]
[ElseIf condition-n Then
[Else
    [elseifstatements]]...
    [elsestatements]]
End If
```

The If...Then...Else statement has these three parts:

PART	DESCRIPTION
condition	A numeric or string expression that is either `True` or `False`. If condition is `Null`, it is treated as `False`.
statements	One or more statements that execute if *condition* is `True`. The statements must appear on one line when using the simple syntax.
condition-n	Similar to condition.
elseifstatements	One or more statements that execute if the associated *condition-n* is `True`.
elsestatements	One or more statements execute if no previous condition or condition-n expression is `True`.

Comments

For short simple tests, the use of the single line If...Else statement is fine. However, the multiple line form provides more structure and flexibility and is easier to read and debug. It will be used in most programming situations.

The single line syntax may execute several statements as a result of an If...Then, provided they all lie on the same line. The following example is thus acceptable:

```
If strAnimal = "Dog" Then intNo_Dog = intNo_Dog + 1 : intNo_Animals =
intNo_Animals + 1
```

In a block If, the condition is evaluated and the statements following the Then execute if the condition is True; otherwise, the ElseIf conditions are evaluated in turn. If none of the ElseIf condition is True, the statements following the Else command execute. After executing the statements following Then or Else, execution of the remainder of the script continues after End If. All block statements must be terminated with an End If command.

You can have as many ElseIf statements as you want in an If block, but none can appear after the Else clause. Block Ifs can be nested like other VBScript constructs.

If anything other than a comment appears after a Then statement, the statement is treated as a single-line syntax.

Let Statement

Assigns the value of an expression to a variable or property.

Syntax

```
[Let] varname = expression
```

The Let syntax has the following components:

PART	DESCRIPTION
varname	Name of the variable or property being assigned to; follows standard variable naming conventions.
expression	Value assigned to the variable or property.

Comments

The Let keyword is optional and is usually omitted.

The Set statement is used to assign object references to variables.

Example

```
Let foxyChick = "Anita Delafield"
```

Related Items

Set Statement

LSet Statement

Left aligns a string within a string variable.

Syntax

LSet *stringvar* = *string*

The LSet statement syntax has these parts:

PART	DESCRIPTION
stringvar	Name of target string variable.
string	String expression to be left-aligned within *stringvar*.

Comments

LSet replaces any leftover characters in *stringvar* with spaces. If *string* is longer than *stringvar*, Lset places as many of the leftmost characters in *stringvar* as it can.

Mid Statement

Replaces a specified number of characters in a variable with characters from another string.

Syntax

```
Mid(stringvar,start[,length]) = string
```

The Mid statement has the following arguments:

PART	DESCRIPTION
stringvar	Name of variable to be altered.
start	Character position in *stringvar* where the text will be replaced.
length	Number of characters that will be replaced. If omitted, all of *string* is used.
string	String expression that replaces part of *stringvar*.

Comments

The number of characters replaced is always <= number of characters in *stringvar*.

If you want to replace the byte data contained in a string, you should use the MidB statement, with *start* and *length* being the position and length in terms of bytes rather than characters.

Related Items

```
Mid Function
```

On Error Resume Next Statement

Enables an error-handling routine which stops run-time errors from being fatal. The error should be handled by some user-defined script code.

Syntax

```
On Error Resume Next
```

Comments

If you don't use an On Error Resume Next statement, any run-time error that occurs is fatal. In other words, an error message is displayed and execution stops.

On Error Resume Next causes execution to continue at the statement immediately following the statement that caused the run-time error; or, with the statement immediately following the most recent call out of the procedure containing the On Error Resume Next statement. This allows execution to continue despite a run-time error. You can then build the error-handling routine inline within the procedure. An On Error Resume Next statement becomes inactive when another procedure is called, so you should execute an On Error Resume Next statement in each called routine if you want inline error handing within that routine. See Chapter 8, "Handling Errors with VBScript" for a detailed explanation.

Private Statement

Used at script level to declare private variables and allocate storage space.

Syntax

```
Private varname[([subscripts])][, varname[([subscripts])]]...
```

The Private declaration contains these items:

PART	DESCRIPTION
varname	Name of the variable.
subscripts	Dimensions of an array variable. Up to 60 dimensions may be declared. The lower bound of an array is zero unless otherwise specified.

Comments

Private variables are only available to the script in which they have been declared.

The Private statement can also be used with empty parentheses to declare a dynamic array. Once the array has been declared, the ReDim statement is used to define the number of dimensions and elements in the array. If you try to redeclare a dimension for a static array variable, an error occurs.

When the Private statement is used in a procedure, it is conventionally placed at the beginning of the procedure.

Example

```
<SCRIPT LANGUAGE = "VBScript">
Private intValue, statArray(100), dynArray()
...
</SCRIPT>
```

Related Items

Array Function, **Dim** Statement, **Function** Statement, Public Statement, **ReDim** Statement, **Set** Statement, **Static** Statement, **Sub** Statement

Public Statement

Used at script level to declare public variables and allocate storage space.

Syntax

```
Public varname[([subscripts])][, varname[([subscripts])]]...
```

The Public declaration consists of these parts:

PART	DESCRIPTION
varname	Name of the variable.
subscripts	Dimensions of an array variable. Up to 60 dimensions may be declared. The lower bound of an array is zero unless otherwise specified.

Comments

Public variables are available to all procedures in all scripts in the document.

The Public statement can also be used with empty parentheses to declare a dynamic array. Once the array has been declared, the ReDim statement is used to define the number of dimensions and elements in the array. If you try to redeclare a dimension for a static array variable, an error occurs.

Example

```
<SCRIPT LANGUAGE = "VBScript">
```

```
Public intValue, statArray(100), dynArray()
...
</SCRIPT>
```

Related Items

Array Function, **Dim** Statement, **Private** Statement, **ReDim** Statement, **Set** Statement, **Static** Statement

Randomize Statement

Initializes the random number generator.

Syntax

```
Randomize [number]
```

The number argument can be any valid numeric expression.

Comments

Randomize uses *number* to initialize the Rnd function's random-number generator. It gives it a new seed value. If *number* is not specified, the system timer's current value is used as the seed value for the generator.

If Randomize is not used before the Rnd function is called, the same random number sequence will generate every time.

See Rnd() function for more details.

Related Items

Rnd Function

ReDim Statement

Declares dynamic array and allocates or reallocates storage space for an array variable.

Syntax

```
ReDim [Preserve] varname(subscripts)[, varname(subscripts)]...
```

The ReDim statement has the following arguments:

PART	DESCRIPTION
Preserve	Preserves the data in an existing array when the size of the last dimension is changed.
varname	Name of the array variable.
subscripts	Dimensions of an array variable. Up to 60 dimensions may be declared. The lower bound of an array is zero unless specified otherwise.

Comments

The ReDim statement is usually used to allocate space for an empty dynamic array that has been declared using a Private, Public, or Dim statement with empty parentheses. ReDim can also be used repeatedly to change the number of elements and dimensions of an array.

The Preserve keyword limits the flexibility available to the programmer— you can resize only the last array dimension and you can't change the number of dimensions at all. For example, if an array has only one dimension, it can be resized because it is the only (and therefore the last) dimension. However, if an array has two or more dimensions, only the size of the last dimension can be modified without destroying the original contents of the array. The following example shows how you can increase the size of the last dimension of a dynamic array without erasing any existing data contained in the array.

Note: If you make the array smaller than the original, data in the eliminated elements is lost.

Example

```
Dim arrData()
ReDim arrData(20,20,10)
...
ReDim Preserve arrData(20,20,15)
```

Related Items

Array Function, **Dim** Statement, **Private** Statement, **Public** Statement, **Set** Statement, **Static** Statement

Rem Statement

Used to include explanatory remarks in a section of code.

Syntax

Rem *comment*

or 'comment

The comment section is any text you include as a comment. After the Rem keyword, a space before comment is required.

Comments

The Rem statement must appear on a line of its own, or after a colon. Comments can also be added using the apostrophe option. This is preferable to the Rem statement as it allows comments to be added to a specific line of code.

Example

```
intValue = intValue \ 3          ' integer division has been used here
```

RSet Statement

Right aligns a string within a string variable.

Syntax

```
RSet stringvar = string
```

The RSet statement syntax has these parts:

PART	DESCRIPTION
stringvar	Name of a variable string to contain the right-aligned string.
string	String expression to be right-aligned within *stringvar.*

Comments

The resulting string will have any white space characters from the end of *string* shifted to the beginning, thus right aligning it.

Example

```
Rset strMessage = "Kazza The Great    " returns "    Kazza The Great"
```

Related Items

LSet Statement

Set Statement

Assigns an object reference to a variable or property.

Syntax

Set *objectvar* = {*objectexpression* | **Nothing**}

The Set statement has the following arguments:

PART	DESCRIPTION
objectvar	Name of the variable or property.
objectexpression	Expression which evaluates to an object instance.
Nothing	Discontinues association of *objectvar* with an specific object. Assigning Nothing to *objectvar* releases all the memory and systemresources associated with the previously referenced object if no other variable refers to it.

Comments

The Dim, Private, Public, ReDim, and Static statements can only be used to declare a variable that refers to an object. You need to use the Set statement to assign a specific object to a variable.

Example

```
Dim objButton
...
Set objButton = Document.Form1.Button1
...
objButton.Value = "button text"
```

Related Items

Dim Statement, **Let** Statement, **Private** Statement, **Public** Statement, **ReDim** Statement, **Static** Statement

Static Statement

Declares variables and allocates storage space at the procedure level. Variables declared with the Static statement hold on to their values as long as the code is running, no matter how many times the procedure is called.

Syntax

```
Static varname[([subscripts])][, varname[([subscripts])]]...
```

The Static statement syntax has these parts:

PART	DESCRIPTION
varname	Name of the variable.
subscripts	Dimensions of an array variable to be declared. Up to 60 dimensions may be declared. The lower bound of an array is zero unless specified otherwise.

Comments

Use the Static statement in nonstatic procedures to explicitly declare Static variables.

The Static statement and the Static keyword affect the lifetime of variables differently. If you declare a procedure using the Static keyword, the storage space for all local procedure variables is set aside at the beginning of execution and the value of the variables is preserved for the entire time the program is running. For nonstatic procedures, storage space for variables is allocated and released each time the procedure executes. The Static statement is used to declare variables within nonstatic procedures which permanently retain their values.

When using a Static statement in a procedure, it is conventional to put the Static statement at the beginning of the procedure with any Dim statements.

Related Items

Array Function, **Dim** Statement, **Function** Statement, **Private** Statement, **Public** Statement, **ReDim** Statement, **Sub** Statement

Sub Statement

Declares the name, arguments, and code that form the body of a Sub procedure.

Syntax

```
[Static] Sub name[(arglist)]
[statements]
[Exit Sub]
[statements]
End Sub
```

The Sub statement has the following parts:

PART	DESCRIPTION
`Static`	Indicates that the `Sub` procedure's local variables are preserved between calls. The `Static` attribute doesn't affect global variables declared outside the procedure, even if they are used in the procedure.
name	Name of the procedure.
arglist	List of variables representing arguments that are passed to the `Sub` procedure when it is called. Multiple variables are separated by commas.

PART	DESCRIPTION
statements	Any group of VBScript statements to be executed within the body of the `Sub` procedure.

The arglist argument has the following syntax and parts:
[ByVal | ByRef] varname[()]

PART	DESCRIPTION
ByVal	Indicates that the argument is passed by value.
ByRef	Indicates that the argument is passed by reference. This means that changes to the variable in the procedure is reflected by the calling code.
varname	Name of the variable representing the argument. The optional parentheses indicate that an array is being passed.

Comments

Sub procedures are public by default. If Static is not used, the value of local variables is not preserved between calls.

All executable code should be contained in procedures or functions. A Sub procedure cannot be defined within another Sub or Function procedure.

The Exit Sub keyword causes immediate exit from a Sub procedure. Program execution continues directly after the statement which invoked the Sub procedure. Any number of Exit Sub statements can appear in a Sub procedure.

Unlike a Function procedure, which returns a value, a Sub procedure cannot be used in an expression, and procedure calls should be written as separate statements.

A procedure is called by using the Call statement or by writing the procedure name followed by the argument list and no parentheses.

Caution should be taken when using recursive procedures. These are procedures that call themselves and are iterated to obtain a result.

Recursion can lead to stack overflow, so the Static keyword is usually not used with recursive Sub procedures.

Variables that are explicitly declared in a procedure (using Dim or the equivalent) are always local to the procedure. Variables that are implicitly declared within a procedure are also local. If your procedure refers to an undeclared variable that has the same name as another procedure, constant, or variable, it is assumed that your procedure is referring to that script-level name. Explicitly declared variables to avoid this kind of conflict, and should be used at all times.

Example

```
Sub Link1_MouseOver(shift, button, x, y)
    Dim intTemp
    ....
    If button <> 1 Then Exit Sub
    ....
End Sub
```

Related Items

Call Statement, **Dim** Statement, **Function** Statement

While...Wend Statement

Executes a block of statements as long as a given condition is True.

Syntax

```
While condition
[statements]
Wend
```

The While...Wend statement syntax has these parts:

PART	DESCRIPTION
condition	A VBScript expression which evaluates to `True` or `False`. If *condition* is `Null`, condition is treated as `False`.
statements	One or more statements executed while condition is `True`.

Comments

If *condition* is initially True, all statements in the block are executed until the Wend statement is encountered. Control then returns to the While statement and condition is checked again. If *condition* is still True, the process is repeated. If the *condition* expression has become False, execution resumes with the line of code following the Wend statement.

While…Wend loops can be nested to any level. Each Wend matches the most recent While. Microsoft is phasing out this construct, and recommmends that you use Do...Loop instead.

Example

```
While (not End_of_Input())
...
Wend
```

Related Items

Do...Loop Statement

APPENDIX C

VBScript Language Reference—Operators

+ Operator

Used to add two values together.

Syntax

```
result = expression1 + expression2
```

The + operator syntax has these parts:

PART	DESCRIPTION
result	Any numeric or string variable
expression1	Any VBScript expression
expression2	Any VBScript expression

Comments

Although the + operator can be used to concatenate (join) two character strings, you should use the & operator for concatenation to eliminate ambiguity and provide self-documenting code.

The underlying subtype of the expressions determines the behavior of the + operator:

IF	THEN
Both expressions are numeric	Add
Both expressions are strings	Concatenate
One expression is numeric and one string	Add

If one or both expressions is Null, *result* is Null. If both expressions are Empty, *result* is an Integer subtype. However, if only one expression is Empty, the other expression returns unchanged as *result*.

See Also

`& Operator, - Operator, Arithmetic Operators, Concatenation Operators`

– Operator

Used to find the difference between two numbers or as a unary minus operator.

Syntax

```
result = number1 - number2
```

and

```
-number
```

Comments

The – operator has these parts:

PART	DESCRIPTION
result	Any numeric variable.
number	Any numeric expression.
number1	Any numeric expression.
number2	Any numeric expression.

When the–operator is used for subtraction, the difference between two numbers returns. The alternative use of it is as the unary negation operator which indicates the negative value of an expression.

If one or both expressions are Null expressions, *result* is Null. If an expression is Empty, it is treated as if it were 0.

See Also

`+ Operator, Arithmetic Operators`

X Operator

Used to multiply two quantities together.

Syntax

```
result =  number1 * number2
```

The × operator has the following components:

PART	DESCRIPTION
result	Any numeric variable
number1	Any numeric expression
number2	Any numeric expression

Comments

If either expression is Null, result is Null. If an expression is Empty, it is treated as if it were 0.

See Also

`\ Operator, Arithmetic Operators`

\ Operator

Used to perform integer division.

Syntax

```
result = number1 \ number2
```

The \ operator syntax has these parts:

PART	DESCRIPTION
result	Any numeric variable
number1	Numeric expression to be divided
number2	Numeric expression to divide *number1* by

Comments

Before division performs, numeric expressions are rounded to Byte, Integer, or Long subtype expressions.

If either expression is Null, result is also Null. Any expression that is Empty is treated as 0.

See Also

`* Operator, / Operator, Arithmetic Operators`

/ Operator

Used to perform a floating point division.

Syntax

```
result = number1 / number2
```

The / operator syntax has the following parts:

PART	DESCRIPTION
result	Any numeric expression
number1	Numeric expression to be divided
number2	Any numeric expression to divide *number1* by.

Comments

If one or both of the expressions are Null, result is Null. Any expression that is Empty is treated as 0.

See Also

`* Operator,\ Operator, Arithmetic Operators`

^ Operator

Used to raise a number to a power.

Syntax

```
result = number ^ exponent
```

The ^ operator syntax is as follows:

PART	DESCRIPTION
result	Any numeric variable
number	Numeric expression to be exponentiated
exponent	Any numeric expression representing the power to raise *number* to

Comments

Number can be negative only if exponent is an integer value. When more than one exponentiation is performed in a single expression, the ^ operator is evaluated as it is encountered from left to right. So, 3^2^4 is equivalent to 9^4 and not 3^16.

If either *number* or *exponent* is a Null expression, *result* is also Null.

See Also

`Arithmetic Operators`

And Operator

Used to perform a logical conjunction of two expressions

Syntax

```
result = expression1 And expression2
```

The And operator syntax has these parts:

PART	DESCRIPTION
result	Any numeric variable
expression1	Any expression
expression2	Any expression

Comments

If, and only if, both expressions evaluate to True, result is True. If either expression evaluates to False, result is False. The following table illustrates how the result is determined:

IF *EXPRESSION1* IS	AND *EXPRESSION2* IS	THE *RESULT* IS
`True`	`True`	`True`
`True`	`False`	`False`
`True`	`Null`	`Null`
`False`	`True`	`False`
`False`	`False`	`False`
`False`	`Null`	`False`
`Null`	`True`	`Null`
`Null`	`False`	`False`
`Null`	`Null`	`Null`

The And operator also performs a bit-wise comparison of identically positioned bits in two numeric expressions and sets the corresponding bit in result according to the following truth table:

IF BIT IN *EXPRESSION1* IS	AND BIT IN *EXPRESSION2* IS	THE *RESULT* IS
0	0	0
0	1	0
1	0	0
1	1	1

Example

```
If (strAnswer = "") And (intLoop = 100) Then ...
```

or

```
intSet = intFlag And &H84
```

See Also

Logical Operators, **Not** Operator, **Or** Operator, **Xor** Operator

& Operator

Used to concatenate (join) two string expressions.

Syntax

```
result = expression1 & expression2
```

The **&** operator syntax has the following parts:

PART	DESCRIPTION
result	Any variable
expression1	Any expression
expression2	Any expression

Comments

Whenever an expression is not a string, it converts to a String subtype. if both expressions are Null, result is also Null. However, if only one expression is Null, that expression is treated as a zero-length string when concatenated with the other expression. Any expression that is Empty is also treated as a zero-length string.

Example

```
"Hannah" & " Young" results in the string "Hannah Young"
```

See Also

```
Concatenation Operators
```

Eqv Operator

Used to perform a logical equivalence on two expressions.

Syntax

```
result = expression1 Eqv expression2
```

The Eqv operator syntax is as follows:

PART	DESCRIPTION
result	Any numeric variable
expression1	Any expression
expression2	Any expression

Comments

If either expression is Null, *result* is also Null. When neither expression is Null, *result* is determined according to the following table:

IF *EXPRESSION1* IS	AND *EXPRESSION2* IS	THE *RESULT* IS
`True`	`True`	`True`
`True`	`False`	`False`
`False`	`True`	`False`
`False`	`False`	`True`

The Eqv operator performs a bit-wise comparison of identically positioned bits in two numeric expressions and sets the corresponding bit in result according to the following truth table:

IF BIT IN *EXPRESSION1* IS	AND BIT IN *EXPRESSION2* IS	THE *RESULT* IS
0	0	1
0	1	0
1	0	0
1	1	1

See Also

`Imp` Operator, Logical Operators

Imp Operator

Used to perform a logical implication operation with two expressions.

Syntax

```
result = expression1 Imp expression2
```

The Imp operator syntax has these parts:

PART	DESCRIPTION
result	Any numeric variable
expression1	Any expression
expression2	Any expression

Comments

The following table illustrates how result is determined:

IF *EXPRESSION1* IS	AND *EXPRESSION2* IS	THE *RESULT* IS
`True`	`True`	`True`
`True`	`False`	`False`
`True`	`Null`	`Null`
`False`	`True`	`True`
`False`	`False`	`True`
`False`	`Null`	`True`
`Null`	`True`	`True`
`Null`	`False`	`Null`
`Null`	`Null`	`Null`

The Imp operator also performs a bit-wise comparison of identically positioned bits in two numeric expressions and sets the corresponding bit in result according to the following truth table:

IF BIT IN *EXPRESSION1* IS	AND BIT IN *EXPRESSION2* IS	THE *RESULT* IS
0	0	1
0	1	1
1	0	0
1	1	1

Related Function

Eqv Operator, Logical Operators

Is Operator

Used to compare two variables containing reference to objects.

Syntax

```
result = object1 Is object2
```

The Is operator syntax has these parts:

PART	DESCRIPTION
result	Any numeric variable
object1	Any object expression
object2	Any object expression

Comments

If *object1* and *object2* both refer to the same object, *result* is True; if they do not, result is False. Two variables can be made to refer to the same object by using the Set function.

See Also

Comparison Operators

Mod Operator

Used to divide two numbers and return only the integer remainder.

Syntax

```
result = number1 Mod number2
```

The Mod operator syntax has these parts:

PART	DESCRIPTION
result	Any numeric variable
number1	Any numeric expression
number2	Any numeric expression

Comments

The modulus operator divides *number1* by *number2* (rounding floating point numbers to integers) and returns only the remainder as *result*.

If any expression is Null, *result* is Null. Any expression that is Empty is treated as 0.

Example

```
intRemainder = 19 mod 6.7
```

This makes intRemainder a value of 5.

See Also

```
Arithmetic Operators
```

Not Operator

Used to perform logical negation on an expression.

Syntax

Result = Not expression

The Not operator syntax has these parts:

PART	DESCRIPTION
result	Any numeric variable.
expression	Any expression.

Comments

The following table illustrates how result is determined:

IF EXPRESSION IS	THEN RESULT IS
`True`	`False`
`False`	`True`
`Null`	`Null`

In addition, the Not operator inverts the bit values of any variable and sets the corresponding bit in result according to the following truth table:

BIT IN *EXPRESSION*	BIT IN *RESULT*
0	1
1	0

See Also

`And Operator, Logical Operators, **Or** Operator, **Xor** Operator`

Or Operator

Used to perform a logical disjunction on two expressions.

Syntax

result = *expression1* **Or** *expression2*

The Or operator syntax is as follows:

PART	DESCRIPTION
result	Any numeric variable
expression1	Any expression
expression2	Any expression

Comments

If either expression evaluate to True , result is True. The following table shows how *result* is determined:

IF *EXPRESSION1* IS	AND *EXPRESSION2* IS	THE *RESULT* IS
`True`	`True`	`True`
`True`	`False`	`True`
`True`	`Null`	`True`
`False`	`True`	`True`

IF *EXPRESSION1* IS	AND *EXPRESSION2* IS	THE *RESULT* IS
`False`	`False`	`False`
`False`	`Null`	`Null`
`Null`	`True`	`True`
`Null`	`False`	`Null`
`Null`	`Null`	`Null`

The Or operator performs a bit-wise comparison of identically positioned bits in two numeric expressions and sets the corresponding bit in result according to the following truth table:

IF BIT IN *EXPRESSION1* IS	AND BIT IN *EXPRESSION2* IS	THE *RESULT* IS
0	0	0
0	1	1
1	0	1
1	1	1

Used to perform a logical equivalence on two expressions.

See Also

`And Operator, Logical Operators,` **`Not`** `Operator,` **`Xor`** `Operator`

Xor Operator

Used to perform logical exclusion on two expressions.

Syntax

`result = expression1` **`Xor`** *`expression2`*

The Xor operator syntax is as follows:

PART	DESCRIPTION
result	Any numeric variable
expression1	Any expression
expression2	Any expression

Comments

If one, and only one, of the expressions is True, result is True. However, if either expression is Null, result is also Null. When neither expression is Null, result is determined by the following table.

IF *EXPRESSION1* IS	AND *EXPRESSION2* IS	THE *RESULT* IS
`True`	`True`	`False`
`True`	`False`	`True`
`False`	`True`	`True`
`False`	`False`	`False`

The Xor operator performs a bit-wise comparison of identically positioned bits in two numeric expressions and sets the corresponding bit in result according to the following truth table:

IF BIT IN *EXPRESSION1* IS	AND BIT IN *EXPRESSION2* IS	THE *RESULT* IS
0	0	0
0	1	1
1	0	1
1	1	0

Xor is useful for making sure that two Boolean values are not equal.

See Also

And Operator, Logical Operators, **Not** Operator, **Or** Operator

APPENDIX D

What's on the CD?

The CD that accompanies this book contains numerous tools and utilities to assist Webmasters and developers in managing information and creating content. You will find HTML editors, tools, add-ons, Windows utilities, and more. Examples and source code from the book are included as well.

Running the CD

To make the CD more user-friendly and take up less of your disk space, no installation is required. This means that the only files transferred to your hard disk are the ones you choose to copy.

CAUTION Significant differences between the various Windows operating systems (Windows 3.1, Windows 95, and Windows NT) sometimes render files that work in one Windows environment inoperable in another. Prima Publishing has made every effort to insure that this problem is minimized. However, it is not possible to eliminate it entirely. Therefore you may find that some files or directories appear to be missing from the CD. Those files are, in reality, on the CD, but remain hidden from the operating system. To confirm this, view the CD using a different Windows operating system.

Note: This problem most often occurs while viewing the CD in Windows 3.1.

Windows 3.1

To run the CD:

1. Insert the CD in the CD-ROM Drive.
2. From File Manager select File, Run to open the Run window.
3. In the Command Line text box, type **D:\primacd.exe** (where D:\ is the CD-ROM drive).
4. Select OK.

Windows 95

Since there is no install routine, running the CD in Windows 95 is breeze, especially if you have autorun enabled. Simply insert the CD in the CD-ROM drive, close the tray, and wait for the CD to load.

If you have disabled autorun place the CD in the drive and follow these steps:

1. From the Start menu select Run.
2. Type **D:\primacd.exe** (where D:\ is the CD-ROM drive).
3. Select OK.

The Prima User Interface

Prima's user interface is designed to make viewing and using the CD contents quick and easy. It contains five category buttons, four options buttons, and a display window. Select a category button to show a list of available titles in the display window. Highlight a title in the window and choose an option button to perform the desired action.

Category Buttons

Examples — The entire example World Wide Web Sites.

HTML Tools — A large collection of HTML editors, templates, and add-ons to help you create sophisticated Web pages.

Internet Tools — Web browsers, FTP clients, and other tools for getting the most from the Internet.

Multimedia — A variety of graphics and WAV editors.

Misc — File and system utilities to help manage your system and improve its performance.

Options Buttons

Install/Run. If the highlighted title contains an install routine, selecting this option begins the installation process. If the title has no install procedure, but contains an executable file the executable is run. If neither an install nor an executable file is present (as in the case of a graphics library) the folder containing the information is shown. In the event that an application contains an executable file that will not run from the CD, the entire application is placed in a compressed zip file, which can be accessed by installing WinZip (included on the CD).

NOTE *You can install some of the shareware programs that do not have installation routines by copying the program files from the CD to your hard drive and running the executable (.exe) file.*

Information — Data about the selection is shown, if available. This information is usually in the form of a readme or help file.

Explore — This option allows you to view the folder containing the program files.

Exit — When you're finished and ready to move on, select exit.

The Software

This section gives you a brief description of some of the software you'll find on the CD. This is just a sampling. As you browse the CD, you will find much more.

Cool Edit — A full-featured wave editor for Windows.

CuteFTP — Cute or not, it's a straightforward and easy to use FTP application.

Drag and View Gold — A handy utility that lets you drag, drop, and view word processing, spreadsheet, database, and graphics files without opening the parent application.

Frame-IT! — A feature-packed HTML frame generator, which allows you to generate complex HTML frames, using only your mouse.

HotDog — A stand alone HTML editor that supports extensions from Microsoft and Netscape as well as proposed HTML 3.0 elements.

HTML Assistant — A simple Web publishing tool for creating HTML Web pages.

Kenn Nesbitt's Webedit — The popular HTML editor for novices and pros.

Live Markup — It's as close as you can get to a WYSIWYG HTML editor.

LView Pro — A versatile Windows graphics editor.

Mapedit — A WYSIWYG (What You See Is What You Get) editor for imagemap files.

Microsoft ActiveX SDK — Tools to help you develop Internet ActiveX controls.

Microsoft Internet Explorer 3.0 — Microsoft's full-featured Web browser with support for HTML, ActiveX, Java, and plug-ins.

Paint Shop Pro — The popular bitmap image editor from JASC, Inc.

Vram — speed up your system performance with this 32-bit virtual RAM file system driver for Windows 95.

Vision Storyboard — A developer tool that assists in planning, documenting, and presenting Microsoft's Visual Basic application.

Web Graphics Library — A collection of graphics from Blue Sky Software.

Web Graphics Locator — Find graphics files anywhere on your system in a GIFfy.

Web Weaver — An easy to use HTML text editor.

WinHelp Inspector — Browse your Help files and display statistics such as name, date, and size of the Help file, as well as keywords and fonts used.

WinZip — One of the leading file compression utilities for Windows 95, NT, and Windows 3.1.

Index

T

U

V

Notes

Notes

Notes

Notes

Notes

Notes

Notes

Notes

Notes

Notes

To Order Books

Please send me the following items:

Quantity	Title	Unit Price	Total
______	______________________________	$ ______	$ ______
______	______________________________	$ ______	$ ______
______	______________________________	$ ______	$ ______
______	______________________________	$ ______	$ ______
______	______________________________	$ ______	$ ______

Shipping and Handling depend on Subtotal.

Subtotal	Shipping/Handling
$0.00–$14.99	$3.00
$15.00–$29.99	$4.00
$30.00–$49.99	$6.00
$50.00–$99.99	$10.00
$100.00–$199.99	$13.50
$200.00+	Call for Quote

Foreign and all Priority Request orders:
Call Order Entry department
for price quote at 916/632-4400

This chart represents the total retail price of books only (before applicable discounts are taken).

Subtotal $ ______

Deduct 10% when ordering 3-5 books $ ______

7.25% Sales Tax (CA only) $ ______

8.25% Sales Tax (TN only) $ ______

5.0% Sales Tax (MD and IN only) $ ______

Shipping and Handling* $ ______

Total Order $ ______

By Telephone: With MC or Visa, call 800-632-8676, 916-632-4400. Mon-Fri, 8:30-4:30.
WWW {http://www.primapublishing.com}

Orders Placed Via Internet E-mail {sales@primapub.com}

By Mail: Just fill out the information below and send with your remittance to:

Prima Publishing
P.O. Box 1260BK
Rocklin, CA 95677

My name is ______________________________

I live at ______________________________

City ______________________ State ______ Zip ______

MC/Visa# ______________________ Exp. ______

Check/Money Order enclosed for $ ______________ Payable to Prima Publishing

Daytime Telephone ______________________________

Signature ______________________________

Other Books from Prima Publishing, Computer Products Division

ISBN	Title	Price	Release Date
0-7615-0801-5	ActiveX	$35.00	Available Now
0-7615-0680-2	America Online Complete Handbook and Membership Kit	$24.99	Available Now
0-7615-0915-1	Building Intranets with Internet Information Server and FrontPage	$40.00	Available Now
0-7615-0417-6	CompuServe Complete Handbook and Membership Kit	$24.95	Available Now
0-7615-0849-X	Corporate Intranet Development	$40.00	Fall '96
0-7615-0692-6	Create Your First Web Page in a Weekend	$24.99	Available Now
0-7615-0503-2	Discover What's Online!	$24.95	Available Now
0-7615-0693-4	Internet Information Server	$40.00	Available Now
0-7615-0815-5	Introduction to ABAP/4 Programming for SAP	$45.00	Available Now
0-7615-0678-0	Java Applet Powerpack	$30.00	Available Now
0-7615-0685-3	JavaScript	$35.00	Available Now
0-7615-0901-1	Leveraging Visual Basic with ActiveX Controls	$45.00	Available Now
0-7615-0682-9	LiveWire Pro Master's Handbook	$40.00	Fall '96
0-7615-0755-8	Moving Worlds	$35.00	Available Now
0-7615-0690-X	Netscape Enterprise Server	$40.00	Available Now
0-7615-0691-8	Netscape FastTrack Server	$40.00	Available Now
0-7615-0852-X	Netscape Navigator 3 Complete Handbook	$24.99	Available Now
0-7615-0751-5	Windows NT Server Administrator's Guide	$50.00	Available Now
0-7615-0759-0	Professional Web Design	$40.00	Available Now
0-7615-0773-6	Programming Internet Controls	$45.00	Available Now
0-7615-0780-9	Programming Web Server Applications	$40.00	Available Now
0-7615-0063-4	Researching on the Internet	$29.95	Available Now
0-7615-0686-1	Researching on the World Wide Web	$24.99	Available Now
0-7615-0695-0	The Essential Photoshop Book	$35.00	Available Now
0-7615-0752-3	The Essential Windows NT Book	$27.99	Available Now
0-7615-0689-6	The Microsoft Exchange Productivity Guide	$24.99	Available Now
0-7615-0684-5	VBscript Web Page Interactivity	$35.00	Available Now
0-7615-0903-8	Visual FoxPro 5 Enterprise Development	$45.00	Available Now
0-7615-0814-7	Visual J++	$35.00	Available Now
0-7615-0383-8	Web Advertising and Marketing	$34.95	Available Now
0-7615-0726-4	Webmaster's Handbook	$40.00	Available Now

License Agreement/Notice of Limited Warranty

By opening the sealed disk container in this book, you agree to the following terms and conditions. If, upon reading the following license agreement and notice of limited warranty, you cannot agree to the terms and conditions set forth, return the unused book with unopened disk to the place where you purchased it for a refund.

License:

The enclosed software is copyrighted by the copyright holder(s) indicated on the software disk. You are licensed to copy the software onto a single computer for use by a single concurrent user and to a backup disk. You may not reproduce, make copies, or distribute copies or rent or lease the software in whole or in part, except with written permission of the copyright holder(s). You may transfer the enclosed disk only together with this license, and only if you destroy all other copies of the software and the transferee agrees to the terms of the license. You may not decompile, reverse assemble, or reverse engineer the software.

Notice of Limited Warranty:

The enclosed disk is warranted by Prima Publishing to be free of physical defects in materials and workmanship for a period of sixty (60) days from end user's purchase of the book/disk combination. During the sixty-day term of the limited warranty, Prima will provide a replacement disk upon the return of a defective disk.

Limited Liability:

THE SOLE REMEDY FOR BREACH OF THIS LIMITED WARRANTY SHALL CONSIST ENTIRELY OF REPLACEMENT OF THE DEFECTIVE DISK. IN NO EVENT SHALL PRIMA OR THE AUTHORS BE LIABLE FOR ANY OTHER DAMAGES, INCLUDING LOSS OR CORRUPTION OF DATA, CHANGES IN THE FUNCTIONAL CHARACTERISTICS OF THE HARDWARE OR OPERATING SYSTEM, DELETERIOUS INTERACTION WITH OTHER SOFTWARE, OR ANY OTHER SPECIAL, INCIDENTAL, OR CONSEQUENTIAL DAMAGES THAT MAY ARISE, EVEN IF PRIMA AND/OR THE AUTHORS HAVE PREVIOUSLY BEEN NOTIFIED THAT THE POSSIBILITY OF SUCH DAMAGES EXISTS.

Disclaimer of Warranties:

PRIMA AND THE AUTHORS SPECIFICALLY DISCLAIM ANY AND ALL OTHER WARRANTIES, EITHER EXPRESS OR IMPLIED, INCLUDING WARRANTIES OF MERCHANTABILITY, SUITABILITY TO A PARTICULAR TASK OR PURPOSE, OR FREEDOM FROM ERRORS. SOME STATES DO NOT ALLOW FOR EXCLUSION OF IMPLIED WARRANTIES OR LIMITATION OF INCIDENTAL OR CONSEQUENTIAL DAMAGES, SO THESE LIMITATIONS MAY NOT APPLY TO YOU.

Other:

This Agreement is governed by the laws of the State of California without regard to choice of law principles. The United Convention of Contracts for the International Sale of Goods is specifically disclaimed. This Agreement constitutes the entire agreement between you and Prima Publishing regarding use of the software.